More praise from across the nation for the JobBank series:

"One of the better publishers of e............................lia
Corporation ... publisher of *The Metropolitan*............
named directories of employers in Texas, Boston, Chicago, Northern and
Southern California, and Washington DC. A good buy...."

**-Wall Street Journal's
National Business Employment Weekly**

"*JobBank* books are all devoted to specific job markets. This is helpful if
you are thinking about working in cities like San Antonio, Washington, Boston, or
states such as Tennessee or the Carolinas. You can use them for research, and
a particularly useful feature is the inclusion of the type of positions that are
commonly offered at the companies listed."

**-Karen Ronald, Library Director
Wilton Library, Wilton, CT**

"If you are looking for a job ... before you go to the newspapers and the
help-wanted ads, listen to Bob Adams, publisher *of The Metropolitan New York
JobBank.*"

-Tom Brokaw, NBC

"Since 1985 the Adams *JobBank Series* has proven to be the
consummate tool for the efficient job search."

**-Mel Rappleyea, Human Resources Director
Starbucks Coffee Company**

"Having worked in the Career Services field for 10 years, I know the
quality of Adams publications."

**-Philip Meade, Director of Graduate Career Services
Baruch School of Business (New York NY)**

"I read through the 'Basics of Job Winning' and 'Resumes' sections [in
The Dallas-Fort Worth JobBank] and found them to be very informative, with
some positive tips for the job searcher. I believe the strategies outlined will bring
success to any determined candidate."

**-Camilla Norder, Professional Recruiter
Presbyterian Hospital of Dallas**

"The ultimate in a superior series of job hunt directories."

**-Cornell University Career Center's
*Where to Start***

"Help on the job hunt ... Anyone who is job-hunting in the New York area can find a lot of useful ideas in a new paperback called *The Metropolitan New York JobBank*...."

-Angela Taylor, *New York Times*

"A timely book for Chicago job hunters follows books from the same publisher that were well received in New York and Boston ... [*The Chicago JobBank* is] a fine tool for job hunters...."

-Clarence Peterson, *Chicago Tribune*

"Because our listing is seen by people across the nation, it generates lots for resumes for us. We encourage unsolicited resumes. We'll always be listed [in *The Chicago JobBank*] as long as I'm in this career."

**-Tom Fitzpatrick, Director of Human Resources
Merchandise Mart Properties, Inc.**

"Job hunting is never fun, but this book can ease the ordeal ...[*The Los Angeles JobBank*] will help allay fears, build confidence, and avoid wheel-spinning."

-Robert W. Ross, *Los Angeles Times*

"*The Seattle JobBank* is an essential resource for job hunters."

**-Gil Lopez, Staffing Team Manager
Battelle Pacific Northwest Laboratories**

"*The Phoenix JobBank* is a first-class publication. The information provided is useful and current."

**-Lyndon Denton
Director of Human Resources and Materials Management
Apache Nitrogen Products, Inc.**

"*The Florida JobBank* is an invaluable job-search reference tool. It provides the most up-to-date information and contact names available for companies in Florida. I should know – it worked for me!"

**-Rhonda Cody, Human Resources Consultant
Aetna Life and Casualty**

"I read through the 'Basics of Job Winning' and 'Resumes' sections [in *The Dallas-Fort Worth JobBank*] and found them to be very informative, with some positive tips for the job searcher. I believe the strategies outlined will bring success to any determined candidate."

**-Camilla Norder, Professional Recruiter
Presbyterian Hospital of Dallas**

"Through *The Dallas-Fort Worth JobBank,* we've been able to attract high-quality candidates for several positions."

**-Rob Bertino, Southern States Sales Manager
CompuServe**

What makes the JobBank series the nation's premier line of employment guides?

With vital employment information on thousands of employers across the nation, the JobBank series is the most comprehensive and authoritative set of career directories available today.

Each book in the series provides information on **dozens of different industries** in a given city or area, with the primary employer listings providing contact information, telephone and fax numbers, e-mail addresses, Websites, a summary of the firm's business, internships, and in many cases descriptions of the firm's typical professional job categories.

All of the reference information in the JobBank series is as up-to-date and accurate as possible. Every year, the entire database is thoroughly researched and verified by mail and by telephone. Adams Media Corporation publishes **more local employment guides more often** than any other publisher of career directories.

The JobBank series offers **20 regional titles**, from Boston to San Francisco. All of the information is organized geographically, because most people look for jobs in specific areas of the country.

A condensed, but thorough, review of the entire job search process is presented in the chapter **The Basics of Job Winning**, a feature that has received many compliments from career counselors. In addition, each JobBank directory includes a section on **resumes and cover letters** the *New York Times* has acclaimed as "excellent."

The JobBank series gives job hunters the most comprehensive, timely, and accurate career information, organized and indexed to facilitate your job search. An entire career reference library, JobBank books are designed to help you find optimal employment in any market.

Top career publications from Adams Media

The JobBank Series:
each JobBank book is $17.95

The Atlanta JobBank, 15th Ed.
The Austin/San Antonio JobBank, 4th Ed.
The Boston JobBank, 20th Ed.
The Carolina JobBank, 7th Ed.
The Chicago JobBank, 19th Ed.
The Colorado JobBank, 13th Ed.
The Connecticut JobBank, 3rd Ed.
The Dallas-Fort Worth JobBank, 14th Ed.
The Florida JobBank, 16th Ed.
The Houston JobBank, 12th Ed.
The Los Angeles JobBank, 17th Ed.
The New Jersey JobBank, 3rd Ed.
The Metropolitan New York JobBank, 19th Ed.
The Ohio JobBank, 11th Ed.
The Greater Philadelphia JobBank, 14th Ed.
The Phoenix JobBank, 9th Ed.
The San Francisco Bay Area JobBank, 17th Ed.
The Seattle JobBank, 13th Ed.
The Virginia JobBank, 4th Ed.
The Metropolitan Washington DC JobBank, 16th Ed.

The National JobBank, 2006
  (Covers the entire U.S.: $475.00 hc)

Other Career Titles:
The Adams Businesses You Can Start Almanac ($14.95)
The Adams Cover Letter Almanac ($12.95)
The Adams Internet Job Search Almanac, 6th Ed. ($12.95)
The Adams Job Interview Almanac, 2nd Ed. ($17.95)

The Adams Resume Almanac, 2nd Ed. ($17.95)
Business Etiquette in Brief ($7.95)
College Grad Job Hunter, 5th Ed. ($14.95)
The Complete Resume & Job Search Book for College Students, 2nd Ed. ($12.95)
Cover Letters That Knock 'em Dead, 6th Ed. ($12.95)
The Everything Alternative Careers Book ($14.95)
The Everything Cover Letter Book, 2nd Ed. ($14.95)
The Everything Get-A-Job Book ($12.95)
The Everything Job Interview Book ($14.95)
The Everything Leadership Book ($12.95)
The Everything Managing People Book ($14.95)
The Everything Online Job Search Book ($12.95)
The Everything Practice Interview Book ($12.95)
The Everything Resume Book, 2nd Ed. ($14.95)
The Everything Selling Book ($14.95)
The Everything Start Your Own Business Book ($14.95)
Knock 'em Dead, 2005 ($14.95)
Knock 'em Dead Business Presentations ($12.95)
Knock 'em Dead Management ($14.95)
Market Yourself and Your Career, 2nd Ed. ($12.95)
The New Professional Image ($14.95)
Resume Buzz Words ($9.95)
The Resume Handbook, 4th Ed. ($9.95)
Resumes That Knock 'em Dead, 6th Ed. ($12.95)
The Road to CEO ($10.95)
The 250 Job Interview Questions You'll Most Likely Be Asked ($9.95)

If you cannot find these titles at your favorite book outlet, you may order them directly from the publisher.

BY PHONE: Call 800/872-5627 (in Massachusetts 508/427-7100).
We accept Visa, Mastercard, and American Express.
$4.95 will be added to your total for shipping and handling.

BY MAIL: Write out the full titles of the books you'd like to order and send payment, including $4.95 for shipping and handling to:
Adams Media, 57 Littlefield Street, Avon MA 02322.

BY FAX: 800/872-5628. **BY E-MAIL:** orders@adamsmedia.com

30-day money back guarantee.

Discounts available for standing orders.

VISIT OUR WEBSITE
www.adamsmedia.com

20th Edition

THE

Boston
JobBank

adams
media

Published by Adams Media, an F+W Publications Company
57 Littlefield Street, Avon, MA 02322 U.S.A.
www.adamsmedia.com

ISBN: 1-59337-442-9
ISSN: 1098-9757
Manufactured in USA

Copyright © 2005 F+W Publications, Inc. All rights reserved. This book, or parts thereof, may not be reproduced or used in any form or by any means, electronic or mechanical, including photocopying, recording, or by any information storage retrieval system without permission from the publisher. Exceptions are made for brief excerpts used in published reviews.

The Boston JobBank, 20th Edition and its cover design are trademarks of F+W Publications, Inc.

Product or brand names used in this book are proprietary property of the applicable firm, subject to trademark protection, and registered with government offices. Any use of these names does not convey endorsement by or other affiliation with the name holder.

Because addresses and telephone numbers of smaller companies change rapidly, we recommend you call each company and verify the information before mailing to the employers listed in this book. Mass mailings are not recommended.

While the publisher has made every reasonable effort to obtain and verify accurate information, occasional errors are possible due to the magnitude of the data. Should you discover an error, or if a company is missing, please write the editors at the above address so that we may update future editions.

"This publication is designed to provide accurate and authoritative information with regard to the subject matter covered. It is sold with the understanding that the publisher is not engaged in rendering legal, accounting, or other professional advice. If legal advice or other expert assistance is required, the services of a competent professional person should be sought."
--From a Declaration of Principles jointly adopted by a Committee of the American Bar Association and a Committee of Publishers and Associations

This book is available on standing order and at quantity discounts for bulk purchases. For information, call 800/872-5627 (in Massachusetts, 508/427-7100).

TABLE OF CONTENTS

SECTION ONE: INTRODUCTION

How to Use This Book/12
An introduction to the most effective way to use *The Boston JobBank*.

SECTION TWO: THE JOB SEARCH

The Basics of Job Winning/16
A review of the elements of a successful job search campaign. Includes advice on developing effective strategies, time planning, and preparing for interviews. Special sections address situations faced by jobseekers who are currently employed, those who have lost a job, and graduates conducting their first job search.

Resumes and Cover Letters/30
Advice on creating strong resumes and cover letters with examples.

SECTION THREE: PRIMARY EMPLOYERS

The Employers/49
The Boston JobBank is organized according to industry. Many listings include the address and phone number of each major firm listed, along with a description of the company's basic product lines and services, and, in many cases, a contact name and other relevant hiring information.

- Physical Fitness Facilities
- Professional Sports Clubs; Sporting and Recreational Camps
- Public Golf Courses and Racing and Track Operations
- Theatrical Producers and Services

Automotive/74
- Automotive Repair Shops
- Automotive Stampings
- Industrial Vehicles and Moving Equipment
- Motor Vehicles and Equipment
- Travel Trailers and Campers

Banking, Savings and Loans, & Other Depository Institutions/76
- Banks
- Bank Holding Companies and Associations
- Lending Firms/Financial Services Institutions

Biotechnology, Pharmaceuticals, and Scientific R&D/81
- Clinical Labs
- Lab Equipment Manufacturers
- Pharmaceutical Manufacturers and Distributors

Business Services and Non-Scientific Research/94
- Adjustment and Collection Services
- Cleaning, Maintenance, and Pest Control Services
- Credit Reporting Services
- Detective, Guard, and Armored Car Services/Security Systems Services
- Miscellaneous Equipment Rental and Leasing
- Secretarial and Court Reporting Services

Charities and Social Services/97
- Social and Human Service Agencies
- Job Training and Vocational Rehabilitation Services
- Nonprofit Organizations

Chemicals, Rubber, and Plastics/102
- Adhesives, Detergents, Inks, Paints, Soaps, Varnishes
- Agricultural Chemicals and Fertilizers
- Carbon and Graphite Products
- Chemical Engineering Firms
- Industrial Gases

Communications: Telecommunications and Broadcasting/105
- Cable/Pay Television Services
- Communications Equipment
- Radio and Television Broadcasting Stations
- Telephone, Telegraph, and Other Message Communications

Computer Hardware, Software, and Services/110
- Computer Components and Hardware Manufacturers
- Consultants and Computer Training Companies
- Internet and Online Service Providers
- Networking and Systems Services
- Repair Services/Rental and Leasing
- Resellers, Wholesalers, and Distributors
- Software Developers/Programming Services

Educational Services/139
- Business/Secretarial/Data Processing Schools

HOW TO USE THIS BOOK

Right now, you hold in your hands one of the most effective job-hunting tools available anywhere. In *The Boston JobBank*, you will find valuable information to help you launch or continue a rewarding career. But before you open to the book's employer listings and start calling about current job openings, take a few minutes to learn how best to use the resources presented in *The Boston JobBank*.

The Boston JobBank will help you to stand out from other jobseekers. While many people looking for a new job rely solely on newspaper help-wanted ads, this book offers you a much more effective job-search method -- direct contact. The direct contact method has been proven twice as effective as scanning the help-wanted ads. Instead of waiting for employers to come looking for you, you'll be far more effective going to them. While many of your competitors will use trial and error methods in trying to set up interviews, you'll learn not only how to get interviews, but what to expect once you've got them.

In the next few pages, we'll take you through each section of the book so you'll be prepared to get a jump-start on your competition.

Basics of Job Winning

Preparation. Strategy. Time management. These are three of the most important elements of a successful job search. *Basics of Job Winning* helps you address these and all the other elements needed to find the right job.

One of your first priorities should be to define your personal career objectives. What qualities make a job desirable to you? Creativity? High pay? Prestige? Use *Basics of Job Winning* to weigh these questions. Then use the rest of the chapter to design a strategy to find a job that matches your criteria.

In *Basics of Job Winning,* you'll learn which job-hunting techniques work, and which don't. We've reviewed the pros and cons of mass mailings, help-wanted ads, and direct contact. We'll show you how to develop and approach contacts in your field; how to research a prospective employer; and how to use that information to get an interview and the job.

Also included in *Basics of Job Winning*: interview dress code and etiquette, the "do's and don'ts" of interviewing, sample interview questions, and more. We also deal with some of the unique problems faced by those jobseekers who are currently employed, those who have lost a job, and college students conducting their first job search.

Resumes and Cover Letters

The approach you take to writing your resume and cover letter can often mean the difference between getting an interview and never being noticed. In this section, we discuss different formats, as well as what to put on (and what to leave off) your resume. We review the benefits and drawbacks of professional resume writers, and the importance of a follow-up letter. Also included in this section are sample resumes and cover letters which you can use as models.

The Employer Listings

Employers are listed alphabetically by industry. When a company does business under a person's name, like "John Smith & Co.," the company is usually listed by the surname's spelling (in this case "S"). Exceptions occur when a company's name is widely recognized, like "JCPenney" or "Howard Johnson Motor Lodge." In those cases, the company's first name is the key ("J" and "H" respectively).

The Boston JobBank covers a very wide range of industries. Each company profile is assigned to one of the industry chapters listed below.

Accounting and Management Consulting
Advertising, Marketing, and Public
   Relations
Aerospace
Apparel, Fashion, and Textiles
Architecture, Construction, and Engineering
Arts, Entertainment, Sports, and Recreation
Automotive
Banking/Savings and Loans
Biotechnology, Pharmaceuticals, and
   Scientific R&D
Business Services and Non-Scientific
   Research
Charities and Social Services
Chemicals/Rubber and Plastics
Communications: Telecommunications and
   Broadcasting
Computer Hardware, Software, and
   Services
Educational Services
Electronic/Industrial Electrical Equipment
   and Components

Environmental and Waste Management
   Services
Fabricated/Primary Metals and Products
Financial Services
Food and Beverages/Agriculture
Government
Health Care: Services, Equipment, and
   Products
Hotels and Restaurants
Insurance
Legal Services
Manufacturing: Miscellaneous Consumer
Manufacturing: Miscellaneous Industrial
Mining/Gas/Petroleum/Energy Related
Paper and Wood Products
Printing and Publishing
Real Estate
Retail
Stone, Clay, Glass, and Concrete Products
Transportation/Travel
Utilities: Electric/Gas/Water
Miscellaneous Wholesaling

Many of the company listings offer detailed company profiles. In addition to company names, addresses, and phone numbers, these listings also include contact names or hiring departments, and descriptions of each company's products and/or services. Many of these listings also feature a variety of additional information including:

Positions advertised - A list of open positions the company was advertising at the time our research was conducted. Note: Keep in mind that *The Boston JobBank* is a directory of major employers in the area, not a directory of openings currently available. Positions listed in this book that were advertised at the time research was conducted may no longer be open. Many of the companies listed will be hiring, others will not. However, since most professional job openings are filled without the placement of help-wanted ads, contacting the employers in this book directly is still a more effective method than browsing the Sunday papers.

Special programs - Does the company offer training programs, internships, or apprenticeships? These programs can be important to first time jobseekers and college students looking for practical work experience. Many employer profiles will include information on these programs.

Parent company - If an employer is a subsidiary of a larger company, the name of that parent company will often be listed here. Use this information to supplement your company research before contacting the employer.

Number of employees - The number of workers a company employs.

Company listings may also include information on other U.S. locations and any stock exchanges the firm may be listed on.

A note on all employer listings that appear in *The Boston JobBank*: This book is intended as a starting point. It is not intended to replace any effort that you, the jobseeker, should devote to your job hunt. Keep in mind that while a great deal of effort has been put into collecting and verifying the company profiles provided in this book, addresses and contact names change regularly. Inevitably, some contact names listed herein have changed even before you read this. We recommend you contact a company before mailing your resume to ensure nothing has changed.

Industry Associations

This section includes a select list of professional and trade associations organized by industry. Many of these associations can provide employment advice and job-search help, offer magazines that cover the industry, and provide additional information or directories that may supplement the employer listings in this book.

Index of Primary Employers

The Boston JobBank index is listed alphabetically by company name.

THE JOB SEARCH

THE BASICS OF JOB WINNING: A CONDENSED REVIEW

This chapter is divided into four sections. The first section explains the fundamentals that every jobseeker should know, especially first-time jobseekers. The next three sections deal with special situations faced by specific types of jobseekers: those who are currently employed, those who have lost a job, and college students.

THE BASICS:
Things Everyone Needs to Know

Career Planning

The first step to finding your ideal job is to clearly define your objectives. This is better known as career planning (or life planning if you wish to emphasize the importance of combining the two). Career planning has become a field of study in and of itself.

If you are thinking of choosing or switching careers, we particularly emphasize two things. First, choose a career where you will enjoy most of the day-to-day tasks. This sounds obvious, but most of us have at some point found the idea of a glamour industry or prestigious job title attractive without thinking of the key consideration: Would we enjoy performing the *everyday* tasks the position entails?

The second key consideration is that you are not merely choosing a career, but also a lifestyle. Career counselors indicate that one of the most common problems people encounter in jobseeking is that they fail to consider how well-suited they are for a particular position or career. For example, some people, attracted to management consulting by good salaries, early responsibility, and high-level corporate exposure, do not adapt well to the long hours, heavy travel demands, and constant pressure to produce. Be sure to ask yourself how you might adapt to the day-to-day duties and working environment that a specific position entails. Then ask yourself how you might adapt to the demands of that career or industry as a whole.

Choosing Your Strategy

Assuming that you've established your career objectives, the next step of the job search is to develop a strategy. If you don't take the time to develop a plan, you may find yourself going in circles after several weeks of randomly searching for opportunities that always seem just beyond your reach.

The most common jobseeking techniques are:

- following up on help-wanted advertisements (in the newspaper or online)
- using employment services
- relying on personal contacts
- contacting employers directly (the Direct Contact method)

Each of these approaches can lead to better jobs. However, the Direct Contact method boasts twice the success rate of the others. So unless you have specific reasons to employ other strategies, Direct Contact should form the foundation of your job search.

If you choose to use other methods as well, try to expend at least half your energy on Direct Contact. Millions of other jobseekers have already proven that Direct Contact has been twice as effective in obtaining employment, so why not follow in their footsteps?

Setting Your Schedule

Okay, so now that you've targeted a strategy it's time to work out the details of your job search. The most important detail is setting up a schedule. Of course, since job searches aren't something most people do regularly, it may be hard to estimate how long each step will take. Nonetheless, it is important to have a plan so that you can monitor your progress.

When outlining your job search schedule, have a realistic time frame in mind. If you will be job-searching full-time, your search could take at least two months or more. If you can only devote part-time effort, it will probably take at least four months.

You probably know a few people who seem to spend their whole lives searching for a better job in their spare time. Don't be one of them. If you are presently working and don't feel like devoting a lot of energy to jobseeking right now, then wait. Focus on enjoying your present position, performing your best on the job, and storing up energy for when you are really ready to begin your job search.

> **The first step in beginning your job search is to clearly define your objectives.**

Those of you who are currently unemployed should remember that *job-hunting is tough work, both physically and emotionally*. It is also intellectually demanding work that requires you to be at your best. So don't tire yourself out by working on your job campaign around the clock. At the same time, be sure to discipline yourself. The most logical way to manage your time while looking for a job is to keep your regular working hours.

If you are searching full-time and have decided to choose several different strategies, we recommend that you divide up each week, designating some time for each method. By trying several approaches at once, you can evaluate how promising each seems and alter your schedule accordingly. Keep in mind that the *majority of openings are filled without being advertised*. Remember also that positions advertised on the Internet are just as likely to already be filled as those found in the newspaper!

If you are searching part-time and decide to try several different contact methods, we recommend that you try them sequentially. You simply won't have enough time to put a meaningful amount of effort into more than one method at once. Estimate the length of your job search, and then allocate so many weeks or months for each contact method, beginning with Direct Contact. The purpose of setting this schedule is not to rush you to your goal but to help you periodically evaluate your progress.

The Direct Contact Method

Once you have scheduled your time, you are ready to begin your search in earnest. Beginning with the Direct Contact method, the first step is to develop a checklist for categorizing the types of firms for which you'd like to work. You might categorize firms by product line, size, customer type (such as industrial or consumer), growth prospects, or geographical location. Keep in mind, the shorter the list the easier it will be to locate a company that is right for you.

Next you will want to use this *JobBank* book to assemble your list of potential employers. Choose firms where *you* are most likely to be able to find a job. Try matching your skills with those that a specific job demands. Consider where your skills might be in demand, the degree of competition for employment, and the employment outlook at each company.

Separate your prospect list into three groups. The first 25 percent will be your primary target group, the next 25 percent will be your secondary group, and the remaining names will be your reserve group.

After you form your prospect list, begin working on your resume. Refer to the Resumes and Cover Letters section following this chapter for more information.

Once your resume is complete, begin researching your first batch of prospective employers. You will want to determine whether you would be happy working at the firms you are researching and to get a better idea of what their employment needs might be. You also need to obtain enough information to sound highly informed about the company during phone conversations and in mail correspondence. But don't go all out on your research yet! You probably won't be able to arrange interviews with some of these firms, so save your big research effort until you start to arrange interviews. Nevertheless, you should plan to spend several hours researching each firm.

The more you know about a company, the more likely you are to catch an interviewer's eye. (You'll also face fewer surprises once you get the job!)

Do your research in batches to save time and energy. Start with this book, and find out what you can about each of the firms in your primary target group. For answers to specific questions, contact any pertinent professional associations that may be able to help you learn more about an employer. Read industry publications looking for articles on the firm. (Addresses of associations and names of important publications are listed after each section of employer listings in this book.) Then look up the company on the Internet or try additional resources at your local library. Keep organized, and maintain a folder on each firm.

Information to look for includes: company size; president, CEO, or owner's name; when the company was established; what each division does; and benefits that are important to you. An abundance of company information can now be found electronically, through the World Wide Web or commercial online services. Researching companies online is a convenient means of obtaining information quickly and easily. If you have access to the Internet, you can search from your home at any time of day.

You may search a particular company's Website for current information that may be otherwise unavailable in print. In fact, many companies that maintain a site update their information daily. In addition, you may also search articles written about the company online. Today, most of the nation's largest newspapers, magazines, trade publications, and regional business periodicals have online versions of their publications. To find additional resources, use a search engine like Yahoo! or Alta Vista and type in the keyword "companies" or "employers."

If you discover something that really disturbs you about the firm (they are about to close their only local office), or if you discover that your chances of getting a job there are practically nil (they have just instituted a hiring freeze), then cross them off your prospect list. If possible, supplement your research efforts by contacting individuals who know the firm well. Ideally you should make an informal contact with someone at that particular firm, but often a direct competitor or a major customer will be able to supply you with just as much information. At the very least, try to obtain whatever printed information the company has available -- not just annual reports, but product brochures, company profiles, or catalogs. This information is often available on the Internet.

Getting the Interview

Now it is time to make Direct Contact with the goal of arranging interviews. If you have read any books on job-searching, you may have noticed that most of these books tell you to avoid the human resources office like the plague. It is said that the human resources office never hires people; they screen candidates. Unfortunately, this is often the case. If you can identify the appropriate manager with the authority to hire you, you should try to contact that person directly.

The obvious means of initiating Direct Contact are:

* Mail (postal or electronic)
* Phone calls

Mail contact is a good choice if you have not been in the job market for a while. You can take your time to prepare a letter, say exactly what you want, and of course include your resume. Remember that employers receive many resumes every day. Don't be surprised if you do not get a response to your inquiry, *and don't spend weeks waiting for responses that may never come*. If you do send a letter, follow it up (or precede it) with a phone call. This will increase your impact, and because of the initial research you did, will underscore both your familiarity with and your interest in the firm. Bear in mind that your goal is to make your name a familiar one with prospective employers, so that when a position becomes available, your resume will be one of the first the hiring manager seeks out.

DEVELOPING YOUR CONTACTS: NETWORKING

Some career counselors feel that the best route to a better job is through somebody you already know or through somebody to whom you can be introduced. These counselors recommend that you build your contact base beyond your current acquaintances by asking each one to introduce you, or refer you, to additional people in your field of interest.

The theory goes like this: You might start with 15 personal contacts, each of whom introduces you to three additional people, for a total of 45 additional contacts. Then each of these people introduces you to three additional people, which adds 135 additional contacts. Theoretically, you will soon know every person in the industry.

Of course, developing your personal contacts does not work quite as smoothly as the theory suggests because some people will not be able to introduce you to anyone. The further you stray from your initial contact base, the weaker your references may be. So, if you do try developing your own contacts, try to begin with as many people that you know personally as you can. Dig into your personal phone book and your holiday greeting card list and locate old classmates from school. Be particularly sure to approach people who perform your personal business such as your lawyer, accountant, banker, doctor, stockbroker, and insurance agent. These people develop a very broad contact base due to the nature of their professions.

If you send a fax, always follow with a hard copy of your resume and cover letter in the mail. Often, through no fault of your own, a fax will come through illegibly and employers do not often have time to let candidates know.

Another alternative is to make a "cover call." Your cover call should be just like your cover letter: concise. Your first statement should interest the employer in you. Then try to subtly mention your familiarity with the firm. Don't be overbearing; keep your introduction to three sentences or less. Be pleasant, self-confident, and relaxed. This will greatly increase the chances of the person at the other end of the line developing the conversation. But don't press. If you are asked to follow up with "something in the mail," this signals the conversation's natural end. Don't try to prolong the conversation once it has ended, and don't ask what they want to receive in the mail. Always send your resume and a highly personalized follow-up letter, reminding the addressee of the phone conversation. *Always* include a cover letter if you are asked to send a resume, and treat your resume and cover letter as a total package. Gear your letter toward the specific position you are applying for and prove why you would be a "good match" for the position.

> **Always include a cover letter if you are asked to send a resume.**

Unless you are in telephone sales, making smooth and relaxed cover calls will probably not come easily. Practice them on your own, and then with your friends or relatives.

DON'T BOTHER WITH MASS MAILINGS OR BARRAGES OF PHONE CALLS

Direct Contact does not mean burying every firm within a hundred miles with mail and phone calls. Mass mailings rarely work in the job hunt. This also applies to those letters that are personalized -- but dehumanized -- on an automatic typewriter or computer. Don't waste your time or money on such a project; you will fool no one but yourself.

The worst part of sending out mass mailings, or making unplanned phone calls to companies you have not researched, is that you are likely to be remembered as someone with little genuine interest in the firm, who lacks sincerity -- somebody that nobody wants to hire.

If you obtain an interview as a result of a telephone conversation, be sure to send a thank-you note reiterating the points you made during the conversation. You will appear more professional and increase your impact. However, unless specifically requested, don't mail your resume once an interview has been arranged. Take it with you to the interview instead.

You should never show up to seek a professional position without an appointment. Even if you are somehow lucky enough to obtain an interview, you will appear so unprofessional that you will not be seriously considered.

HELP WANTED ADVERTISEMENTS

Only a small fraction of professional job openings are advertised. Yet the majority of jobseekers -- and quite a few people not in the job market -- spend a lot of time studying the help wanted ads. As a result, the competition for advertised openings is often very severe.

A moderate-sized employer told us about their experience advertising in the help wanted section of a major Sunday newspaper:

It was a disaster. We had over 500 responses from this relatively small ad in just one week. We have only two phone lines in this office and one was totally knocked out. We'll never advertise for professional help again.

If you insist on following up on help wanted ads, then research a firm before you reply to an ad. Preliminary research might help to separate you from all of the other professionals responding to that ad, many of whom will have only a passing interest in the opportunity. It will also give you insight about a particular firm, to help you determine if it is potentially a good match. That said, your chances of obtaining a job through the want ads are still much smaller than they are with the Direct Contact method.

Preparing for the Interview

As each interview is arranged, begin your in-depth research. You should arrive at an interview knowing the company upside-down and inside-out. You need to know the company's products, types of customers, subsidiaries, parent company, principal locations, rank in the industry, sales and profit trends, type of ownership, size, current plans, and much more. By this time you have probably narrowed your job search to one industry. Even if you haven't, you should still be familiar with common industry terms, the trends in the firm's industry, the firm's principal competitors and their relative performance, and the direction in which the industry leaders are headed.

Dig into every resource you can! Surf the Internet. Read the company literature, the trade press, the business press, and if the company is public, call your stockbroker (if you have one) and ask for additional information. If possible, speak to someone at the firm before the

> **You should arrive at an interview knowing the company upside-down and inside-out.**

interview, or if not, speak to someone at a competing firm. The more time you spend, the better. Even if you feel extremely pressed for time, you should set aside several hours for pre-interview research.

If you have been out of the job market for some time, don't be surprised if you find yourself tense during your first few interviews. It will probably happen every time you re-enter the market, not just when you seek your first job after getting out of school.

Tension is natural during an interview, but knowing you have done a thorough research job should put you more at ease. Make a list of questions that you think might be asked in each interview. Think out your answers carefully and practice them with a friend. Tape record your responses to the problem questions. (*See also in this chapter: Informational Interviews.*) If you feel particularly unsure of your interviewing skills, arrange your first interviews at firms you are not as interested in. (But remember it is common courtesy to seem enthusiastic about the possibility of working for any firm at which you interview.) Practice again on your own after these first few interviews. Go over the difficult questions that you were asked.

Take some time to really think about how you will convey your work history. Present "bad experiences" as "learning experiences." Instead of saying "I hated my position as a salesperson because I had to bother people on the phone," say "I realized that cold-calling was not my strong suit. Though I love working with people, I decided my talents would be best used in a more face-to-face atmosphere." Always find some sort of lesson from previous jobs, as they all have one.

Interview Attire

How important is the proper dress for a job interview? Buying a complete wardrobe, donning new shoes, and having your hair styled every morning are not enough to guarantee you a career position as an investment banker. But on the other hand, if you can't find a clean, conservative suit or won't take the time to wash your hair, then you are just wasting your time by interviewing at all.

Personal grooming is as important as finding appropriate clothes for a job interview. Careful grooming indicates both a sense of thoroughness and self-confidence. This is not the time to make a statement -- take out the extra earrings and avoid any garish hair colors not found in nature. Women should not wear excessive makeup, and both men and women should refrain from wearing any perfume or cologne (it only takes a small spritz to leave an allergic interviewer with a fit of sneezing and a bad impression of your meeting). Men should be freshly shaven, even if the interview is late in the day, and men with long hair should have it pulled back and neat.

Men applying for any professional position should wear a suit, preferably in a conservative color such as navy or charcoal gray. It is easy to get away with wearing the same dark suit to consecutive interviews at the same company; just be sure to wear a different shirt and tie for each interview.

Women should also wear a business suit. Professionalism still dictates a suit with a skirt, rather than slacks, as proper interview garb for women. This is usually true even at companies where pants are acceptable attire for female employees. As much as you may disagree with this guideline, the more prudent time to fight this standard is after you land the job.

The final selection of candidates for a job opening won't be determined by dress, of course. However, inappropriate dress can quickly eliminate a first-round candidate. So while you shouldn't spend a fortune on a new wardrobe, you should be sure that your clothes are appropriate. The key is to dress at least as or slightly more formally and conservatively than the position would suggest.

What to Bring

Be complete. Everyone needs a watch, a pen, and a notepad. Finally, a briefcase or a leather-bound folder (containing extra, *unfolded*, copies of your resume) will help complete the look of professionalism.

Sometimes the interviewer will be running behind schedule. Don't be upset, be sympathetic. There is often pressure to interview a lot of candidates and to quickly fill a demanding position. So be sure to come to your interview with good reading material to keep yourself occupied and relaxed.

The Interview

The very beginning of the interview is the most important part because it determines the tone for the rest of it. Those first few moments are especially crucial. Do you smile when you meet? Do you establish enough eye contact, but not too much? Do you walk into the office with a self-assured and confident stride? Do you shake hands firmly? Do you make small talk easily without being garrulous? It is human nature to judge people by that first impression, so make sure it is a good one. But most of all, try to be yourself.

BE PREPARED:
Some Common Interview Questions

Tell me about yourself.

Why did you leave your last job?

What excites you in your current job?

Where would you like to be in five years?

How much overtime are you willing to work?

What would your previous/present employer tell me about you?

Tell me about a difficult situation that you
faced at your previous/present job.

What are your greatest strengths?

What are your weaknesses?

Describe a work situation where you took initiative
and went beyond your normal responsibilities.

Why should we hire you?

Often the interviewer will begin, after the small talk, by telling you about the company, the division, the department, or perhaps, the position. Because of your detailed research, the information about the company should be repetitive for you, and the interviewer would probably like nothing better than to avoid this regurgitation of the company biography. So if you can do so tactfully, indicate to the interviewer that you are very familiar with the firm. If he or she seems intent on providing you with background information, despite your hints, then acquiesce.

But be sure to remain attentive. If you can manage to generate a brief discussion of the company or the industry at this point, without being forceful, great. It will help to further build rapport, underscore your interest, and increase your impact.

> ## The interviewer's job is to find a reason to turn you down; your job is to not provide that reason.
>
> -John L. LaFevre, author, *How You Really Get Hired*
>
> Reprinted from the 1989/90 *CPC Annual*, with permission of the National Association of Colleges and Employers (formerly College Placement Council, Inc.), copyright holder.

Soon (if it didn't begin that way) the interviewer will begin the questions, many of which you will have already practiced. This period of the interview usually falls into one of two categories (or somewhere in between): either a structured interview, where the interviewer has a prescribed set of questions to ask; or an unstructured interview, where the interviewer will ask only leading questions to get you to talk about yourself, your experiences, and your goals. Try to sense as quickly as possible in which direction the interviewer wishes to proceed. This will make the interviewer feel more relaxed and in control of the situation.

Remember to keep attuned to the interviewer and make the length of your answers appropriate to the situation. If you are really unsure as to how detailed a response the interviewer is seeking, then ask.

As the interview progresses, the interviewer will probably mention some of the most important responsibilities of the position. If applicable, draw parallels between your experience and the demands of the position as detailed by the interviewer. Describe your past experience in the same manner that you do on your resume: emphasizing results and achievements and not merely describing activities. But don't exaggerate. Be on the level about your abilities.

The first interview is often the toughest, where many candidates are screened out. If you are interviewing for a very competitive position, you will have to make an impression that will last. Focus on a few of your greatest strengths that are relevant to the position. Develop these points carefully, state them again in different words, and then try to summarize them briefly at the end of the interview.

Often the interviewer will pause toward the end and ask if you have any questions. Particularly in a structured interview, this might be the one chance to really show your knowledge of and interest in the firm. Have a list prepared of specific questions that are of real interest to you. Let your questions subtly show your research and your knowledge of the firm's activities. It is wise to have an extensive list of questions, as several of them may be answered during the interview.

Do not turn your opportunity to ask questions into an interrogation. Avoid reading directly from your list of questions, and ask questions that you are fairly certain the interviewer can answer (remember how you feel when you cannot answer a question during an interview).

Even if you are unable to determine the salary range beforehand, do not ask about it during the first interview. You can always ask later. Above all, don't ask about fringe benefits until you have been offered a position. (Then be sure to get all the details.)

Try not to be negative about anything during the interview, particularly any past employer or any previous job. Be cheerful. Everyone likes to work with someone who seems to be happy. Even if you detest your current/former job or manager, do not make disparaging comments. The interviewer may construe this as a sign of a potential attitude problem and not consider you a strong candidate.

Don't let a tough question throw you off base. If you don't know the answer to a question, simply say so -- do not apologize. Just smile. Nobody can answer every question -- particularly some of the questions that are asked in job interviews.

Before your first interview, you may be able to determine how many rounds of interviews there usually are for positions at your level. (Of course it may differ quite a bit even within the different levels of one firm.) Usually you can count on attending at least two or three interviews, although some firms are known to give a minimum of six interviews for all professional positions. While you should be more relaxed as you return for subsequent interviews, the pressure will be on. The more prepared you are, the better.

Depending on what information you are able to obtain, you might want to vary your strategy quite a bit from interview to interview. For instance, if the first interview is a screening interview, then be sure a few of your strengths really stand out. On the other hand, if later interviews are primarily with people who are in a position to veto your hiring, but not to push it forward, then you should primarily focus on building rapport as opposed to reiterating and developing your key strengths.

If it looks as though your skills and background do not match the position the interviewer was hoping to fill, ask him or her if there is another division or subsidiary that perhaps could profit from your talents.

After the Interview

Write a follow-up letter immediately after the interview, while it is still fresh in the interviewer's mind (see the sample follow-up letter format found in the Resumes and Cover Letters chapter). Not only is this a thank-you, but it also gives you the chance to provide the interviewer with any details you may have forgotten (as long as they can be tactfully added in). If you haven't heard back from the interviewer within a week of sending your thank-you letter, call to stress your continued interest in the firm and the position. If you lost any points during the interview for any reason, this letter can help you regain footing. Be polite and make sure to stress your continued interest and competency to fill the position. Just don't forget to proofread it thoroughly. If you are unsure of the spelling of the interviewer's name, call the receptionist and ask.

THE BALANCING ACT:
Looking for a New Job While Currently Employed

For those of you who are still employed, job-searching will be particularly tiring because it must be done in addition to your normal work responsibilities. So don't overwork yourself to the point where you show up to interviews looking exhausted or start to slip behind at your current job. On the other hand, don't be tempted to quit your present job! The long hours are worth it. Searching for a job while you have one puts you in a position of strength.

Making Contact

If you must be at your office during the business day, then you have additional problems to deal with. How can you work interviews into the business day? And if you work in an open office, how can you even call to set up interviews? Obviously, you should keep up the effort and the appearances on your present job. So maximize your use of the lunch hour, early mornings, and late afternoons for calling. If you keep trying, you'll be surprised how often you will be able to reach the executive you are trying to contact during your out-of-office hours. You can catch people as early as 8 a.m. and as late as 6 p.m. on frequent occasions.

Scheduling Interviews

Your inability to interview at any time other than lunch just might work to your advantage. If you can, try to set up as many interviews as possible for your lunch hour. This will go a long way to creating a relaxed atmosphere. But be sure the interviews don't stray too far from the agenda on hand.

Lunchtime interviews are much easier to obtain if you have substantial career experience. People with less experience will often find no alternative to taking time off for interviews. If you have to take time off, you have to take time off. But try to do this as little as possible. Try to take the whole day off in order to avoid being blatantly obvious about your job search, and try to schedule two to three interviews for the same day. (It is very difficult to maintain an optimum level of energy at more than three interviews in one day.) Explain to the interviewer why you might have to juggle your interview schedule; he/she should honor the respect you're showing your current employer by minimizing your days off and will probably appreciate the fact that another prospective employer is interested in you.

> **Try calling as early as 8 a.m. and as late as 6 p.m. You'll be surprised how often you will be able to reach the executive you want during these times of the day.**

References

What do you tell an interviewer who asks for references from your current employer? Just say that while you are happy to have your former employers contacted, you are trying to keep your job search confidential and would rather that your current employer not be contacted until you have been given a firm offer.

IF YOU'RE FIRED OR LAID OFF:
Picking Yourself Up and Dusting Yourself Off

If you've been fired or laid off, you are not the first and will not be the last to go through this traumatic experience. In today's changing economy, thousands of professionals lose their jobs every year. Even if you were terminated with just cause, do not lose heart. Remember, being fired is not a reflection on you as a person. It is usually a reflection of your company's staffing needs and its perception of your recent job performance and attitude. And if you were not performing up to par or enjoying your work, then you will probably be better off at another company anyway.

> **Be prepared for the question "Why were you fired?" during job interviews.**

A thorough job search could take months, so be sure to negotiate a reasonable severance package, if possible, and determine to what benefits, such as health insurance, you are still legally entitled. Also, register for unemployment compensation immediately. Don't be surprised to find other professionals collecting unemployment compensation -- it is for everyone who has lost their job.

Don't start your job search with a flurry of unplanned activity. Start by choosing a strategy and working out a plan. Now is not the time for major changes in your life. If possible, remain in the same career and in the same geographical location, at least until you have been working again for a while. On the other hand, if the only industry for which you are trained is leaving, or is severely depressed in your area, then you should give prompt consideration to moving or switching careers.

Avoid mentioning you were fired when arranging interviews, but be prepared for the question "Why were you fired?" during an interview. If you were laid off as a result of downsizing, briefly explain, being sure to reinforce that your job loss was not due to performance. If you were in fact fired, be honest, but try to detail the reason as favorably as possible and portray what you have learned from your mistakes. If you are confident one of your past managers will give you a good reference, tell the interviewer to contact that person. Do not to speak negatively of your past employer and try not to sound particularly worried about your status of being temporarily unemployed.

Finally, don't spend too much time reflecting on why you were let go or how you might have avoided it. Think positively, look to the future, and be sure to follow a careful plan during your job search.

THE COLLEGE STUDENT:
Conducting Your First Job Search

While you will be able to apply many of the basics covered earlier in this chapter to your job search, there are some situations unique to the college student's job search.

THE GPA QUESTION

You are interviewing for the job of your dreams. Everything is going well: You've established a good rapport, the interviewer seems impressed with your qualifications, and you're almost positive the job is yours. Then you're asked about your GPA, which is pitifully low. Do you tell the truth and watch your dream job fly out the window?

Never lie about your GPA (they may request your transcript, and no company will hire a liar). You can, however, explain if there is a reason you don't feel your grades reflect your abilities, and mention any other impressive statistics. For example, if you have a high GPA in your major, or in the last few semesters (as opposed to your cumulative college career), you can use that fact to your advantage.

Perhaps the biggest problem college students face is lack of experience. Many schools have internship programs designed to give students exposure to the field of their choice, as well as the opportunity to make valuable contacts. Check out your school's career services department to see what internships are available. If your school does not have a formal internship program, or if there are no available internships that appeal to you, try contacting local businesses and offering your services. Often, businesses will be more than willing to have an extra pair of hands (especially if those hands are unpaid!) for a day or two each week. Or try contacting school alumni to see if you can "shadow" them for a few days, and see what their daily duties are like.

Informational Interviews

Although many jobseekers do not do this, it can be extremely helpful to arrange an informational interview with a college alumnus or someone else who works in your desired industry. You interview them about their job, their company, and their industry with questions you have prepared in advance. This can be done over the phone but is usually done in person. This will provide you with a contact in the industry who may give you more valuable information -- or perhaps even a job opportunity -- in the future. Always follow up with a thank you letter that includes your contact information.

The goal is to try to begin building experience and establishing contacts as early as possible in your college career.

What do you do if, for whatever reason, you weren't able to get experience directly related to your desired career? First, look at your previous jobs and see if there's anything you can highlight. Did you supervise or train other employees? Did you reorganize the accounting system, or boost productivity in some way? Accomplishments like these demonstrate leadership, responsibility, and innovation -- qualities that most companies look for in employees. And don't forget volunteer activities and school clubs, which can also showcase these traits.

On-Campus Recruiting

Companies will often send recruiters to interview on-site at various colleges. This gives students a chance to interview with companies that may not have interviewed them otherwise. This is particularly true if a company schedules "open" interviews, in which the only screening process is who is first in line at the sign-ups. Of course, since many more applicants gain interviews in this format, this also means that many more people are rejected. The on-campus interview is generally a screening interview, to see if it is worth the company's time to invite you in for a second interview. So do everything possible to make yourself stand out from the crowd.

The first step, of course, is to check out any and all information your school's career center has on the company. If the information seems out of date, check out the company on the Internet or call the company's headquarters and ask for any printed information.

Many companies will host an informational meeting for interviewees, often the evening before interviews are scheduled to take place. DO NOT MISS THIS MEETING. The recruiter will almost certainly ask if you attended. Make an effort to stay after the meeting and talk with the company's representatives. Not only does this give you an opportunity to find out more information about both the company and the position, it also makes you stand out in the recruiter's mind. If there's a particular company that you had your heart set on, but you weren't able to get an interview with them, attend the information session anyway. You may be able to persuade the recruiter to squeeze you into the schedule. (Or you may discover that the company really isn't the right fit for you after all.)

Try to check out the interview site beforehand. Some colleges may conduct "mock" interviews that take place in one of the standard interview rooms. Or you may be able to convince a career counselor (or even a custodian) to let you sneak a peek during off-hours. Either way, having an idea of the room's setup will help you to mentally prepare.

Arrive at least 15 minutes early to the interview. The recruiter may be ahead of schedule, and might meet you early. But don't be surprised if previous interviews have run over, resulting in your 30-minute slot being reduced to 20 minutes (or less). Don't complain or appear anxious; just use the time you do have as efficiently as possible to showcase the reasons *you* are the ideal candidate. Staying calm and composed in these situations will work to your advantage.

LAST WORDS

A parting word of advice. Again and again during your job search you will face rejection. You will be rejected when you apply for interviews. You will be rejected after interviews. For every job offer you finally receive, you probably will have been rejected many times. Don't let rejections slow you down. Keep reminding yourself that the sooner you go out, start your job search, and get those rejections flowing in, the closer you will be to obtaining the job you want.

RESUMES AND COVER LETTERS

When filling a position, an employer will often have 100-plus applicants, but time to interview only a handful of the most promising ones. As a result, he or she will reject most applicants after only briefly skimming their resumes.

Unless you have phoned and talked to the employer -- which you should do whenever you can -- you will be chosen or rejected for an interview entirely on the basis of your resume and cover letter. *Your cover letter must catch the employer's attention, and your resume must hold it.* (But remember -- a resume is no substitute for a job search campaign. *You* must seek a job. Your resume is only one tool, albeit a critical one.)

RESUME FORMAT:
Mechanics of a First Impression

The Basics

Employers dislike long resumes, so unless you have an unusually strong background with many years of experience and a diversity of outstanding achievements, keep your resume length to one page. If you must squeeze in more information than would otherwise fit, try using a smaller typeface or changing the margins. Watch also for "widows" at the end of paragraphs. You can often free up some space if you can shorten the information enough to get rid of those single words taking up an entire line. Another tactic that works with some word processing programs is to decrease the font size of your paragraph returns and changing the spacing between lines.

Print your resume on standard 8 1/2" x 11" paper. Since recruiters often get resumes in batches of hundreds, a smaller-sized resume may be lost in the pile. Oversized resumes are likely to get crumpled at the edges, and won't fit easily in their files.

First impressions matter, so make sure the recruiter's first impression of your resume is a good one. Never hand-write your resume (or cover letter)! Print your resume on quality paper that has weight and texture, in a conservative color such as white, ivory, or pale gray. Good resume paper is easy to find at many stores that sell stationery or office products. It is even available at some drug stores. Use *matching* paper and envelopes for both your resume and cover letter. One hiring manager at a major magazine throws out all resumes that arrive on paper that differs in color from the envelope!

Do not buy paper with images of clouds and rainbows in the background or anything that looks like casual stationery that you would send to your favorite aunt. Do not spray perfume or cologne on your resume. Do not include your picture with your resume unless you have a specific and appropriate reason to do so.

Another tip: Do a test print of your resume (and cover letter), to make sure the watermark is on the same side as the text so that you can read it. Also make sure it is right-side up. As trivial as this may sound, some recruiters check for this! One recruiter at a law firm in New Hampshire sheepishly admitted this is the first thing he checks. *"I open each envelope and check the watermarks on the resume and cover letter. Those candidates that have it wrong go into a different pile."*

Getting it on Paper

Modern photocomposition typesetting gives you the clearest, sharpest image, a wide variety of type styles, and effects such as italics, bold-facing, and book-like justified margins. It is also too expensive for many jobseekers. The quality of today's laser printers means that a computer-generated resume can look just as impressive as one that has been professionally typeset.

A computer with a word processing or desktop publishing program is the most common way to generate your resume. This allows you the flexibility to make changes almost instantly and to store different drafts on disk. Word processing and desktop publishing programs also offer many different fonts to choose from, each taking up different amounts of space. (It is generally best to stay between 9-point and 12-point font size.) Many other options are also available, such as bold-facing or italicizing for emphasis and the ability to change and manipulate spacing. It is generally recommended to leave the right-hand margin unjustified as this keeps the spacing between the text even and therefore easier to read. It is not wrong to justify both margins of text, but if possible try it both ways before you decide.

For a resume on paper, the end result will be largely determined by the quality of the printer you use. Laser printers will generally provide the best quality. Do not use a dot matrix printer.

Many companies now use scanning equipment to screen the resumes they receive, and certain paper, fonts, and other features are more compatible with this technology. White paper is preferable, as well as a standard font such as Courier or Helvetica. You should use at least a 10-point font, and avoid bolding, italics, underlining, borders, boxes, or graphics.

Household typewriters and office typewriters with nylon or other cloth ribbons are *not* good enough for typing your resume. If you don't have access to a quality word processing program, hire a professional with the resources to prepare your resume for you. Keep in mind that businesses such as Kinko's (open 24 hours) provide access to computers with quality printers.

Don't make your copies on an office photocopier. Only the human resources office may see the resume you mail. Everyone else may see only a copy of it, and copies of copies quickly become unreadable. Furthermore, sending photocopies of your resume or cover letter is completely unprofessional. Either print out each copy individually, or take your resume to a professional copy shop, which will generally offer professionally-maintained, extra-high-quality photocopiers and charge fairly reasonable prices. You want your resume to represent <u>you</u> with the look of polished quality.

Proof with Care

Whether you typed it or paid to have it produced professionally, mistakes on resumes are not only embarrassing, but will usually remove you from consideration (particularly if something obvious such as your name is misspelled). No matter how much you paid someone else to type, write, or typeset your resume, *you* lose if there is a mistake. So proofread it as carefully as possible. Get a friend to help you. Read your draft aloud as your friend checks the proof copy. Then have your friend read aloud while you check. Next, read it letter by letter to check spelling and punctuation.

If you are having it typed or typeset by a resume service or a printer, and you don't have time to proof it, pay for it and take it home. Proof it there and bring it back later to get it corrected and printed.

If you wrote your resume with a word processing program, use the built-in spell checker to double-check for spelling errors. Keep in mind that a spell checker will not find errors such as "to" for "two" or "wok" for "work." Many spell check programs do not recognize missing or misused punctuation, nor are they set to check the spelling of capitalized words. It's important that you still proofread your resume to check for grammatical mistakes and other problems, even after it has been spellchecked. If you find mistakes, do not make edits in pen or pencil or use white-out to fix them on the final copy!

Electronic Resumes

As companies rely increasingly on emerging technologies to find qualified candidates for job openings, you may opt to create an electronic resume in order to remain competitive in today's job market. Why is this important? Companies today sometimes request that resumes be submitted by e-mail, and many hiring managers regularly check online resume databases for candidates to fill unadvertised job openings. Other companies enlist the services of electronic employment database services, which charge jobseekers a nominal fee to have their resumes posted to the database to be viewed by potential employers. Still other companies use their own automated applicant tracking systems, in which case your resume is fed through a scanner that sends the image to a computer that "reads" your resume, looking for keywords, and files it accordingly in its database.

Whether you're posting your resume online, e-mailing it directly to an employer, sending it to an electronic employment database, or sending it to a company you suspect uses an automated applicant tracking system, you must create some form of electronic resume to take advantage of the technology. Don't panic! An electronic resume is simply a modified version of your conventional resume. An electronic resume is one that is sparsely formatted, but filled with keywords and important facts.

In order to post your resume to the Internet -- either to an online resume database or through direct e-mail to an employer -- you will need to change the way your resume is formatted. Instead of a Word, WordPerfect, or other word processing document, save your resume as a plain text, DOS, or ASCII file. These three terms are basically interchangeable, and describe text at its simplest, most basic level, without the formatting such as boldface or italics that most jobseekers use to make their resumes look more interesting. If you use e-mail, you'll notice that all of your messages are written and received in this format. First, you should remove all formatting from your resume including boldface, italics, underlining, bullets, differing font sizes, and graphics. Then, convert and save your resume as a plain text file. Most word processing programs have a "save as" feature that allows you to save files in different formats. Here, you should choose "text only" or "plain text."

Another option is to create a resume in HTML (hypertext markup language), the text formatting language used to publish information on the World Wide Web. However, the real usefulness of HTML resumes is still being explored. Most of the major online databases do not accept HTML resumes, and the vast majority of companies only accept plain text resumes through their e-mail.

Finally, if you simply wish to send your resume to an electronic employment database or a company that uses an automated applicant tracking system, there is no need to convert your resume to a plain text file. The only change you need to make is to organize the information in your resume by keywords. Employers are likely to do keyword searches for information, such as degree held or knowledge of particular types of software. Therefore, using the right keywords or key phrases in your resume is critical to its ultimate success. Keywords are usually nouns or short phrases that the computer searches for which refer to experience, training, skills, and abilities. For example, let's say an employer searches an employment database for a sales representative with the following criteria:

BS/BA
exceeded quota
cold calls
high energy
willing to travel

Even if you have the right qualifications, neglecting to use these keywords would result in the computer passing over your resume. Although there is no way to know for sure which keywords employers are most likely to search for, you can make educated guesses by checking the help-wanted ads or online job postings for your type of job. You should also arrange keywords in a keyword summary, a paragraph listing your qualifications that immediately follows your name and address (see sample letter in this chapter). In addition, choose a nondecorative font with clear, distinct characters, such as Helvetica or Times. It is more difficult for a scanner to accurately pick up the more unusual fonts. Boldface and all capital letters are best used only for major section headings, such as "Experience" and "Education." It is also best to avoid using italics or underlining, since this can cause the letters to bleed into one another.

Types of Resumes

The most common resume formats are the functional resume, the chronological resume, and the combination resume. (Examples can be found at the end of this chapter.) A functional resume focuses on skills and de-emphasizes job titles, employers, etc. A functional resume is best if you have been out of the work force for a long time or are changing careers. It is also good if you want to highlight specific skills and strengths, especially if all of your work experience has been at one company. This format can also be a good choice if you are just out of school or have no experience in your desired field.

Choose a chronological format if you are currently working or were working recently, and if your most recent experiences relate to your desired field. Use reverse chronological order and include dates. To a recruiter your last job and your latest schooling are the most important, so put the last first and list the rest going back in time.

A combination resume is perhaps the most common. This resume simply combines elements of the functional and chronological resume formats. This is used by many jobseekers with a solid track record who find elements of both types useful.

Organization

Your name, phone number, e-mail address (if you have one), and a complete mailing address should be at the top of your resume. Try to make your name stand out by using a slightly larger font size or all capital letters. Be sure to spell out everything. Never abbreviate St. for Street or Rd. for Road. If you are a college student, you should also put your home address and phone number at the top. Change your message on your answering machine if necessary – RUSH blaring in the background or your sorority sisters screaming may not come across well to all recruiters. If you think you may be moving within six months then include a second address and phone number of a trusted friend or relative who can reach you no matter where you are.

Remember that employers will keep your resume on file and may contact you months later if a position opens that fits your qualifications. All too often, candidates are unreachable because they have moved and had not previously provided enough contact options on their resume.

Next, list your experience, then your education. If you are a recent graduate, list your education first, unless your experience is more important than your education. (For example, if you have just graduated from a teaching school, have some business experience, and are applying for a job in business, you would list your business experience first.)

Keep everything easy to find. Put the dates of your employment and education on the left of the page. Put the names of the companies you worked for and the schools you attended a few spaces to the right of the dates. Put the city and state, or the city and country, where you studied or worked to the right of the page.

The important thing is simply to break up the text in some logical way that makes your resume visually attractive and easy to scan, so experiment to see which layout works best for your resume. However you set it up, *stay consistent*. Inconsistencies in fonts, spacing, or tenses will make your resume look sloppy. Also, be sure to use tabs to keep your information vertically lined up, rather than the less precise space bar.

RESUME CONTENT:
Say it with Style
Sell Yourself

You are selling your skills and accomplishments in your resume, so it is important to inventory yourself and know yourself. If you have achieved something, say so. Put it in the best possible light, but avoid subjective statements, such as "I am a hard worker" or "I get along well with my coworkers." Just stick to the facts.

While you shouldn't hold back or be modest, don't exaggerate your achievements to the point of misrepresentation. <u>Be honest</u>. Many companies will immediately drop an applicant from consideration (or fire a current employee) upon discovering inaccurate or untrue information on a resume or other application material.

Write down the important (and pertinent) things you have done, but do it in as few words as possible. Your resume will be scanned, not read, and short, concise phrases are much more effective than long-winded sentences. Avoid the use of "I" when emphasizing your accomplishments. Instead, use brief phrases beginning with action verbs.

While some technical terms will be unavoidable, you should try to avoid excessive "technicalese." Keep in mind that the first person to see your resume may be a human resources person who won't necessarily know all the jargon -- and how can they be impressed by something they don't understand?

Keep it Brief

Also, try to hold your paragraphs to six lines or less. If you have more than six lines of information about one job or school, put it in two or more paragraphs.

A short resume will be examined more carefully. Remember: Your resume usually has between eight and 45 seconds to catch an employer's eye. So make every second count.

Job Objective

A functional resume may require a job objective to give it focus. One or two sentences describing the job you are seeking can clarify in what capacity your skills will be best put to use. Be sure that your stated objective is in line with the position you're applying for.

Examples:

> An entry-level editorial assistant position in the publishing industry.
> A senior management position with a telecommunications firm.

Don't include a job objective on a chronological resume unless your previous work experiences are <u>completely</u> unrelated to the position for which you're applying. The presence of an overly specific job objective might eliminate you from consideration for other positions that a recruiter feels are a better match for your qualifications. But even if you don't put an objective on paper, having a career goal in mind as you write can help give your resume a solid sense of direction.

USE ACTION VERBS

How you write your resume is just as important as *what* you write. In describing previous work experiences, the strongest resumes use short phrases beginning with action verbs. Below are a few you may want to use. (This list is not all-inclusive.)

achieved	developed	integrated	purchased
administered	devised	interpreted	reduced
advised	directed	interviewed	regulated
arranged	distributed	launched	represented
assisted	established	managed	resolved
attained	evaluated	marketed	restored
budgeted	examined	mediated	restructured
built	executed	monitored	revised
calculated	expanded	negotiated	scheduled
collaborated	expedited	obtained	selected
collected	facilitated	operated	served
compiled	formulated	ordered	sold
completed	founded	organized	solved
computed	generated	participated	streamlined
conducted	headed	performed	studied
consolidated	identified	planned	supervised
constructed	implemented	prepared	supplied
consulted	improved	presented	supported
controlled	increased	processed	tested
coordinated	initiated	produced	trained
created	installed	proposed	updated
determined	instructed	published	wrote

Some jobseekers may choose to include both "Relevant Experience" and "Additional Experience" sections. This can be useful, as it allows the jobseeker to place more emphasis on certain experiences and to de-emphasize others.

Emphasize continued experience in a particular job area or continued interest in a particular industry. De-emphasize irrelevant positions. It is okay to include one opening line providing a general description of each company you've worked at. Delete positions that you held for less than four months (unless you are a very recent college grad or still in school). Stress your <u>results</u> and your achievements, elaborating on how you contributed in your previous jobs. Did you increase sales, reduce costs, improve a product, implement a new program? Were you promoted? Use specific numbers (i.e., quantities, percentages, dollar amounts) whenever possible.

Education

Keep it brief if you have more than two years of career experience. Elaborate more if you have less experience. If you are a recent college graduate, you may choose to include any high school activities that are directly relevant to your career. If you've been out of school for a while you don't need to list your education prior to college.

Mention degrees received and any honors or special awards. Note individual courses or projects you participated in that might be relevant for employers. For example, if you are an English major applying for a position as a business writer, be sure to mention any business or economics courses. Previous experience such as Editor-in-Chief of the school newspaper would be relevant as well.

If you are uploading your resume to an online job hunting site such as CareerCity.com, action verbs are still important, but the key words or key nouns that a computer would search for become more important. For example, if you're seeking an accounting position, key nouns that a computer would search for such as "Lotus 1-2-3" or "CPA" or "payroll" become very important.

Highlight Impressive Skills

Be sure to mention any computer skills you may have. You may wish to include a section entitled "Additional Skills" or "Computer Skills," in which you list any software programs you know. An additional skills section is also an ideal place to mention fluency in a foreign language.

Personal Data

This section is optional, but if you choose to include it, keep it brief. A one-word mention of hobbies such as fishing, chess, baseball, cooking, etc., can give the person who will interview you a good way to open up the conversation.

Team sports experience is looked at favorably. It doesn't hurt to include activities that are somewhat unusual (fencing, Akido, '70s music) or that somehow relate to the position or the company to which you're applying. For instance, it would be worth noting if you are a member of a professional organization in your industry of interest. Never include information about your age, alias, date of birth, health, physical characteristics, marital status, religious affiliation, or political/moral beliefs.

References

The most that is needed is the sentence "References available upon request" at the bottom of your resume. If you choose to leave it out, that's fine. This line is not really necessary. It is understood that references will most likely be asked for and provided by you later on in the interviewing process. Do not actually send references with your resume and cover letter unless specifically requested.

HIRING A RESUME WRITER:
Is it the Right Choice for You?

If you write reasonably well, it is to your advantage to write your own resume. Writing your resume forces you to review your experiences and figure out how to explain your accomplishments in clear, brief phrases. This will help you when you explain your work to interviewers. It is also easier to tailor your resume to each position you're applying for when you have put it together yourself.

If you write your resume, everything will be in your own words; it will sound like you. It will say what you want it to say. If you are a good writer, know yourself well, and have a good idea of which parts of your background employers are looking for, you should be able to write your own resume better than someone else. If you decide to write your resume yourself, have as many people as possible review and proofread it. Welcome objective opinions and other perspectives.

When to Get Help

If you have difficulty writing in "resume style" (which is quite unlike normal written language), if you are unsure which parts of your background to emphasize, or if you think your resume would make your case better if it did not follow one of the standard forms outlined either here or in a book on resumes, then you should consider having it professionally written.

Even some professional resume writers we know have had their resumes written with the help of fellow professionals. They sought the help of someone who could be objective about their background, as well as provide an experienced sounding board to help focus their thoughts.

If You Hire a Pro

The best way to choose a writer is by reputation: the recommendation of a friend, a personnel director, your school placement officer, or someone else knowledgeable in the field.

Important questions:
· "How long have you been writing resumes?"
· "If I'm not satisfied with what you write, will you go over it with me and change it?"
· "Do you charge by the hour or a flat rate?"

There is no sure relation between price and quality, except that you are unlikely to get a good writer for less than $50 for an uncomplicated resume and you shouldn't have to pay more than $300 unless your experience is very extensive or complicated. There will be additional charges for printing. Assume nothing no matter how much you pay. It is your career at stake if there are mistakes on your resume!

Few resume services will give you a firm price over the phone, simply because some resumes are too complicated and take too long to do for a predetermined price. Some services will quote you a price that applies to almost all of their customers. Once you decide to use a specific writer, you should insist on a firm price quote *before* engaging their services. Also, find out how expensive minor changes will be.

COVER LETTERS:
Quick, Clear, and Concise

Always mail a cover letter with your resume. In a cover letter you can show an interest in the company that you can't show in a resume. You can also point out one or two of your skills or accomplishments the company can put to good use.

Make it Personal

The more personal you can get, the better, so long as you keep it professional. If someone known to the person you are writing has recommended that you contact the company, get permission to include his/her name in the letter. If you can get the name of a person to send the letter to, address it directly to that person (after first calling the company to verify the spelling of the person's name, correct title, and mailing address). Be sure to put the person's name and title on both the letter and the envelope. This will ensure that your letter will get through to the proper person, even if a new person now occupies this position. It will not always be possible to get the name of a person. Always strive to get at least a title.

Be sure to mention something about why you have an interest in the company -- *so many candidates apply for jobs with no apparent knowledge of what the company does!* This conveys the message that they just want any job.

Type cover letters in full. Don't try the cheap and easy ways, like using a computer mail merge program or photocopying the body of your letter and typing in the inside address and salutation. You will give the impression that you are mailing to a host of companies and have no particular interest in any one.

Print your cover letter on the same color and same high-quality paper as your resume.

Cover letter basic format

<u>Paragraph 1:</u> State what the position is that you are seeking. It is not always necessary to state how you found out about the position -- often you will apply without knowing that a position is open.
<u>Paragraph 2:</u> Include what you know about the company and why you are interested in working there. Mention any prior contact with the company or someone known to the hiring person if relevant. Briefly state your qualifications and what you can offer. (Do not talk about what you cannot do).
<u>Paragraph 3:</u> Close with your phone number and where/when you can be reached. Make a request for an interview. State when you will follow up by phone (or mail or e-mail if the ad requests no phone calls). Do not wait long -- generally five working days. If you say you're going to follow up, then actually do it! This phone call can get your resume noticed when it might otherwise sit in a stack of 225 other resumes.

Cover letter do's and don'ts

- *Do* keep your cover letter brief and to the point.
- *Do* be sure it is error-free.
- *Do* accentuate what you can offer the company, not what you hope to gain.

- *Do* be sure your phone number and address is on your cover letter just in case it gets separated from your resume (this happens!).
- *Do* check the watermark by holding the paper up to a light -- be sure it is facing forward so it is readable -- on the same side as the text, and right-side up.
- *Do* sign your cover letter (or type your name if you are sending it electronically). Blue or black ink are both fine. Do not use red ink.
- *Don't* just repeat information verbatim from your resume.
- *Don't* overuse the personal pronoun "I."
- *Don't* send a generic cover letter -- show your personal knowledge of and interest in that particular company.

THANK YOU LETTERS:
Another Way to Stand Out

As mentioned earlier, *always* send a thank you letter after an interview (see the sample later in this section). So few candidates do this and it is yet another way for you to stand out. Be sure to mention something specific from the interview and restate your interest in the company and the position.

It is generally acceptable to handwrite your thank you letter on a generic thank you card (but *never* a postcard). Make sure handwritten notes are neat and legible. However, if you are in doubt, typing your letter is always the safe bet. If you met with several people it is fine to send them each an individual thank you letter. Call the company if you need to check on the correct spelling of their names.

Remember to:
- Keep it short.
- Proofread it carefully.
- Send it *promptly*.

FUNCTIONAL RESUME

C.J. RAVENCLAW
129 Pennsylvania Avenue
Washington DC 20500
202/555-6652
e-mail: ravenclaw@dcpress.net

Objective
A position as a graphic designer commensurate with my acquired skills and expertise.

Summary
Extensive experience in plate making, separations, color matching, background definition, printing, mechanicals, color corrections, and personnel supervision. A highly motivated manager and effective communicator. Proven ability to:

- **Create Commercial Graphics**
- **Produce Embossed Drawings**
- **Color Separate**
- **Control Quality**
- **Resolve Printing Problems**
- **Analyze Customer Satisfaction**

Qualifications
Printing:
Knowledgeable in black and white as well as color printing. Excellent judgment in determining acceptability of color reproduction through comparison with original. Proficient at producing four- or five-color corrections on all media, as well as restyling previously reproduced four-color artwork.

Customer Relations:
Routinely work closely with customers to ensure specifications are met. Capable of striking a balance between technical printing capabilities and need for customer satisfaction through entire production process.

Specialties:
Practiced at creating silk screen overlays for a multitude of processes including velo bind, GBC bind, and perfect bind. Creative design and timely preparation of posters, flyers, and personalized stationery.

Personnel Supervision:
Skillful at fostering atmosphere that encourages highly talented artists to balance high-level creativity with maximum production. Consistently beat production deadlines. Instruct new employees, apprentices, and students in both artistry and technical operations.

Experience
Graphic Arts Professor, Ohio State University, Columbus OH (1998-2002).
Manager, Design Graphics, Washington DC (2003-present).

Education
Massachusetts Conservatory of Art, Ph.D. 1996
University of Massachusetts, B.A. 1994

CHRONOLOGICAL RESUME

HARRY SEABORN
557 Shoreline Drive
Seattle, WA 98404
(206) 555-6584
e-mail: hseaborn@centco.com

EXPERIENCE

THE CENTER COMPANY   Seattle, WA
Systems Programmer   2002-present
- Develop and maintain customer accounting and order tracking database using a Visual Basic front end and SQL server.
- Plan and implement migration of company wide transition from mainframe-based dumb terminals to a true client server environment using Windows NT Workstation and Server.
- Oversee general local and wide area network administration including the development of a variety of intranet modules to improve internal company communication and planning across divisions.

INFO TECH, INC.   Seattle, WA
Technical Manager   1996-2002
- Designed and managed the implementation of a network providing the legal community with a direct line to Supreme Court cases across the Internet using SQL Server and a variety of Internet tools.
- Developed a system to make the entire library catalog available on line using PERL scripts and SQL.
- Used Visual Basic and Microsoft Access to create a registration system for university registrar.

EDUCATION

SALEM STATE UNIVERSITY   Salem, OR
     M.S. in Computer Science.   1999
     B.S. in Computer Science.   1997

COMPUTER SKILLS

- Programming Languages: Visual Basic, Java, C++, SQL, PERL
- Software: SQL Server, Internet Information Server, Oracle
- Operating Systems: Windows NT, UNIX, Linux

FUNCTIONAL RESUME

Donna Hermione Moss
703 Wizard's Way
Chicago, IL 60601
(312) 555-8841
e-mail: donna@cowfire.com

OBJECTIVE:
To contribute over five years of experience in promotion, communications, and administration to an entry-level position in advertising.

SUMMARY OF QUALIFICATIONS:
- Performed advertising duties for small business.
- Experience in business writing and communications skills.
- General knowledge of office management.
- Demonstrated ability to work well with others, in both supervisory and support staff roles.
- Type 75 words per minute.

SELECTED ACHIEVEMENTS AND RESULTS:
Promotion:
Composing, editing, and proofreading correspondence and public relations materials for own catering service. Large-scale mailings.

Communication:
Instruction; curriculum and lesson planning; student evaluation; parent-teacher conferences; development of educational materials. Training and supervising clerks.

Computer Skills:
Proficient in MS Word, Lotus 1-2-3, Excel, and Filemaker Pro.

Administration:
Record-keeping and file maintenance. Data processing and computer operations, accounts receivable, accounts payable, inventory control, and customer relations. Scheduling, office management, and telephone reception.

PROFESSIONAL HISTORY:
Teacher; Self-Employed (owner of catering service); Floor Manager; Administrative Assistant; Accounting Clerk.

EDUCATION:
Beloit College, Beloit, WI, BA in Education, 1997

CHRONOLOGICAL RESUME

PERCY ZIEGLER
16 Josiah Court
Marlborough CT 06447
203/555-9641 (h)
203/555-8176, x14 (w)

EDUCATION   Keene State College, Keene NH
Bachelor of Arts in Elementary Education, 2003
• Graduated *magna cum laude*
• English minor
• Kappa Delta Pi member, inducted 2001

EXPERIENCE   Elmer T. Thienes Elementary School, Marlborough CT
September 2003- *Part-time Kindergarten Teacher*
Present   • Instruct kindergartners in reading, spelling, language   arts, and
music.
• Participate in the selection of textbooks and learning aids.
• Organize and supervise class field trips and coordinate in-class
presentations.

Summers   Keene YMCA, Youth Division, Keene NH
2000-2002   *Child-care Counselor*
• Oversaw summer program for low-income youth.
• Budgeted and coordinated special events and field trips,
working with Program Director to initiate variations in the
program.
• Served as Youth Advocate in cooperation with social worker to
address the social needs and problems of participants.

Spring 2002   Wheelock Elementary School, Keene NH
Student Teacher
• Taught third-grade class in all elementary subjects.
• Designed and implemented a two-week unit on Native
Americans.
• Assisted in revision of third-grade curriculum.

Fall 2001   Child Development Center, Keene NH
Daycare Worker
• Supervised preschool children on the playground and during art
activities.
• Created a "Wishbone Corner," where children could quietly
look at books or take a voluntary "time-out."

ADDITIONAL INTERESTS
Martial arts, Pokemon, politics, reading, skiing, writing.

ELECTRONIC RESUME

GRIFFIN DORE
69 Dursley Drive
Cambridge, MA 02138
(617) 555-5555

KEYWORD SUMMARY

Senior financial manager with over ten years experience in Accounting and Systems Management, Budgeting, Forecasting, Cost Containment, Financial Reporting, and International Accounting. MBA in Management. Proficient in Lotus, Excel, Solomon, and Windows.

EXPERIENCE

COLWELL CORPORATION, Wellesley, MA
Director of Accounting and Budgets, 1995 to present
　Direct staff of twenty in General Ledger, Accounts Payable, Accounts Receivable, and International Accounting.
　Facilitate month-end closing process with parent company and auditors.
　Implemented team-oriented cross-training program within accounting group, resulting in timely month-end closings and increased productivity of key accounting staff.
　Developed and implemented a strategy for Sales and Use Tax Compliance in all fifty states.
　Prepare monthly financial statements and analyses.

FRANKLIN AND DELANEY COMPANY, Melrose, MA
Senior Accountant, 1993-1996
　Managed Accounts Payable, General Ledger, transaction processing, and financial reporting. Supervised staff of five.

Staff Accountant, 1991-1993
　Managed Accounts Payable, including vouchering, cash disbursements, and bank reconciliation.
　Wrote and issued policies.
　Maintained supporting schedules used during year-end audits.
　Trained new employees.

EDUCATION

MBA in Management, Northeastern University, Boston, MA, 1995
BS in Accounting, Boston College, Boston, MA, 1991

ASSOCIATIONS

National Association of Accountants

GENERAL MODEL
FOR A COVER LETTER

Your mailing address
Date

Contact's name
Contact's title
Company
Company's mailing address

Dear Mr./Ms. _____:

Immediately explain why your background makes you the best candidate for the position that you are applying for. Describe what prompted you to write (want ad, article you read about the company, networking contact, etc.). Keep the first paragraph short and hard-hitting.

Detail what you could contribute to this company. Show how your qualifications will benefit this firm. Describe your interest in the corporation. Subtly emphasizing your knowledge about this firm and your familiarity with the industry will set you apart from other candidates. Remember to keep this letter short; few recruiters will read a cover letter longer than half a page.

If possible, your closing paragraph should request specific action on the part of the reader. Include your phone number and the hours when you can be reached. Mention that if you do not hear from the reader by a specific date, you will follow up with a phone call. Lastly, thank the reader for their time, consideration, etc.

Sincerely,

(signature)

Your full name (typed)

Enclosure (use this if there are other materials, such as your resume, that are included in the same envelope)

SAMPLE COVER LETTER

16 Josiah Court
Marlborough CT 06447
January 16, 2006

Ms. Leona Malfoy
Assistant Principal
Laningham Elementary School
43 Mayflower Drive
Keene NH 03431

Dear Ms. Malfoy:

Toby Potter recently informed me of a possible opening for a third grade teacher at Laningham Elementary School. With my experience instructing third-graders, both in schools and in summer programs, I feel I would be an ideal candidate for the position. Please accept this letter and the enclosed resume as my application.

Laningham's educational philosophy that every child can learn and succeed interests me, since it mirrors my own. My current position at Elmer T. Thienes Elementary has reinforced this philosophy, heightening my awareness of the different styles and paces of learning and increasing my sensitivity toward special needs children. Furthermore, as a direct result of my student teaching experience at Wheelock Elementary School, I am comfortable, confident, and knowledgeable working with third-graders.

I look forward to discussing the position and my qualifications for it in more detail. I can be reached at 203/555-9641 evenings or 203/555-8176, x14 weekdays. If I do not hear from you before Tuesday of next week, I will call to see if we can schedule a time to meet. Thank you for your time and consideration.

Sincerely,

Percy Ziegler

Percy Ziegler

Enclosure

GENERAL MODEL FOR A
THANK YOU/FOLLOW-UP LETTER

Your mailing address
Date

Contact's name
Contact's title
Company
Company's mailing address

Dear Mr./Ms._____:

Remind the interviewer of the reason (i.e., a specific opening, an informational interview, etc.) you were interviewed, as well as the date. Thank him/her for the interview, and try to personalize your thanks by mentioning some specific aspect of the interview.

Confirm your interest in the organization (and in the opening, if you were interviewing for a particular position). Use specifics to re-emphasize that you have researched the firm in detail and have considered how you would fit into the company and the position. This is a good time to say anything you wish you had said in the initial meeting. Be sure to keep this letter brief; a half page is plenty.

If appropriate, close with a suggestion for further action, such as a desire to have an additional interview, if possible. Mention your phone number and the hours you can be reached. Alternatively, you may prefer to mention that you will follow up with a phone call in several days. Once again, thank the person for meeting with you, and state that you would be happy to provide any additional information about your qualifications.

Sincerely,

(signature)

Your full name (typed)

PRIMARY EMPLOYERS

ACCOUNTING & MANAGEMENT CONSULTING

**You can expect to find the following types of companies
in this section:**
Consulting and Research Firms • Industrial Accounting Firms • Management
Services • Public Accounting Firms • Tax Preparation Companies

ABT ASSOCIATES INC.
55 Wheeler Street, Cambridge MA 02138. 617/492-7100. **Fax:** 617/492-5219.
Contact: Human Resources. **E-mail address:** abtassoc@rpc.webhire.com.
World Wide Web address: http://www.abtassoc.com. **Description:** One of the
largest government and business consulting and research firms in the country.
The company offers policy analysis, technical assistance, program evaluation,
and program operation services to governmental clients and provides
organizational development, service quality measurement and management,
strategic planning, management consulting, and new product development
services to business clients. ABT Associates conducts its business through four
main practice areas: international economic policy research; business research
and consulting; and ABT Associates Clinical Trials. Founded in 1965. **Positions
advertised include:** Analyst; Research Assistant; Medical Associate; MIS
Director; Programmer Analyst; Research Project Manager; Accounts Payable
Clerk; Informational Payroll Manager; Administrative Assistant; Principal
Associate; Biostatistician. **NOTE:** Applicants can mail resumes with appropriate
source code found on website to this address for consideration: Abt Associates
Inc., Source Code, P.O. Box 369 Burlington MA 01803. **Corporate
headquarters location:** This location. **Other area locations:** Lexington MA;
Hadley MA. **Other U.S. locations:** Washington DC; Chicago IL; Bethesda MD.
International locations: Egypt; South Africa. **Operations at this facility
include:** Administration; Research and Development. **Annual sales/revenues:**
More than $100 million. **Number of employees worldwide:** 1,000.

BDO SEIDMAN, LLP
40 Broad Street, Suite 500, Boston MA 02109. 617/422-7576. **Fax:** 617/422-
7570. **Contact:** Katie Rojik, Office Manager. **World Wide Web address:**
http://www.bdo.com. **Description:** A public accounting and consulting firm.
Positions advertised include: Administrative Assistant; Senior Tax Consultant.

BAIN & COMPANY, INC.
131 Dartmouth Street, Boston MA 02116. 617/572-2000. **Contact:** Human
Resources. **World Wide Web address:** http://www.bain.com. **Description:** An
international management consulting firm that helps major companies achieve
higher levels of competitiveness and profitability. Founded in 1973. **Corporate
headquarters location:** This location. **Other U.S. locations:** Nationwide.
International locations: Worldwide. **Number of employees nationwide:** 1,000.
Number of employees worldwide: 2800.

CERIDIAN EMPLOYER SERVICES
401 Edgewater Place, Suite 220, Wakefield MA 01880. 781/213-8000. **Contact:**
Human Resources. **World Wide Web address:** http://www.ceridian.com.
Description: An accounting and auditing services company. **Positions
advertised include:** Client Service Analyst. **Parent company:** Ceridian
Corporation (Minneapolis MN.)

ERNST & YOUNG LLP
200 Clarendon Street, Boston MA 02116. 617/266-2000. **Contact:** Personnel Manager. **World Wide Web address:** http://www.ey.com. **Description:** A certified public accounting firm that also provides management consulting services. Services include data processing, financial modeling, financial feasibility studies, production planning and inventory management, management sciences, health care planning, human resources, cost accounting, and budgeting systems. **Other U.S. locations:** Nationwide. **International locations:** Worldwide. **Number of employees worldwide:** 77,000.

THE FORUM CORPORATION
One Exchange Place, 3rd Floor, Boston MA 02109. 617/523-7300. **Toll-free phone:** 800/367-8611. **Fax:** 617/973-2005. **Contact:** Human Resources. **E-mail address:** careers@forum.com. **World Wide Web address:** http://www.forum.com. **Description:** An international training and consulting firm. Founded in 1971. **Special programs:** Internships. **Office hours:** Monday - Friday, 9:00 a.m. - 5:30 p.m. **Corporate headquarters location:** This location. **Other U.S. locations:** San Francisco CA; Wilmington DE; Chicago IL; Landover MD; New York NY. **International locations:** Australia; Canada; England; Hong Kong; Korea; New Zealand; Singapore. **CEO:** Pippa Wicks. **Number of employees at this location:** 115. **Number of employees nationwide:** 260.

GRANT THORNTON LLP
98 North Washington Street, Boston MA 02114-1913. 617/723-7900. **Contact:** Human Resources. **World Wide Web address:** http://www.grantthornton.com. **Description:** An international certified public accounting organization offering consulting and accounting services as well as strategic and tactical planning assistance to a diversified client base. Founded in 1924. **Positions advertised include:** Auditor; Experienced Tax Manager; Tax Associate; State & Local Tax Manager. **Corporate headquarters location:** Chicago IL. **Other U.S. locations:** Nationwide. **International locations:** Worldwide.

H&R BLOCK
77 Main Street, Andover MA 01810. 978/686-1371. **Contact:** Human Resources. **World Wide Web address:** http://www.hrblock.com. **Description:** Engaged in consumer tax preparation. H&R Block operates more than 9,500 offices nationwide, and prepares more than 10 million tax returns each year. The company has offices in over 750 Sears stores in both the United States and Canada. Many offices operate as franchises, and some operate on a seasonal basis. H&R Block is also engaged in a number of other tax-related activities, including group tax programs, premium tax service, tax training schools, and real estate tax awareness seminars. **Corporate headquarters location:** Kansas City MO. **Other U.S. locations:** Nationwide. **Listed on:** New York Stock Exchange. **Stock exchange symbol:** HRB. **President/CEO:** Mark Ernst.

H&R BLOCK
157 Centre Street, Malden MA 02148. 781/322-7453. **Contact:** Human Resources. **World Wide Web address:** http://www.hrblock.com. **Description:** Engaged in consumer tax preparation. H&R Block operates more than 9,500 offices nationwide, and prepares more than 10 million tax returns each year. The company has offices in over 750 Sears stores in both the United States and Canada. Many offices operate as franchises, and some operate on a seasonal basis. H&R Block is also engaged in a number of other tax-related activities, including group tax programs, premium tax service, tax training schools, and real estate tax awareness seminars. **Corporate headquarters location:** Kansas City

MO. **Other U.S. locations:** Nationwide. **Listed on:** New York Stock Exchange. **Stock exchange symbol:** HRB. **President/CEO:** Mark Ernst.

H&R BLOCK
1515 Dorchester Avenue, Fields Corner, Dorchester MA 02122. 617/825-4514. **Contact:** Human Resources. **World Wide Web address:** http://www.hrblock.com. **Description:** Engaged in consumer tax preparation. H&R Block operates more than 9,500 offices nationwide, and prepares more than 10 million tax returns each year. The company has offices in over 750 Sears stores in both the United States and Canada. Many offices operate as franchises, and some operate on a seasonal basis. H&R Block is also engaged in a number of other tax-related activities, including group tax programs, premium tax service, tax training schools, and real estate tax awareness seminars. **Corporate headquarters location:** Kansas City MO. **Other U.S. locations:** Nationwide. **Listed on:** New York Stock Exchange. **Stock exchange symbol:** HRB. **President/CEO:** Mark Ernst.

KPMG
99 High Street, Boston MA 02110-2371. 617/988-1000. **Contact:** Human Resources. **World Wide Web address:** http://www.kpmg.com. **Description:** Delivers a wide range of value-added assurance, tax, and consulting services. **Positions advertised include:** Tax Associate; Transactions Services Manager; Internal Auditor; IT Audit Associate; Corporate Tax Associate; Corporate Tax Associate; Office Services Supervisor; Auditor; Corporate Recovery Associate. **Corporate headquarters location:** Montvale NJ. **Other U.S. locations:** Nationwide. **International locations:** Worldwide. **Parent company:** KPMG International is a leader among professional services firms engaged in capturing, managing, assessing, and delivering information to create knowledge that will help its clients maximize shareholder value. **Number of employees worldwide:** 100,000.

A.T. KEARNEY, INC.
One Memorial Drive, 14th Floor, Cambridge MA 02142-1301. 617/374-2600. **Contact:** Human Resources. **World Wide Web address:** http://www.atkearney.com. **Description:** A general management consulting firm. **NOTE:** Visit website for more information concerning recruiting process. **Parent company:** EDS.

ARTHUR D. LITTLE, INC.
25 Acorn Park, Cambridge MA 02140. 617/498-5290. **Fax:** 617/498-7005. **Contact:** Human Resources. **E-mail address:** careers.mc@adlittle.com. **World Wide Web address:** http://www.adl.com. **Description:** An employee-owned international management and technology consulting firm. The company offers services in three areas: management consulting; technology and product development; and environmental, health, and safety consulting. Services include cost reduction, total quality management consulting, market assessments, logistics management, telecommunications management, auditing, safety programs, software development, and toxicology. Clients operate in a variety of industries including aerospace, automobiles, telecommunications, electronics, and consumer products. Founded in 1886. **Positions advertised include:** Business Analyst; Consultant. **Corporate headquarters location:** This location. **Other U.S. locations:** Cupertino CA; Irvine CA; Palo Alto CA Ventura CA; Philadelphia PA; Charleston SC; Houston TX; Arlington VA. **International locations:** Asia; Europe; Middle East; South America. **Operations at this facility include:** Administration; Manufacturing; Research and Development.

Number of employees at this location: 1,000. **Number of employees nationwide:** 2,500.

MICROCAL LLC.
222 Industrial Drive East, Northampton MA 01060-2327. 413/586-7720. **Toll-free phone:** 800/633-3115. **Fax:** 413/586-0149. **Contact:** Bill Plumley. **E-mail address:** billplumley@microcalorimetry.com. **World Wide Web address:** http://www.microcalorimetry.com. **Description:** A high-tech manufacturer. **Positions advertised include:** Accountant; Human Resources Specialist.

PRICEWATERHOUSECOOPERS LLP
160 Federal Street, Boston MA 02110. 617/439-4390. **Contact:** Director of Recruiting. **World Wide Web address:** http://www.pwcglobal.com. **Description:** One of the largest certified public accounting firms in the world. PricewaterhouseCoopers provides public accounting, business advisory, management consulting, and taxation services. **Positions advertised include:** Data Quality Manager; Manager; Executive Assistant; Actuarial Life Manager; Service Center Clerk; Instructor Trainee; Information Technology Manager. **Special programs:** Internships. **Corporate headquarters location:** New York NY. **Other U.S. locations:** Nationwide. **Number of employees at this location:** 540.

GT REILLY & COMPANY
424 Adams Street, Milton MA 02186-4358. 617/696-8900. **Fax:** 617/698-1803. **Contact:** Director of Personnel. **E-mail address:** pjf@gtreilly.com. **World Wide Web address:** http://www.gtreilly.com. **Description:** A 45-year-old growing regional accounting firm. **Positions advertised include:** Public Accounting Professional.

ADVERTISING, MARKETING, AND PUBLIC RELATIONS

You can expect to find the following types of companies in this section:
Advertising Agencies • Direct Mail Marketers • Market Research Firms • Public Relations Firms

---

ALLIED ADVERTISING
545 Boylston Street, 11th Floor, Boston MA 02116. 617/859-4800. **Contact:** Human Resources. **Description:** An advertising agency. **Other U.S. locations:** Washington DC; St. Louis MO; New York City NY; Syracuse NY; Cleveland OH; Philadelphia PA. **International locations:** Toronto.

ARNOLD WORLDWIDE
101 Huntington Avenue, Boston MA 02199. 617/587-8000. **Fax:** 617/587-8070. **Contact:** Human Resources. **World Wide Web address:** http://www.arn.com. **Description:** An advertising, marketing, and public relations firm.

BBK COMMUNICATIONS
320 Needham Street, Suite 150, Newton MA 02464. 617/630-4477. **Contact:** Human Resources. **World Wide Web address:** http://www.bbkweb.com. **Description:** BBK is an integrated advertising and public relations firm serving the health policies, technologies, managed care, and pharmaceutical fields. **NOTE:** Please indicate the department to which you are applying. **Corporate headquarters location:** This location. **Listed on:** Privately held. **Number of employees at this location:** 30.

BRODEUR PORTER NOVELLI
855 Boylston Street, 8th Floor, Boston MA 02116. 617/587-2800. **Contact:** Human Resources. **World Wide Web address:** http://www.brodeur.com. **Description:** A public relations firm. **Office hours:** Monday - Friday, 8:30 a.m. - 5:30 p.m.

CITIGATE CUNNINGHAM INC.
One Memorial Drive, 9th Floor, Cambridge MA 02142. 617/494-8202. **Contact:** Human Resources. **E-mail address:** careers@citigatecunningham.com. **World Wide Web address:** http://www.citigatecunningham.com. **Description:** A public relations firm that also offers organization strategies, research, and brand positioning. **Parent company:** Incepta Group plc.

COMMONWEALTH CREATIVE ASSOCIATES
345 Union Avenue, Framingham MA 01702. 508/620-6664. **Contact:** Human Resources. **World Wide Web address:** http://www.commcreative.com. **Description:** A full-service advertising agency. **Corporate headquarters location:** This location. **Operations at this facility include:** Administration; Sales. **Listed on:** Privately held. **Number of employees at this location:** 10.

CONE INC.
90 Canal Street, 6th Floor, Boston MA 02114. 617/227-2111. **Contact:** Human Resources. **E-mail address:** hr@coneinc.com. **World Wide Web address:** http://www.conenet.com. **Description:** A strategic marketing communications firm. **Positions advertised include:** Crisis Prevention Planning & Management Position; Cause Branding Account Director.

CYRK, INC.
201 Edgewater Drive, Suite 225, Wakefield MA 01880. 781/876-5800. **Fax:** 360/805-2671. **Contact:** Human Resources. **E-mail address:** careers@cyrk.com. **World Wide Web address:** http://www.cyrk.com. **Description:** Designs, develops, manufactures, and distributes products for promotional programs. The company also provides integrated marketing services to national and international clients. Founded in 1976. **Positions advertised include:** Account Manager; Field Sales Representative. **Corporate headquarters location:** This location. **Other U.S. locations:** Nationwide. **Annual sales/revenues:** More than $100 million.

DM COMMUNICATIONS, INC.
651 Clapboardtree Street, Westwood MA 02090. 781/329-7799. **Fax:** 781/461-8266. **Contact:** Human Resources. **World Wide Web address:** http://www.ad-pr-dm.com. **Description:** A marketing and public relations firm.

DEVINE & PEARSON COMMUNICATIONS
300 Congress Street, Suite 201, Quincy MA 02169. 617/472-2700. **Contact:** Charlotte Delaney, Office Manager. **World Wide Web address:** http://www.devine-pearson.com. **Description:** An advertising and public relations agency that also offers design and consulting services.

THE FIELD COMPANIES
P.O. Box 78, Watertown MA 02471-0078. 617/926-5550. **Toll-free phone:** 800/369-1593. **Physical address:** 385 Pleasant Street, Watertown MA 02472. **Fax:** 617/924-9011. **E-mail address:** info@fieldcompanies.com. **World Wide Web address:** http://www.fieldcompanies.com. **Contact:** Mr. J. McDonald, Human Resources Representative. **Description:** Provides direct mail services such as list procurement and post office delivery. **NOTE:** Entry-level positions are offered. **Corporate headquarters location:** This location. **Listed on:** Privately held. **Number of employees at this location:** 70.

GRAY RAMBUSCH, INC.
One Washington Mall, 10th Floor, Boston MA 02108-2603. 617/367-0100. **Contact:** Human Resources. **Description:** An advertising firm.

HILL, HOLLIDAY
200 Clarendon Street, Boston MA 02116. 617/437-1600. **Contact:** Director of Human Resources. **E-mail address:** careers@hhcc.com. **World Wide Web address:** http://www.hhcc.com. **Description:** An advertising agency. **Other U.S. locations:** New York NY; San Francisco CA.

BERNARD HODES ADVERTISING
215 First Street, Cambridge MA 02142. 617/576-2131. **Contact:** Human Resources. **World Wide Web address:** http://www.hodes.com. **Description:** An advertising agency specializing in recruitment and employee communications. **Corporate headquarters location:** New York NY. **Other U.S. locations:** Nationwide. **International locations:** Worldwide. **Parent company:** Omnicom.

KHJ INTEGRATED MARKETING
One Constitution Plaza, Boston MA 02129-2025. 617/241-8000. **Contact:** Diana Richards, Human Resources. **E-mail address:** drichards@khj.com. **World Wide Web address:** http://www.khj.com. **Description:** An advertising and public relations firm.

LOWE GROB HEALTH & SCIENCE

200 Clarendon Street 42nd Floor, Boston MA 02138. 617/876-9300. **Fax:** 617/859-4233. **Contact:** Human Resources. **E-mail address:** info@lowegrob.com. **World Wide Web address:** http://www.lowegrob.com. **Description:** Provides advertising, consulting, market research, and public relations services to companies primarily in the biotechnical, health, medical, and scientific industries. **Positions advertised include:** Art Director Supervisor. **NOTE:** Entry-level positions are offered. **Special programs:** Internships. **Number of employees at this location:** 25.

MULLEN AGENCY

36 Essex Street, Wenham MA 01984. 978/468-1155. **Contact:** Human Resources. **E-mail address:** jobs@mullen.com. **World Wide Web address:** http://www.mullen.com. **Description:** A leading advertising and public relations firm. **Positions advertised include:** Interactive Account Executive; Mullen Media; Direct Account Executive; Direct Resource Art Director. **Other U.S. locations:** Detroit MI; Winston-Salem NC; Pittsburgh PA.

PAN COMMUNICATIONS INC.

300 Brickstone Square, Andover MA 01810. 978/474-1900. **Fax:** 978/474-1903. **Contact:** Personnel. **E-mail address:** info@pancomm.com. **World Wide Web address:** http://www.pancommunications.com. **Description:** A full-service public relations agency specializing in four portfolios: business-to-business, high-technology, fashion and consumer products, and trade shows. Founded in 1995. **NOTE:** Entry-level positions offered. **Company slogan:** Partners in public relations. **Positions advertised include:** Associate; Junior Associate; Account Manager; Senior Account Manager; Director. **Special programs:** Internships. **Corporate headquarters location:** This location. **Annual sales/revenues:** Less than $5 million. **Number of employees at this location:** 45.

TMP WORLDWIDE

63 Kendrick Street, Suite 201, Needham MA 02494. 978/461-5999. **Contact:** Human Resources. **World Wide Web address:** http://www.tmpw.com. **Description:** An advertising agency specializing in human resources and employee communications. **Other U.S. locations:** Santa Monica CA; Sausalito CA. **Listed on:** NASDAQ. **Stock exchange symbol:** TMPW.

WEBER SHANDWICK WORLDWIDE

101 Main Street, Cambridge MA 02142. 617/661-7900. **Contact:** Human Resources. **E-mail address:** jobscambridge@webershandwick.com. **World Wide Web address:** www.webershandwick.com. **Description:** Weber Shandwick is one of the world's leading public relations and communications management firms. **Corporate headquarters location:**

AEROSPACE

You can expect to find the following types of companies in this section:
Aerospace Products and Services • Aircraft Equipment and Parts

---

AMETEK, INC.
50 Fordham Road, Wilmington MA 01887. 978/988-4101. **Contact:** Human Resources. **E-mail address:** corps.jobs@ametek.com. **World Wide Web address:** http://www.ametek.com. **Description:** AMETEK is a global manufacturing company that serves a variety of industrial and commercial markets. The company produces and sells its products through its Electromechanical, Precision Instruments, and Industrial Materials groups. The Electromechanical Group manufactures electric motors for vacuum cleaners and floor care equipment and technical motor products for computer, medical, and other markets. **Corporate headquarters location:** Philadelphia PA. **International locations:** Denmark; England; Italy; Mexico. **Operations at this facility include:** This location manufactures aircraft parts and auxiliary equipment. **Listed on:** New York Stock Exchange. **Stock exchange symbol:** AME. **Number of employees worldwide:** 6,000.

B & E TOOL COMPANY, INC.
10 Hudson Drive, P.O. Box 40, Southwick MA 01077. 413/569-5585. **Fax:** 413/569-6543. **Contact:** Human Resources. **E-mail address:** info@betool.com. **World Wide Web address:** http://www.betool.com. **Description:** Manufactures aircraft components and parts for aircraft engines and controls. Founded in 1954. **Corporate headquarters location:** This location.

THE BOEING COMPANY
81 Hartwell Avenue, Lexington MA 02141. 781/863-5454. **Toll-free phone:** 800/254-1591. **Contact:** Human Resources. **E-mail address:** employmentoperations@boeing.com. **World Wide Web address:** http://www.boeing.com. **Description:** The Boeing Company is one of the largest aerospace firms in the United States, one of the nation's top exporters, and one of the world's leading manufacturers of commercial jet transports. The company is a major U.S. government contractor, with capabilities in missile and space, electronic systems, military aircraft, helicopters, and information systems management. Boeing is divided into four business segments: Commercial Aircraft, Space & Communications, Military Aircraft and Missiles, and Shared Services. **Corporate headquarters location:** Chicago IL. **Operations at this facility include:** This location is a marketing office. **Subsidiaries include:** Boeing Information Services, Inc. (Vienna VA) develops and manages large-scale information systems for selected agencies of the federal government. **Listed on:** New York Stock Exchange. **Stock exchange symbol:** BA.

COX ENGINEERING COMPANY
35 Industrial Drive, Canton MA 02021. 781/302-3300. **Contact:** Human Resources. **Description:** Engaged in mechanical engineering and sheetmetal work for the aerospace industry.

DYNAMICS RESEARCH CORPORATION (DRC)
60 Frontage Road, Andover MA 01810. 978/475-9090. **Fax:** 978/470-0201. **Contact:** Human Resources. **World Wide Web address:** http://www.drc.com.

Description: Provides systems engineering and analysis, operations research, logistics, and database systems support for the Department of Defense. Applications include acquisition management, inertial navigation and guidance, human resources requirements analyses, software systems, and logistic support analyses. The company also manufactures rotary and linear optical incremental encoders and precision patterned glass and metal products including precision measuring scales, reticles, and optical pick-offs for computer peripheral and optical equipment OEMs. **Positions advertised include:** Compensation Administrator; Credit Collection Manager; Accounting Assistant; EBS Business Analyst. **Corporate headquarters location:** This location. **Other area locations:** Bedford MA; West Newton MA; Wilmington MA. **Other U.S. locations:** Nationwide. **Operations at this facility include:** Administration; Research and Development; Sales; Service. **Listed on:** NASDAQ. **Stock exchange symbol:** DRCO.

FENWAL SAFETY SYSTEMS
700 Nickerson Road, Marlborough MA 01752-4602. 508/481-5800. **Contact:** Human Resources. **World Wide Web address:** http://www.fenwalsafety.com. **Description:** Manufactures aircraft explosion protection equipment.

GENERAL ELECTRIC COMPANY
1000 Western Avenue, Building 174AD, Mail Drop 14515, Lynn MA 01910. 781/594-0100. **Fax:** 781/594-1917. **Contact:** Mary Welsh, Personnel Technician. **World Wide Web address:** http://www.ge.com. **Description:** General Electric operates in the following areas: aircraft engines including jet engines, replacement parts, and repair services for commercial, military, executive, and commuter aircraft; appliances; broadcasting (NBC); industrial through lighting products, electrical distribution and control equipment, transportation systems products, electric motors and related products, a broad range of electrical and electronic industrial automation products, and a network of electrical supply houses; materials including plastics, ABS resins, silicones, superabrasives, and laminates; power systems including products for the generation, transmission, and distribution of electricity; technical products and systems including medical systems and equipment, as well as a full range of computer-based information and data interchange services for both internal use and external commercial and industrial customers; and capital services including consumer services; financing; and specialty insurance. **Corporate headquarters location:** Fairfield CT. **Operations at this facility include:** This facility manufactures aircraft engines and engine parts. **Listed on:** New York Stock Exchange. **Stock exchange symbol:** GE. **Number of employees worldwide:** 230,000.

JET AVIATION OF AMERICA
380 Hanscom Drive, Hanscom Field, Bedford MA 01730. 781/274-0030. **Fax:** 781/274-6573. **Contact:** Human Resources. **World Wide Web address:** http://www.jetaviation.com. **Description:** Manages a fleet of 100 aircraft and provides a wide range of aviation services including airframe and engine maintenance, and FBO services to business aircraft. **Corporate headquarters location:** West Palm Beach FL. **Other U.S. locations:** Burbank CA; Chicago IL; Teterboro NJ; Dallas TX. **International locations:** Bermuda.

LKM INDUSTRIES
44 Sixth Road, Woburn MA 01801. 781/935-9210. **Contact:** Human Resources. **World Wide Web address:** http://www.lkm.com. **Description:** Manufactures parts for aircraft engines and cooling systems.

MERCURY AIR CENTER
180 Hanscom Drive, Bedford MA 01730. 781/274-0010. **Contact:** Human Resources. **World Wide Web address:** http://www.mercuryairgroup.com. **Description:** Sells and maintains aircraft and parts, and provides ground support services.

MIDDLETON AEROSPACE CORPORATION
206 South Main Street, Middleton MA 01949. 978/774-6000. **Fax:** 978/777-5640. **Contact:** Human Resources. **E-mail address:** sales@midaero.com. **World Wide Web address:** http://www.midaero.com. **Description:** Manufactures aircraft engine components.

PARKER HANNIFIN NICHOLS AIRBORNE DIVISION
14 Robbins Pond Road, Ayer MA 01432-5641. 978/784-1200. **Contact:** Human Resources. **World Wide Web address:** http://www.parker.com. **Description:** Parker Hannifin Corporation makes motion control products including fluid power systems, electromechanical controls, and related components. The Motion and Control Group manufactures hydraulic pumps, power units, control valves, accumulators, cylinders, actuators, and automation devices to remove contaminants from air, fuel, oil, water, and other fluids. The Fluid Connectors Group manufactures connectors, tube and hose fittings, hoses, and couplers that transmit fluid. The Seal Group manufactures sealing devices, gaskets, and packing that insure leak-proof connections. The Automotive and Refrigeration Group manufactures components for use in industrial and automotive air conditioning and refrigeration systems. **Operations at this facility include:** This location manufactures fuel systems and components for aircraft. **Listed on:** New York Stock Exchange. **Stock exchange symbol:** PH.

WYMAN-GORDON COMPANY
244 Worcester Street, Box 8001, North Grafton MA 01536-8001. 508/839-4441. **Contact:** Human Resources. **World Wide Web address:** http://www.wyman-gordon.com. **Description:** Wyman-Gordon uses forging and investment casting technologies to produce components for applications such as jet turbine engines and airframes, and designs and produces prototype products using composite technologies. **Corporate headquarters location:** This location. **Subsidiaries include:** Wyman-Gordon Investment Castings, Inc. uses automated, high-volume production equipment and both air-melt and vacuum-melt furnaces to produce a wide variety of complex investment castings. WGIC investment castings are made from a range of metal alloys including aluminum and magnesium, steel, titanium, and high-temperature-based alloys. The company's composites operation, Scaled Composites, Inc., plans, proposes, designs, fabricates, and tests prototypes for aerospace, automotive, and other customers. **Operations at this facility include:** This location manufactures metal components for aerospace applications. **Number of employees at this location:** 725. **Number of employees nationwide:** 2,600. **Number of employees worldwide:** 3,000.

YANKEE AVIATION SERVICES INC.
246 South Meadow Road, Box 11, Plymouth Airport, Plymouth MA 02360. 508/746-5511. **Contact:** Human Resources Department. **World Wide Web address:** http://www.yankeeaviation.com. **Description:** Services and maintains aircraft.

APPAREL, FASHION, AND TEXTILES

You can expect to find the following types of companies in this section:
Broadwoven Fabric Mills • Knitting Mills • Yarn and Thread Mills • Curtains and Draperies • Footwear • Nonwoven Fabrics • Textile Goods and Finishing

ARLEY CORPORATION
1115 West Chestnut Street, Brockton MA 02301-7501. 508/580-4245. **Contact:** Human Resources. **World Wide Web address:** http://www.arley.com. **Description:** A curtain and drapery manufacturer.

CONVERSE, INC.
1 High Street, Andover MA 01845. 978/983-3300. **Fax:** 978/664-7472. **Contact:** Human Resources. **E-mail address:** jobs@converse.com. **World Wide Web address:** http://www.converse.com. **Description:** Manufactures men's, women's, and children's footwear. **Positions advertised include:** Application Programmer; Creative Director; Designer; Marketing Communications Manager; Public Relations Manager. **Special programs:** Internships. **Corporate headquarters location:** This location. **Other U.S. locations:** Nationwide. **Operations at this facility include:** Administration; Research and Development; Sales; Service. **Number of employees at this location:** 400. **Number of employees nationwide:** 2,000.

DEXTER SHOE COMPANY
1230 Washington Street, West Newton MA 02465-2129. 617/332-4300. **Contact:** Office Manager. **E-mail address:** jobs@dextershoe.com. **World Wide Web address:** http://www.dextershoe.com. **Description:** Manufactures men's and women's footwear. **Corporate headquarters location:** Dexter ME. **Parent company:** Berkshire Hathaway. **Operations at this facility include:** Administration.

HARODITE INDUSTRIES, INC.
66 South Street, Taunton MA 02780. 508/824-6961. **Contact:** Human Resources. **E-mail address:** jjardin@harodite.com. **World Wide Web address:** http://www.harodite.com. **Description:** One of the oldest textile manufacturing companies in New England. Products include a complete range of woven and nonwoven fabrics. Founded in 1908. **Corporate headquarters location:** This location. **Other U.S. locations:** Taylors SC. **Operations at this facility include:** Administration; Manufacturing. **Listed on:** Privately held. **Annual sales/revenues:** $5 - $10 million. **Number of employees at this location:** 130.

THE J. JILL GROUP, INC.
4 Batterymarch Park, Quincy MA 02169. 617/376-4300. **Fax:** 617/376-4479. **Contact:** Human Resources. **E-mail address:** jobs@jjillgroup.com. **World Wide Web address:** http://www.jjillgroup.com. **Description:** A leading retailer of women's apparel, shoes, gifts, and accessories. The company sells its products through catalogs, retail stores, and an e-commerce Website. Founded in 1987. **Office hours:** Monday - Friday, 8:30 a.m. - 5:00 p.m. **Corporate headquarters location:** This location. **Listed on:** NASDAQ. **Stock exchange symbol:** JILL. **Number of employees nationwide:** 825.

MAXWELL SHOE COMPANY INC.

P.O. Box 37, Hyde Park MA 02137-0037. 617/364-5090. **Physical address:** 101 Sprague Street, Hyde Park MA 02136. **Toll-free phone:** 800/326-6687. **Fax:** 617/364-9058. **Contact:** Human Resources. **E-mail address:** hr@maxwellshoe.com. **World Wide Web address:** http://www.maxwellshoe.com. **Description:** Designs, develops, and markets moderately priced casual and dress footwear for women under the A Line Anne Klein, Anne Klein2, Mootsies Tootsies, Sam & Libby, J.G. Hook, and Dockers brand names and for children under the Mootsies Kids brand name. The company also designs and develops private label footwear for selected retailers. **Corporate headquarters location:** This location. **Listed on:** NASDAQ. **Stock exchange symbol:** MAXS. **Chairman and CEO:** Mark J. Cocozza.

NATIONAL NONWOVENS

P.O. Box 150, Easthampton MA 01027. 413/527-3445. **Physical address:** 180 Pleasant Street, Easthampton MA 01027. **Toll-free phone:** 800/333-3469. **Fax:** 413/527-9570. **Contact:** Personnel. **World Wide Web address:** http://www.nationalnonwovens.com. **Description:** Develops, markets, and manufactures needle punch and other nonwoven textiles. **Corporate headquarters location:** This location. **Operations at this facility include:** Administration; Manufacturing; Research and Development; Sales. **Listed on:** Privately held. **Annual sales/revenues:** $21 - $50 million. **Number of employees at this location:** 200.

NEW BALANCE ATHLETIC SHOE INC.

Brighton Landing, 20 Guest Street, Brighton MA 02135. 617/783-4000. **Contact:** Human Resources. **World Wide Web address:** http://www.newbalance.com. **Description:** Manufactures and distributes running and other athletic shoes. **Positions advertised include:** Administrative Assistant; Billing Specialist; Lead Programming Analyst; Network Engineer; Associate Product Manager; Marketing Manager; Designer; Retail Sales Associate. **Corporate headquarters location:** This location. **International locations:** Worldwide. **Number of employees worldwide:** 2,400.

QUAKER FABRIC CORPORATION

941 Grinnell Street, Fall River MA 02721. 508/678-1951. **Fax:** 508/646-2429. **Contact:** Personnel. **World Wide Web address:** http://www.quakerfabric.com. **Description:** Manufactures textile upholstery fabrics and yarn. **Positions advertised include:** Textile Designer; Process Engineer; Lab Manager; Quality Engineer; Entry Level Engineer; Health & Wellness Specialist; Employee Development Specialist; Human Resources Representative; Benefits Coordinator; Manufacturing Supervisor; Marketing Professional. **Corporate headquarters location:** This location. **Operations at this facility include:** Administration; Divisional Headquarters; Manufacturing; Regional Headquarters; Research and Development; Service. **Listed on:** NASDAQ. **Stock exchange symbol:** QFAB. **Number of employees at this location:** 1,500.

RADICI SPANDEX CORPORATION

125 Hartwell Street, Fall River MA 02721. 508/674-3585. **Fax:** 508/674-3580. **Contact:** Personnel. **World Wide Web address:** http://www.radicispandex.com. **Description:** A manufacturer and worldwide marketer of rubber threads and synthetic spandex fibers. Customers include apparel, textile, and nonwoven manufacturers. **Corporate headquarters location:** This location.

REEBOK INTERNATIONAL LTD.
1895 J.W. Foster Boulevard, Canton MA 02021. 781/401-5000. **Contact:** Human Resources. **World Wide Web address:** http://www.reebok.com. **Description:** A leading worldwide designer, marketer, and distributor of sports, fitness, and casual footwear, apparel, and equipment. Principal operating units include the Reebok Division, Avia Group International, Inc., and The Rockport Company, Inc. **Positions advertised include:** Human Resources Assistant; Apparel Designer; Creative Director; Designer; Product Planning Manager; Technical Designer; Associate Product Line Manager; Production Manager. **Corporate headquarters location:** This location. **Listed on:** New York Stock Exchange. **Stock exchange symbol:** RBK.

THE ROCKPORT COMPANY, LLC
1895 J.W. Foster Boulevard, Canton MA 02021. 781/401-5000. **Toll-free phone:** 800/ROCKPORT. **Contact:** Human Resources. **World Wide Web address:** http://www.rockport.com. **Description:** Designs, markets, and sells men's and women's shoes. **Corporate headquarters location:** This location. **Parent company:** Reebok International Ltd. **Operations at this facility include:** Administration; Research and Development; Sales; Service. **Annual sales/revenues:** More than $100 million.

SPALDING SPORTS WORLDWIDE
425 Meadow Street, Chicopee MA 01021. 413/536-1200. **Contact:** Human Resources. **World Wide Web address:** http://www.spalding.com. **Description:** Manufactures performance athletic footwear specializing in golf, tennis, soccer, and basketball shoes. **Annual sales/revenues:** More than $100 million. **Number of employees at this location:** 80.

STEVENS LINEN ASSOCIATES, INC.
P.O. Box 95, Dudley MA 01571. 508/943-0813x38. **Fax:** 800/339-1569. **Contact:** Human Resources. **E-mail address:** info@stevenslinen.com. **World Wide Web address:** http://www.stevenslinen.com. **Description:** Engaged in linen screen-printing. Products include calendar towels, tea towels, pot holders, and other domestic goods. Founded in 1846. **NOTE:** Entry-level positions are offered. **Office hours:** Monday - Friday, 8:00 a.m. - 5:00 p.m. **Corporate headquarters location:** This location. **Listed on:** Privately held. **President:** Greg Kline. **Facilities Manager:** Michael Burzynski. **Number of employees at this location:** 100.

WILLIAM E. WRIGHT LIMITED PARTNERSHIP
85 South Street, West Warren MA 01092. 413/436-7732. **Toll-free phone:** 877/597-4445. **Fax:** 413/436-9510. **Contact:** Human Resources. **E-mail address:** pgancorz@wrights.com. **World Wide Web address:** http://www.wrights.com. **Description:** Manufactures and markets fashion trimmings for its home sewing, home furnishing, and decorative packaging customers. **Positions advertised include:** Assembly Machine Operator; Winder; Order Packer; Material Handler; Associate; Buyer; Inventory Return Clerk.

Rawlings ?

ARCHITECTURE, CONSTRUCTION, AND ENGINEERING

**You can expect to find the following types of companies
in this section:**
Architectural and Engineering Services • Civil and Mechanical Engineering Firms
• Construction Products, Manufacturers, and Wholesalers • General
Contractors/Specialized Trade Contractors

ABBOT BUILDING RESTORATION COMPANY, INC.
28 Allerton Street, Boston MA 02119. 617/445-0274. **Contact:** Human
Resources Department. **Description:** Specializes in building restoration.
Services include brick masonry and concrete repair.

AMERICAN BILTRITE INC.
57 River Street, Wellesley Hills MA 02481. 781/237-6655. **Fax:** 781/237-6880.
Contact: Human Resources. **E-mail address:** info@ambilt.com. **World Wide
Web address:** http://www.ambilt.com. **Description:** Manufactures hard floor
coverings including asphalt felt-based linoleum. **NOTE:** Hiring is conducted
through a subsidiary of American Biltrite. Please forward all inquiries to Bonnie
Posnak, Vice President of Human Resources, Ideal Tape, 1400 Middlesex
Street, Lowell MA 01851. **Listed on:** American Stock Exchange. **Stock
exchange symbol:** ABL.

ARCADD, INC.
1185 Washington Street, West Newton MA 02465. 617/332-1200. **Fax:** 617/969-
3362. **Contact:** Employment. **E-mail address:** arcaddinc@aol.com. **World Wide
Web address:** http://www.arcadd.com. **Description:** An architectural design
firm.

BALCO INC.
306 Northern Avenue, Boston MA 02210. 617/482-0100. **Contact:** Human
Resources. **Description:** A heating, ventilation, air conditioning, and refrigeration
contractor engaged in construction and residential building maintenance
services. **Corporate headquarters location:** This location. **Other U.S.
locations:** Birmingham AL; Rockville MD; Harrisburg PA. **Parent company:**
Energy Systems, Inc. **Operations at this facility include:** Administration; Sales;
Service. **Number of employees at this location:** 500.

BEALS & THOMAS, INC.
144 Turnpike Road, Southborough MA 01772-2104. 508/786-5431. **Fax:**
508/366-4391. **Contact:** Human Resources. **E-mail address:** hr@btiweb.com.
World Wide Web address: http://www.btiweb.com. **Description:** A civil
engineering firm offering a variety of services including surveying, site planning,
and landscape architecture. **Positions advertised include:** Geographic
Information Systems Manager; Land Surveyor; Staff Level Civil Engineer; Civil
Engineer. **NOTE:** Users can submit resume online.

R.W. BECK, INC.
P.O. Box 9344, Framingham MA 01701-9344. 508/935-1600. **Fax:** 508/935-
1888. **Physical address:** 550 Cochituate Road, Framingham MA. **Fax:** 508/935-
1666. **Contact:** William G. LaBonte, Director of Administration and Human
Resources. **E-mail address:** boston@rwbeck.com. **World Wide Web address:**
http://www.rwbeck.com. **Description:** A diversified professional, technical, and

management consulting firm. The company provides construction, environmental, technical, energy, solid waste, and water/wastewater services nationwide. Founded in 1942. **Positions advertised include:** Senior Water Practice Consultant. **Corporate headquarters location:** Seattle WA. **Other area locations:** Waltham MA. **Operations at this facility include:** Divisional Headquarters; Regional Headquarters. **Listed on:** Privately held. **Number of employees at this location:** 100. **Number of employees nationwide:** 500.

WILLIAM A. BERRY & SON, INC.
99 Conifer Hill Drive, Suite 410, Danvers MA 01923. 978/774-1057. **Toll-free phone:** 877/774-1057. **Fax:** 978/777-9024. **Contact:** Human Resources. **E-mail address:** contactus@berry.com. **World Wide Web address:** http://www.waberry.com. **Description:** A construction management firm. Founded in 1857. **Positions advertised include:** Senior Project Manager; Project Manager; Project/Lead Estimator; HVAC Project Engineer; Project Coordinator.

BRYANT ASSOCIATES, INC.
160 North Washington Street, Suite 700, Boston MA 02114-2127. 617/248-0300. **Fax:** 617/248-0212. **Contact:** Human Resources. **E-mail address:** jobs@bryant-engrs.com. **World Wide Web address:** http://www.bryant-engrs.com. **Description:** An engineering and surveying firm. Founded in 1976. **Positions advertised include:** Operations Manager. **Other U.S. locations:** New Ipswich NH; Syracuse NY; Lincoln RI.

CANNON DESIGN
One Center Plaza, Boston MA 02108. 617/742-5440. **Contact:** Human Resources. **World Wide Web address:** http://www.cannondesign.com. **Description:** An architectural, interior design, and engineering firm. **Positions advertised include:** Engineer; Project Architect; Educational Planner. **Corporate headquarters location:** Grand Island NY. **Other U.S. locations:** Los Angeles CA; Washington DC; Jacksonville FL; Chicago IL; Baltimore MD; St. Louis MO.

CARLSON ASSOCIATES, INC.
959 Concord Street, 2nd Floor, Framingham MA 01701. 508/370-0100. **Fax:** 508/626-2390. **Contact:** Ms. Saroj Patel, Personnel Manager. **Description:** Provides a variety of architectural services. **Corporate headquarters location:** This location. **Other U.S. locations:** CA; FL; NC. **Subsidiaries include:** Carlson Design/Construction Corporation. **Parent company:** Carlson Holdings Company. **Operations at this facility include:** Administration. **Number of employees at this location:** 40. **Number of employees nationwide:** 95.

CLARK CONSTRUCTION
263 Summer Street, Boston MA 02210. 617/439-0073. **Contact:** Human Resources. **World Wide Web address:** http://www.clarkus.com. **Description:** A general construction contractor. Founded in 1906. **Positions advertised include:** Project Manager; Superintendent; Field Engineer; Office Engineer. **Corporate headquarters location:** Bethesda MD. **Other U.S. locations:** Irvine CA; Oakland CA; Tampa FL; Chicago IL.

COLONIAL SAW

P.O. Box A 122 Pembroke Street, Kingston MA 02364. 781/585-4364. **Fax:** 781/585-9375. **Contact:** Human Resources: **E-mail address:** info@csaw.com. **World Wide Web address:** http://www.csaw.com. **Description:** Produces the worlds most advanced woodworking and tool grinding technology.

CUTTING EDGE TECHNOLOGIES

250 Nicks Rock Road, Plymouth MA 02360. 508/746-6900. **Toll-free phone:** 800/233-9956. **Fax:** 508/747-4339. **Contact:** Human Resources. **E-mail address:** toolsales@cetdirect.com. **World Wide Web address:** http://www.cetdirect.com. **Description:** 1SO 9002 certified company to make cutting tools that meet standard or special tolerances.

DEWBERRY & GOODKIND

31 St. James Avenue, 3rd Floor, Boston MA 02116. 617/695-3400. **Fax:** 617/695-3310. **Contact:** Personnel. **World Wide Web address:** http://www.dewberry.com. **Description:** An engineering firm specializing in architectural design, environmental consulting, and construction administration. Founded in 1922. **Positions advertised include:** Architectural Project Manager; Senior Traffic Engineer; Structural Project Engineer.

ECKLAND CONSULTANTS

131 Tremont Street, Boston MA 02111. 617/423-1100. **Fax:** 617/423-1188. **Contact:** Human Resources. **World Wide Web address:** http://www.eckland.com. **Description:** An architecture and engineering consulting firm that specializes in property and environmental assessments for real estate agencies and banks. **Other U.S. locations:** Nationwide.

EDWARDS & KELCEY

The Schrafft Center, 529 Main Street, Suite 203, Boston MA 02129. 617/242-9222. **Contact:** Human Resources. **E-mail address:** corphr@ekmail.com. **World Wide Web address:** http://www.ekcorp.com. **Description:** An engineering firm specializing in road/highway, traffic, and structural projects. **Positions advertised include:** Marketing Coordinator; Structural Engineer. **Corporate headquarters location:** Morristown NJ. **Other U.S. locations:** Nationwide. **International locations:** The Netherlands; Puerto Rico.

EXPONENT, INC.

21 Strathmore Road, Natick MA 01760. 508/652-8500. **Contact:** Human Resources Department. **E-mail address:** hr@exponent.com. **World Wide Web address:** http://www.exponent.com. **Description:** A technical consulting firm dedicated to the investigation, analysis, and prevention of accidents and failures of an engineering or scientific nature. The company provides a multidisciplinary approach to analyze how failures occur. The company specializes in accident reconstruction, biomechanics, construction/structural engineering, aviation and marine investigations, environmental assessment, materials and product testing, warning and labeling issues, accident statistical data analysis, and risk prevention/mitigation. Founded in 1967. **Positions advertised include:** Engineer; Managing Scientist Engineer; Lab Technician; Managing Engineer. **NOTE:** All hiring is conducted through corporate headquarters. Please send resumes to: Exponent, Inc., Human Resources, 149 Commonwealth Drive, Menlo Park CA 94025. **Other U.S. locations:** Nationwide. **Parent company:** Exponent, Inc. **Listed on:** NASDAQ. **Stock exchange symbol:** EXPO.

FAY, SPOFFORD & THORNDIKE, INC.
5 Burlington Woods, Burlington MA 01803. 781/221-1000. **Fax:** 781/221-1025. **Contact:** Human Resources. **E-mail:** hr@fstinc.com. **World Wide Web address:** http://www.fstinc.com. **Description:** Engaged in civil, electrical, environmental, and mechanical engineering. **Corporate headquarters location:** This location. **Other U.S. locations:** Cromwell CT; Boston MA; Bedford NH; West Caldwell NJ; Melville NY; New York NY; Whippany NY; Fort Washington PA. **Number of employees at this location:** 175.

GALE ASSOCIATES, INC.
163 Libbey Parkway, P.O. Box 890189, Weymouth, MA 02189. 781/335-6465. **Toll-free phone:** 800/659-4753. **Fax:** 781/335-6467. **Contact:** Kathleen A. Forrand, Human Resources Manager. **E-mail address:** kaf@gainc.com. **World Wide Web address:** http://www.gainc.com. **Description:** A national architecture and engineering firm that specializes in the improvement of existing buildings, sites, and infrastructures for both public and private clients. This location also hires seasonally. Founded in 1964. **NOTE:** Entry-level positions and part-time jobs are offered. **Positions advertised include:** Corporate Inspector; Civil Engineer; Project Manager; Structural Engineer; Engineer; Architect. **Special programs:** Training; Co-ops; Summer Jobs. **Office hours:** Monday - Friday, 8:00 a.m. - 5:00 p.m. **Corporate headquarters location:** This location. **Other U.S. locations:** Mountain View CA; Oakland CA; Winter Park FL; Baltimore MD; Bedford NH. **Operations at this facility include:** Divisional Headquarters. **Listed on:** Privately held. **President:** Harold E. Flight. **Accounting Manager:** Bruce P. White. **Annual sales/revenues:** $5 - $10 million. **Number of employees at this location:** 60. **Number of employees nationwide:** 100.

GANNETT FLEMING
150 Wood Road, Braintree MA 02184. 781/380-7750. **Contact:** Donald B. Nicholas, Human Resources. **E-mail address:** dnicholas@gfnet.com. **World Wide Web address:** http://www.gannettfleming.com. **Description:** An engineering firm offering a wide variety of services including structural, geo-technical, environmental, hazardous waste, bridge design, and tunnel design. **Positions advertised include:** Environmental Engineer; Resident Engineer. **Other U.S. locations:** Nationwide.

GRACE CONSTRUCTION PRODUCTS
62 Whittemore Avenue, Cambridge MA 02140. 617/876-1400. **Contact:** Human Resources. **E-mail address:** careers@grace.com. **World Wide Web address:** http://www.grace.com. **Description:** As part of W.R. Grace & Company, Grace Construction Products manufactures concrete additives, waterproofing products and systems, and fire protection products. The company has more than 125 plants and sales offices worldwide. **NOTE:** Entry-level positions are offered. **Special programs:** Internships. **Corporate headquarters location:** Columbia MD. **Subsidiaries include:** Darex Container Products (Belgium; Lexington MA); Davison Chemicals (Canada; Columbia MD); Performance Chemicals (Cambridge MA). **Listed on:** New York Stock Exchange. **Stock exchange symbol:** GRA. **CEO:** Paul Norris.

HDR ENGINEERING, INC.
7 Winthrop Square, Boston MA 02111. 617/357-7700. **Contact:** Human Resources. **E-mail address:** careers@hdrinc.com. **World Wide Web address:** http://www.hdrinc.com. **Description:** HDR Engineering, Inc. provides water, transportation, waste, and energy services including studies, design, and implementation for complex projects. **Positions advertised include:** Civil Section Manager; Civil Roadway Engineer; Rail Engineer; Civil Engineer.

Corporate headquarters location: Omaha NE. **Operations at this facility include:** This location specializes in a variety of transportation-related engineering projects including bridges, roads, and tunnels. **Parent company:** HDR, Inc.

HNTB CORPORATION
75 State Street, Boston MA 02109. 617/542-6900. **Contact:** Human Resources. **World Wide Web address:** http://www.hntb.com. **Description:** An architectural engineering firm specializing in the design of highways and bridges. **Corporate headquarters location:** Kansas City MO. **Other U.S. locations:** Nationwide.

HARVEY INDUSTRIES, INC.
400 Main Street, Waltham MA 02451-9180. 781/899-3500. **Toll-free phone:** 800/9HARVEY. **Contact:** Human Resources. **E-mail address:** jobs@harveyind.com. **World Wide Web address:** http://www.harveyind.com. **Description:** Manufactures windows and doors. The company is also a wholesale distributor of building materials. **Positions advertised include:** Administrative Assistant; New Business Sales Representative.

HAYES ENGINEERING
603 Salem Street, Wakefield MA 01880. 781/246-2800. **Fax:** 781/246-7596. **Contact:** Human Resources. **E-mail address:** jogren@hayeseng.com. **World Wide Web address:** http://www.hayeseng.com. **Description:** A civil and environmental engineering firm that also provides land surveying services.

JACOBS SVERDRUP
2 Center Plaza, 7th Floor, Boston MA 02108. 617/742-8060. **Contact:** Human Resources. **World Wide Web address:** http://www.sverdrup.com. **Description:** A civil engineering firm engaged in the operation of environmental, transportation, and water resources projects.

LEMESSURIER CONSULTANTS
675 Massachusetts Avenue, Cambridge MA 02139. 617/868-1200. **Fax:** 617/661-7520. **Contact:** Peter Cheevers, Personnel Director. **World Wide Web address:** http://www.lemessurier.com. **Description:** Provides structural engineering consulting services. Founded in 1961. **Positions advertised include:** Experienced CAD Operators.

MAGUIRE GROUP, INC.
225 Foxborough Boulevard, Foxborough MA 02035. 508/543-1700. **Contact:** Jan Washburn, Human Resources Manager. **World Wide Web address:** http://www.maguiregroup.com. **Description:** An architectural, engineering, and planning firm, serving domestic and international clients. Maguire Group, Inc. is engaged in the design and construction management of industrial commercial buildings; environmental facilities including sewers and treatment plants; hydroelectric power plants; highways, bridges, airports, and mass transit projects; and port and marine facilities. **Positions advertised include:** Environmental Specialist. **Corporate headquarters location:** This location. **Other U.S. locations:** New Britain CT; Portland ME; Portsmouth NH; Atlantic City NJ; Lawrenceville NJ; Harrisburg PA; Philadelphia PA; Pittsburgh PA; State College PA; Providence RI. **International locations:** St. Croix, U.S. Virgin Islands.

MASSACHUSETTS ELECTRIC CONSTRUCTION COMPANY
180 Guest Street, Boston MA 02135-2028. 617/254-1015. **Contact:** Human Resources. **World Wide Web address:** http://www.masselec.com. **Description:**

An electrical contractor. Services include construction management, value engineering, design, and consultation. **Other U.S. locations:** Nationwide.

NATIONAL ENGINEERING SERVICE CORPORATION
10 Cedar Street, Suite 27, Woburn MA 01801. 781/938-4747. **Contact:** Human Resources. **Description:** A contract engineering firm engaged primarily in civil engineering projects.

PARSONS
30 Dan Road, Canton MA 02021. 781/401-3200. **Contact:** Human Resources. **World Wide Web address:** http://www.parsons.com. **Description:** An engineering and construction company specializing in power generation and utilities, general industrial engineering, and environmental engineering. Founded in 1944. **Other U.S. locations:** Nationwide. **International locations:** Worldwide.

PARSONS BRINCKERHOFF INC.
75 Arlington Street, Boston MA 02116. 617/348-2950. **Contact:** Human Resources. **World Wide Web address:** http://www.pbworld.com. **Description:** An engineering and design firm engaged in the design of bridges, tunnels, rapid transit systems, hydroelectric facilities, water supply systems, and marine facilities. **Positions advertised include:** Architectural Inspector. **Other U.S. locations:** Nationwide.

PERINI CORPORATION
73 Mt. Wayte Avenue, Framingham MA 01701. 508/628-2000. **Fax:** 508/628-2960. **Contact:** Human Resources. **E-mail address:** dtanner@perini.com. **World Wide Web address:** http://www.perini.com. **Description:** One of the largest heavy and building construction firms in the United States. Worldwide projects include bridges and roads, mass transportation and airport construction, and commercial building construction. Perini also provides engineering and consulting services. Founded in 1894. **Positions advertised include:** Scheduler; Estimator; Project Engineer. **Corporate headquarters location:** This location. **Operations at this facility include:** Administration. **Listed on:** American Stock Exchange. **Stock exchange symbol:** PCR.

SASAKI ASSOCIATES, INC.
64 Pleasant Street, Watertown MA 02472. 617/926-3300. **Fax:** 617/924-2748. **Contact:** Human Resources. **World Wide Web address:** http://www.sasaki.com. **Description:** An architectural and design firm that specializes in architecture, civil engineering, graphic design, interior design, landscape architecture, and urban design. Founded in 1953. **Positions advertised include:** Interior Design; Marketing Coordinator. **Corporate headquarters location:** This location. **Other U.S. locations:** San Francisco CA; Dallas TX. **Number of employees at this location:** 155. **Number of employees nationwide:** 200.

STONE & WEBSTER ENGINEERING CORPORATION
100 Technology Center Drive, Stoughton MA 02072. 617/589-5111. **Fax:** 617/589-1587. **Contact:** Human Resources Department. **World Wide Web address:** http://www.shawgrp.com/stonewebster. **Description:** Provides construction, consulting, engineering, environmental, and procurement services to a variety of industries worldwide. **Positions advertised include:** Principal Mechanical Engineer; Lead Mechanical Engineer. **NOTE:** Apply online. **Office hours:** Monday - Friday, 8:00 a.m. - 4:45 p.m. **Corporate headquarters location:** This location. **Other U.S. locations:** Denver CO; Cherry Hill NJ; New York NY; Chattanooga TN; Houston TX. **Parent company:** The Shaw Group,

Inc. **Listed on:** New York Stock Exchange. **Stock exchange symbol:** SGR. **Number of employees at this location:** 1,200. **Number of employees nationwide:** 6,000.

TIGHE & BOND
53 Southampton Road, Westfield MA 01085. 413/562-1600. **Contact:** April Lassard, Administrative Assistant. **E-mail address:** alassard@tighebond.com. **World Wide Web address:** http://www.tighebond.com. **Description:** Offers environmental and civil engineering consulting services. **Positions advertised include:** Site Civil Engineer; Geotechnical Engineer; Structural Engineer.

WASHINGTON GROUP INTERNATIONAL, INC.
One Broadway, Cambridge MA 02142. 617/494-7000. **Contact:** Human Resources. **World Wide Web address:** http://www.wgint.com. **Description:** Provides design, engineering, and construction services to chemical, petroleum, and other related industrial customers. **Positions advertised include:** Engineer.

ARTS, ENTERTAINMENT, SPORTS, AND RECREATION

You can expect to find the following types of companies in this section:
Botanical and Zoological Gardens • Entertainment Groups • Motion Picture and Video Tape Production and Distribution • Museums and Art Galleries • Physical Fitness Facilities • Professional Sports Clubs; Sporting and Recreational Camps • Public Golf Courses and Racing and Track Operations • Theatrical Producers and Services

---

AMERICAN REPERTORY THEATRE
Loeb Drama Center, 64 Brattle Street, Cambridge MA 02138. 617/495-2668. **Contact:** Robert Orchard, Managing Director. **E-mail address:** info@amrep.org. **World Wide Web address:** http://www.amrep.org. **Description:** A nonprofit theater. **Special programs:** Internships. **Office hours:** Monday - Friday, 9:00 a.m. - 5:00 p.m.

BOSTON BALLET
19 Clarendon Street, Boston MA 02116. 617/695-6950. **Fax:** 617/695-6995. **Contact:** Human Resources. **E-mail address:** diane@bostonballet.com. **World Wide Web address:** http://www.bostonballet.org. **Description:** One of the largest dance companies in the United States. Boston Ballet performs a mix of classic story ballets, contemporary ballets, and avant-garde works. Founded in 1965. **Positions advertised include:** Major Gifts Officer; Data Coordinator; Managing Director; Male Principal Dancer; Resident Director.

BOSTON BRUINS
One Fleet Center Place, Suite 250, Boston MA 02114. 617/624-1050. **Contact:** Human Resources. **World Wide Web address:** http://www.bostonbruins.com. **Description:** Administrative and publicity offices for the National Hockey League team. **Corporate headquarters location:** This location.

BOSTON RED SOX BASEBALL CLUB
Fenway Park, 4 Yawkey Way, Boston MA 02215. 617/267-9440. **Contact:** Human Resources. **World Wide Web address:** http://boston.redsox.mlb.com. **Description:** Operates the Boston Red Sox, an American League professional baseball franchise.

BOSTON SPORTS CLUB — *Google*
201 Brookline Avenue, Boston MA 02215. 617/266-7400. **Contact:** Human Resources. **Description:** A fully equipped fitness center with free weights, nautilus equipment, a pool, massage therapy, and exercise classes including sports conditioning, aerobics, and yoga.

BOSTON SYMPHONY ORCHESTRA, INC.
301 Massachusetts Avenue, Boston MA 02115. 617/266-1492. **Contact:** Human Resources. **World Wide Web address:** http://www.bso.org. **Description:** Administrative offices for the Boston Symphony Orchestra.

CRANBERRY VALLEY GOLF COURSE
183 Oak Street, Harwich MA 02645. 508/430-5234. **Contact:** Human Resources. **World Wide Web address:** http://www.cranberryvalley.com. **Description:** A town owned and operated golf course.

THE CAPITAL THEATRE
204 Massachusetts Avenue, Arlington MA 02174. 781/648-6022. **Contact:** Manager. **Description:** An independently owned, six-screen movie theater. Founded in 1925. **Corporate headquarters location:** This location.

JACOB'S PILLOW DANCE FESTIVAL, INC.
P.O. Box 287, Lee MA 01238-0287. 413/637-1322. **Fax:** 413/243-4744. **Contact:** Connie Chin, Company Manager. **E-mail address:** info@jacobspillow.org. **World Wide Web address:** http://www.jacobspillow.org. **Description:** One of America's oldest dance festivals, presenting 10 weeks of dance performances and conducting a professional dance school each summer. Founded in 1942. **Positions advertised include:** Director of Marketing & PR; Audience Engagement Liaison; Development Manager for Institutional Support; Nurse; Emergency Medical Technician; Housekeeper; Driver. . **Special programs:** Internships. **Internship information:** Internships are offered in the following areas: archives/preservation; business office; development; documentation; education; marketing/press; operations; programming; technical/theatre production; and ticket services. Applicants are asked to send a resume, two work-related references with phone numbers, two letters of recommendation, and a cover letter. The cover letter should indicate a primary area of interest and describe goals and expectations for the internship. Applicants for marketing, development, education, and programming must include at least two writing samples, maximum two pages in length each. Please call the organization to find out deadline information.

MEDIEVAL MANOR
246 East Berkeley Street, Boston MA 02118. 617/423-4900. **Contact:** Manager. **World Wide Web address:** http://www.medievalmanor.com. **Description:** A dinner/theater restaurant with a medieval theme.

MUSEUM OF FINE ARTS - BOSTON
465 Huntington Avenue, Boston MA 02115. 617/267-9300. **Contact:** Sandra Matthews, Human Resources. **World Wide Web address:** http://www.mfa.org. **Description:** One of the largest museums in New England, with a wide spectrum of permanent and featured exhibits. **Positions advertised include:** Assistant Curator for Chinese Art; Registrar Assistant, Exhibitions and Loans; Grants Officer; Director of Marketing; MFA Fund Officer. **Positions advertised include:** Curatorial Specialist. **Corporate headquarters location:** This location.

NATIONAL AMUSEMENTS INC.
200 Elm Street, Dedham MA 02026. 781/461-1600. **Fax:** 781/407-0052.**Contact:** Maureen Dixon, Personnel Manager. **E-mail address:** mdixon@nationalamusements.com. **World Wide Web address:** http://www.nationalamusements.com. **Description:** National Amusements operates the Showcase and Multiplex movie theater chains. **Positions advertised include:** Cashier; Usher; Concession Attendant. **Parent company:** Viacom is a diversified entertainment and communications company with operations in four principal segments: Viacom Networks operates three advertiser-supported basic cable television program services: MTV, VH-1, and Nickelodeon/Nick at Nite; and three premium subscription television services, SHOWTIME, The Movie Channel, and FLIX; Viacom Entertainment distributes television series, feature films, made-for-television movies, miniseries, and movies for prime time broadcast network television. Viacom Entertainment also acquires and distributes television series for initial exhibition on a first-run basis; and develops, produces, distributes, and markets interactive software for the

stand-alone and other multimedia marketplaces; Viacom Cable Television owns and operates cable television systems in California, the Pacific Northwest, and Midwest; Viacom Broadcasting owns and operates 5 network-affiliated television stations and 14 radio stations. **Operations at this facility include:** This location houses administrative offices.

NEW ENGLAND AQUARIUM
Central Wharf, Boston MA 02110. 617/973-5200. **Contact:** Human Resources. **World Wide Web address:** http://www.neaq.org. **Description:** An aquarium offering a variety of educational programs, outdoor shows, whale watching trips, and the Aquarium Medical Center. Founded in 1969. **Positions advertised include:** Visitor Assistant; Sales Associate; Lead Sales Associate; Alternate Lead Visitor Attendant; IMAX Theatre Host; Reservation Assistant; Administrative Assistant.

NEW ENGLAND PATRIOTS FOOTBALL CLUB
60 Washington Street, Foxboro MA 02035. 508/543-8200. **Contact:** Human Resources. **World Wide Web address:** http://www.patriots.com. **Description:** Houses the executive offices of the New England Patriots, a member of the National Football League.

OLD STURBRIDGE VILLAGE
One Old Sturbridge Village Road, Sturbridge MA 01566. 508/347-3362. **Fax:** 508/347-0254. **Contact:** Human Resources. **World Wide Web address:** http://www.osv.org. **Description:** An outdoor history museum representing rural New England during the 1830s. Old Sturbridge Village operates a working farm, a mill, blacksmith and pottery shops, and a variety of other exhibits on 200 acres of land. Old Sturbridge Village also offers a wide range of events including apple cider tasting, archaeology programs, and concerts. **President:** Alberta Sebolt George.

PLIMOTH PLANTATION
P.O. Box 1620, Plymouth MA 02362. 508/746-1622. **Fax:** 508/746-3407. **Contact:** Susan Haverstock, Human Resources. **E-mail address:** shaverstock@plimoth.org. **World Wide Web address:** http://www.plimoth.org. **Description:** An outdoor authentic re-creation of the seventeenth-century Plymouth Colony. The staff plays the parts of the villagers and tour guides. Plimoth Plantation is open seven days a week, 9:00 a.m. - 5:00 p.m. from April through November. Founded in 1947. **Positions advertised include:** Mayflower II Security Officer; Stockroom Supervisor; Wompanoag Food-ways Supervisor; Industrial Advancement Writer; Director of Development.

SANKATY HEAD GOLF CLUB
100 Sankaty Road, Siasconsett MA 02564. 508/257-6655. **Fax:** 508/257-4265. **Contact:** Human Resources. **Description:** A private golf club on Nantucket Island known for its signature hole next to Sankaty Head Light House. **Golf Professional:** Mark Heartfield.

SIX FLAGS NEW ENGLAND
P.O. Box 307, Agawam MA 01001. 413/786-9300. **Fax:** 413/821-0038. **Contact:** Human Resources. **World Wide Web address:** http://www.sixflags.com. **Description:** A 160-acre amusement park with over 100 rides and attractions. Founded in 1940. **NOTE:** Apply online. Applicants must be available to work weekends April and May, daily June though Labor Day, and weekends in September and October. Must be at least 16 years old. Applicants may apply in

person or mail in an application. **Parent company:** Premier Parks (OK) owns and operates 35 theme parks nationwide. **CEO:** Kieran Burke.

SUFFOLK DOWNS
111 Waldemar Avenue, East Boston MA 02128. 617/567-3900. **Contact:** Human Resources. **World Wide Web address:** http://www.suffolkdowns.com. **Description:** A thoroughbred racetrack and entertainment facility offering live racing June through September. In the off-season, the track offers simulcasted broadcasts of races throughout the country.

Museum of Science?

AUTOMOTIVE

You can expect to find the following types of companies in this section:
Automotive Repair Shops • Automotive Stampings • Industrial Vehicles and Moving Equipment • Motor Vehicles and Equipment • Travel Trailers and Campers

ADESA BOSTON
63 Western Avenue, Framingham MA 01702. 508/626-7000. **Contact:** Human Resources. **E-mail address:** email_careers@adesa.com. **World Wide Web address:** http://www.adesa.com. **Description:** Auctions used cars and other vehicles to franchised auto dealerships. Adesa also provides auto reconditioning and vehicle transport services. **NOTE:** Entry-level positions and part-time jobs are offered. **Positions advertised include:** Application Technician; NT Analyst; Senior Financial Analyst. **Office hours:** Monday - Friday, 8:30 a.m. - 5:00 p.m. **Number of employees at this location:** 380. **Number of employees nationwide:** 4,000.

ROBERT BOSCH CORPORATION
101 First Avenue, Waltham MA 02451. 781/890-8282. **Contact:** Human Resources. **World Wide Web address:** http://www.boschusa.com. **Description:** Robert Bosch Corporation operates in three groups: Automotive-Original Equipment, Industrial Group, and Sales-Automotive Aftermarket. The largest segment of the company's business is the Automotive Group, which includes products such as antilock braking systems (ABS), airbag electronics, fuel injectors, and oxygen sensors. The Industrial Group consists of the Packaging Machinery Division, which sells high-technology packaging equipment, primarily to the food processing and pharmaceutical industries; the Surftran Division, which offers a range of deburring services, as well as manufacturing, selling, and servicing cleaning equipment; Weldun International, Inc. manufactures flexible assembly systems and automation products and assembles machinery for the Packaging Machinery Division; and Robert Bosch Fluid Power Corporation, which designs, produces, and markets hydraulic pumps, valves, and power units, and sells a full line of pneumatic products. The Sales Group handles automotive aftermarket, mobile communications, and household goods. Robert Bosch Corporation also participates in three joint ventures. Diesel Technology Company produces electronic and mechanical unit injectors. S-B Power Tool Company markets portable electric power tools and accessories to the industrial, contractor, and do-it-yourself markets. Automotive Electronic Controls Systems, Inc. manufactures parts for fuel-injection systems and automotive transmissions. **Corporate headquarters location:** Broadview IL. **Other U.S. locations:** Nationwide. **Operations at this facility include:** This location provides automotive sales, engineering, and administration as part of Robert Bosch Corporation's Automotive Group.

LO-JACK CORPORATION
200 Lowder Brook Drive, Suite 1000, Westwod MA 02090. 781/326-4700. **Contact:** Human Resources. **World Wide Web address:** http://www.lojack.com. **Description:** Manufactures electronic recovery systems for stolen automobiles. **Positions advertised include:** Automotive Installation Technician; Installation Supervisor; Field Specialist; Quality Control Specialist; Manager of Commercial Sales Division; Customer Service Representative. **NOTE:** Marketing and PR

Internships available. **International locations:** Worldwide. **Number of employees at this location:** 190.

POLLAK
195 Freeport Street, Boston MA 02122. 617/282-9550. **Contact:** Human Resources. **World Wide Web address:** http://www.pollak.com. **Description:** Pollak designs, develops, and produces integral components and systems for virtually every area of the transportation industry. The company creates electronic instrumentation including analog and digital clusters, drive information displays, power supplies, and warning light bars. Pollak manufactures electronic modules including light and HVAC control, panel seat memory, window control, brake monitoring, data acquisition, engine oil life monitor, multiplexing, and network interface. Founded in 1909. **Parent company:** Stoneridge, Inc. (Warren OH). **Operations at this facility include:** This location manufactures actuated automotive parts. **Listed on:** New York Stock Exchange. **Stock exchange symbol:** SRI.

POLLAK
300 Dan Road, Canton MA 02021. 781/830-0340. **Contact:** Human Resources. **World Wide Web address:** http://www.pollak.com. **Description:** Pollak designs, develops, and produces integral components and systems for virtually every area of the transportation industry. The company creates electronic instrumentation including analog and digital clusters, drive information displays, power supplies, and warning light bars. Pollak manufactures electronic modules including light and HVAC control, panel seat memory, window control, brake monitoring, data acquisition, engine oil life monitor, multiplexing, and network interface. Founded in 1909. **Parent company:** Stoneridge, Inc. (Warren OH). **Operations at this facility include:** This location manufactures a variety of automotive parts. **Listen on:** New York Stock Exchange. **Stock exchange symbol:** SRI.

STADIUM AUTO BODY, INC.
305 Western Avenue, Brighton MA 02134. 617/254-6163. **Contact:** Human Resources. **World Wide Web address:** http://www.stadiumauto.com. **Description:** Provides a wide variety of auto body and car repair services. The company also offers 24-hour towing services. **Corporate headquarters location:** This location.

BANKING, SAVINGS & LOANS, AND OTHER DEPOSITORY INSTITUTIONS

You can expect to find the following types of companies
in this section:
Banks • Bank Holding Companies and Associations • Lending Firms/Financial
Services Institutions

ABINGTON SAVINGS BANK
536 Washington Street, Abington MA 02351. 781/982-3200. **Fax:** 781/682-8777.
Contact: Human Resources. **E-mail address:** hradmin@abingtonsavings.com.
World Wide Web address: http://www.abingtonsavings.com. **Description:** A
full-service bank. **Corporate headquarters location:** This location. **Other U.S.
locations:** Halifax MA; Hanover MA; Holbrook MA; Hull MA; Kingston MA;
Pembroke MA; Whitman MA. **Listed on:** NASDAQ. **Stock exchange symbol:**
ABBK.

BANK OF AMERICA
11 Center Street, Burlington MA 01803. 781/273-3783. **Contact:** Human
Resources. **World Wide Web address:** http://www.bankofamerica.com.
Description: A full-service bank. **Positions advertised include:** Premier Client
Manager; Teller. **Corporate headquarters location:** Charlotte NC.

BANK OF AMERICA
460 West Broadway, South Boston MA 02127. 617/268-1936. **Contact:** Joe
Lynch, Branch Manager. **World Wide Web address:**
http://www.bankofamerica.com. **Description:** A full-service bank. **Positions
advertised include:** Premier Client Manager; Teller. **Corporate headquarters
location:** Charlotte NC.

BANK OF AMERICA
100 Federal Street, Boston MA 02110. 617/434-2200. **Fax:** 617/434-1941.
Contact: Human Resources. **World Wide Web address:**
http://www.bankofamerica.com. **Description:** Operates a full-service bank,
serving the commercial and consumer banking needs of individuals,
corporations, institutions, and government in the Northeast. **Positions
advertised include:** Branch Manager; F/A Invest Operator Assistant; Premium
Client Manager; Sales & Service Representative; Regional Sales Director;
Administrative Assistant. **Corporate headquarters location:** Charlotte NC.
Note: Please send resumes to: One Federal Street, Boston MA 02110.

BANKNORTH MASSACHUSETTS
153 Merrimack Street, Haverhill MA 01830. 978/374-1911. **Contact:** Human
Resources. **Description:** Operates a full-service bank providing residential
mortgage lending, commercial lending, construction lending, and savings. **Other
U.S. locations:** MA; NH. **Parent company:** Banknorth, N.A.

BERKSHIRE BANK
P.O. Box 1308, Pittsfield MA 01202. 413/443-5601. **Toll-free phone:** 800/773-
5601. **Fax:** 413/447-1830. **Physical address:** 24 North Street, Pittsfield MA
01201. **Contact:** Human Resources. **E-mail address:**
resumes@berkshirebank.com. **World Wide Web address:**
http;//www.berkshirebank.com. **Description:** A full-service mutual savings bank.

Corporate headquarters location: This location. **Operations at this facility include:** Administration. **Number of employees at this location:** 150.

BOSTON FEDERAL SAVINGS BANK
17 New England Executive Park, Burlington MA 01803. 781/273-0300. **Fax:** 781/229-0282. **Contact:** Human Resources. **World Wide Web address:** http://www.bfsb.com. **Description:** A full-service federal savings bank with several branch locations throughout the greater Boston area. **Positions advertised include:** Loan Services Representative; Teller; Assistant Branch Manager; Loan Investment Specialist; Floating Assistant Manager; Floating Assistant Manager; Construction Loan Services; Brand Administrative Specialist. **Corporate headquarters location:** This location. **Other area locations:** Arlington MA; Bedford MA; Billerica MA; Boston MA; Lexington MA; Peabody MA; Wellesley MA; Woburn MA. **Operations at this facility include:** Administration.

BROOKLINE SAVINGS BANK
P.O. Box 470469, Brookline MA 02477. 617/730-3500. **Toll-free phone:** 877/668-2265. **Physical address:** 24 Webster Place, Brookline MA 02477. **Contact:** Jack Nealon, Personnel Director. **World Wide Web address:** http://www.brooklinesavings.com. **Description:** A full-service savings bank. **Positions advertised include:** Teller; Customer Service Representative. **Corporate headquarters location:** This location.

CAMBRIDGE SAVINGS BANK
P.O. Box 380206, Cambridge MA 02238-0206. 617/864-8700. **Physical Address:** 1374 Massachusetts Avenue, Cambridge MA 02138. **Fax:** 617/441-4171. **Contact:** Human Resources. **E-mail address:** jobs@csb.usa.com. **World Wide Web address:** http://www.cambridgesavings.com. **Description:** Operates a full-service savings bank. **Positions advertised include:** Teller; Corporate Lending Administrator; Messenger/Driver; Underwriter; WebBank Product Manager. **Special programs:** Internships. **Corporate headquarters location:** This location. **Operations at this facility include:** Administration; Sales; Service. **Number of employees at this location:** 265.

CAMBRIDGEPORT BANK
1380 Soldiers Field Road, Brighton MA 02135. 617/779-2900. **Fax:** 617/779-2729. **Contact:** Human Resources. **E-mail address:** HumanResource@Cambridgeport.com. **World Wide Web address:** http://www.host.theeditors.com/cp-bank. **Description:** A full service community bank providing personal and business financial services. **Other area locations:** Arlington MA; Newton MA; Lexington MA; Wellesley MA; Needham MA; Winchester MA; Natick MA; Westwood MA.

CAPE COD FIVE CENTS SAVINGS BANK
P.O. Box 10, Orleans MA 02653. 508/240-0555. **Contact:** Human Resources. **World Wide Web address:** http://www.capecodfive.com. **Description:** A full-service savings bank.

CENTURY BANK
400 Mystic Avenue, Medford MA 02155. 781/393-4613. **Toll-free phone:** 800/442-1859. **Fax:** 781/393-4220. **Contact:** Kathleen McGillicuddy, Human Resources. **E-mail address:** kmcgillicuddy@century-bank.com. **World Wide Web address:** http://www.century-bank.com. **Description:** A bank holding company. Founded in 1969. **NOTE:** Entry-level positions and part-time jobs are offered. This location also hires seasonally. **Positions advertised include:** Head

Teller; Assistant Manager; Branch Manager; Service Counselor; Item Process Supervisor; Customer Service Representative; Accounts Receivable Specialist; Balance & Reconciliation Specialist; Sorter Operator. **Office hours:** Monday - Friday, 8:30 a.m. - 5:00 p.m. **Corporate headquarters location:** This location. **Other area locations:** Beverly MA; Boston MA; Braintree MA; Brighton MA; Brookline MA; Burlington MA; Cambridge MA; Everett MA; Lynn MA; Malden MA; Medford MA; Newton MA; Peabody MA; Quincy MA; Salem MA; Somerville MA. **Subsidiaries include:** Century Bank and Trust Company offers a full range of banking services to individuals, businesses, and municipal customers. The bank operates through 16 branches in the greater Boston area. **Listed on:** NASDAQ. **Stock exchange symbol:** CNBKA. **Chairman/President/CEO:** Marshall Sloane. **Number of employees at this location:** 150. **Number of employees nationwide:** 300.

CITIZENS BANK
28 State Street, Boston MA 02108. 617/725-5500. **Contact:** Human Resources. **World Wide Web address:** http://www.citizensbank.com. **Description:** A commercial bank holding company. Citizens Bank maintains more than 700 branch locations and more than 1,490 ATMs in Connecticut, Massachusetts, New Hampshire, Rhode Island, Pennsylvania, and Delaware. **Corporate headquarters location:** Providence RI. **Other area locations:** Brighton, Chestnut Hill, Arlington, Braintree, Concord, Groton, Littleton, Brookline, Framingham, Newton, Newton Centre, Quincy, Norwell and many other locations. **Parent company:** Citizens Financial Group, Inc. **Number of employees nationwide:** 12,500.

COMPASSBANK
141 North Main Street, Fall River MA 02720. 508/994-5000. **Toll-free phone:** 800/322-9313. **Fax:** 508/646-3425. **Contact:** Linda Empoliti, Director of Human Resources. **E-mail address:** hresources@compassbank.com. **World Wide Web address:** http://www.compassbank.com. **Description:** Operates a full-service savings bank. Founded in 1855. **Corporate headquarters location:** New Bedford MA. **Other area locations:** Assonet MA; Buzzards Bay MA; Carver MA; Cedarville MA; Chatham MA; Chilmark MA; Dartmouth MA; Edgartown MA; Fairhaven MA; Falmouth MA; Hyannis MA; Mattapoisett MA; Oak Bluffs MA; Orleans MA; Plymouth MA; Pocasset MA; Sandwich MA; Seekonk MA; Somerset MA; South Dennis MA; South Sandwich MA; South Yarmouth MA; Swansea MA; Vineyard Haven MA; Wareham MA; West Tisbury MA; Westport MA. **Parent company:** Seacoast Financial Services Corporation. **Listed on:** NASDAQ. **Stock exchange symbol:** SCFS.

EASTERN BANK
195 Market Street, Lynn MA 01901. 781/598-7899. **Contact:** Human Resources. **World Wide Web address:** http://www.easternbank.com. **Description:** Operates a full-service savings bank. **Corporate headquarters location:** This location. **Other area locations:** Beverly MA; Boston MA; Braintree MA; Brockton MA; Burlington MA; Canton MA; Danvers MA; Hanover MA; Hingham MA; Lynnfield MA; Malden MA; Marblehead MA; Marshfield MA; Medford MA; Melrose MA; Newburyport MA; Norwell MA; Peabody MA; Quincy MA; Randolph MA; Reading MA; Salem MA; Saugus MA; South Boston MA; Stoneham MA; Stoughton MA; Swampscott MA; Wakefield MA; Weymouth MA. **Positions advertised include:** Data Entry Clerk; Quality Control Clerk; Teller; Human Resources Officer; Mortgage Production Specialist.

MASSBANK CORPORATION

123 Haven Street, Reading MA 01867. 781/662-0100. **Contact:** Human Resources. **World Wide Web address:** http://www.massbank.com. **Description:** A savings and loan corporation. **NOTE:** Please send resumes to: Human Resources, MASSBANK Corporation, 50 Central Street, Lowell MA 01852. **Number of employees at this location:** 150.

METROWEST BANK

420 Franklin Street, Framingham MA 01702. 508/879-7525. **Contact:** Human Resources. **World Wide Web address:** http://www.metrowestbank.com. **Description:** A full-service savings bank. **Parent company:** Banknorth, N.A.

MIDDLESEX SAVINGS BANK

6 Main Street, Natick MA 01760. 508/653-0300. **Toll-free phone:** 877/463-6287. **Fax:** 508/651-9026. **Contact:** Personnel. **E-mail address:** careers@middlesexbank.com. **World Wide Web address:** http://www.middlesexbank.com. **Description:** A savings bank. **Positions advertised include:** Commercial Banking Officer; Commercial Real Estate Analyst; Vice President Commercial Real Estate. **Corporate headquarters location:** This location. **Other U.S. locations:** Acton MA; Ashland MA; Concord MA; Framingham MA; Groton MA; Holliston MA; Hopkinton MA; Littleton MA; Maynard MA; Medfield MA; Millis MA; Natick MA; Southborough MA; Sudbury MA; Wayland MA; Wellesley MA; Westford MA.

NANTUCKET BANK

104 Pleasant Street, Nantucket Island MA 02554. 508/228-0580. **Toll-free phone:** 800/533-9313. **Fax:** 508/228-1322. **Contact:** Human Resources. **E-mail address:** lmccandless@nantucketbank.com. **World Wide Web address:** http://www.nantucketbank.com. **Description:** A local island bank.

PLYMOUTH SAVINGS BANK

151 Campanelli Drive, P.O. Box 1439, Middleboro MA 02346. 508/946-3000. **Contact:** Personnel. **World Wide Web address:** http://www.plymouthsavings.com. **Description:** A full-service savings bank with 17 branch offices. **Positions advertised include:** Teller; Mortgage Officer; Assistant Manager. **Corporate headquarters location:** This location. **Other area locations:** Duxbury MA; Falmouth MA; Lakeville MA; Marion MA; Mashpee MA; Mattapoisett MA; Raynham MA; Sandwich MA. **Parent company:** Plymouth Bancorp, Inc.

ROCKLAND TRUST

288 Union Street, Rockland MA 02370. 781/878-6100. **Fax:** 781/982-6424. **Contact:** Paul McDonough, Employment Manager. **World Wide Web address:** http://www.rocklandtrust.com. **Description:** Rockland Trust is a commercial bank with 44 offices offering retail and commercial banking services, trust and estate planning, investment, and employee benefit services. Founded in 1907. **NOTE:** Entry-level positions are offered. **Positions advertised include:** Customer Service Agent; Mortgage Originator. **Special programs:** Training. **Corporate headquarters location:** This location. **Other area locations:** Statewide. **Parent company:** Independent Bank Corp. **Listed on:** NASDAQ. **Stock exchange symbol:** INDB. **Number of employees at this location:** 570.

SLADE'S FERRY BANCORP
SLADE'S FERRY BANK

P.O Box 390, Somerset MA 02726. 508/675-2121. **Physical address:** 100 Slade's Ferry Avenue, Somerset MA 02726. **Fax:** 508/675-1751. **Contact:**

Charlene Jarest, Vice President of Human Resources. **World Wide Web address:** http://www.sladesferry.com. **Description:** A holding company. This location also houses a branch of Slade's Ferry Bank. Founded in 1989. **Positions advertised include:** Teller; Assistant Branch Manager. **Corporate headquarters location:** This location. **Other area locations:** Fairhaven MA; Fall River MA; New Bedford MA; Seekonk MA; Swansea MA. **Subsidiaries include:** Slade's Ferry Trust Company. **Listed on:** NASDAQ. **Stock exchange symbol:** SFBC. **President/CEO:** James Carey. **Number of employees nationwide:** 250.

SOVEREIGN BANK

One Harvard Street, Brookline Village MA 02446. 617/232-0467. **Toll-free phone:** 877/768-2265. **Contact:** Human Resources. **World Wide Web address:** http://www.sovereignbank.com. **Description:** A $55 billion financial institution with nearly 600 community banking offices and 1,000 ATMs in Connecticut, Massachusetts, New Hampshire, New Jersey, New York, Pennsylvania, and Rhode Island. **Parent company:** Sovereign Bancorp, Inc. **Listed on:** New York Stock Exchange. **Stock exchange symbol:** SOV. **Number of employees nationwide:** 9,500.

SOVEREIGN BANK

75 State Street, Boston MA 02109. 617/757-3410. **Toll-free phone:** 877/768-2265. **Contact:** Human Resources. **World Wide Web address:** http://www.sovereignbank.com. **Description:** A $55 billion financial institution with nearly 600 community banking offices and 1,000 ATMs in Connecticut, Massachusetts, New Hampshire, New Jersey, New York, Pennsylvania, and Rhode Island. **Positions advertised include:** Anti – Money Laundering Analyst; Community Banking Manager; Customer Service Representative; Teller; Deposit Manager; Executive Assistant; Financial Assistant. **Parent company:** Sovereign Bancorp, Inc. **Listed on:** New York Stock Exchange. **Stock exchange symbol:** SOV. **Number of employees nationwide:** 9,500.

U.S. FEDERAL RESERVE BANK OF BOSTON

600 Atlantic Avenue, Employment Unit T-3, Boston MA 02106. 617/973-3518. **Contact:** Human Resources. **World Wide Web address:** http://www.bos.frb.org. **Description:** One of 12 regional Federal Reserve banks that, along with the Federal Reserve Board of Governors (Washington DC) and the Federal Open Market Committee, comprise the Federal Reserve System. As the nation's central bank, the Federal Reserve is charged with three major responsibilities: monetary policy, banking supervision and regulation, and processing payments.

BIOTECHNOLOGY, PHARMACEUTICALS, AND SCIENTIFIC R&D

You can expect to find the following types of companies in this section:
Clinical Labs • Lab Equipment Manufacturers • Pharmaceutical Manufacturers and Distributors

---

ABBOTT BIORESEARCH CENTER
100 Research Drive, Worcester MA 01605. 508/849-2500. **Fax:** 508/755-8511 **Contact:** Human Resources. **E-mail address:** abcjobs@abbott.com. **World Wide Web address:** http://www.abbott.com. **Description:** Engaged in immunology and oncology research for the development of pharmaceuticals. **Positions advertised include:** Process Engineer; Director of Translation; Validation Specialist; Research Associate; Scientist; Quality Assurance Specialist. **Corporate headquarters location:** Abbott Park IL. **Parent company:** Abbott Laboratories. **Other U.S. locations:** Nationwide. **International locations:** Worldwide.

ACAMBIS INC.
38 Sidney Street, 4th Floor, Cambridge MA 02139. 617/761-4200. **Fax:** 617/494-1741. **Contact:** Human Resources. **World Wide Web address:** http://www.acambis.com. **Description:** Discovers and develops oral vaccines and noninjected antibody products to prevent and treat diseases that infect the human body at its mucous membranes. These tissues include the linings of the gastrointestinal, respiratory, and genitourinary tracts and the surfaces of the eyes. Acambis is pursuing three principal product development programs that target diseases that have high rates of incidence including viral pneumonia in children, peptic ulcer disease, and antibiotic-associated diarrhea and colitis. **Positions advertised include:** Accounting Manager; Network Engineer; IT Manager; Clinical Regulatory Manager; Clinical Trial Manager. **Corporate headquarters location:** Cambridge, England. **Listed on:** NASDAQ. **Stock exchange symbol:** ACAM.

ADVANCED MAGNETICS, INC.
61 Mooney Street, Cambridge MA 02138. 617/497-2070. **Fax:** 617/547-2445. **Contact:** Human Resources. **E-mail address:** contactus@advancedmagnets.com. **World Wide Web address:** http://www.advancedmagnetics.com. **Description:** Engaged in the development and manufacture of MRI contrast agents for the detection of cancer and other diseases. **Listed on:** American Stock Exchange. **Stock exchange symbol:** AVM.

ALKERMES, INC.
64 Sidney Street, Cambridge MA 02139. 617/494-0171. **Contact:** Peter Maguire, Director of Human Resources. **World Wide Web address:** http://www.alkermes.com. **Description:** A pharmaceutical company that produces drug delivery systems for pharmaceutical agents. Alkermes produces four proprietary delivery systems including Cereport blood-brain permeabilizer, ProLease and Medisorb injectable sustained-release systems, RingCap and Dose Sipping oral delivery systems, and AIR pulmonary delivery systems. **Positions advertised include:** Clinical Manager; Drug Safety Associate; Medical Director; Statistical Programmer; Development Engineer; Scientist;

Quality Control Microbiologist Supervisor; Regulatory Affairs Director; Regulatory Affairs Manager; Strategic Procurement Manager. **NOTE: A**pply and submit resumes online. Resumes should be sent to Peter Maguire at 840 Memorial Drive, Cambridge MA 02139. **Corporate headquarters location:** This location. **Other U.S. locations:** Cincinnati OH. **Listed on:** NASDAQ. **Stock exchange symbol:** ALKS.

AMERICAN SCIENCE & ENGINEERING, INC.

829 Middlesex Turnpike, Billerica MA 01821. 978/262-8700. **Fax:** 978/262-8896. **Contact:** Human Resources. **E-mail address:** service@as-e.com. **World Wide Web address:** http://www.as-e.com. **Description:** Researches, develops, produces, and sells instrumentation for X-ray research for use in government space science programs and other scientific applications. The company also manufactures and sells a load management and automatic remote meter-reading system for public utilities; and develops, manufactures, and markets X-ray equipment. **Positions advertised include:** Corporate Counsel; Field Service Engineer; Project Manager; Project Cost Accountant. **Corporate headquarters location:** This location. **Operations at this facility include:** Administration; Manufacturing; Research and Development; Sales; Service. **Listed on:** American Stock Exchange. **Stock exchange symbol:** ASE.

ANIKA THERAPEUTICS

236 West Cummings Parkway, Woburn MA 01801. 781/932-6616. **Fax:** 781/935-4120. **Contact:** Personnel. **World Wide Web address:** http://www.anikatherapeutics.com. **Description:** Develops and commercializes products using hyaluronic acid (HA) for medical and therapeutic applications. Products include AMVISC, a high molecular weight HA product that is used as a viscoelastic agent in ophthalmic surgical procedures including cataract extraction and intraocular lens implantation; HYVISC, a high molecular weight HA product used for the treatment of joint dysfunction in horses due to noninfectious synovitis associated with equine osteoarthritis; ORTHOVISC, a high molecular weight, injectable HA product for the symptomatic treatment of osteoarthritis of the knee; and INCERT, a chemically modified, cross-linked form of HA designed to prevent the formation of post-surgical wound adhesions. Founded in 1993. **Positions advertised include:** Process Development Engineer; Quality Engineer; Scientist. **NOTE:** Entry-level positions and second and third shifts are offered. **Special programs:** Internships. **Corporate headquarters location:** This location. **Listed on:** NASDAQ. **Stock exchange symbol:** ANIK. **CEO:** Douglas R. Potter.

ANTIGENICS INC.

3 Forbes Road, Lexington MA 02421-7305. 781/674-4400. **Fax:** 781/674-4200. **Contact:** Human Resources. **E-mail address:** recruiter@antigenics.com. **World Wide Web address**: http://www.antigenics.com. **Description:** Develops diagnostic and vaccine products to fight AIDS, cancer, and other diseases. **Positions advertised include:** Research Associate; Paralegal; Process Development; Scientist; Research Associate; Web Producer; Payroll Specialist. **Corporate headquarters location:** New York City NY. **Other area locations:** Woburn, MA. **International locations:** The Netherlands. **Listed on:** NASDAQ. **Stock exchange symbol:** AGEN.

APPLIED SCIENCE LABORATORIES

175 Middlesex Turnpike, Bedford MA 01730. 781/275-4000. **Fax:** 781/275-3388. **Contact:** Human Resources. **E-mail address:** asl@a-s-l.com. **World Wide Web address:** http://www.a-s-l.com. **Description:** Develops and manufactures eye tracking systems and technology. The company also provides contract research.

Corporate headquarters location: This location. **Parent company:** Applied Science Group, Inc.

ARIAD PHARMACEUTICALS, INC.
26 Landsdowne Street, Cambridge MA 02139. 617/494-0400. **Contact:** Human Resources. **E-mail address:** human.resources@ariad.com. **World Wide Web address:** http://www.ariad.com. **Description:** A biopharmaceutical company that uses gene regulation and signal transduction to develop therapeutic products. Founded in 1991. **Positions advertised include:** Medical Director; Pharmaceutical Affairs Manager; Quality Assurance Manager; Quality Assurance Manager; Quality Control Specialist; Research Associate; Analytical Chemistry; Research Associate. **NOTE:** When mailing resumes, address to Job Code:___ before the above address. Job codes can be found on the website. **Corporate headquarters location:** This location. **Listed on:** NASDAQ. **Stock exchange symbol:** ARIA.

ASTRAZENECA
50 Otis Street, Westborough MA 01581. 508/366-1100. **Contact:** Human Resources. **World Wide Web address:** http://www.astrazeneca.com. **Description:** Develops pharmaceuticals to fight infections, cardiovascular and gastrointestinal diseases, cancer, and asthma and other respiratory problems. Other products developed by AstraZeneca are used as anesthetics and to control pain. **Positions advertised include:** Research Associate; Pharmaceutical Sales; Principal Scientist; Purchasing Manager; Administrative Coordinator; Facilities Technician; Product Operation; Machine Adjuster; CAD Leader; Patent Attorney; Chemist; Training Specialist; Scientist.

ATHENA DIAGNOSTICS, INC.
4 Biotechnology Research Park, 377 Plantation Street, Worcester MA 01605. 508/756-2886. **Toll-free phone:** 800/394-4493. **Fax:** 508/753-5601. **Contact:** Human Resources. **E-mail address:** employment@athenadiognostics.com. **World Wide Web address:** http://www.athenadiagnostics.com. **Description:** A reference laboratory that develops and commercializes diagnostics and therapeutics for neurological and neurogenic disorders. **Corporate headquarters location:** South San Francisco CA. **Parent company:** Elan Pharmaceuticals, Inc. **Operations at this facility include:** Administration; Manufacturing; Research and Development; Sales; Service. **Listed on:** NASDAQ. **Annual sales/revenues:** $11 - $20 million. **Number of employees at this location:** 65.

AVANT IMMUNOTHERAPEUTICS, INC.
119 Fourth Avenue, Needham MA 02194-2725. 781/433-0771. **Fax:** 781/433-3113. **Contact:** Human Resources. **E-mail address:** info@avantimmune.com. **World Wide Web address:** http://www.avantimmune.com. **Description:** A biopharmaceutical company specializing in the understanding and treatment of diseases caused by misregulation of the body's natural defense systems. **Positions advertised include:** Document Control Manager; Manufacturing Manager. **Corporate headquarters location:** This location. **Other area locations:** Fall River MA. **Listed on:** NASDAQ. **Stock exchange symbol:** AVAN.

BAYER DIAGNOSTICS
63 North Street, Medfield MA 02052. 508/359-7711. **Contact:** Human Resources. **World Wide Web address:** http://www.bayerds.com. **Description:** Develops, manufactures, and sells clinical diagnostic systems. Bayer Diagnostics specializes in critical care, laboratory, and point-of-care testing. **International**

locations: Worldwide. **Parent company:** Bayer Group. **Number of employees nationwide:** 4,500.

BIOGEN CORPORATION
14 Cambridge Center, Cambridge MA 02142. 617/252-9200. **Fax:** 617/679-2546. **Contact:** Human Resources. **E-mail address:** resumes@biogen.com. **World Wide Web address:** http://www.biogen.com. **Description:** Develops and commercializes drugs produced by genetic engineering. Products include alpha interferon, sold by Schering-Plough, and Hepatitis B vaccines, sold by Merck and SmithKline Beecham. **Positions advertised include:** Associate Customer Service Director; Manufacturing Associate; Commodity Analyst; Medical Coder; Sales Analyst; Data Support Administrator; Web Architect; Associate Scientist; Business Analyst; Business Project Manager; Development Engineer; Documentation Specialist. **Special programs:** Internships. **Corporate headquarters location:** This location. **Other U.S. locations:** Research Triangle Park NC. **International locations:** France. **Operations at this facility include:** Administration; Manufacturing; Research and Development. **Listed on:** NASDAQ. **Stock exchange symbol:** BGEN. **Number of employees nationwide:** 430.

BIOPURE CORPORATION
11 Hurley Street, Cambridge MA 02141. 617/234-6500. **Contact:** Personnel. **E-mail address:** hr@biopure.com. **World Wide Web address:** http://www.biopure.com. **Description:** A pharmaceutical company that develops oxygen-based therapeutic products. **Positions advertised include:** Biostatistics Data Manager; Clinical Project Manager; Clinical Operations Director; Regulatory Affairs Drug Safety Specialist. **Listed on:** NASDAQ. **Stock exchange symbol:** BPUR.

BIOSPHERE MEDICAL INC.
1050 Hingham Street, Rockland MA 02370. 781/681-7900. **Fax:** 781/792-2745. **Contact:** Human Resources. **World Wide Web address:** http://www.biospheremed.com. **Description:** Biomedical company focused on embolotherapy. **Other locations:** France.

BIOTRANSPLANT, INC.
Building 75, Third Avenue, Charlestown Navy Yard, Charlestown MA 02129. 617/241-5200. **Contact:** Human Resources. **World Wide Web address:** http://www.biotransplant.com. **Description:** Engaged in the research and development of pharmaceuticals. Products are designed to help the human body to accept transplants; to increase the potential for more nonhuman to human transplants; and to treat rejection of transplanted organs and tissues. **Listed on:** NASDAQ. **Stock exchange symbol:** BTRN.

BOSTON BIOMEDICA, INC.
375 West Street, West Bridgewater MA 02379. 508/580-1900. **Contact:** Human Resources. **World Wide Web address:** http://www.bbii.com. **Description:** A clinical laboratory that provides diagnostic testing specifically for HIV-1 (AIDS), HTLV-1, HIV-2, and Viral Hepatitis. **Other U.S. locations:** Garden Grove CA; Gaithersburg MD. **Listed on:** NASDAQ. **Stock exchange symbol:** BBII.

BRISTOL-MYERS SQUIBB COMPANY
331 Treble Cove Road, Building 300-2, Billerica, MA 01862. 978/667-9531. **Contact:** Human Resources. **World Wide Web address:** http://www.bms.com. **Description:** Manufactures pharmaceuticals including Coumadin, Sinemet, Cardiolite, Thallium, and I.V. Persantine. **Positions advertised include:**

International Brand Manager Cardiolite; Research Scientist Assistant; Technical Transfer Representative; Accounts Receivable Representative; Process Engineer; Technician Principal; Principal Quality Scientist; Planner; Buyer; Assistant Vet Services Technician; Occupational Health; Purchase Agent; Customer Service Representative; Lead Person; Project Custodian. **Corporate headquarters location:** New York NY. **Listed on:** New York Stock Exchange. **Stock exchange symbol:** BMY.

CENTER FOR BLOOD RESEARCH LABORATORIES, INC.

800 Huntington Avenue, Boston MA 02115. 617/731-6470. **Contact:** Human Resources. **World Wide Web address:** http://www.cbrlabs.com. **Description:** Provides molecular diagnostic and genetic typing services for the purpose of identity testing, matching potential donors for patients, and diagnosis of inherited diseases. The company also provides blood testing services to detect diseases for early treatment, as well as the testing new medical treatments and diagnostic products. **Special programs:** Internships. **Corporate headquarters location:** This location. **Parent company:** The Center for Blood Research (CBR) is a nonprofit organization affiliated with Harvard Medical School that conducts research on the functions and uses of components of blood and other tissue and trains medical and scientific personnel in research. **Operations at this facility include:** Research and Development. **Number of employees at this location:** 150.

CHARLES RIVER LABORATORIES

251 Ballardvale Street, Wilmington MA 01887. 978/658-6000. **Contact:** Human Resources Manager. **E-mail address:** jobs@criver.com. **World Wide Web address:** http://www.criver.com. **Description:** A commercial supplier of laboratory animals including mice, rats, and guinea pigs for use in medical and scientific research. Users include chemical and pharmaceutical companies, government agencies, universities, commercial testing laboratories, hospitals, and others. **Positions advertised include:** Manager, Computer Operations & Operating Systems; Product Marketing Administrator, Transgenics; Sr. Analyst, Corporate Accounting; Sr. Technologist, Diagnostic Support; Administrator, Corporate Engineering. **Corporate headquarters location:** This location. **Operations at this facility include:** Administration; Manufacturing; Research and Development; Sales; Service. **Listed on:** New York Stock Exchange. **Stock exchange symbol:** CRL. **Number of employees nationwide:** 1,100.

CORNING INC.

Life Sciences, 45 Nagog Park, Acton MA 01720-3413. 978/635-2200. **Contact:** Human Resources. **World Wide Web address:** http://www.corning.com. **Description:** Corning's Science Products Division is engaged in the design, development, manufacture, and sale of disposable plastic research labware. **Positions advertised include:** Business Development Manager; Midwest Area Sales Manager. **NOTE:** Summer internships are available, search the website for more information and apply online. **Other U.S. locations:** Nationwide. **International locations:** Worldwide. **Operations at this facility include:** This location houses the company's administrative offices. **Listed on:** New York Stock Exchange. **Stock exchange symbol:** GLW.

CUBIST PHARMACEUTICALS

65 Hayden Avenue, Lexington MA 02421. 781/860-8660. **Fax:** 781/861-0566. **Contact:** Human Resources. **E-mail address:** hr@cubist.com. **World Wide Web address:** http://www.cubist.com. **Description:** Pharmaceutical company focused on the production of antiinfective drugs. **Corporate headquarters location:** This location.

CHARLES STARK DRAPER LABORATORY, INC.
555 Technology Square, Mail Stop 44, Cambridge MA 02139-3563. 617/258-1000. **Contact:** Personnel. **E-mail address:** hr@draper.com. **World Wide Web address:** http://www.draper.com. **Description:** A private, nonprofit corporation dedicated to scientific research, development, and education. **Positions advertised include:** Test Engineer; Systems Engineer; Communications Engineer; Software Engineer. **Corporate headquarters location:** This location.

DYAX CORPORATION
One Kendall Square, Building 600, Suite 623, Cambridge MA 02139. 617/225-2500. **Contact:** Human Resources. **World Wide Web address:** http://www.dyax.com. **Description:** Engaged in producing protein and peptide separations as well as screening technology products. Dyax Corporation also develops nuclear medicine to help alleviate clotting problems. **Positions advertised include:** Procurement Manager; Program Management Director; System Administrator. Subsidiaries include: Dyax s.a. (Belgium); Biotage Division (Charlottesville VA); Biotage UK (England). Listed on: New York Stock Exchange. Stock exchange symbol: DYAX.

GPC BIOTECH
610 Lincoln Street, Waltham MA 02451. 781/890-9007. **Fax:** 781/890-9005. **Contact:** Human Resources. **E-mail address:** hr.waltham@gpc-biotech.com. **World Wide Web address:** http://www.gpc-biotech.com. **Description:** A transatlantic genomics drug discovery company that specializes in proprietary genomics, proteomics, and drug discovery technologies designed to improve the process of drug development. Founded in 1992. **Positions advertised include:** Scientist; Chemist. **Office hours:** Monday - Friday, 8:30 a.m. - 5:00 p.m. **Listed on:** Privately held. **Number of employees at this location:** 75.

GENOME THERAPEUTICS CORPORATION
100 Beaver Street, Waltham MA 02453-8443. 781/398-2300. **Fax:** 781/893-9535. **Contact:** Personnel. **World Wide Web address:** http://www.genomecorp.com. **Description:** Engaged in the research, analysis, and commercial development of genetic information. Founded in 1961. **NOTE:** Entry-level positions and second and third shifts are offered. **Positions advertised include:** Accounts Payable Administrator; Vice President Corporate Capability Registration Compliance; Vice President Drug Safety; Clinical Trials Manager; Product Manager; Associate Director. **Office hours:** Monday - Friday 8:30 a.m. - 5:00 p.m. **Corporate headquarters location:** This location. **Operations at this facility include:** Administration; Research and Development. **Listed on:** NASDAQ. **Stock exchange symbol:** GENE. **President/CEO:** Steven Rauscher. **Annual sales/revenues:** $21 - $50 million. **Number of employees at this location:** 200.

GENVEC INC.
Building 96, 13th Street, Charlestown Navy Yard, Charlestown MA 02129. 617/242-9100. **Fax:** 617/242-0070. **Contact:** Human Resources. **E-mail address:** resume@genvec.com. **World Wide Web address:** http://www.genvec.com. **Description:** A biotechnology company that specializes in cell transplantation technology designed to treat diseases characterized by cell dysfunction or cell death. Founded in 1989. **Positions advertised include:** Research Scientist; Research Assistant; Research Assistant Biochemistry. **Special programs:** Co-ops. **Office hours:** Monday - Friday, 8:00 a.m. - 5:30 p.m.

GENZYME BIOSURGERY

64 Sidney Street, Cambridge MA 02139-4136. 617/494-8484. **Contact:** Human Resources. **World Wide Web address:** http://www.genzyme.com. **Description:** Develops tissues grown from human cells for medical use. **Corporate headquarters location:** Cambridge MA. **Other U.S. locations:** Nationwide. **International locations:** Worldwide. **Parent company:** Genzyme Corporation (Cambridge MA). **Listed on:** NASDAQ. **Stock exchange symbol:** GENZ. **Annual sales/revenues:** $51 - $100 million. **Number of employees nationwide:** 3,140. **Number of employees worldwide:** 3,700.

GENZYME CORPORATION

One Kendall Square, Building 1400, Cambridge MA 02139-1562. 617/252-7500. **Contact:** Human Resources. **World Wide Web address:** http://www.genzyme.com. **Description:** An international, diversified health care products company focused on developing and delivering practical solutions to specific medical needs. The company's activities and products are organized into six primary business areas: Therapeutics, Surgical Products, Genetics, Pharmaceuticals, Diagnostic Services, and Tissue Repair. Founded in 1981. **Special programs:** Internships; Co-ops; Summer Jobs. **Office hours:** Monday - Friday, 8:30 a.m. - 5:00 p.m. **Corporate headquarters location:** This location. **Other U.S. locations:** Nationwide. **International locations:** Worldwide. **Listed on:** NASDAQ. **Stock exchange symbol:** GENZ. **Annual sales/revenues:** $51 - $100 million. **Number of employees nationwide:** 3,140. **Number of employees worldwide:** 3,700.

GENZYME CORPORATION

One Mountain Road, P.O. Box 9322, Framingham MA 01701-9322. 508/872-8400. **Contact:** Human Resources. **World Wide Web address:** http://www.genzyme.com. **Description:** Genzyme Corporation is an international, diversified health care products company dedicated to developing and delivering practical solutions to specific medical needs. **Corporate headquarters location:** Cambridge MA. **Other U.S. locations:** Nationwide. **International locations:** Worldwide. **Operations at this facility include:** This location is engaged in the application of transgenic technology to the development and production of recombinant proteins for therapeutic and diagnostic uses. . **Listed on:** NASDAQ. **Stock exchange symbol:** GENZ. **Annual sales/revenues:** $51 - $100 million. **Number of employees nationwide:** 3,140. **Number of employees worldwide:** 3,700.

HYBRIDON, INC.

345 Vassar Street, Cambridge MA 02139. 617/679-5500. **Contact:** Human Resources. **E-mail address:** hr@hybridon.com. **World Wide Web address:** http://www.hybridon.com. **Description:** A pharmaceutical research and development company focused on the treatment of viral diseases, cancer, and diseases of the eye. **Positions advertised include:** Manager Clinical Research.

IMMUNOGEN INC.

128 Sidney Street, Cambridge MA 02139. 617/995-2500. **Fax:** 617/995-2510. **Contact:** Human Resources. **E-mail address:** resume@immunogen.com. **World Wide Web address:** http://www.immunogen.com. **Description:** ImmunoGen Inc. is engaged in the research and development of pharmaceuticals, primarily for the treatment of cancer. The company's product line consists of proprietary toxins or drugs coupled with highly specific targeting agents. **Positions advertised include:** Patent Agent; Validation Engineer; Principal Development Director; Analytical Development Scientist/ Chemistry Scientist; Chemistry Research Associate; Process Development Research

Associate. **Corporate headquarters location:** This location. **Operations at this facility include:** This location is a research facility. **Listed on:** NASDAQ. **Stock exchange symbol:** IMGN.

IMMUNOGEN INC.
333 Providence Highway, Norwood MA 02062. 781/769-4242. **Fax:** 781/255-1489. **Contact:** Human Resources. **E-mail address:** resume@immunogen.com. **World Wide Web address:** http://www.immunogen.com. **Description:** ImmunoGen is engaged in the research and development of pharmaceuticals, primarily for the treatment of cancer. The company's product line consists of proprietary toxins or drugs coupled with highly specific targeting agents. The drugs, called immunoconjugates, are designed to identify, bind to, and destroy target cells. **Positions advertised include:** Patent Agent; Validation Engineer; Principal Development Director; Analytical Development Scientist/ Chemistry Scientist; Chemistry Research Associate; Process Development Research Associate. **Other U.S. locations:** Cambridge MA. **Operations at this facility include:** This location is a manufacturing facility. **Listed on:** NASDAQ. **Stock exchange symbol:** IMGN.

INTERNEURON PHARMACEUTICALS, INC.
One Ledgemont Center, 99 Hayden Avenue, Suite 200, Lexington MA 02421. 781/861-8444. **Contact:** Human Resources, Tessa Cooper. **E-mail address:** hr@interneuron.com. **World Wide Web address:** http://www.interneuron.com. **Description:** Develops medical products to treat neurological and behavioral disorders. **Corporate headquarters location:** This location. **Subsidiaries include:** Intercardia, Inc.; Progenitor, Inc.; and Transcell Technologies, Inc. develop products and technologies that treat cardiovascular disease, and are used for gene therapy, stem cell production, oligosaccharide synthesis, and drug transport. **Listed on:** NASDAQ. **Stock exchange symbol:** IPIC.

KLA-TENCOR
200 Friberg Parkway, Westborough MA 01581. 508/616-0412. **Contact:** Human Resources. **World Wide Web address:** http://www.kla-tencor.com. **Description:** Manufactures electron scanning microscopes.

MIT LINCOLN LABORATORY
244 Wood Street, Lexington MA 02420-9108. 781/981-7066. **Fax:** 781/981-7086. **Contact:** Human Resources Department. **E-mail address:** resume@ll.mit.edu. **World Wide Web address:** http://www.ll.mit.edu. **Description:** A federally funded, nonprofit research center of the Massachusetts Institute of Technology (MIT). Lincoln Laboratory applies science, by means of advanced technology, to critical problems of national security. Problems focus on space surveillance, tactical systems, free space and terrestrial optical communications, and air traffic control systems. Founded in 1951. **NOTE:** Resumes must be in a scannable format and may be e-mailed (ASCII text file) or faxed. **Positions advertised include:** Engineer; Analyst; Laboratory Assistant; Biologist. **Office hours:** Monday - Friday, 8:30 a.m. - 5:00 p.m. **Corporate headquarters location:** This location. **Operations at this facility include:** Research and Development. **Number of employees at this location:** 2,200.

MACROCHEM CORPORATION
110 Hartwell Avenue, Lexington MA 02421-3134. 781/862-4003. **Fax:** 781/862-4338. **Contact:** Human Resources. **E-mail address:** hr@macrochem.com. **World Wide Web address:** http://www.macrochem.com. **Description:** Engaged in the development and commercialization of advanced drug delivery systems for the transdermal delivery of enzyme, protein, and drug compounds for

therapeutic, over-the-counter, and cosmetic applications. SEPA, MacroChem's worldwide-patented compound, accelerates the passage of drugs through the skin and other biomembranes. **Corporate headquarters location:** This location. **Listed on:** NASDAQ. **Stock exchange symbol:** MCHM.

MATRITECH, INC.

330 Nevada Street, Newton MA 02460. 617/928-0820. **Toll-free phone:** 800/320-2521. **Fax:** 617/928-0821. **Contact:** Human Resources. **World Wide Web address:** http://www.matritech.com. **Description:** A biotechnology company using proprietary nuclear matrix protein technology to develop and commercialize innovative serum-, cell-, and urine-based NMP diagnostics that enable physicians to detect and monitor the presence of bladder, breast, colorectal, cervical, and prostate cancers. The company's other primary focus is the development of additional serum assays for lung, liver, pancreatic, stomach, and renal cancer. Founded in 1987. **NOTE:** Entry-level positions are offered. **Positions advertised include:** Biochemist; Research Assistant. **Corporate headquarters location:** This location. **Listed on:** NASDAQ. **Stock exchange symbol:** NMPS. **CEO:** Stephen D. Chubb. **Annual sales/revenues:** Less than $5 million. **Number of employees at this location:** 55.

MILLENNIUM PHARMACEUTICALS, INC.

640 Memorial Drive, Cambridge MA 02139. 617/679-7000. **Toll-free phone:** 800/390-566.3. **Fax:** 617/663-3735. **Contact:** Human Resources. **E-mail:** info@minm.com. **World Wide Web address:** http://www.mlnm.com. **Description:** Engaged in genomics research and development. **Other U.S. locations:** San Diego CA. **International locations:** England; Japan. **Listed on:** NASDAQ. **Stock exchange symbol:** MLNM.

MILLIPORE CORPORATION

17 Cherry Hill Drive, Danvers MA 01923. 978/777-3622. **Contact:** Human Resources. **World Wide Web address:** http://www.millipore.com. **Description:** Manufactures microporous filters and filtration devices used for the analysis, separation, and purification of fluids. Products are used in the fields of health care, pharmaceuticals, micro-electronics, biological sciences, and genetic engineering. **Positions advertised include:** Product & Process Development Engineer; Product Manager. **Corporate headquarters location:** Bedford MA. **International locations:** Canada; Japan. **Operations at this facility include:** District Headquarters; Manufacturing. **Listed on:** New York Stock Exchange. **Stock exchange symbol:** MIL. **Number of employees worldwide:** 4,200.

MILLIPORE CORPORATION

80 Ashby Road, Bedford MA 01730. 781/533-6000. **Contact:** Employment Manager. **World Wide Web address:** http://www.millipore.com. **Description:** Manufactures microporous filters and filtration devices used for the analysis, separation, and purification of fluids. Products are used in the fields of health care, pharmaceuticals, micro-electronics, biological sciences, and genetic engineering. **Positions advertised include:** Process Engineer; Software Engineer; Development Engineer. **Corporate headquarters location:** This location. **Listed on:** New York Stock Exchange. **Stock exchange symbol:** MIL. **Number of employees worldwide:** 4,200.

NEW ENGLAND BIOLABS, INC.

32 Tozer Road, Beverly MA 01915. 978/927-5054. **Contact:** Human Resources. **E-mail address:** kong@neb.com. **World Wide Web address:** http://www.neb.com. **Description:** A medical research laboratory that manufactures products for molecular biology research with a specialization in

restriction endonucleases. **Positions advertised include:** Executive Director; Organic Chemist; Post Doctoral Fellow.

NUTRAMAX PRODUCTS INC.
51 Blackburn Drive, Gloucester MA 01930. 978/283-1800. **Fax:** 978/282-3794. **Contact:** Human Resources. **E-mail address:** hr@nutramax.com. **World Wide Web address:** http://www.nutramax.com. **Description:** Manufactures pharmaceutical and personal care products. **Positions advertised include:** Domestic Sales Representative; International Sales Representative. **Corporate headquarters location:** This location. **Operations at this facility include:** Administration; Manufacturing; Sales. **Number of employees at this location:** 250. **Number of employees nationwide:** 525.

ORGANOGENESIS INC.
150 Dan Road, Canton MA 02021. 781/575-0775. **Fax:** 781/401-1299. **Contact:** Human Resources. **World Wide Web address:** http://www.organogenesis.com. **Description:** Designs, develops, and manufactures medical therapeutics containing living cells and/or natural connective tissue components. The company's products are designed to promote the establishment and growth of new tissues to restore, maintain, or improve biological function. Organogenesis's product development focus includes living tissue replacements, organ assist treatments, and guided tissue regeneration scaffolds. **Positions advertised include:** Product Associate; Facilities Technician; Quality Control Microbiologist; Human Resources Director. **Corporate headquarters location:** This location. **Listed on:** AMEX. **Stock exchange symbol:** ORG.

PIERCE BOSTON TECHNOLOGY CENTER
30 Commerce Way, Woburn MA 01801-1059. 781/937-0890. **Fax:** 781/937-3096. **Contact:** Human Resources. **World Wide Web address:** http://www.endogen.com. **Description:** Develops, manufactures, and markets diagnostic test kits that test for HIV and cancer. Products are sold in the United States to private and government institutions, university hospitals, medical centers, and large commercial laboratories via a direct sales force. **Positions advertised include:** Research Associate; Technical Marketing Assistant. **Corporate headquarters location:** Rockford IL. **Parent Company:** Pierce Chemical Corporation. **NOTE:** Please send all resumes to: Pierce Chemical Corporation, P.O. Box 117, Rockford IL 61105.

PSYCHEMEDICS CORPORATION
1280 Massachusetts Avenue, Suite 200, Cambridge MA 02138. 617/868-7455. **Fax:** 617/864-1639. **Contact:** Human Resources Department. **World Wide Web address:** http://www.psychemedics.com. **Description:** A biotechnology company concentrating on diagnostics through the detection and measurement of substances in the body using hair samples. The first commercial product, a testing service for the detection of drugs, is provided principally to private sector companies. This test identifies traces of cocaine, marijuana, opiates, methamphetamines, and PCP. Psychemedics's testing methods use patented technology for performing immunoassays on enzymatically dissolved hair samples with confirmation testing by gas chromatography or mass spectrometry. **Corporate headquarters location:** This location. **Other U.S. locations:** Los Angeles CA; Fort Lauderdale FL; Atlanta GA; Chicago IL; Las Vegas NV; Dallas TX. **Listed on:** American Stock Exchange. **Stock exchange symbol:** PMD. **Number of employees nationwide:** 95.

QUEST DIAGNOSTICS INCORPORATED

415 Massachusetts Avenue, Cambridge MA 02139-4102. 617/547-8900. **Fax:** 617/868-7962. **Contact:** Human Resources. **World Wide Web address:** http://www.questdiagnostics.com. **Description:** One of the largest clinical laboratories in North America, providing a broad range of clinical laboratory services to health care clients that include physicians, hospitals, clinics, dialysis centers, pharmaceutical companies, and corporations. The company offers and performs tests on blood, urine, and other bodily fluids and tissues to provide information for health and well-being. **Positions advertised include:** Phlebotomy Services Representative; Account Manager; Medical Technologist; Billing Supervisor; Processing Associate.

REPLIGEN CORPORATION

41 Seyon Street Building #1, Suite 100, Waltham MA 02453. 781/250-0111. **Toll-free phone:** 800/622-2259. **Fax:** 781/259-0015. **Contact:** Human Resources. **World Wide Web address:** http://www.repligen.com. **Description:** Researches and manufactures pharmaceutical products. **Positions advertised include:** Associate Medical Director; Analytical Biochemist; Quality Affairs Associate; Regulatory Affairs Manager; Clinical Research Associate.

SEPRACOR, INC.

111 Locke Drive, Marlborough MA 01752. 508/481-6700. **Fax:** 508/357-7490. **Contact:** Human Resources. **World Wide Web address:** http://www.sepracor.com. **Description:** Develops new and improved versions of prescription drugs. Sepracor's products are known as Improved Chemical Entities (ICE Pharmaceuticals) and are used in the allergy, asthma, gastroenterology, neurology, psychiatry, and urology markets. **Positions advertised include:** Principal Application Support Center; Validation Support Specialist; Project Coordinator; Purchasing Administrator; Medical Information Manager; Information Technology Administration Assistant; Financial Systems Support Specialist; Human Resources Associate Director; Project Manager; Technical Business Analyst. **Corporate headquarters location:** This location. **Listed on:** NASDAQ. **Stock exchange symbol:** SEPR.

SERONO, INC.

One Technology Place, Rockland MA 02370. 781/982-9000. **Toll-free phone:** 800/283-8088. **Contact:** Human Resources. **World Wide Web address:** http://www.seronousa.com. **Description:** Manufactures prescription pharmaceuticals for the treatment of a variety of diseases including multiple sclerosis and cancer. **Positions advertised include:** Systems Engineer; Managed Marketing Manager; National Account Manager; Postdoctoral Fellow; Accounts Payable Specialist; General Counsel; Distributor; Facilities Operations Manager. **Corporate headquarters location:** This location. **Operations at this facility include:** Administration; Manufacturing; Research and Development; Sales; Service. **Listed on:** Privately held. **Number of employees at this location:** 150. **Number of employees nationwide:** 370.

STERIS-ISOMEDIX SERVICES

435 Whitney Street, Northborough MA 01532. 508/393-9323. **Contact:** Human Resources. **World Wide Web address:** http://www.steris.com. **Description:** Provides contract sterilization services to manufacturers of prepackaged products such as health care and certain consumer products. The company uses gamma radiation and ethylene oxide in these operations. **Positions advertised include:** Field Service Representative. **Corporate headquarters location:** Mentor OH.

THERMEDICS POLYMER PRODUCTS
207 Lowell Street, Wilmington MA 01887. 978/642-5000. **Fax:** 978/657-4371. **Contact:** Human Resources. **E-mail address:** edelehanty@thermadics.com. **World Wide Web address:** http://www.thermedics.com. **Description:** Thermedics Polymer Products is a leading supplier of custom manufactured thermoplastic polyurethanes.

TRANSKARYOTIC THERAPIES, INC.
700 Main Street, Cambridge MA 02139. 617/349-0200. **Contact:** Human Resources. **World Wide Web address:** http://www.tktx.com. **Description:** Engaged in the research and development of gene therapy. **Positions advertised include:** Research & Design Specialist; Quality Control Analyst; Bioengineer; Staff Scientist; Warehouse Manager; Inventory Control Coordinator; Material Planner; Operations Analysis Manager; Financial Planning Analyst; Regulatory Documentation Coordinator. **Listed on:** NASDAQ. **Stock exchange symbol:** TKTX.

VERTEX PHARMACEUTICALS INCORPORATED
40 Allston Street, Cambridge MA 02139-4242. 617/576-3111. **Fax:** 617/577-6444. **Contact:** Human Resources. **World Wide Web address:** http://www.vpharm.com. **Description:** Develops drugs for viral, autoimmune, inflammatory, and neurodegenerative diseases. Vertex Pharmaceuticals also develops oral active pharmaceuticals for drug-resistant cancer and hemoglobin disorders. **Positions advertised include:** Biochemistry Investigator; Principal Biostatistician; Associate Scientist; Staff Investigator; Administrative Assistant; Accountant; Financial Analyst; Compensation Director; Human Resources Manager; Human Resources Administrative Assistant; System Analyst; Staff Investigator; Logistics Manager; Document Management Specialist; Quality Assurance Specialist; Staff Investigator Toxicity. **Corporate headquarters location:** This location. **Subsidiaries include:** Altus Biologics Inc. (Cambridge MA); Versal Technologies, Inc. (Cambridge MA); Vertex Pharmaceuticals (Europe) Limited (United Kingdom); Vertex Securities Corporation (Cambridge MA). **Listed on:** NASDAQ. **Stock exchange symbol:** VRTX.

WATERS CORPORATION
34 Maple Street, Milford MA 01757. 508/478-2000. **Fax:** 508/482-2413. **Recorded jobline:** 508/482-3332. **Contact:** Human Resources. **World Wide Web address:** http://www.waters.com. **Description:** Produces a range of instruments, information management systems, and chromatography products for high-performance liquid chromatography and related applications. Waters Corporation's products are also used in fundamental research directed toward a better understanding of the chemical, physical, and biological composition of compounds, as well as in the detection, measurement, and identification of compounds of interest across a wide range of industries. Founded in 1958. **NOTE:** Entry-level positions and second and third shifts are offered. **Positions advertised include:** Administrative & Support; Chemistry; Electrical Engineer. **NOTE:** Apply Online. **Office hours:** Monday - Friday, 8:00 a.m. - 4:30 p.m. **Corporate headquarters location:** This location. **Other U.S. locations:** Nationwide. **International locations:** Worldwide. **Operations at this facility include:** Regional Headquarters. **Listed on:** New York Stock Exchange. **CEO/President:** Douglas Berthiaume. **Facilities Manager:** William Stares. **Annual sales/revenues:** More than $100 million. **Number of employees at this location:** 950. **Number of employees worldwide:** 2,000.

WHITEHEAD INSTITUTE FOR BIOMEDICAL RESEARCH

9 Cambridge Center, Cambridge MA 02142-1479. 617/258-5000. **Fax:** 617/258-6294. **Contact:** Human Resources **E-mail address:** resumes@wi.mit.edu. **World Wide Web address:** http://www.wi.mit.edu. **Description:** A nonprofit research and teaching institution that specializes in programs regarding AIDS and cancer research, developmental biology, genetics, infectious diseases, and structural biology. **Positions advertised include;** Research Scientist; Programmer; Technical Assistant. **Corporate headquarters location:** This location.

WOODS HOLE OCEANOGRAPHIC INSTITUTION

Mail Stop 15, 14 Maury Lane, Woods Hole MA 02543-1120. 508/457-2000. **Fax:** 508/457-2173. **Contact:** Human Resources. **E-mail address:** hr@whoi.edu. **World Wide Web address:** http://www.whoi.edu. **Description:** A private, nonprofit oceanography research institute. **Positions advertised include:** Assistant Scientist; Chief Scientist; Engineering Assistant; Part Time Helper; Postdoctoral Investigator; Research Assistant; Security Guard; Electrician.

WYETH GENETICS INSTITUTE

35 Cambridge Park Drive, Cambridge MA 02140. 617/876-1170. **Contact:** Human Resources. **World Wide Web address:** http://www.wyeth.com. **Description:** Performs biotechnology research contributing to the application and creation of recombinant DNA technology. **Positions advertised include:** Staff Engineer; Associate Director; Plant Engineer; Senior Maintenance Mechanic; Project Specialist; Process Technician. **Other area locations:** Andover MA. **Other U.S. locations:** St. Louis MO. **International locations:** Germany. **Parent company:** American Home Products Corporation (Madison NJ).

BUSINESS SERVICES & NON-SCIENTIFIC RESEARCH

You can expect to find the following types of companies in this section:
Adjustment and Collection Services • Cleaning, Maintenance, and Pest Control Services • Credit Reporting Services • Detective, Guard, and Armored Car Services • Security Systems Services • Miscellaneous Equipment Rental and Leasing • Secretarial and Court Reporting Services

AM-PM CLEANING CORPORATION
1560 Trapelo Road, Waltham MA 02451. 781/622-1444. **Contact:** Human Resources. **Description:** Provides cleaning and maintenance service. **NOTE:** Entry-level positions and part-time jobs are offered. **Company slogan:** Maintaining an atmosphere of excellence. **Corporate headquarters location:** This location. **General Manager:** J. Kenneth Fosealdo. **Sales Manager:** Karen Perkins. **Annual sales/revenues:** $11 - $20 million. **Number of employees at this location:** 650.

ARAMARK UNIFORM SERVICES
P.O. Box 568, Lawrence MA 01842. 978/685-1936. **Physical Address:** 110 Glenn Street, Lawrence MA 01843. **Contact:** Human Resources. **World Wide Web address:** http://www.aramark-uniform.com. **Description:** Offers uniforms to reinforce corporate identities or to meet specialized demands for static control and flame resistance. The company also provides a variety of products including walk-off mats, cleaning cloths, disposable towels, and other environmental control items. **Parent company:** ARAMARK (Philadelphia PA) is one of the world's leading providers of managed services. The company operates in all 50 states and 10 foreign countries, offering a broad range of services to businesses of all sizes including many *Fortune* 500 companies and thousands of universities, hospitals, and municipal, state, and federal government facilities. The company is employee-owned.

AUTOMATIC DATA PROCESSING (ADP)
225 Second Avenue, Waltham MA 02454. 781/890-2500. **Contact:** Human Resources. **World Wide Web address:** http://www.adp.com. **Description:** A data processing and computing services firm that provides commercial services such as payroll, accounts receivable, accounts payable, financial statement preparation, tax services, and unemployment compensation management; financial services including general and specialized management oriented online services to major corporations, large financial institutions, and the government; dealer services in the auto, truck, and industrial equipment trade; collision estimating services; and pension services. **Positions advertised include:** Consultant; Driver; Night Coordinator; National Sales Manager; Implementation Specialist; Resource Manager; Sales Administrator; New Account Coordinator; Telephone Data Representative; Customer Service Representative; Inventory Control Clerk; Billing Specialist; eTechnical Support. **Corporate headquarters location:** Roseland NJ. **Operations at this facility include:** Service. **Listed on:** New York Stock Exchange. **Stock exchange symbol:** ADP.

CASS INFORMATION SYSTEMS, INC.
P.O. Box 6540, Chelmsford MA 01824-0940. 978/446-0101. **Fax:** 978/323-6624. **Contact:** John A. Luciano, Human Resources. **E-mail address:** humanresourcesbos@cassinfo.com. **World Wide Web address:**

http://www.cassinfo.com. **Description:** Cass Information Services is a provider of information services. These logistics-related services include the processing and payment of freight charges, preparation of transportation management reports, auditing of freight charges, and rating of freight shipments. Cass Information Systems operations are divided between its Payment Systems Group and its Software Systems Group. **NOTE:** Jobseekers should send resumes to: Human Resources, 900 Chelmsford Street, Lowell MA 01851-8101. **Subsidiaries include:** Cass Bank & Trust is a bank that provides a full range of banking services to individual, corporate, and institutional customers. **Parent company:** Cass Commercial Corporation. **Other U.S. locations:** Bridgeton MO; Columbus OH. **Operations at this facility include:** This location operates as part of the Payment Systems Group. **Listed on:** NASDAQ. **Stock exchange symbol:** CASS.

DUN & BRADSTREET, INC.
1800 West Park Drive, Suite 300, Westborough MA 01581. 508/871-8000. **Contact:** Human Resources. **E-mail:** hrsourcing@dnb.com. **World Wide Web address:** http://www.dnb.com. **Description:** Provides business-to-business credit, marketing, and investment management services. **Corporate headquarters location:** Murray Hill NJ. **Parent company:** The Dun & Bradstreet Corporation. **Listed on:** New York Stock Exchange. **Stock exchange symbol:** DNB. **CEO:** Allan Loren. **Number of employees worldwide:** 9,000.

FORRESTER RESEARCH
400 Technology Square, Cambridge MA 02139. 617/497-7090. **Contact:** Human Resources. **World Wide Web address:** http://www.forrester.com. **Description:** An independent research firm that provides technology consulting services to business. **Positions advertised include:** Corporate Communication Manager; Editing Manager; Web Developer; Client Care Specialist; Financial Services Analyst; Research Advisor; Healthcare Analyst; Sales Associate; Healthcare Associate; Applications Analyst; Business Development Director; Account Executive; Research Associate. **Corporate headquarters location:** This location. **Other U.S. locations:** San Francisco CA. **International locations:** England; Germany; The Netherlands. **Listed on:** NASDAQ. **Stock exchange symbol:** FORR.

IRON MOUNTAIN INC.
745 Atlantic Avenue, Boston MA 02111. 617/357-4455. **Fax:** 617/ **Contact:** Human Resources. **Fax:** 617/368-9117. **E-mail address:** jobs@ironmountain.com. **World Wide Web address:** http://www.ironmountain.com. **Description:** One of the nation's largest record management companies. Iron Mountain provides businesses with storage facilities for their records. **Positions advertised include:** Telemarketing Representative; Seibel Design Engineer; Corporate Staff Accountant; Marketing Specialist; Marketing Administration; Systems Engineer; Quality Assurance Manager. **Corporate headquarters location:** This location. **Other U.S. locations:** Nationwide. **Listed on:** NASDAQ. **Stock exchange symbol:** IRM.

MAIL COMPUTER SERVICE INC. (MCS)
321 Manly Street, West Bridgewater MA 02379. 508/584-6490. **Contact:** Human Resources. **E-mail address:** 508/584-2890. **World Wide Web address:** http://www.mailcompserv.com. **Description:** A full-service mail house. Mail Computer Service Inc.'s mass-mailing services include data processing, mail processing, digitizing, lasering, and printing.

MASS BUYING POWER (MBP)

1076 Washington Street, Hanover MA 02339. 781/829-4900. **Contact:** Human Resources. **E-mail address:** massbuy@massbuy.com. **World Wide Web address:** http://www.massbuy.com. **Description:** Provides discount purchasing benefits for employees of member companies. Mass Buying Power offers discounts on a wide variety of products and services including automobiles, major household appliances, furniture, consumer loans, and home improvements. Mass Buying Power also operates a full-service travel agency specializing in discount travel packages. Founded in 1967. **Corporate headquarters location:** This location. **Listed on:** Privately held.

McGRAW-HILL COMPANIES, INC.

24 Hartwell Avenue, Lexington MA 02421. 781/863-5100. **Contact:** Human Resources. **World Wide Web address:** http://www.mcgraw-hill.com. **Description:** McGraw-Hill Companies, Inc. provides computer-accessible economic information, models, forecasts, analyses, software, and consulting services to clients in industry, government, and business. **Positions advertised include:** Market Research Analyst; Economic Analyst; Bid News Coordinator. **Corporate headquarters location:** New York NY. **Listed on:** New York Stock Exchange. **Stock exchange symbol:** MHP.

MILHENCH SUPPLY COMPANY

121 Duchaine Road, New Bedford MA 02745. 508/995-8331. **Toll-free phone:** 800/642-7570. **Fax:** 508/995-4187. **Contact:** Human Resources. **World Wide Web address:** http://www.milhench.com. **Description:** A supplier of janitorial & maintenance, industrial packaging, safety & material handling & storage supplies.

SECURITAS USA

575 Boylston Street, 6th Floor, Boston MA 02116. 617/437-9119. **Contact:** Human Resources. **World Wide Web address:** http://www.securitasusa.com. **Description:** A contract security agency providing uniformed security officers, investigative services, and security system installation.

UNITED RENTALS

133 Southampton Street, Boston MA 02118. 617/445-6750. **Contact:** Human Resources. **E-mail address:** careerinfo@ur.com. **World Wide Web address:** http://www.unitedrentals.com. **Description:** Rents construction equipment and supplies. **Positions advertised include:** District Manager. **Corporate headquarters locations:** Greenwich CT. **Other U.S. locations:** Nationwide. **Listed on:** New York Stock Exchange. **Stock exchange symbol:** URI.

CHARITIES AND SOCIAL SERVICES

You can expect to find the following types of companies in this section:
Social and Human Service Agencies • Job Training and Vocational Rehabilitation Services • Nonprofit Organizations

ACTION FOR BOSTON COMMUNITY DEVELOPMENT (ABCD)
178 Tremont Street, Boston MA 02111. 617/357-6000. **Contact:** Human Resources. **E-mail address:** hr@bostonabc.org. **NOTE:** When sending in applications please have them in Microsoft Word format only. **World Wide Web address:** http://www.bostonabcd.org. **Description:** A nonprofit, community action, human services agency helping low-income residents make the transition from poverty to self-sufficiency. ABCD provides programs and services including job training, education, weatherization, housing services, fuel assistance, the Urban College Program, child care including Head Start and daycare, and elder service programs. **Positions advertised include:** Receptionist; Program Assistant. **Corporate headquarters location:** This location. **Operations at this facility include:** Administration; Research and Development.

ADAMS/CHESHIRE HEADSTART PROJECT
46 Howland Avenue, Adams MA 01220. 413/743-5150. **Contact:** Human Resources. **Description:** A state- and federally funded daycare program for low-income families with children between the ages of three and five.

AIDS ACTION COMMITTEE
294 Washington Street 5th Floor, Boston MA 02108. 617/437-6200. **Fax:** 617/437-6445. **Recorded jobline:** 617/450-1435. **Contact:** Human Resources. **E-mail address:** resumes@aac.org. **World Wide Web address:** http://www.aac.org. **Description:** A nonprofit organization providing services to people living with HIV, and their families; combating the AIDS epidemic through education; and advocating fair and effective AIDS policy and funding. The AIDS Action Committee is the largest AIDS service organization in New England. Founded by a small group of volunteers, the organization now includes a full-time professional staff supported by several thousand volunteers. The group operates through several segments, all of which offer employment and volunteer opportunities. They include clinical services, housing, financial and legal, counseling, education, training, development, fundraising, public policy, government relations, communications, grant writing, administration and finance, AR/AP, human resources, MIS, computer operations, and facilities. Founded in 1983. **Positions advertised include:** Clinical Specialist; Associate Director of Major Gifts; Bilingual Hotline Coordinator; Field Interviewer. **NOTE:** Please call the jobline for current openings. Indicate the position of interest in your cover letter. **Special programs:** Internships. **Corporate headquarters location:** This location. **Operations at this facility include:** Administration. **Number of employees at this location:** 100.

BIG BROTHERS ASSOCIATION
55 Summer Street, 8th Floor, Boston MA 02110. 617/542-9090. **Contact:** Human Resources. **Description:** Provides a mentor program for underprivileged children by pairing them with an adult volunteer.

CATHOLIC CHARITIES
75 Kneeland Street, 8th Floor, Boston MA 02111. 617/482-5440. **Fax:** 617/482-9737. **Contact:** Human Resources. **E-mail address:** resumes@ccab.org. **World Wide Web address:** http://www.ccab.org. **Description:** A social service agency. Services include career counseling, alternative education, immigration refugee services and relief, family guidance, shelter and ministry programs, substance abuse services, and English-as-a-Second-Language (ESL) programs. **Positions advertised include:** Administrative Assistant; Payroll Assistant; Outreach Family Therapy.

CEREBRAL PALSY OF THE SOUTH SHORE
CHILDREN'S DEVELOPMENTAL DISABILITIES CENTER
43 Old Colony Avenue, Quincy MA 02170. 617/479-7443. **Contact:** Human Resources. **Description:** An outpatient rehabilitation and treatment center for children from birth to eight years old who have disabilities. The onsite treatment facilities also include a school and a daycare center. **Positions advertised include:** Nurse; Social Worker; Therapist.

CITIZENS ENERGY CORPORATION
530 Atlantic Avenue, Boston MA 02210. 617/338-6300. **Contact:** Controller. **E-mail address:** inform@citizensenergy.com. **World Wide Web address:** http://www.citizensenergy.com. **Description:** A nonprofit organization aimed at providing needy families with affordable home heating oil.

EDUCATION DEVELOPMENT CENTER, INC.
55 Chapel Street, Newton MA 02458. 617/969-7100. **Contact:** Human Resources. **World Wide Web address:** http://www.edc.org. **Description:** One of the world's leading educational nonprofit research and development firms specializing in early childhood development, K-12 education, health promotion, learning technologies, and institutional reform. Founded in 1958. **Company slogan:** Promoting human development through education. **Positions advertised include:** Office Assistant; Project Coordinator. **Corporate headquarters location:** This location. **Other U.S. locations:** Washington DC; New York NY; Newport RI. **International locations:** The Netherlands. **Listed on:** Privately held. **Annual sales/revenues:** $21 - $50 million. **Number of employees at this location:** 310. **Number of employees nationwide:** 400.

FEDERATED DORCHESTER NEIGHBORHOOD HOUSES
450 Washington Street, Dorchester MA 02124. 617/282-5034. **Fax:** 617/265-6020. **Contact:** Brigette Henry, Human Resources Director. **E-mail address:** hrfdnh@thecia.net. **World Wide Web address:** http://www.fdnh.org. **Description:** A nonprofit, human service agency with eight locations. **NOTE:** Entry-level positions and part-time jobs are offered. **Positions advertised include:** Case Manager; Operations and Administration Coordinator; Community Outreach Coordinator; Teen Recreation Worker. **Special programs:** Internships; Summer Jobs. **Corporate headquarters location:** This location. **Number of employees at this location:** 450.

HABITAT FOR HUMANITY BOSTON
455 Arborway, Jamaica Plain MA 02130. 617/524-8891. **Contact:** Human Resources. **World Wide Web address:** http://www.habitatboston.org. **Description:** A nonprofit organization that builds homes for the homeless. **Corporate headquarters location:** Americus GA. **Other U.S. locations:** Nationwide.

HEAD START PROJECT
62 First Street, Pittsfield MA 01201. 413/499-0137. **Contact:** Human Resources. **E-mail address:** lmcallops@nhsa.org. **World Wide Web address:** http://www.nhsa.org. **Description:** A state- and federally-funded program for low-income families with young children.

THE ITALIAN HOME FOR CHILDREN
1125 Center Street, Jamaica Plain MA 02130. 617/524-3116. **Contact:** Director. **E-mail address:** hr@italianhome.org. **World Wide Web address:** http://www.italianhome.org. **Description:** A residential treatment center for emotionally disturbed children. The Italian Home for Children provides counseling and schooling for approximately 60 youths, aged six to 13. **Positions advertised include:** Childcare Worker; Quality Improvement Associate; Director of Child Care Training Services. **Number of employees at this location:** 100.

JANE DOE INC.
MA COALITION AGAINST SEXUAL ASSAULT & DOMESTIC VIOLENCE
14 Beacon Street, Suite 507, Boston MA 02108. 617/248-0922. **Fax:** 617/248-0902. **Contact:** Human Resources. **E-mail address:** jobs@janedoe.org. **World Wide Web address:** http://www.janedoe.org. **Description:** A nonprofit public education and advocacy organization. Jane Doe Inc. operates more than 30 programs across the state.

MASSACHUSETTS AUDUBON SOCIETY
MOOSE HILL WILDLIFE SANCTUARY
Moosehill Sanctuary, 293 Moose Hill Street, Sharon MA 02067. 781/784-5691. **Contact:** Director. **World Wide Web address:** http://www.massaudubon.org. **Description:** A nonprofit organization involved in educating the community about the environment and promoting conservation efforts. The sanctuary offers a wide range of programs including Owl Prowls, family camp-outs, summer camp for children, and maple sugaring tours. The sanctuary also has its own art gallery featuring bimonthly exhibits of works by local artists. **NOTE:** Moose Hill Wildlife Sanctuary welcomes applicants for volunteer positions. **Positions advertised include:** Development Officer; Administrative Assistant. **NOTE:** For either of these positions send resume to: Mass Audubon Society, 208 South Great Road, Lincoln MA, 01773. Attention: Karen O'Neil. E-mail koneill@massaudubon.org. Education Coordinator: For this position mail resume to Rebecca Taylor, Felix Neck Wildlife Sanctuary, P.O. Box, 494, Vineyard Haven MA, 02568. **Corporate headquarters location:** Lincoln MA.

MELMARK NEW ENGLAND
50 Tower Office Park, Woburn MA 01801. 781/932-9211. **Fax:** 781/932-0189. **Contact:** Recruiting Department. **E-mail address:** recruiter@melmarkne.org. **World Wide Web address:** http://www.melmarkne.org. **Description:** A non-profit organization, serving children with autism, neurological disorders, and acquired brain injuries. **Positions advertised include:** ABA Counselor; Classroom Teacher; Speech Language Pathologist.

MORGAN MEMORIAL GOODWILL INDUSTRIES, INC.
1010 Harrison Avenue, Boston MA 02119-2540. 617/541-1400. **Fax:** 617/541-1495. **Contact:** Toni Preston, Director of Human Resources. **World Wide Web address:** http://www.goodwillmass.org. **Description:** A nonprofit human services agency. Programs include training, employment, and career services for persons with disabilities and others who face barriers to employment; and youth services including a live-in summer camp in central Massachusetts for inner-city youth, ages 7 through 16. The organization also operates nine retail stores. **NOTE:**

Volunteer opportunities are offered. **Positions advertised include:** Human Resources Benefits Coordinator; Accounts Payable Specialist; Manager of Career Counseling; Community Job Placement Specialist; Reporting and Analysis Specialist; Training Instructor; Case Manager. **Special programs:** Internships. **President/CEO:** Joanne K. Hilferty.

OLD COLONY ELDERLY SERVICES, INC.
P.O. Box 4469 Brockton MA 02301 508/584-1561. **Physical address:** 144 Main Street, Brockton MA 02301. **Contact:** Human Resources. **Description:** Provides various services to the elderly including transportation and in-home care.

PINE STREET INN, INC.
434 Harrison Avenue, Boston MA 02118. 617/521-7621. **Fax:** 617/521-7667. **Contact:** Human Resources. **World Wide Web address:** http://www.pinestreetinn.org. **Description:** Provides shelter, transitional programs, and housing for men, women, and children. **Operations at this facility include:** Administration; Service. **Number of employees at this location:** 650.

PROJECT BREAD
WALK FOR HUNGER
145 Border Street, Boston MA 02128. 617/723-5000. **Contact:** Human Resources. **World Wide Web address:** http://www.projectbread.org. **Description:** Supports nearly 500 food pantries, soup kitchens, homeless shelters, food banks, and other emergency feeding programs in 119 Massachusetts communities. Project Bread's Technical Assistance Program trains over 200 volunteers and staff, provides over 100 programs with one-on-one management assistance, and holds training series. Project Bread's transportation program, Food Drive for the Hungry, operated jointly with the American Red Cross, provides transportation to pick up low-cost or donated food. Since it began in 1969, the Walk for Hunger has become one of the nation's largest annual, one-day fundraisers for the hungry.

THE SALVATION ARMY
187 Columbus Avenue, Boston MA 02116-5197. 617/542-5420. **Fax:** 617/338-7990. **Contact:** Divisional Personnel Secretary. **World Wide Web address:** http://www.salvationarmy.org. **Description:** A nonprofit organization providing several service programs including day-care centers, programs for people with disabilities, substance abuse programs and tutoring for at-risk students. The Salvation Army targets its programs to assist alcoholics, battered women, drug addicts, the elderly, the homeless, people with AIDS, prison inmates, teenagers, and the unemployed. **Corporate headquarters location:** Alexandria VA. **Other U.S. locations:** Nationwide. **Operations at this facility include:** Administration; Divisional Headquarters. **Number of employees at this location:** 50.

THE SALVATION ARMY
402 Massachusetts Avenue, P.O. Box 647, Cambridge MA 02139. 617/547-3400. **Contact:** Personnel. **World Wide Web address:** http://www.salvationarmy.org. **Description:** A nonprofit organization providing several service programs including day-care centers, programs for people with disabilities, substance abuse programs and tutoring for at-risk students. The Salvation Army targets its programs to assist alcoholics, battered women, drug addicts, the elderly, the homeless, people with AIDS, prison inmates, teenagers, and the unemployed. **Corporate headquarters location:** Alexandria VA. **Other U.S. locations:** Nationwide.

SOCIETY FOR THE PRESERVATION OF NEW ENGLAND ANTIQUITIES

141 Cambridge Street, Boston MA 02114. 617/227-3956. **Fax:** 617/227-9204. **Contact:** Human Resources. **World Wide Web address:** http://www.spnea.org. **Description:** A nonprofit society founded to preserve New England's domestic buildings and artifacts. It is among the country's largest regional preservation organizations, owning 43 historic properties, 34 of which are open as house museums. Founded in 1910. **Special programs:** Internships. **Corporate headquarters location:** This location. **Other U.S. locations:** CT; ME; NH; RI. **Number of employees at this location:** 45. **Number of employees nationwide:** 100.

UNITED WAY OF MASSACHUSETTS BAY

245 Summer Street, Suite 1401, Boston MA 02210. 617/624-8000. **Fax:** 617/624-9114.**Contact:** Human Resources. **World Wide Web address:** http://www.uwmb.org. **Description:** Through a vast network of volunteers and local charities, the United Way helps to meet the health and human-care needs of millions of people. The United Way is comprised of approximately 1,900 organizations. **Other U.S. locations:** Nationwide.

CHEMICALS, RUBBER, AND PLASTICS

**You can expect to find the following types of companies
in this section:**
Adhesives, Detergents, Inks, Paints, Soaps, Varnishes • Agricultural Chemicals
and Fertilizers • Carbon and Graphite Products • Chemical Engineering Firms •
Industrial Gases

ACUSHNET RUBBER COMPANY
744 Belleville Avenue, New Bedford MA 02745. 508/998-4000. **Contact:** Human
Resources. **World Wide Web address:** http://www.acushnet.com. **Description:**
Manufactures and markets rubber and elastomeric products worldwide.

ADHESIVE PACKAGING SPECIALTIES, INC.
103 Foster Street P.O. Box 31, Peabody MA 01960. 978/531-3300. **Toll-free
phone:** 800/222-1117. **Fax:** 978/532-8901. **Contact:** Human Resources. **E-mail
address:** humanresources@adhesivepackaging.com. **World Wide Web
address:** http://www.adhesivepackaging.com. **Description:** A custom
repackager of resins and adhesives.

ANDERSON POWER PRODUCTS
13 Pratts Junction Road, P.O. Box 579, Sterling MA 01564. 978/422-3600. **Fax:**
978/422-3700. **Contact:** Human Resources. **E-mail address:**
employment@andersonpower.com. **World Wide Web address:**
http;//www.andersonpower.com. **Description:** Designs, manufactures, and
markets high power interconnects and accessories.

APPLIED EXTRUSION TECHNOLOGIES, INC.
3 Centennial Drive, Peabody MA 01960. 978/538-1500. **Contact:** Human
Resources. **World Wide Web address:** http://www.aetfilms.com. **Description:** A
leading manufacturer of a broad range of plastic films, nets, and webs used
primarily in packaging, health care, and environmental settings. The Packaging
Films Division develops, manufactures, and sells oriented polypropylene film for
flexible packaging applications, primarily for the snack food, soft drink, and
confectionery markets. The Specialty Nets and Profiles Divisions develop,
manufacture, and sell oriented aperture film or nets, as well as non-net
thermoplastic products to a number of markets such as health care,
environmental, packaging, and home products. **Corporate headquarters
location:** This location. **Listed on:** NASDAQ. **Stock exchange symbol:** AETC.

BOSTIK FINDLEY, INC.
211 Boston Street, Middleton MA 01949. 978/777-0100. **Fax:** 978/750-7249.
Contact: Human Resources. **E-mail address:** careers@bostikfindley.com.
World Wide Web address: http://www.bostik.com. **Description:** Bostik, Inc. and
Ato Findley, Inc. merged in the Fall of 2000 to become Bostik Findley, Inc. Bostik
Findley produces more than 2,000 formulations of rubber-based, polymer, water-
borne, and epoxy adhesives. Bostik Findley also manufactures sealants, aerosol,
engineering adhesives, maintenance aerosols, and construction grouts and
mastics. Founded in 1889. **Positions advertised include:** Hardwood Product
Manager; Process Specialist. **Corporate headquarters location:** This location.
Other U.S. locations: Long Beach CA; Conyers GA; Marshall MI; Cleveland OH;
Huntingdon Valley PA. **International locations:** Australia; England; France;
Germany; Korea; Mexico; New Zealand; Portugal; Spain; Sweden. **Parent**

company: TotalFinaElf. **Operations at this facility include:** Administration; Divisional Headquarters; Manufacturing; Research and Development; Sales; Service. **Listed on:** Privately held. **Number of employees at this location:** 350. **Number of employees worldwide:** 4500.

A.W. CHESTERTON COMPANY
225 Fallon Road, Stoneham MA 02180. 781/438-7000. **Fax:** 781/481-2530. **Contact:** Human Resources. **E-mail address:** jobs@Chesterton.com. **World Wide Web address:** http://www.chesterton.com. **Description:** Manufactures polishing and cleaning goods. **Corporate headquarters location:** This location. **Other area locations:** Groveland MA; Winchester MA. **Other U.S. locations:** Elmhurst IL; Baton Rouge LA; North Smithfield RI; Pasadena TX. **International locations:** Australia; Canada; Germany; Hungary; Mexico; Poland; Slovakia.

DOE & INGALLS INC.
P.O. Box 560, Medford MA 02155. 781/391-0090. **Physical address:** 25 Commercial Street, Medford MA 02155. **Contact:** Peter Liebman, President. **World Wide Web address:** http://www.doeingalls.com. **Description:** Manufactures and distributes chemicals. Founded in 1921. **Other U.S. locations:** Tampa FL; Durham NC.

EPOXY TECHNOLOGY
14 Fortune Drive, Billerica MA 01821. 978/667-3805. **Fax:** 978/663-9782. **Contact:** Human Resources. **World Wide Web address:** http://www.epotek.com. **Description:** Develops conductive epoxies, adhesives, and coatings for a wide range of industrial uses. Industries served include electronics, optical, medical, and metals.

ITW DEVCON PLEXUS
30 Endicott Street, Danvers MA 01923. 978/777-1100. **Toll-free phone:** 800/851-6692. **Fax:** 978/777-9871. **Contact:** Human Resources. **E-mail address:** jdelisle@devcon.com. **World Wide Web address:** http://www.itwplexus.com. **Description:** Manufactures structural adhesives for the transportation, marine, and engineering construction industries. **Positions advertised include:** Production Worker.

MAINTENANCE CHEMICAL SUPPLIERS INC.
101 Messina Drive, Braintree MA 02184. 781/849-6168. **Contact:** Human Resources. **Description:** Provides maintenance and janitorial services. The company is also involved in the direct sale of industrial chemical products. **Corporate headquarters location:** This location. **Number of employees at this location:** 10.

NYPRO, INC.
101 Union Street, P.O. Box 2005, Clinton MA 01510. 978/365-9721. **Fax:** 978/368-0236. **Contact:** Human Resources. **World Wide Web address:** http://www.nypro.com. **Description:** Manufactures custom injection moldings. **Other U.S. locations:** Nationwide. **International locations:** Worldwide.

PARKS CORPORATION
One West Street, Fall River MA 02720-1336. 508/679-5939. **Toll-free phone:** 800/225-8543. **Fax:** 508/674-8404. **Contact:** Human Resources. **World Wide Web address:** http://www.parkscorp.com. **Description:** Manufactures solvents, cleaners, paint remover, and finish remover. The company markets its products under the brand names Carver Tripp and Parks.

PERKINELMER LIFE SCIENCES INC.
549 Albany Street, Boston MA 02118. 617/482-9595. **Toll-free phone:** 800/446-0035. **Fax:** 617/338-9758. **Contact:** Human Resources. **World Wide Web address:** http://las.perkinelmer.com/. **Description:** Provides radioactive, chemilluminescent and fluorescent labeling and detection products for life science and drug discovery. **Special programs:** Internships; Co-ops. **Other area locations:** Billerica MA; Wellesley MA. **Other U.S. locations:** Beltsville MD; Norton OH. **International locations:** Belgium; Canada; England; Finland. **Number of employees at this location:** 400.

PERMA INC.
605 Springs Road, Bedford MA 01730. 978/667-5161. **Fax:** 978/670-5797. **Contact:** Human Resources. **World Wide Web address:** http://www.perma.com. **Description:** Manufactures specialty chemicals for commercial cleaning applications.

PLYMOUTH RUBBER COMPANY, INC.
104 Revere Street, Canton MA 02021. 781/828-0220. **Contact:** Human Resources. **World Wide Web address:** http://www.plymouthrubber.com. **Description:** Manufactures and markets rubber and vinyl products. The company serves the automotive, electrical supply, and utilities industries. **Listed on:** American Stock Exchange. **Stock exchange symbol:** PLRa.

TILLOTSON CORPORATION
59 Waters Avenue, Everett MA 02149. 617/387-9400. **Contact:** Human Resources. **World Wide Web address:** http://www.thcnet.com. **Description:** Manufactures rubber-based products including molds and gloves.

UFP TECHNOLOGIES, INC.
172 East Main Street, Georgetown MA 01833. 978/352-2200. **Fax:** 978/352-5616. **Contact:** Human Resources. **E-mail address:** hr@ufpt.com. **World Wide Web address:** http://www.ufpt.com. **Description:** Specializes in custom engineered packaging and specialty solutions that are produced by converting a wide range of foam, rigid plastic, fabric, fiber, and other composite materials. Packaging products and services include custom thermoforming plastics and foams; designing and manufacturing precision, 100-percent recycled protective packaging and multimaterial solutions for durable, reusable inter- and intra-plant product shipment; producing interior packaging; manufacturing complex product handling devices; and clean room manufacturing capabilities, which enable particulate, temperature, and humidity controlled manufacturing. Specialty products include precision-molded foams, performance products, laminating and molding, custom footbeds, and medical components. **Positions advertised include:** Packaging Engineer; Manufacturing Engineer; Quality Management; Field Service Engineer; Inside Sales Representative. **Corporate headquarters location:** This location. **Listed on:** NASDAQ. **Stock exchange symbol:** UFPT.

COMMUNICATIONS: TELECOMMUNICATIONS AND BROADCASTING

You can expect to find the following types of companies in this section:
Cable/Pay Television Services • Communications Equipment • Radio and Television Broadcasting Stations • Telephone, Telegraph, and Other Message Communications

---

ARCH WIRELESS, INC.
1800 West Park Drive, Suite 250, Westborough MA 01581-3912. 508/898-0962. **Contact:** Human Resources. **World Wide Web address:** http://www.arch.com. **Description:** Provides telephone paging services. **Positions advertised include:** Senior Auditor; Senior Benefits Administrator. **Corporate headquarters location:** This location.

BACK CHANNEL MEDIA
107 South Street, 2nd Floor, Boston MA 02116. 617/728-3626. **Fax:** 617/728-0511. **Contact:** Human Resources. **E-mail address:** info@backchannelmedia.com. **World Wide Web address:** http://www.backchannelmedia.com. **Description:** Secures full-time cable channel positions on behalf of emerging cable programmers. Back Channel Media also tracks per inquiry sales, and offers interactive television consulting services. Founded in 2000. **Office hours:** Monday - Friday, 9:00 a.m. - 5:00 p.m. **Corporate headquarters location:** This location. **Listed on:** Privately held. **President:** Michael Kokernak. **Annual sales/revenues:** $11 - $20 million. **Number of employees at this location:** 30.

BT CONFERENCING
25 Braintree Hill Park, Suite 200, Braintree MA 02184. 781/843-2002. **Fax:** 781/849-8136. **Contact:** Recruiter. **E-mail address:** jobs@btna.com. **World Wide Web address:** http://www.btconferencing.com. **Description:** Provides communications services to businesses. **Positions advertised include:** Client Relations; Call Center Team Leader; Billing Applications Engineer; Partner Integration Engineer; Customer Service Representative; Inside Sales Manager.

CTC COMMUNICATIONS
220 Bear Hill Road, Waltham MA 02451. 781/466-8080. **Contact:** Human Resources. **World Wide Web address:** http://www.ctcnet.com. **Description:** CTC Communications is an independent sales agent for the Regional Bell Operating Companies. The company markets discounted telephone calling plans, 800-number services, Centrex systems, and data transport networks to mid-sized commercial accounts. The company operates 15 branch offices in the Northeast. **Corporate headquarters location:** This location. **Listed on:** NASDAQ. **Stock exchange symbol:** CPTL. **Number of employees nationwide:** 180.

COMVERSE NETWORK SYSTEMS
100 Quannapowitt Parkway, Wakefield MA 01880. 781/246-9000. **Contact:** Human Resources. **E-mail address:** careeropportunities@comverse.com. **World Wide Web address:** http://www.comverse.com. **Description:** Manufactures and designs networking equipment for the telecommunications industry. **Corporate headquarters location:** This location. **Other U.S.**

locations: Alpharetta GA; Park Ridge IL; Overland Park KS; Florissant MO; New York NY; Woodbury NY; Charlotte NC; Addison TX; Chantilly VA; Bellevue WA; Gig Harbor WA. **International locations:** Worldwide.

CONCERTO SOFTWARE
6 Technology Park Drive, Westford MA 01886. 978/952-0200. **Contact:** Human Resources. **World Wide Web address:** http://www.concerto.com. **Description:** Develops, markets, implements, supports, and services outbound and inbound/outbound management systems for call center operations. These systems consist mainly of predictive dialing products and related autodialing systems responsible for important business applications including credit/collections, customer service, and telephone sales. Concerto Software provides unified call center solutions to banks, consumer finance organizations, retailers, and utilities. **Positions advertised include:** Technical Support Services; New Product Integration; Engineer. **Special programs:** Internships. **Corporate headquarters location:** This location. **Other U.S. locations:** Santa Clara CA; Norcross GA; Newtown PA; Dallas TX. **Listed on:** NASDAQ. **Stock exchange symbol:** DAVX. **Number of employees at this location:** 100. **Number of employees nationwide:** 160.

CONCORD COMMUNICATIONS, INC.
400+600 Nickerson Road, Marlboro MA 01752. 508/460-4646. **Contact:** Human Resources. **World Wide Web address:** http://www.concord.com. **Description:** Manufactures telecommunications equipment. **Positions advertised include:** Director of Sales Engineering; Commission Accountant; Services Product Marketing Specialist; Technical Support Engineer; Global Sales Representative. **Other U.S. locations:** Atlanta GA (formerly Empire Technologies). **Listed on:** NASDAQ. **Stock exchange symbol:** CCRD.

CONSOLIDATED SERVICES GROUP
661 Pleasant Street, Norwood MA 02062. 781/769-4316. **Toll-free phone:** 800/742-7240. **Fax:** 781/769-2144. **Contact:** Human Resources. **E-mail address:** lsalvia@constar.com. **World Wide Web address:** http://www.constar.com. **Description:** A telecommunications and voice data firm. Founded in 1993. **NOTE:** Entry-level positions are offered. **Corporate headquarters location:** This location. **Other U.S. locations:** Nationwide. **Parent company:** Constar International, Inc. **Annual sales/revenues:** $21 - $50 million. **Number of employees at this location:** 100. **Number of employees nationwide:** 175.

EDS (ELECTRONIC DATA SYSTEMS CORPORATION)
5 Clock Tower Place, Suite 300, Maynard MA 01754. 781/487-1000. **Contact:** Human Resources. **World Wide Web address:** http://www.eds.com. **Description:** EDS serves cellular carriers on over 500 U.S. and international markets, specifically in the areas of billing and rating, real-time networking and switching, and new technologies. **Corporate headquarters location:** Plano TX. **Parent company:** General Motors Corporation. **Operations at this facility include:** Divisional Headquarters. **Listed on:** New York Stock Exchange. **Stock exchange symbol:** EDS. **Number of employees at this location:** 390. **Number of employees nationwide:** 77,000. **Number of employees worldwide:** 140,000.

GENERAL DYNAMICS
77 A Street, Needham MA 02494. 781/449-2000. **Contact:** Human Resources Department. **World Wide Web address:** http://www.generaldynamics.com. **Description:** Provides secure communication systems and information solutions

to both commercial and military markets. The Communications Systems division also develops broadband data communications, digital network management systems, and PCS base stations. **Corporate headquarters location:** Taunton MA.

GENERAL DYNAMICS
400 John Quincy Adams Road, Taunton MA 02780. 508/880-4000. **Contact:** Human Resources. **World Wide Web address:** http://www.generaldynamics.com. **Description:** Provides secure communication systems and information solutions to both commercial and military markets. The Communications Systems division also develops broadband data communications, digital network management systems, and PCS base stations. **Corporate headquarters location:** This location.

GREATER MEDIA, INC.
55 Morrissey Boulevard, Boston MA 02125. 617/822-9600. **Contact:** Human Resources. **World Wide Web address:** http://www.greaterbostonradio.com. **Description:** Operates several Boston-area radio broadcasting stations with a variety of formats. Stations include WROR, WBOS, WKLB, WMJX, and WTKK.

MCI
800 Boylston Street, 7th Floor, Boston, MA 02199. 617/867-7400. **Contact:** Human Resources. **World Wide Web address:** http://www.mci.com. **Description:** One of the world's largest suppliers of local, long distance, and international telecommunications services, and a global Internet service provider. MCI services more than 150 countries. **NOTE:** Submit resume and search for positions online. **Positions advertised include:** SBS Account Representative. **Corporate headquarters location:** Ashburn VA.

NMS COMMUNICATIONS
100 Crossing Boulevard, Framingham MA 01702. 508/620-9300. **Contact:** Human Resources. **E-mail address:** resumes@nmss.com. **World Wide Web address:** http://www.nmss.com. **Description:** Designs, manufactures, and markets enabling technology products for the call processing market. These products permit others to efficiently develop and implement high performance, PC-based call processing systems that provide applications in one or a combination of areas such as automated attendant, voicemail, and interactive voice response. Product applications include telephone banking, medical alert services, pay-per-view cable services, and telemarketing. **Positions advertised include:** Principal NT Server & Network Analyst; Principal Hardware Engineer. **Corporate headquarters location:** This location. **Other U.S. locations:** Los Gatos CA. **International locations:** Worldwide. **Listed on:** NASDAQ. **Stock exchange symbol:** NMSS.

OFS FITEL
50 Hall Road, Sturbridge MA 01566. 508/347-2261. **Fax:** 508/347-8668. **Contact:** Human Resources. **Description:** Manufactures communications products including switching, transmission, fiber-optic cable, wireless systems, and operations systems to fulfill the needs of telephone companies and other communications services providers.

POLYCOM, INC.
100 Minuteman Road, Andover MA 01810. 978/292-5000. **Toll-free phone:** 800/POL-YCOM. **Contact:** Personnel. **World Wide Web address:** http://www.polycom.com. **Description:** Develops, manufactures, and markets visual communications systems using advanced video and audio compression

technology. Founded in 1984. **Positions advertised include:** Network Engineer; Product Support Technologist; Staff Engineer; Technical Support Engineer; Web Content Manager. **Corporate headquarters location:** Milipitas CA. **Listed on:** NASDAQ. **Stock exchange symbol:** PLCM. **Number of employees at this location:** 670.

SIGNATRON TECHNOLOGY CORPORATION
29 Domino Drive, Concord MA 01742. 978/371-0550. **Fax:** 978/371-7414. **Contact:** Human Resources. **E-mail address:** jobs@signatron.com. **World Wide Web address:** http://www.signatron.com. **Description:** Engaged in research and development for advanced communication systems and precision radio location systems. **Positions advertised include:** Software Engineer. **Corporate headquarters location:** This location. **Number of employees at this location:** 20.

SPECTEL
200 Minuteman Road, Andover MA 01810. 978/552-6200. **Toll-free phone:** 800/685-8454. **Contact:** Personnel. **World Wide Web address:** http://www.spectel.com. **Description:** Manufactures audio- and videoconferencing products. **Positions advertised include:** Senior Software Engineer. **Corporate headquarters location:** This location. **Other U.S. locations:** Denver CO; Atlanta GA; Chicago IL; New York NY. **International locations:** England; Ireland; Singapore.

TELLABS
30 North Avenue, Burlington MA 01803. 781/273-1400. **Fax:** 781/273-4160. **Contact:** Human Resources. **World Wide Web address:** http://www.tellabs.com. **Description:** Supplies wideband base-station products for wireless communication applications including cellular products and personal computers. **Listed on:** NASDAQ. **Stock exchange symbol:** TLAB. **Annual sales/revenues:** More than $100 million.

WAAF 107.3 FM
P.O. Box 1073, Boston MA 02215. 617/931-1223. **Contact:** Station Manager. **World Wide Web address:** http://www.waaf.com. **Description:** A radio station with a hard rock format.

WBCN 104.1 FM
1265 Boylston Street, Boston MA 02215. 617/266-1111. **Contact:** Dawn McNeil, Business Manager. **World Wide Web address:** http://www.wbcn.com. **Description:** A rock and roll format FM radio station.

WBZ-TV, CHANNEL 4
1170 Soldiers Field Road, Boston MA 02134. **Contact:** Station Manager. **World Wide Web address:** http://www.wbz.com. **Description:** A television station broadcasting to metropolitan Boston and portions of southern New England.

WCVB-TV, CHANNEL 5
5 TV Place, Needham MA 02494. 781/449-0400. **Fax:** 781/449-6682. **Contact:** Human Resources. **World Wide Web address:** http://www.thebostonchannel.com. **Description:** An ABC-affiliated television station. **Special programs:** Internships. **Corporate headquarters location:** New York NY.

WFXT-TV, CHANNEL 25
dba FOX 25
25 Fox Drive, P.O. Box 9125, Dedham MA 02027-9125. 781/326-8825. **Fax:** 781/467-7212. **Contact:** Director of Human Resources. **World Wide Web address:** http://www.fox25.com. **Description:** A television station affiliated with the Fox Broadcasting Network. **Positions advertised include:** Director; Studio Technician; Local Sales Manager; Account Executive; Sales Assistant; Traffic Assistant. **Special programs:** Internships. **Corporate headquarters location:** This location. **Parent company:** Boston Celtics Broadcasting. **Operations at this facility include:** Administration; Sales. **Number of employees at this location:** 60.

WHDH-TV, CHANNEL 7
7 Bulfinch Place, Boston MA 02114. 617/725-0777. **Contact:** Human Resources. **World Wide Web address:** http://www.whdh.com. **Description:** An NBC-affiliated television station.

WLVI-TV, CHANNEL 56 (WB-56)
75 Morrissey Boulevard, Boston MA 02125. 617/265-5656. **Contact:** Human Resources. **World Wide Web address:** http://www.wb56.com. **Description:** A television station offering a variety of programming. WLVI-TV is part of the WB Network.

WSBK-TV, CHANNEL 38 (UPN-38)
83 Leo Birmingham Parkway, Brighton MA 02135. 617/787-7000. **Contact:** Manager. **World Wide Web address:** http://www.upn38.com. **Description:** A television broadcasting station serving metropolitan Boston and parts of southern New England. WSBK-TV's programming format includes entertainment, news, and sports.

COMPUTER HARDWARE, SOFTWARE, AND SERVICES

You can expect to find the following types of companies in this section:
Computer Components and Hardware Manufacturers • Consultants and Computer Training Companies • Internet and Online Service Providers • Networking and Systems Services • Repair Services/Rental and Leasing • Resellers, Wholesalers, and Distributors • Software Developers/Programming Services • Web Technologies

ASA INTERNATIONAL LTD.

10 Speen Street, Framingham MA 01701. 508/626-2727. **Fax:** 508/626-0645. **Contact:** Human Resources. **World Wide Web address:** http://www.asaint.com. **Description:** Designs, develops, and installs proprietary vertical market software. **Special programs:** Internships. **Corporate headquarters location:** This location. **Other U.S. locations:** Nashua NH; Blue Bell PA. **Subsidiaries include:** ASA Legal Systems; ASA Tire Systems. **Listed on:** NASDAQ. **Stock exchange symbol:** ASAA. **Annual sales/revenues:** $21 - $50 million. **Number of employees at this location:** 85. **Number of employees nationwide:** 190.

ABERDEEN GROUP

260 Franklin Street Suite 1700, Boston MA 02108. 617/723-7890. **Toll-free phone:** 800/577-7897. **Contact:** Human Resources. **E-mail address:** inquiry@Aberdeen.com. **World Wide Web address:** http://www.aberdeen.com. **Description:** A computer systems, software, and communications consulting and research firm. Aberdeen Group provides strategic management solutions for domestic and international clients. **Positions advertised include:** Sales Account Manager; Product Marketing Manager; Curriculum Director.

ACCENTURE

100 William Street, Wellesley MA 02481. 617/454-4000. **Contact:** Human Resources. **World Wide Web address:** http://www.accenture.com. **Description:** A management and technology consulting firm. Accenture offers a wide range of services including business re-engineering, customer service system consulting, data system design and implementation, Internet sales systems research and design, and strategic planning. **Positions advertised include:** Oracle Operations Consultant; PeopleSoft Financials Functional Consultant; SAP Technical Architect; Credit & Collections Solutions Consultant; Service Attendant; Transaction Attorneys; Finance Professional; Executive Assistant; Project Administrator. **Corporate headquarters location:** Chicago IL. **Other area locations:** Boston MA. **Other U.S. locations:** Nationwide. **International locations:** Worldwide. **Listed on:** New York Stock Exchange. **Stock exchange symbol:** ACN.

ADVIZEX TECHNOLOGIES

128 Wheeler Road, Burlington MA 01803. 781/229-2419. **Toll-free phone:** 800/366-6096. **Fax:** 781/229-9991. **Contact:** Human Resources. **E-mail address:** jobs@advizex.com. **World Wide Web address:** http://www.advizex.com. **Description:** Provides open systems technology integration along with other business services including IT planning and developing, and computer reselling. **Positions advertised include:** Oracle Apps Data Base Administrator; Project Manager; Storage Consultant; Oracle Solution Architect; Unix Consultant; Account Executive.

AEGIS ASSOCIATES, INC.
98 Galen Street, Watertown MA 02472. 617/923-2500. **Fax:** 617/926-7050. **Contact:** Marie Stefanik, Human Resources Coordinator. **E-mail address:** hr2@aegis-inc.com. **World Wide Web address:** http://www.aegis-inc.com. **Description:** A computer reseller and network integrator that provides custom computer systems, networks, and related services. This location also hires seasonally. Founded in 1989. **NOTE:** Entry-level positions are offered. **Company slogan:** Your technology experts. **Positions advertised include:** Account Executive; Inside sales Representative. **Special programs:** Training. **Office hours:** Monday - Friday, 8:30 a.m. - 5:00 p.m. **Corporate headquarters location:** This location. **Annual sales/revenues:** $5 - $10 million.

AIRVANA, INC.
19 Alpha Road, Chelmsford MA 01824. 866/344-7437. **Fax:** 978/250-3910. **Contact:** Human Resources. **E-mail address:** information@airvananet.com. **World Wide Web address:** http://www.arivananet.com. **Description:** Develops All-IP 3G Radio Access Network infrastructure equipment for wireless carriers and global infrastructure suppliers such as Nortel Networks and Ericsson. **Positions advertised include:** Automation Test Engineer; Consulting Systems Engineer; Customer Network Engineer; General Counsel; Marketing Manager; Mobile IP Architect; QA Engineer.

ALPHA SOFTWARE CORPORATION
83 Cambridge Street, Suite 3B, Burlington MA 01803. 781/229-4500. **Fax:** 781/272-4876. **Contact:** Human Resources. **E-mail address:** jobs@alphasoftware.com. **World Wide Web address:** http://www.alphasoftware.com. **Description:** Develops and markets business software for IBM personal computers and compatibles. The company distributes its products to Canada and Europe. **Positions advertised include:** Customer Service Representatives.

ANALYSIS AND COMPUTER SYSTEMS INC.
One Van de Graaff Drive, Burlington MA 01803. 781/272-8841. **Contact:** Human Resources. **World Wide Web address:** http://www.acsi1.com. **Description:** Offers software consulting. Analysis and Computer Systems provides support services to the U.S. government and commercial organizations.

APOGEE TECHNOLOGY INC.
129 Morgan Drive, Norwood MA 02062. 781/551-9450. **Fax:** 781/440-9528. **Contact:** Human Resources. **World Wide Web address:** http://www.apogeeddx.com. **Description:** A silicon based semiconductor manufacturer specializing in audio technology.

APPLIX, INC.
289 Turnpike Road, Westborough MA 01581. 508/870-0300. **Contact:** Human Resources. **E-mail address:** jobs@applix.com. **World Wide Web address:** http://www.applix.com. **Description:** Develops and markets software applications for the UNIX market. **Positions advertised include:** Localization Engineer; Systems Engineer. **Corporate headquarters location:** This location. **Other U.S. locations:** Warren NJ; Vienna VA. **International locations:** Worldwide. **Listed on:** NASDAQ. **Stock exchange symbol:** APLX.

ARBOR NETWORKS
430 Bedford Street, Suite 160, Lexington MA 02420. 781/684-0900. **Toll-free phone:** 866/212-7267. **Fax:** 781/768-3299. **Contact:** Human Resources. **World

Wide Web address: http://www.arbornetworks.com. **Description:** Develops network integrity systems for enterprises and service providers. **Positions advertised include:** Consulting Engineer; Staff Accountant. **Corporate headquarters location:** This location. **Other U.S. locations:** Ann Arbor MI.

ARTESYN TECHNOLOGIES
125 Newbury Street, Framingham MA 01701. 508/628-5600. **Fax:** 508/424-2752. **Contact:** Human Resources. **E-mail address:** Jackie.kallman@artsesyn.com. **World Wide Web address:** http://www.artesyn.com. **Description:** Offers repair services for computer and peripheral manufacturers. The company also manufactures power conversion products. **Positions advertised include:** Engineering Manager; Key Account Manager for Medical Industry; Design Engineer; SAP Control Lead; SAP Sales & Distributor; Electrical Design Engineer. **Other international locations:** Worldwide. **Listed on:** NASDAQ. **Stock exchange symbol:** ATSN.

ARTISOFT, INC.
5 Cambridge Center, 3rd Floor, Cambridge MA 02142. 617/354-0600. **Fax:** 617/354-7744. **Contact:** Personnel. **E-mail address:** jobs@artisoft.com. **World Wide Web address:** http://www.artisoft.com. **Description:** A provider of networking solutions for businesses. The company offers the LANtastic network operating system as well as network management, backup, and multiplatform connectivity systems. **Positions advertised include:** Channel Development Representative. **Corporate headquarters location:** This location. **Listed on:** NASDAQ. **Stock exchange symbol:** ASFT.

ASCENTIAL SOFTWARE
50 Washington Street, Westborough MA 01581. 508/366-3888. **Fax:** 508/389-8955. **Contact:** Human Resources Manager. **E-mail address:** staffing@ascentialsoftware.com. **World Wide Web address:** http://www.ascentialsoftware.com. **Description:** Manufactures a wide range of software products including database systems and warehouse development tools. Ascential serves government and business customers in the manufacturing, health care, telecommunications, aerospace, defense, financial services, and utilities industries. **Positions advertised include:** Solutions Architect; SQA Engineer; Software Engineering Web Services; Software Engineer; Tax Analyst; Manager of Marketing Communication & Services; Account Development Representative; Help Desk Analyst; Account Executive; District Sales Manager; IBM Alliance Director. **Corporate headquarters location:** This location. **Other U.S. locations:** CA; CO; GA; IL; NC; NJ; TX; WA. **International locations:** Australia; Brazil; Canada; France; Germany; Hong Kong; Japan; South Africa; United Kingdom. **Listed on:** NASDAQ. **Stock exchange symbol:** ASCL.

ASPENTECH
10 Canal Park, Cambridge MA 02141-2201. 617/949-1000. **Fax:** 617/949-1030. **Contact:** Human Resources. **World Wide Web address:** http://www.aspentech.com. **Description:** Supplies chemical engineering software to the chemicals, petroleum, pharmaceuticals, metals, minerals, food products, consumer products, and utilities industries. **Positions advertised include:** Oil & Gas Solutions Director; Software Quality Engineer; Accounts Receivable Clerk; Collections Specialist; Accountant; Director Computer & Network Operations; Sales Operations Director. **Corporate headquarters location:** This location. **Other U.S. locations:** Nationwide. **International locations:** Worldwide. **Listed on:** NASDAQ. **Stock exchange symbol:** AZPN.

ATEX MEDIA SOLUTIONS
15 Crosby Drive, Bedford MA 01730. 781/275-2323. **Fax:** 781/276-1254. **Contact:** Human Resources. **E-mail address:** jobs.bedford@atexmediacommand.com. **World Wide Web address:** http://www.atex.com. **Description:** Designs, develops, and sells computer software products for the newspaper, magazine, and prepress publishing markets worldwide. **Positions advertised include:** Vice President of Customer Support Services. **Corporate headquarters location:** This location. **Other U.S. locations:** Nationwide. **International locations:** Worldwide. **Operations at this facility include:** Administration; Research and Development; Sales; Service. **Listed on:** Privately held. **Number of employees at this location:** 240. **Number of employees nationwide:** 400.

ATLANTIC DATA SERVICES
One Batterymarch Park, Quincy MA 02169. 617/770-3333. **Contact:** Director of Human Resources. **E-mail address:** joinourteam@adsfs.com. **World Wide Web address:** http://www.atlanticdataservices.com. **Description:** A professional services firm providing computer consulting and project management services to the banking and financial industries. **Positions advertised include:** Project Consultant; Business Development Manager. **Corporate headquarters location:** This location. **Other U.S. locations:** Nationwide. **Listed on:** NASDAQ. **Stock exchange symbol:** ADSC. **Annual sales/revenues:** $21 - $50 million. **Number of employees nationwide:** 200.

AVID TECHNOLOGY, INC.
Avid Technology Park, 1925 Andover Street (Building 2), Tewksbury MA 01876. 978/640-6789. **Contact:** Human Resources. **World Wide Web address:** http://www.avid.com. **Description:** A leading provider of digital audio and video tools. Products include digital editing systems and networking and shared storage systems. The company's products are used for various media and entertainment applications. Founded in 1987. **Positions advertised include:** Customer Service & Technical Support Representative; Broadcast Engineer; Post Engineer; Workgroup & Storage Engineer; Finance & Accounting Representative; Human Resources Representative; Information Systems Representative; Manufacturing Representative; Marketing Representative; Product Marketing Representative. **Corporate headquarters location:** This location. **International locations:** Worldwide. **Listed on:** NASDAQ. **Stock exchange symbol:** AVID.

AVOCENT CORPORATION
4 Meeting House Road, Chelmsford MA 01824. 978/244-2000. **Toll-free phone:** 800/264-9443. **Fax:** 978/244-0334. **Contact:** Human Resources. **World Wide Web address:** http://www.avocent.com. **Description:** Develops and markets connectivity solutions for businesses, data centers, service providers, and financial institutions. Avocent Corporation's products include KVM switching, remote access, and video display solutions. **Positions advertised include:** Software Engineer. **NOTE:** Jobseekers should send resumes to: Human Resources, 4991 Corporate Drive, Huntsville AL 35805. **Corporate headquarters location:** Huntsville AL. **Other U.S. locations:** Huntsville AL; Sunrise FL; Austin TX; Redmond WA. **International locations:** Canada; Germany; Hong Kong; Ireland. **Listed on:** NASDAQ. **Stock exchange symbol:** AVCT.

AWARE INC.
40 Middlesex Turnpike, Bedford MA 01730. 781/276-4000. **Fax:** 781/276-4001. **Contact:** Human Resources. **E-mail address:** jobs@aware.com. **World Wide**

Web address: http://www.aware.com. **Description:** A world leader in the development of xDSL technology for high-speed, broadband modems. Founded in 1986. **Other U.S. locations:** Lafayette CA. **Listed on:** NASDAQ. **Stock exchange symbol:** AWRE. **Annual sales/revenues:** $5 - $10 million. **Number of employees at this location:** 80.

AXIS COMPUTER SYSTEMS
201 Boston Post Road West, Marlborough MA 01752. 508/481-9600. **Toll-free phone:** 800/370-AXIS. **Contact:** Human Resources. **E-mail address:** hr@axiscomp.com. **World Wide Web address:** http://www.axiscomp.com. **Description:** Develops software for manufacturing facilities in the metals industry. **Positions advertised include:** Software Developer; Development Manager; Software Quality Assurance Manager; Customer Service Consultant; Product Support Specialist; Sales Professional; Support Specialist.

BMC SOFTWARE
Waltham Woods, 880 Winter Street, Building 4, Waltham MA 02454. 781/891-0000. **Contact:** Human Resources. **World Wide Web address:** http://www.bmc.com. **Description:** Manufactures, sells, and supports software used for MIS and business productivity. The integrated software is written for IBM, IBM compatible VAX/VMS mainframes and RS/6000 workstations, new applications, and network performance management. The company distributes its products across North America, South America, Europe, the Middle East, and the Pacific Rim. **Positions advertised include:** Software Consultant; Administrative Support Assistant. **Other U.S. locations:** Nationwide. **International locations:** Worldwide. **Listed on:** New York Stock Exchange. **Stock exchange symbol:** BMC. **Number of employees at this location:** 180.

BITSTREAM, INC.
245 First Street 17th Floor, Cambridge MA 02142. 617/497-6222. **Contact:** Human Resources. **E-mail address:** careers@bitstream.com. **World Wide Web address:** http://www.bitstream.com. **Description:** Develops and markets digital font software packages for original equipment manufacturers and end users. Products include fonts used in graphic arts image setters, printers, and screen displays for both personal computer and Macintosh platforms. Founded in 1981.

BROADVISION
400 Fifth Avenue, Waltham MA 02451. 781/290-0710. **Contact:** Human Resources. **World Wide Web address:** http://www.broadvision.com. **Description:** BroadVision creates communications and marketing applications for business and governmental entities. **Positions advertised include:** Sales Representative. **Special programs:** Internships. **Corporate headquarters location:** Redwood City CA. **Other U.S. locations:** Nationwide. **International locations:** Brazil; Canada; Mexico. **Operations at this facility include:** This location develops document management systems and solutions software. **Listed on:** NASDAQ. **Stock exchange symbol:** BVSN.

BROOKTROUT TECHNOLOGY, INC.
250 First Avenue, Needham MA 02494. 781/449-4100. **Fax:** 781/433-9596. **Contact:** Human Resources. **E-mail address:** hr@brooktout.com. **World Wide Web address:** http://www.brooktrout.com. **Description:** Designs, manufactures, and markets software, hardware, and systems solutions for electronic messaging applications in telecommunications and networking environments worldwide. These products help integrate voice, fax, and data communications across networks. **Positions advertised include:** Principal Hardware Engineer; Principal Engineer; Product Manager. **Corporate headquarters location:** This location.

Other U.S. locations: Nationwide. **International locations:** Worldwide. **Subsidiaries include:** Brooktrout Networks Group, Inc. (Texas); Brooktrout Securities Corporation; Brooktrout Technology Europe, Ltd. **Listed on:** NASDAQ. **Stock exchange symbol:** BRKT. **Number of employees nationwide:** 60.

BRYLEY SYSTEMS INC.

12 Main Street, Hudson MA 01749. 978/562-6077. **Fax:** 978/562-5680. **Contact:** Human Resources. **E-mail address:** humanresources@bryley.com. **World Wide Web address:** http://www.bryley.com. **Description:** A network systems integrator that provides computer network/telephone solutions to businesses throughout New England. The company provides analysts, consulting, design, and installation services. **Positions advertised include:** Account Executives.

BULL HN INFORMATION SYSTEMS INC.

300 Concord Road, Billerica MA 01821-4199. 978/294-6000. **Fax:** 978/294-6601. **Contact:** Human Resources. **E-mail address:** job.opportunities@bull.com. **World Wide Web address:** http://www.bull.com. **Description:** Bull HN Information Systems is a major systems and technologies integrator with a comprehensive range of solutions, services, and support capabilities. Bull's strategy, the Distributed Computing Model, allows users to integrate multivendor systems in a flexible, open environment. **Corporate headquarters location:** This location. **International locations:** Worldwide. **Parent company:** Groupe Bull (France).

BYTEX CORPORATION

495 Commerce Park, 113 Cedar Street, Suite 2, Milford MA 01757. 508/422-9422. **Fax:** 508/422-9410. **Contact:** Human Resources. **E-mail address:** personell@bytex.com. **World Wide Web address:** http://www.bytex.com. **Description:** A data communications and internetworking company providing manufacturing, sales, and service of an intelligent switching hub used in both local and wide area computer networks. **Other U.S. locations:** Columbia MD; Minnetonka MI. **Operations at this facility include:** Engineering and Design; Manufacturing; Marketing; Service. **Number of employees at this location:** 200. **Number of employees nationwide:** 1,300.

CGI INFORMATION SYSTEMS

600 Federal Street, Andover MA 01810. 978/682-5500. **Contact:** Human Resources. **World Wide Web address:** http://www.cgi.ca. **Description:** Provides systems integration, outsourcing, consulting, and business solutions to the financial, telecommunications, manufacturing, government, health care, and utilities industries. **Other U.S. locations:** Nationwide. **International locations:** Worldwide. **Listed on:** New York Stock Exchange. **Stock exchange symbol:** GIB.

CMGI

100 Brickstone Square, Andover MA 01810. 978/684-3600. **Contact:** Human Resources. **World Wide Web address:** http://www.cmgi.com. **Description:** Develops and integrates a variety of advanced Internet and database management technologies. **Corporate headquarters location:** This location. **Other area locations:** Wilmington MA. **International locations:** Worldwide. **Subsidiaries Include:** AltaVista; CMGion; Engage, Inc.; Equilibrium; NaviSite; SalesLink; Tallan; uBid.com; yesmail.com. **Listed on:** NASDAQ. **Stock exchange symbol:** CMGI.

CSC CONSULTING & SYSTEMS
275 Second Avenue, Waltham MA 02451. 781/890-7446. **Fax:** 781/890-1208. **Contact:** Patricia Bleheen, Recruiting Manager. **World Wide Web address:** http://www.csc.com. **Description:** A consulting firm specializing in systems integration, systems design, and applications development for the commercial and private sectors. Founded in 1959. **Positions advertised include:** Business Process Architect; Application Developer; Business Analyst; Network Engineer; System Administrator; Application Manager; Application Designer; Enterprise Package Solution Specialist; Application Designer; Payroll Specialist; Accountant. **Corporate headquarters location:** El Segundo CA. **Other U.S. locations:** Nationwide. **Parent company:** Computer Sciences Corporation. **Listed on:** New York Stock Exchange. **Stock exchange symbol:** CSC. **Annual sales/revenues:** More than $100 million. **Number of employees at this location:** 300. **Number of employees worldwide:** 44,000.

CSPI
43 Manning Road, Billerica MA 01821. 978/663-7598. **Toll-free phone:** 800/325-3110. **Fax:** 978/663-0150. **E-mail address:** hr@cspi.com. **Contact:** Karen Lacroix, Human Resources Manager. **World Wide Web address:** http://www.cspi.com. **Description:** CSPI designs, manufactures, and markets digital signal processing, high-performance, multiprocessing systems for real-time applications. These low-power, special purpose computers enhance a system's ability to perform high-speed arithmetic and are primarily used for defense, medical, industrial, and real-time applications. **Special programs:** Co-ops. **Corporate headquarters location:** This location. **Other U.S. locations:** CA; FL; MD; VA. **Subsidiaries include:** MODCOMP, Inc. sells real-time process control systems and legacy solutions; Scanalytics, Inc. is focused on hardware and software products for scientific imaging. **Listed on:** NASDAQ. **Stock exchange symbol:** CSPI. **Number of employees at this location:** 60. **Number of employees nationwide:** 150.

CADENCE DESIGN SYSTEMS, INC.
270 Billerica Road, Chelmsford MA 01824. 978/262-6000. **Contact:** Human Resources. **World Wide Web address:** http://www.cadence.com. **Description:** Develops automation software for wireless computers and telecommunication devices. **Positions advertised include:** Marketing Program Manager; Sales Technical Leader. **Corporate headquarters location:** San Jose CA. **Other U.S. locations:** Nationwide. **International locations:** Worldwide. **Listed on:** New York Stock Exchange. **Stock exchange symbol:** CDN.

CAMBEX CORPORATION
115 Flanders Road, Westborough MA 01581. 508/983-1200. **Toll-free phone:** 800/325-5565. **Fax:** 508/983-0255. **Contact:** Human Resources. **World Wide Web address:** http://www.cambex.com. **Description:** Cambex Corporation develops, manufactures, and markets a variety of direct access storage products that improve the performance of large- and mid-size IBM computers. These products include central and expanded memory, controller cache memory, disk array systems, disk and tape subsystems, and related software products. **Positions advertised include:** Sales Executive; Regional Sales Manager; Telemarketing Representative. **Corporate headquarters location:** This location. **Other U.S. locations:** Scottsdale AZ; Thousand Oaks CA; Walnut Creek CA; Westport CT; Clearwater FL; Roswell GA; Schaumburg IL; Troy MI; Chesterfield MO; Charlotte NC; Clark NJ; Cincinnati OH; Blue Bell PA; Dallas TX; Reston VA. **Operations at this facility include:** Administration; Manufacturing; Research and Development; Sales; Service.

CAMBRIDGE TECHNOLOGY PARTNERS

8 Cambridge Center, Cambridge MA 02142. 617/374-9800. **Contact:** Human Resources. **World Wide Web address:** http://www.ctp.com. **Description:** Provides information technology consulting and software development services to organizations with large-scale information processing and distribution needs that are utilizing or migrating to open systems computing environments. **Positions advertised include:** Technical Account Manager. **Corporate headquarters location:** This location. **Other U.S. locations:** Nationwide. **International locations:** Worldwide. **Parent company:** Novell, Inc.

CHANNEL 1 INTERNET

P.O. Box 338, Cambridge MA 02238. 617/864-0100. **Fax:** 617/354-3100. **Physical address:** 14 Arrow Street, Cambridge MA 02138. **Contact:** Human Resources. **World Wide Web address:** http://www.channel1.com. **Description:** Designs Websites and virtual stores.

COGNEX CORPORATION

One Vision Drive, Natick MA 01760. 508/650-3000. **Fax:** 508/650-3340. **Recorded jobline:** 508/650-3232. **Contact:** Human Resources. **E-mail address:** human.resources@cognex.com. **World Wide Web address:** http://www.cognex.com. **Description:** Designs, develops, manufactures, and markets machine vision systems used to automate a wide range of manufacturing processes. Cognex machine vision systems are used in the electronics, semiconductor, pharmaceutical, health care, aerospace, automotive, packaging, and graphic arts industries to gauge, guide, inspect, and identify products in manufacturing operations. Founded in 1981. **NOTE:** Entry-level positions and part-time jobs are offered. **Company slogan:** To preserve and enhance vision. **Positions advertised include:** End User Sales; Cost Accounting Manager; Principal Product Marketing Manager; HW Engineer; PC Specialist; Account Specialist; Credit Collection Specialist; Project Engineer. **Special programs:** Internships; Training; Co-ops; Summer Jobs. **Office hours:** Monday - Friday, 8:00 a.m. - 5:00 p.m. **Corporate headquarters location:** This location. **Other U.S. locations:** Alameda CA; Mountain View CA; Naperville IL; Novi MI; Portland OR; Wayne PA; Austin TX; West Allis WI. **International locations:** Worldwide. **Listed on:** NASDAQ. **Stock exchange symbol:** CGNX. **President/CEO:** Dr. Robert Shillman. **Number of employees at this location:** 300. **Number of employees nationwide:** 450. **Number of employees worldwide:** 600.

COGNOS CORPORATION

15 Wayside Road, Burlington MA 01803. 781/229-6600. **Toll-free phone:** 800/426-4667. **Fax:** 781/229-9844. **Contact:** Human Resources. **World Wide Web address:** http://www.cognos.com. **Description:** Develops a line of business management software. **Positions advertised include:** Accounting Manager; Account Executive; Commission System Supervisor; Business Analyst; Business Development Representative; Service Operations Advisor; Solutions Architect. **Corporate headquarters location:** This location. **Other U.S. locations:** Nationwide. **International locations:** Worldwide. **Listed on:** NASDAQ. **Stock exchange symbol:** COGN.

COMPUREX SYSTEMS

P.O. Box 2000, Easton MA 02334. 508/230-3700. **Fax:** 508/238-8250. **Contact:** Human Resources. **World Wide Web address:** http://www.compurex.com. **Description:** Rents, sells, and leases new and used Compaq and Digital Equipment Corporation systems, peripherals, and compatibles.

COMPUTER ASSOCIATES INTERNATIONAL, INC.
100 Staples Drive, Framingham MA 01702. 508/628-8000. **Contact:** Human Resources. **World Wide Web address:** http://www.cai.com. **Description:** Computer Associates International, Inc. is one of the world's leading developers of client/server and distributed computing software. The company develops, markets, and supports enterprise management, database and applications development, business applications, and consumer software products for a broad range of mainframe, midrange, and desktop computers. The company serves major business, government, research, and educational organizations. **Positions advertised include:** Development Manager; Principal Consultant; Systems Engineer. **Corporate headquarters location:** Islandia NY. **Other U.S. locations:** Nationwide. **International locations:** Worldwide. **Operations at this facility include:** This location develops software. **Listed on:** New York Stock Exchange. **Stock exchange symbol:** CA.

COMPUTER CORPORATION OF AMERICA, INC.
500 Old Connecticut Path, Framingham MA 01701. 508/270-6666. **Contact:** Human Resources. **World Wide Web address:** http://www.cca-int.com. **Description:** Develops high-speed database software. **Corporate headquarters location:** This location. **International locations:** Canada; England.

COMPUTER HORIZONS CORPORATION
35 Braintree Hill Park, Suite 108, Braintree MA 02184. 781/356-7800. **Toll-free phone:** 800/773-3496. **Fax:** 781/356-8899. **Contact:** Human Resources. **World Wide Web address:** http://www.computerhorizons.com. **Description:** A full-service technology solutions company offering contract staffing, outsourcing, re-engineering, migration, downsizing support, and network management. The company has a worldwide network of 33 offices. Founded in 1969. **Corporate headquarters location:** Mountain Lakes NJ. **Other U.S. locations:** Nationwide. **International locations:** Canada. **Listed on:** NASDAQ. **Stock exchange symbol:** CHRZ. **Number of employees nationwide:** 1,500. **Number of employees worldwide:** 3,000.

THE COMPUTER MERCHANT, LTD.
95 Longwater Circle, Norwell MA 02061. 781/878-1070. **Toll-free phone:** 800/617-6172. **Fax:** 781/878-4712. **Contact:** Human Resources. **World Wide Web address:** http://www.tcml.com. **Description:** Provides software consulting services. **NOTE:** Part-time jobs are offered. **Positions advertised include:** Tester; Engineer; Project Manager; Business Analyst; Programmer; Database Administrator; Network Service Support Technician. **Special programs:** Internships; Summer Jobs. **Listed on:** Privately held. **CEO:** John Danieli. **Information Systems Manager:** Donna Cash. **Annual sales/revenues:** More than $100 million. **Number of employees at this location:** 80.

CONTINENTAL RESOURCES, INC.
175 Middlesex Turnpike, P.O. Box 9137, Bedford MA 01730-9137. 781/275-0850. **Toll-free phone:** 800/937-4688. **Fax:** 781/533-0212. **Contact:** Human Resources. **World Wide Web address:** http://www.conres.com. **Description:** Configures, integrates, sells, services, and supports computer systems and electronic test equipment. **NOTE:** Entry-level positions are offered. **Special programs:** Internships. **Corporate headquarters location:** This location. **Other U.S. locations:** Milpitas CA; Torrance CA; Orlando FL; Wood Dale IL; Silver Spring MD; Mount Laurel NJ; Somerset NJ; New York NY. **Subsidiaries include:** Wall Industries manufactures AC/DC power sources and DC/DC converters; Continental Leasing is a lease financing company. **Operations at this facility include:** Administration; Manufacturing; Sales; Service. **Annual**

sales/revenues: More than $100 million. **Number of employees at this location:** 120. **Number of employees nationwide:** 275.

DATA DIRECT, INC.
27 Charles Street, Needham Heights MA 02494. 781/444-9290. **Contact:** Human Resources. **Description:** Distributes products and services for the software manufacturing industry including software duplication systems, data recording media, and CD-ROMs. The company offers data recording products from suppliers including 3M, Maxell, and Sony.

DATA SET CABLE COMPANY
ADD-ON DATA
323 Andover Street, Wilmington MA 01887. 978/988-1900. **Contact:** Human Resources. **Description:** Data Set Cable Company manufactures custom computer cable assemblies. Add-On Data (also at this location) resells computers.

DATA TRANSLATION
100 Locke Drive, Marlborough MA 01752-1192. 508/481-3700. **Fax:** 508/481-5670. **Contact:** Human Resources. **E-mail address:** hresources@datx.com. **World Wide Web address:** http://www.datatranslation.com. **Description:** Designs, develops, and manufactures high-performance digital media, data acquisition, and imaging products. The company's principal products are digital signal processing boards and software, which use personal computers to receive analog signals, convert them to digital form, and process the digital data. One product, Media 100, enables video producers to produce broadcast quality videos on a Macintosh computer. **Positions advertised include:** Test Operator. **Corporate headquarters location:** This location. **Subsidiaries include:** Data Translation, GmbH (Germany); Data Translation Ltd. (England). **Listed on:** NASDAQ. **Stock exchange symbol:** DATX.

DATACUBE, INC.
300 Rosewood Drive, Danvers MA 01923. 978/777-4200. **Fax:** 978/777-3117. **Contact:** Human Resources. **World Wide Web address:** http://www.datacube.com. **Description:** A manufacturer of board- and system-level hardware for image processing. **NOTE:** Entry-level positions are offered. **Positions advertised include:** Principal/Senior Software Engineer. **Corporate headquarters location:** This location. **Listed on:** Privately held. **Annual sales/revenues:** $11 - $20 million. **Number of employees at this location:** 140.

DATAWATCH CORPORATION
175 Cabot Street, Suite 503, Lowell MA 01854. 978/441-2200. **Contact:** Human Resources. **World Wide Web address:** http://www.datawatch.com. **Description:** Designs, manufactures, markets, and supports personal computer software including Monarch, which provides data access, translation, and reporting capability to users of network PCs, and VIREX, which detects, repairs, and monitors virus infections for Macintosh computers. **Positions advertised include:** Sales Executive; Product Manager. **Subsidiaries include:** Datawatch Europe Ltd. (England); Datawatch GmbH (Germany); Datawatch International Ltd. (England); Datawatch Pty Ltd. (Australia); Datawatch Sarl (France). **Listed on:** NASDAQ. **Stock exchange symbol:** DWCH.

DELPHI FORUMS INC.
1030 Massachusetts Avenue, Cambridge MA 02138. 617/576-3690. **Fax:** 617/995-3032. **Contact:** Human Resources. **E-mail address:** jobs@delphi.com.

World Wide Web address: http://www.delphiforums.com. **Description:** Manages a Website that hosts online forums and supports thousands of special interest communities including free do-it-yourself message boards, chat rooms, and personal home pages. Delphi Forums has more than 2 million registered users of approximately 80,000 forums. **Corporate headquarters location:** This location.

EAD SYSTEMS CORPORATION
300 Congress Street #304, Quincy MA 02169. 617/328-5258. **Fax:** 617/328-4941. **Contact:** Human Resources. **World Wide Web address:** http://www.ead.com. **Description:** Repairs computer monitors. **Other U.S. locations:** Fremont CA.

EMC CORPORATION
P.O. Box 9103, Hopkinton MA 01748-9103. 508/435-1000. **Fax:** 508/435-8884. **Contact:** Human Resources. **E-mail address:** resumes@emc.com. **World Wide Web address:** http://www.emc.com. **Description:** EMC designs, manufactures, markets, and supports high-performance data storage products. The company also provides related services for selected mainframe and mid-range computer systems primarily manufactured by IBM and Unisys. **Positions advertised include:** District Administration; Functional Program Manager; Software Release Administrator; Speechwriter; PR Specialist; Corporate Systems Engineer; Lead Corporation Systems Engineer; Product Manager; Controller; Financial Analyst; Cost Accounting Supervisor; Global Solutions; Mechanical Engineer; Materials Quality Engineer; HR Operation Manager; IT Program Research; Paralegal. **NOTE:** Applicants should mail their resumes to: EMC Corporation, Attn: Employment Opportunities, 5 Technology Drive, Milford, MA 01757. **Corporate headquarters location:** This location. **Listed on:** New York Stock Exchange. **Stock exchange symbol:** EMC. **Annual sales/revenues:** More than $100 million. **Number of employees at this location:** 1,500.

EASTMAN KODAK COMPANY
900 Chelmsford Street, Lowell MA 01851. 978/323-7600. **Contact:** Human Resources. **World Wide Web address:** http://www.kodak.com. **Description:** Develops color management software. **Subsidiaries include:** Eastman Software (Billerica MA).

EDOCS INC.
One Apple Hill, Suite 301, Natick MA 01760. 508/652-8600. **Fax:** 508/652-8601. **Contact:** Human Resources. **World Wide Web address:** http://www.edocs.com. **Description:** A software manufacturer that designs programs for customer self-service and e-billing. **Parent company:** Siebel Solutions.

ELCOM INTERNATIONAL INC.
10 Oceana Way, Norwood MA 02062. 781/762-0202. **Contact:** Human Resources. **E-mail address:** hr@elcon.com. **World Wide Web address:** http://www.elcom.com. **Description:** Elcom International Inc. produces products for the electronic commerce software market. The company's software is designed to support the sales of computer products, as well as aid companies in the production of electronic catalogs and ordering systems. **Corporate headquarters location:** This location. **Other U.S. locations:** San Diego CA; Washington DC; Tampa FL; Chicago IL; New York NY. **International locations:** Brazil; England; India; South Africa. **Operations at this facility include:** This location resells computers.

EPSILON
50 Cambridge Street, Burlington MA 01803. 781/273-0250. **Fax:** 781/685-0807. **Contact:** Human Resources. **E-mail address:** jobs@epsilon.com. **World Wide Web address:** http://www.epsilon.com. **Description:** Designs, implements, and supports database marketing programs in a variety of industries including financial services, retail, health care, technology, telecommunications, and nonprofit. Founded in 1970. **NOTE:** Entry-level positions and second and third shifts are offered. **Special programs:** Internships; Summer Jobs. **Office hours:** Monday - Friday, 8:30 a.m. - 5:30 p.m. **Corporate headquarters location:** This location. **Other U.S. locations:** Timonium MD; Earth City MO; Carrollton TX; Dallas TX; Salt Lake City UT; Arlington VA. **Operations at this facility include:** Administration; Divisional Headquarters; Research and Development; Sales; Service. **Listed on:** Privately held. **Annual sales/revenues:** More than $100 million. **Number of employees at this location:** 600. **Number of employees nationwide:** 700.

EROOM TECHNOLOGY, INC.
725 Concord Avenue, Cambridge MA 02138. 617/497-6300. **Contact:** Human Resources. **World Wide Web address:** http://www.eroom.com. **Description:** A leading Web-based project management application. **Corporate headquarters location:** This location.

FUNK SOFTWARE, INC.
222 Third Street, Suite 2163, Cambridge MA 02142. 617/497-6339. **Fax:** 617/547-1031. **Contact:** Human Resources. **E-mail address:** hr@funk.com. **World Wide Web address:** http://www.funk.com. **Description:** Develops remote access and LAN-based communications software. Products include Steel-Belted Radius for NetWare which provides centralized authentication for dial-in users; WanderLink remote access software for NetWare; Proxy remote control software, which allows remote operation of PCs; and AppMeter II, a software usage metering product. Founded in 1982. **Positions advertised include:** SBR Engineer; Quality Assurance Project Lead; Software Engineer; Radius Territory Manager; Renewal Sales Representative. **Corporate headquarters location:** This location. **Listed on:** Privately held.

GCC PRINTERS, INC.
209 Burlington Road, Bedford MA 01730. 781/275-5800. **Contact:** Human Resources. **World Wide Web address:** http://www.gcctech.com. **Description:** Manufactures printers for use with personal computers. GCC also does research in the areas of computer graphics, VLSI design, consumer robotics, and digital sound generation. **NOTE:** Applicants must show proven ability in one or more of the following areas: real-time programming for microprocessors; applications software for personal computers; or computer graphics. **Positions advertised include:** Direct Sales Representative; Education Account Manager; Administrative Assistant; PCB Repair & Test Technician; Hardware Engineer; Software Engineer; Networking Software Engineer. **Corporate headquarters location:** This location. **Operations at this facility include:** Administration; Manufacturing; Research and Development; Sales; Service. **Number of employees at this location:** 150.

GALAXY INTERNET SERVICES
188 Needham Street, Suite 110R, Newton MA 02164. 617/558-0909. **Contact:** Human Resources. **World Wide Web address:** http://www.gis.net. **Description:** Offers services including Web page design, technical support, and business connectivity. **Positions advertised include:** Director of Sales; Broadband Sales; Dialup Sales Representatives; Technical Support Specialist

GENERAL ELECTRIC FANUC AUTOMATION
325 Foxboro Boulevard, Foxboro MA 02035. 508/698-3322. **Fax:** 508/698-8391. **Contact:** Human Resources. **World Wide Web address:** http://www.gefanucautomation.com/. **Description:** Develops industrial automation solutions software. **Parent company:** Emerson Process Management (St. Louis MO).

GLOBALWARE SOLUTIONS
200 Ward Hill Avenue, Haverhill MA 01835. 978/469-7500. **Fax:** 979/469-7555. **Contact:** Personnel. **E-mail address:** jobs@globalwaresolutions.com. **World Wide Web address:** http://www.globalwaresolutions.com. **Description:** Develops e-business solutions for the delivery and management of digital content products. **Positions advertised include:** Sales Executive; Web Applications Developer.

HARTE-HANKS DATA TECHNOLOGIES
25 Linnell Circle, Billerica MA 01821. 978/436-8981. **Fax:** 978/663-3576. **Contact:** David Lobley, Human Resources Representative. **World Wide Web address:** http://www.harte-hanks.com. **Description:** A leading provider of database marketing services and software for database marketing uses. Harte-Hanks Data Technologies supports corporations in banking, insurance, retail, and technology. Founded in 1968. **Company slogan:** Directly ahead. **Positions advertised include:** Account Executive; Business Developer; Business Development Director; Database Marketing Practice Leader; Database Marketing RFP manager; Director of Information & Network Security; Education Consultant; Field Marketing Manager; Product Marketing Manager; Quality Assurance Engineer; Technical Writer; Web Marketing Manager. **Special programs:** Internships; Training. **Corporate headquarters location:** San Antonio TX. **Other U.S. locations:** Nationwide. **International locations:** Asia; Australia; Canada; South America; United Kingdom. **Parent company:** Harte-Hanks Communications. **Listed on:** New York Stock Exchange. **Stock exchange symbol:** HHS. **Annual sales/revenues:** More than $100 million. **Number of employees at this location:** 550. **Number of employees nationwide:** 6,000. **Number of employees worldwide:** 7,000.

HEWLETT PACKARD
200 Forest Street, Marlborough MA 01752. 978/493-5111. **Contact:** Human Resources. **World Wide Web address:** http://www.hp.com. **Description:** Designs, manufactures, sells, and services computers and associated peripheral equipment, and related software and supplies. Applications and programs include scientific research, computation, communications, education, data analysis, industrial control, time sharing, commercial data processing, graphic arts, word processing, health care, instrumentation, engineering, and simulation. **Positions advertised include:** Sales Representative; Direct Deployment Specialist; Pre Sales Consultant; Director Client Manager; Lead Solutions Architect; Inbound Operation Manager; Web Manager; End User Sales Representative; Director Client Manager; Business Systems Analyst; Information Technology Technical Lead; Logistics Individual Contributor; Market Researcher; HP Services Tax Manager. **Other U.S. locations:** Nationwide.

HITACHI AMERICA, LTD.
200 Lowder Brook Drive, Suite 2200, Westwood MA 02090. 781/461-8300. **Toll-free phone:** 800/441-4832. **Fax:** 781/461-8664. **Contact:** Human Resources. **World Wide Web address:** http://www.hitachidisplays.com. **Description:** This location is a sales office and imports and distributes computer monitors. **NOTE:**

Entry-level positions are offered. **Annual sales/revenues:** $51 - $100 million. **Number of employees at this location:** 30. **Number of employees nationwide:** 155.

HITACHI COMPUTER PRODUCTS

1601 Trapelo Road, 3rd Floor, Waltham MA 02451. 781/890-0444. **Toll-free phone:** 800/745-4056. **Fax:** 781/890-4998. **Contact:** Human Resources. **E-mail address:** cssc@hitachisoftware.com. **World Wide Web address:** http://www.hi.com. **Description:** Develops electronic commerce software. **International locations:** England; Japan.

I-LOGIX, INC.

3 Riverside Drive, Andover MA 01810. 978/682-2100. **Toll-free phone:** 888/BILOGIX. **Fax:** 978/682-5995. **Contact:** Human Resources. **E-mail address:** info@ilogix.com. **World Wide Web address:** http://www.ilogix.com. **Description:** Manufactures software for high-technology applications. **International locations:** England; France; Germany; Israel.

IDX SYSTEMS CORPORATION

116 Huntington Avenue, Boston MA 02116. 617/424-6800. **Fax:** 617/266-5419. **Contact:** Human Resources. **World Wide Web address:** http://www.idx.com. **Description:** Develops medical software for hospitals. IDX Systems Corporation provides health care information to physician groups and academic medical centers across the country. **Positions advertised include:** Project Manager; Implementation Lead; eCommerce Software Engineer; Project Manager; Technical Writer. **NOTE:** Entry-level positions are offered. **Office hours:** Monday - Friday, 8:30 a.m. - 5:15 p.m. **Corporate headquarters location:** Burlington VT. **Other U.S. locations:** San Francisco CA; Deerfield Beach FL; Atlanta GA; Chicago IL; Louisville KY; Dallas TX; Arlington VA; Seattle WA. **Listed on:** NASDAQ. **Stock exchange symbol:** IDXC. **Annual sales/revenues:** More than $100 million. **Number of employees at this location:** 550. **Number of employees nationwide:** 3,600.

ITG INC.

44 Farnsworth Street, 9th Floor, Boston MA 02210. 617/728-2800. **Toll-free phone:** 800/983-4484. **Contact:** Human Resources. **E-mail address:** itg_hr@itginc.com. **World Wide Web address:** http://www.itginc.com. **Description:** Provides automated securities trade execution and analysis services to institutional equity investors. ITG's two main services are POSIT, the largest automated stock crossing system operated during trading hours; and QuantEX, a proprietary software that enhances customers' trading efficiencies, access to market liquidity, and portfolio analysis capabilities. **Corporate headquarters location:** New York NY. **Other U.S. locations:** Los Angeles CA. **International locations:** London, England. **Parent company:** Investment Technology Group. **Listed on:** New York Stock Exchange. **Stock exchange symbol:** ITG.

IMARKET, INC.

460 Totten Pond Road, 7th Floor, Waltham MA 02451. 781/672-9200. **Toll-free phone:** 800/590-0085. **Fax:** 781/672-9290. **Contact:** Personnel. **World Wide Web address:** http://www.imarketinc.com. **Description:** Develops desktop marketing software that allows companies to computerize their marketing efforts. Products include MarketPlace, which gives the user desktop access to the Dun & Bradstreet marketing database.

INFINIUM SOFTWARE
25 Communication Way, P.O. Box 6000, Hyannis MA 02601. 508/778-2000. **Contact:** Human Resources. **World Wide Web address:** http://www.infinium.com. **Description:** Develops software for business applications. **Corporate headquarters location:** This location. **Other area locations:** Marlboro MA. **Other U.S. locations:** Irvine CA; Alpharetta GA; Lisle IL; Las Vegas NV; Bend OR. **International locations:** Mexico. **Listed on:** NASDAQ. **Stock exchange symbol:** INFMC.

INTEGRATED IT SOLUTIONS
290 Vanderbilt Avenue, Norwood MA 02494. 781/453-5100. **Fax:** 781/449-7897. **Contact:** Human Resources. **E-mail address:** jobs@integratedit.com. **World Wide Web address:** http://www.integratedit.com. **Description:** A full-service consulting firm. Integrated IT Solutions offers information and consultation on system choice, network configurations, the Internet, and e-business solutions. **Positions advertised include:** Sales Engineer; Field Service Engineer; Account Executive. **Corporate headquarters location:** This location.

INTEL NETWORK SYSTEMS
75 Reed Road, Hudson MA 01749. 978/553-4000. **Contact:** Human Resources. **World Wide Web address:** http://www.intel.com. **Description:** Produces a line of direct-dial products and remote access servers. **NOTE:** Apply online. **Other area locations:** Boston MA; Framingham MA; Lowell MA; Shrewsbury MA; Waltham MA; Springfield MA. **Other U.S. location:** Nationwide. **International locations:** Worldwide.

INTRANET, INC.
One Gateway Center, Suite 700, Newton MA 02458. 617/527-7020. **Contact:** Human Resources. **World Wide Web address:** http://www.intranet.com. **Description:** Manufactures networking software. **Positions advertised include:** Senior Technical Writer. **NOTE:** Search and apply for open positions online. **Parent company:** Transaction Systems Architects, Inc.

KEANE, INC.
10 City Square, Boston MA 02129. 617/241-9200. **Contact:** Human Resources. **World Wide Web address:** http://www.keane.com. **Description:** Designs, develops, and manages software for corporations and health care facilities. Keane, Inc.'s services enable clients to leverage existing information systems and develop and manage new software applications more rapidly and proficiently. Founded in 1965. **Positions advertised include:** Web Developer; Web Applications Developer; Technical Recruiter; Administrative Assistant; Proposal Writer; Technical Support Manager; Business Analyst; Client Server Developer; Recruiting Associate; Quality Assurance Analyst; Sales Associate. **Corporate headquarters location:** This location. **Other U.S. locations:** Nationwide. **Listed on:** American Stock Exchange. **Stock exchange symbol:** KEA. **Number of employees at this location:** 100.

KEMA
3 Burlington Woods, Burlington MA 01803-4543. 781/273-5700. **Fax:** 781/229-4867. **Contact:** Paula LaRue, Director of Human Resources. **World Wide Web address:** http://www.kema.com. **Description:** Develops software products for utilities and energy companies.

KRONOS INC.
297 Billerica Road, Chelmsford MA 01824. 978/250-9800. **Contact:** Human Resources. **World Wide Web address:** http://www.kronos.com. **Description:**

Designs, develops, and markets labor management software and computerized systems that measure employee attendance and schedules. Founded in 1977. **Positions advertised include:** Information Systems Manager; Software Quality Assurance Engineer; Software Engineer; Prospect Marketing Representative; Marketing Writer; Solutions Consultant; Financial Analyst; Enterprise Account Manager; Vice President of Marketing; Network Security Officer; Technical Support Engineer; Events Specialist; Software Product Manager. **Special programs:** Internships. **Corporate headquarters location:** This location. **Other U.S. locations:** Nationwide. **International locations:** Worldwide. **Operations at this facility include:** Administration; Research and Development; Sales; Service. **Listed on:** NASDAQ. **Stock exchange symbol:** KRON. **Annual sales/revenues:** More than $100 million. **Number of employees at this location:** 900.

KUBOTEK USA
100 Locke Drive, Marlborough MA 01752. 508/229-2020. **Fax:** 508/229-2121. **Contact:** Human Resources. **World Wide Web address:** http://www.kubotekusa.com. **Description:** A developer of 3-D mechanical design software for CAD systems. **Corporate headquarters location:** This location.

LANGUAGE ENGINEERING CORPORATION
385 Concord Avenue, Belmont MA 02478. 617/489-4000. **Fax:** 617/489-3850. **Contact:** Human Resources. **E-mail address:** info@hq.lec.com. **World Wide Web address:** http://www.lec.com. **Description:** Develops Logovista Internet software that translates English Web pages into Japanese.

LIANT SOFTWARE CORPORATION
354 Waverly Street, Framingham MA 01702. 508/872-8700. **Fax:** 508/626-2221. **Contact:** Human Resources. **World Wide Web address:** http://www.liant.com. **Description:** A developer of network-based programming and software development tools that enhance client/server systems and architectures. **Corporate headquarters location:** This location. **Other U.S. locations:** Austin TX. **International locations:** London, England. **Listed on:** Privately held. **Number of employees worldwide:** 60.

LOGICA NORTH AMERICA, INC.
32 Hartwell Avenue, Lexington MA 02421. 617/476-8000. **Contact:** Andrea Merurio, Human Resources. **World Wide Web address:** http://www.logica.com. **Description:** Provides computer programming systems, design, and consulting services for the banking, insurance, and telecommunications industries. **Other U.S. locations:** San Francisco CA; New York NY; Dearborn MI; Pittsburgh PA; Dallas TX; Houston TX; Bellevue WA. **International locations:** Worldwide.

LOTUS DEVELOPMENT CORPORATION
One Rogers Street, Cambridge MA 02142. 617/577-8500. **Toll-free phone:** 800/796-9876. **Contact:** Personnel. **World Wide Web address:** http://www.lotus.com/jobs. **Description:** Lotus develops, manufactures, and markets applications software and services that meet the evolving technology and business application needs for individuals, work groups, and entire organizations. Products include Lotus Notes, a software application that provides groupware links allowing workers to share information. **Positions advertised include:** Associate Project Manager; Lead Consultant. **NOTE:** Visit: http://www-1.ibm.com/employment/ for current positions. **Corporate headquarters location:** This location. **Parent company:** IBM. **Number of employees nationwide:** 4,400.

LUCENT TECHNOLOGIES INTERNETWORKING SYSTEMS
One Robbins Road, Westford MA 01886. 978/952-1600. **Fax:** 978/392-9682. **Contact:** Human Resources. **World Wide Web address:** http://www.lucent.com. **Description:** Develops, manufactures, markets, and supports a family of high performance, multiservice wide area network (WAN) switches that enable public carrier providers and private network managers to provide cost-effective, high-speed, enhanced data communications services. These products direct and manage data communications across wide area networks that utilize different network architectures and services, and are designed to support, on a single platform, the major high-speed packet data communications services. These services include frame relay, switched multimegabit data service, and asynchronous transfer mode. The company markets its products to public network providers, including interexchange carriers, local exchange carriers, competitive access providers, other public network providers, and private network managers. **Positions advertised include:** Security Consultant; Logistics Strategy Manager; EMEA Regional PEC Leader; CALA Regional PEC Leader. **Corporate headquarters location:** Murray Hill NJ. **Other U.S. locations:** Nationwide. **Listed on:** New York Stock Exchange. **Stock exchange symbol:** LU. **Number of employees at this location:** 650.

LYCOS, INC.
400-2 Totten Pond Road, Waltham MA 02451-2000. 781/370-2700. **Contact:** Human Resources. **World Wide Web address:** http://www.lycos.com. **Description:** An Internet search engine that finds, indexes, and filters information from the World Wide Web. **Corporate headquarters location:** This location. **Listed on:** NASDAQ. **Stock exchange symbol:** LCOS.

MRO SOFTWARE, INC.
100 Crosby Drive, Bedford MA 01730. 781/280-2000. **Contact:** Human Resources. **World Wide Web address:** http://www.mro.com. **Description:** Develops, markets, and supports enterprisewide client/server applications software used to assist in maintaining and developing high-value capital assets such as facilities, systems, and production equipment. The company's products enable customers to reduce downtime, control maintenance expenses, cut spare parts inventories, improve purchasing efficiency, shorten product development cycles, and deploy productive assets and personnel more effectively. **Positions advertised include:** Consultant Information Technology Asset Management. **Corporate headquarters location:** This location. **International locations:** Worldwide. **Listed on:** NASDAQ. **Stock exchange symbol:** MROI.

MRV COMMUNICATIONS
295 Foster Street, Littleton MA 01460. 978/952-4700. **Contact:** Tracy Flory, Human Resources. **E-mail address:** hr@mrv.com. **World Wide Web address:** http://www.mrv.com. **Description:** Designs, manufactures, markets, and supports high-performance data communications network systems. **Listed on:** NASDAQ. **Stock exchange symbol:** MRVC.

MACROMEDIA, INC.
275 Grove Street, Newton MA 02466. 617/219-2000. **Fax:** 617/219-2100. **Contact:** Human Resources. **World Wide Web address:** http://www.macromedia.com. **Description:** Develops and supports application development and server software that allow businesses to develop e-commerce systems. **Corporate headquarters location:** San Francisco.

MATH WORKS

3 Apple Hill Drive, Natick MA 01760. 508/647-7000. **Fax:** 508/647-7001. **Contact:** Human Resources. **World Wide Web address:** http://www.mathworks.com. **Description:** Develops mathematical software packages. **Positions advertised include:** Applications Support Engineer; FPC Manager; MATLAB Software Developer; Software Engineer; Release Engineer; Principal Tools Engineer; Business Systems Administration; Physical Modeling Developer; Communications Quality Engineer; Applications Engineer.

MATHSOFT ENGINEERING & EDUCATION, INC.

101 Main Street, 16th Floor, Cambridge MA 02142. 617/577-1017. **Fax:** 617/444-8001. **Contact:** Human Resources. **E-mail address:** hrjobs@mathsoft.com. **World Wide Web address:** http://www.mathsoft.com. **Description:** A leading developer of mathematical software and electronic books for desktop computers. Products include Mathcad, a live interactive environment for mathematics work in a wide variety of fields including engineering, science, and education. MathSoft also publishes the Mathcad Library of Electronic Books, Maple V symbolic computation software, and other third-party mathematical software. Founded in 1984. **Positions advertised include:** Math CAD Author; Math CAD Reviewer. **Corporate headquarters location:** This location. **International locations:** England; Germany. **Annual sales/revenues:** $11 - $20 million. **Number of employees at this location:** 60. **Number of employees nationwide:** 150.

McKESSONHBOC

3 Bridle Road, Chelmsford MA 01824. 978/256-1655. **Contact:** Human Resources. **World Wide Web address:** http://www.hboc.com. **Description:** An information solutions company that provides information systems and technology to health care enterprises including hospitals, integrated delivery networks, and managed care organizations. McKesson HBOC's primary products are Pathway 2000, a family of client/server-based applications that allows for the integration and uniting of health care providers; STAR, Series, and HealthQuest transaction systems; TRENDSTAR decision support system; and QUANTUM enterprise information system. The company also offers outsourcing services that include strategic information systems planning, data center operations, receivables management, business office administration, and major system conversions. **Positions advertised include:** Night Warehouse Supervisor; Sales Manager; Vice President Business Solutions; Radiology Information Systems; Department Liaison; Driver. **Corporate headquarters location:** San Francisco CA.

MEDITECH (MEDICAL INFORMATION TECHNOLOGY, INC.)

One MEDITECH Circle, Westwood MA 02090. 781/821-3000. **Contact:** Human Resources. **E-mail address:** jobs@meditech.com. **World Wide Web address:** http://www.meditech.com. **Description:** Develops, sells, installs, and supports computer software designed to help the medical community share critical information. **NOTE:** Entry-level positions are offered. **Positions advertised include:** Marketing Consultant; Marketing Consultant Nursing; Marketing Support Representative; Application Specialist; Programmer; Accounts Receivable Specialist. **Office hours:** Monday - Friday, 9:00 a.m. - 5:30 p.m. **Corporate headquarters location:** This location. **Other U.S. locations:** Canton MA; Framingham MA; Norwood MA. **Operations at this facility include:** Administration; Research and Development; Sales; Service. **Number of employees nationwide:** 1,900.

MENTOR GRAPHICS

300 Nickerson Road, Suite 200, Marlborough MA 01752. 508/480-0881. **Toll-free phone:** 800/592-2210. **Contact:** Human Resources. **World Wide Web**

address: http://www.mentor.com. **Description:** A leader in electronic hardware and software design solutions, providing products, consulting services and support for electronics and semiconductor companies. **Positions advertised include:** Director of Marketing; Product Marketing Manager; Technical Marketing Engineer; Software Development Engineer; Financial Analyst. **Special programs:** Internships.

MERCURY COMPUTER SYSTEMS, INC.
199 Riverneck Road, Chelmsford MA 01824. 978/256-1300. **Contact:** Human Resources. **World Wide Web address:** http://www.mc.com. **Description:** A leading provider of high-performance, real-time, embedded solutions for diverse applications including medical imaging, defense electronics, and shared storage configurations. **NOTE:** Entry-level positions are offered. **Positions advertised include:** Component Engineer; Director of Systems Architecture; Engineer. **Special programs:** Internships; Co-ops; Summer Jobs. **Corporate headquarters location:** This location. **Listed on:** NASDAQ. **Stock exchange symbol:** MRCY. **Annual sales/revenues:** $51 - $100 million. **Number of employees nationwide:** 370.

MERCURY INTERACTIVE CORPORATION
25 Burlington Mall Road, Burlington MA 01803. 800/837-8911. **Contact:** Personnel. **World Wide Web address:** http://www.mercuryinteractive.com. **Description:** Mercury Interactive Corporation is a developer of automated software quality (ASQ) tools for enterprise applications testing. The company's products are used to isolate software and system errors prior to application deployment. **Positions advertised include:** Product Marketing Manager; Product Manager; Brand Manager; ITG Applications Engineer; Technical Support Application Engineer; Commercial Counsel; Contract Negotiation; Stock Administrator; Financial Analyst; Treasury Operations Manager; Accountant. **NOTE:** Resumes should be sent to: Human Resources, 1325 Borregas Avenue, Sunnyvale CA 94089. **Corporate headquarters location:** Sunnyvale CA. **Operations at this facility include:** This location is a sales office. **Listed on:** NASDAQ. **Stock exchange symbol:** MERQ. **Annual sales/revenues:** More than $100 million.

META SOFTWARE CORPORATION
125 Cambridge Park Drive, Cambridge MA 02140. 617/576-6920. **Toll-free phone** 800/227-4106. **Fax:** 617/661-2008. **Contact:** Human Resources. **E-mail address:** resumes@metasoft.com. **World Wide Web address:** http://www.metasoftware.com. **Description:** Develops business process re-engineering software and provides consulting services. Founded in 1985. **Positions advertised include:** Senior Consultant; Technical Support Specialist; Programmer/Analyst. **Corporate headquarters location:** This location. **President/CEO:** Robert Seltzer.

MICROTIME COMPUTER DISTRIBUTION, INC.
300 Wildwood Avenue, Woburn MA 01801. 781/938-6699. **Fax:** 781/938-5599. **Contact:** Human Resources. **Description:** Wholesales and distributes computer peripherals and components to the reseller market. The company also assembles custom-built PCs.

MICROWAY, INC.
Plymouth Industrial Park 12 Richards Road, Plymouth MA 02360. 508/746-7341. **Fax:** 508/746-4678. **Contact:** Human Resources. **E-mail address:** info@microway.com. **World Wide Web address:** http://www.microway.com. **Description:** Designs state-of-the-art, high quality Linux clusters, servers, and

RAID storage solutions for universities, life sciences, Fortune 500 companies and research agencies worldwide. **NOTE:** Check http://www.monster.com for latest job postings.

NX NETWORKS
9 Technology Drive, Westborough MA 01581. 508/898-2800. **Contact:** Human Resources. **E-mail address:** hr@nsgdata.com. **World Wide Web address:** http://www.nxnetworks.com. **Description:** Provides secure voice and data networking products to corporations, government agencies, and service providers worldwide. **Corporate headquarters location:** Herndon VA. **International locations:** England; Hong Kong.

NATIONAL DATACOMPUTER, INC.
900 Middlesex Turnpike, Building 5, Billerica MA 01821. 978/663-7677. **Fax:** 978/667-1869. **Contact:** Human Resources. **E-mail:** tferra@ndcomputer.com. **World Wide Web address:** http://www.ndcomputer.com. **Description:** Designs, manufactures, and markets computerized systems used to automate the collection, processing, and communication of information related to product sales, distribution, and inventory control. The company's products and services include data communication networks, application-specific software, hand-held computers and related peripherals, and associated training and support services. The company's products facilitate rapid and accurate data collection, data processing, and two-way communication of information with a customer's host information system.

NETEGRITY INC.
201 Jones Road, Waltham MA 02451. 781/890-1700. **Fax:** 781/487-7791. **Contact:** Human Resources. **E-mail address:** swjobs@netegrity.com. **World Wide Web address:** http://www.netegrity.com. **Description:** Designs and markets data and voice intra and extranet security products. **Other U.S. locations:** New York NY; Reston VA; San Mateo CA; Los Angeles CA; Rosemount IL. **International locations:** Worldwide. **Parent company:** Computer Associates.

NETEZZA CORPORATION
200 Crossing Boulevard, 5th Floor, Framingham MA 01702. 508/665-6800. **Fax:** 508/665-6811. **Contact:** Human Resources. **World Wide Web address:** http://www.netezza.com. **Description:** A provider of enterprise-class data warehouse solutions that integrate database, server, and storage in one appliance. **Positions advertised include:** Software Engineer, Storage Manager; Sr. Software Engineer, Project Leader; Sr. Customer Service Engineer; System Product Manager; Sr. Software Quality Engineer; Channels Manager.

NETSILICON
411 Waverley Oaks Road, Suite 304, Waltham MA 02452. 781/647-1234. **Toll-free phone:** 800/243-2333. **Fax:** 781/893-1338. **Contact:** Personnel. **E-mail address:** staffing@netsilicon.com. **World Wide Web address:** http://www.netsilicon.com. **Description:** Develops and markets hardware and software that allows copiers, fax machines, printers, and scanners to communicate over internal and external networks. NETsilicon also offers technical support and consulting services. **Corporate headquarters location:** This location. **International locations:** Germany; Japan; Korea. **Listed on:** NASDAQ. **Stock exchange symbol:** NSIL.

NORTEL NETWORKS
8 Federal Street, Billerica MA 01821. 978/670-8888. **Contact:** Human Resources. **World Wide Web address:** http://www.nortel.com. **Description:** Designs, produces, and supports multimedia access devices for use in building corporate, public and Internet networks. The primary focus of the company's services is the consolidation of voice, fax, video, and data and multimedia traffic into a single network link. **Positions advertised include:** Software Engineer; Technical Support Engineer; Account Manager; Product Line Manager; Software Routing Manager; Shasta Routing Project Lead; Service Delivery GSM, BTS Engineer. **Other U.S. locations:** Nationwide. **International locations:** Worldwide. **Listed on:** New York Stock Exchange. **Stock exchange symbol:** NT.

ORACLE CORPORATION
10 Van De Graaff Drive, Burlington MA 01803. 781/744-0000. **Contact:** Human Resources. **World Wide Web address:** http://www.oracle.com. **Description:** Designs and manufactures database and information management software for businesses. The company also provides consulting services. **Positions advertised include:** Staff Sales Consultant; Contracts Administrator; Product Manager; Telesales Representative; Contracts Manager; Field Support Sales; Applications Developer; Technical Writer; Quality Assurance Engineer; Manager Business Development. **Corporate headquarters location:** Redwood Shores CA. **Other U.S. locations:** Nationwide. **Listed on:** NASDAQ. **Stock exchange symbol:** ORCL.

OVID TECHNOLOGIES
100 River Ridge Drive, Norwood MA 02062. 781/769-2599. **Fax:** 781/769-8763. **Contact:** Amy Narcotta, Human Resources. **E-mail address:** resumes@ovid.com. **World Wide Web address:** http://www.ovid.com. **Description:** Publishes and distributes over 225 authoritative databases. Ovid Technologies also publishes CD-ROMs and develops software systems for data retrieval and full text linking. Founded in 1985. **NOTE:** Entry-level positions are offered. **Positions advertised include:** Database Design Analyst; Technical Support Specialist. **Corporate headquarters location:** New York NY. **Other U.S. locations:** New York NY; Salt Lake City UT. **International locations:** Berlin, Germany; Bologna, Italy; Hong Kong; London, England; Paris, France; Sydney, Australia. **Listed on:** Privately held. **Annual sales/revenues:** $51 - $100 million. **Number of employees at this location:** 200. **Number of employees nationwide:** 240.

PARAMETRIC TECHNOLOGY CORPORATION
140 Kendrick Street, Needham MA 02494. **Fax:** 781/370-6000. **Contact:** Human Resources. **World Wide Web address:** http://www.ptc.com. **Description:** Designs and develops fully integrated software products for mechanical engineering and automated manufacturing based upon a parametric solids modeling system. **Positions advertised include:** Inside Sales Representative; Strategic Account Representative; Administrative Assistant; Corporate Visiting Center Coordinator; Product Development Consultant; French Localization Specialist; Korean Localization Specialist; German Localization Specialist; Business Systems Analyst; Associate Technologist Support Engineer. **Corporate headquarters location:** This location. **International locations:** Worldwide. **Listed on:** NASDAQ. **Number of employees at this location:** 500. **Number of employees nationwide:** 1,600.

PASSKEY INTERNATIONAL INC.
180 Old Colony Avenue, Quincy MA 02170. 617/237-8200. **Fax:** 617/328-12121. **Contact:** Human Resources. **E-mail address:** hr@passkey.com. **World Wide Web address:** http://www.passkey.com. **Description:** Provides web-based solutions for processing group hotel reservations. **Corporate headquarters location:** This location.

PEGASYSTEMS INC.
101 Main Street, Cambridge MA 02142-1590. 617/374-9600. **Fax:** 617/374-9620. **Contact:** Personnel. **World Wide Web address:** http://www.pegasystems.com. **Description:** Develops software for the financial industry. **Listed on:** NASDAQ. **Stock exchange symbol:** PEGA.

PERCUSSION SOFTWARE, INC.
600 Unicorn Park Drive, Woburn MA 01801. 781/438-9900. **Toll-free phone:** 800/283-0800. **Fax:** 781/438-9955. **Contact:** Human Resources. **World Wide Web address:** http://www.percussion.com. **Description:** Develops enterprise content management software. **NOTE:** See website for positions and contact information. **Positions advertised include:** QA Engineer; Software Engineer; Technical Trainer; JAVA/Domino Consultant; Content Management Consultant; Pre-Sales Manager.

PHOENIX TECHNOLOGIES LTD.
320 Norwood Park South, Norwood MA 02062. 781/792-4760. **Fax:** 781/551-4000. **Contact:** Human Resources. **World Wide Web address:** http://www.phoenix.com. **Description:** Designs, develops, and markets systems software and end user software products. The Peripherals Division designs, develops, and supplies printer emulation software, page distribution languages, and controller hardware designs for the printing industry. The PhoenixPage imaging software architecture enables printer manufacturers to offer products that are compatible with the PostScript language, the PCL printer language, and other imaging standards. Phoenix Technologies' PC Division works with leading vendors and standards committees to ensure that Phoenix products enable manufacturers to develop and deploy next-generation PCs quickly and cost effectively. The company's Package Products Division is a single-source publisher of MS-DOS, Windows, and other software packages. **Corporate headquarters location:** San Jose CA. **Listed on:** NASDAQ. **Stock exchange symbol:** PTEC. **Number of employees at this location:** 330.

PRIMUS MANAGED HOSTING SOLUTIONS
330 Lynnway, Lynn MA 01901. 781/586-6100. **Fax:** 781/593-6858. **Contact:** Human Resources. **World Wide Web address:** http://www.shore.net. **Description:** Provides Internet access and other online services including dial-up networking, Web design, and scripting. **Positions advertised include:** Customer Account Manager; Agent Channel Marketing; Help Desk Technician; Inside Accounting Representative; Internal Auditor; Legal Secretary; Manager Training Quality Assistant.

PROGRESS SOFTWARE CORPORATION
14 Oak Park, Bedford MA 01730. 781/280-4000. **Contact:** Human Resources. **World Wide Web address:** http://www.progress.com. **Description:** Manufactures and supplies application development software to business and government customers worldwide. Products include PROGRESS, a complete, integrated environment for developing and deploying mission-critical applications that are scalable, portable, and reconfigurable across a wide range of computing environments including client/server, host-based, and mixed. **Positions**

advertised include: Data Integration; Facilities Manager; Inside Sales Representative; International Accounting Supervisor; International Financial Analyst; Research Assistant. **Listed on:** NASDAQ. **Stock exchange symbol:** PRGS. **Number of employees nationwide:** 630.

QRS CORPORATION
17 Rogers Street, Gloucester MA 01930. 978/283-9505. **Contact:** Human Resources. **E-mail address:** careers@qrs.com. **World Wide Web address:** http://www.qrs.com. **Description:** Develops supply chain management software. **Corporate headquarters location:** Richmond CA. **Listed on:** NASDAQ. **Stock exchange symbol:** QRSI.

RSA SECURITY, INC.
20 Crosby Drive, Bedford MA 01730. 781/687-7000. **Contact:** Human Resources. **World Wide Web address:** http://www.rsasecurity.com. **Description:** Develops and markets software for security applications. **Positions advertised include:** Systems Engineer; Inside Sales Representative; Account Manager; Executive Assistant; Accountant; Business Analyst; Administrative Assistant; Quality Assurance Performance Test Engineer; Product Manager; Financial Analyst; Strategic Web Manager; Programming Analyst. **Corporate headquarters location:** This location. **Listed on:** NASDAQ. **Stock exchange symbol:** RSAS.

RATIONAL SOFTWARE CORPORATION
20 Maguire Road, Lexington MA 02421. 781/676-2400. **Contact:** Human Resources. **World Wide Web address:** http://www.rational.com. **Description:** Rational Software develops, markets, and supports embedded software products for Web and e-commerce applications. The company's products operate on both Windows and UNIX systems. **Positions advertised include:** Air Force C2 Systems Engineer; Contracts Negotiator; Financial Planning & Analysis; Quality Assurance Engineer; Principal Budget Analyst; Systems Engineer; Environmental Test Engineer; Supply Chain Source Specialist; Process Working Group Lead; Communication Systems Engineer; Field Engineer. **International locations:** Worldwide. **Operations at this facility include:** This location is the North American sales center. **Listed on:** NASDAQ. **Stock exchange symbol:** RATL.

SAP AMERICA, INC.
950 Winter Street, Suite 3800, Waltham MA 02451. 781/672-6500. **Fax:** 781/672-6683. **Contact:** Human Resources. **World Wide Web address:** http://www.sap.com. **Description:** Develops a variety of client/server computer software packages including programs for finance, human resources, and materials management applications. Founded in 1972. **Positions advertised include:** Administrative Assistant. **Special programs:** Internships; Summer Jobs. **Corporate headquarters location:** Newtown Square PA. **Other U.S. locations:** Nationwide. **International locations:** Germany. **Parent company:** SAP AG. **Annual sales/revenues:** More than $100 million. **Number of employees at this location:** 200. **Number of employees nationwide:** 3,000. **Number of employees worldwide:** 13,000.

SEA CORPORATION
20 Vernon Street, Norwood MA 02062. 781/762-9252. **Contact:** Human Resources. **World Wide Web address:** http://www.seacorp.com. **Description:** Provides systems integration and networking services under government contract.

SPSS INC.
One Alewife Center, Cambridge MA 02140. 617/665-9200. **Contact:** Human Resources. **World Wide Web address:** http://www.spss.com. **Description:** Develops software that allows businesses to analyze and predict online consumer behavior. **Positions advertised include:** Business Development Manager; Product Manager. **NOTE:** Apply online. **Other U.S. locations:** San Francisco CA; Miami FL; Newton MA; New York NY; Cincinnati OH; Arlington VA.

SAPIENT CORPORATION
One Memorial Drive, 3rd Floor, Cambridge MA 02142. 617/621-0200. **Contact:** Director of Hiring. **World Wide Web address:** http://www.sapient.com. **Description:** Provides systems integration, consulting, and software integration services. Founded in 1991. **Positions advertised include:** Billing Associate; Payroll Associate; Finance Manager; Technology Developer; Internal Audit Finance Manager; Technology Associate; People Strategy Manager. **Corporate headquarters location:** This location. **Other U.S. locations:** Los Angeles CA; San Francisco CA; Denver CO; Washington DC; Atlanta GA; Chicago IL; Portland ME; Minneapolis MN; Jersey City NJ; Austin TX; Dallas TX. **International locations:** Australia; England; Germany; India; Italy; Japan. **Listed on:** NASDAQ. **Stock exchange symbol:** SAPE. **Annual sales/revenues:** More than $100 million.

SCANSOFT, INC.
9 Centennial Drive, Peabody MA 01960. 978/977-2000. **Toll-free phone:** 800/248-6550. **Fax:** 978/977-2129. **Contact:** Human Resources. **World Wide Web address:** http://www.scansoft.com. **Description:** Manufactures TextBridge and Pagis scanning software and OCR (Optical Character Recognition) software. **NOTE:** Entry-level positions are offered. **Positions advertised include:** Internal Audit & Compliance Director; Telecommunications Manager; Product Marketing Manager; Inside Sales Representative; Outbound Sales Representative. **Special programs:** Internships; Training; Co-ops; Summer Jobs. **Corporate headquarters location:** This location. **Other U.S. locations:** Nationwide. **Operations at this facility include:** Divisional Headquarters. **Listed on:** NASDAQ. **Stock exchange symbol:** SSFT. **President/CEO:** Mike K. Tivnan. **Annual sales/revenues:** $21 - $50 million. **Number of employees at this location:** 120.

SEAPORT GRAPHICS
12 Channel Street, Suite 802, Marine Industrial Park, Boston MA 02210. 617/330-1200. **Contact:** Human Resources. **E-mail address:** employment@seaportgraphics.com. **World Wide Web address:** http://www.seaportgraphics.com. **Description:** Manufactures presentation graphics software and workstation products. Seaport Graphics also creates imaging systems for personal computers and Macintosh desktop packages, color electronic prepress systems, and overnight slide services. **Positions advertised include:** Sales Representative; Account Manager.

SELECT, INC.
31 Dartmouth Street, Westwood MA 02090. 781/326-8600. **Toll-free phone:** 800/634-1806. **Contact:** Human Resources. **World Wide Web address:** http://www.select.com. **Description:** Manufactures and sells network servers.

SIEMENS BUSINESS SERVICES
45 Shawmut Road, Canton MA 02021-1408. 781/830-2200. **Contact:** Human Resources. **World Wide Web address:** http://www.sbs-usa.siemens.com.

Description: A manufacturer of computer systems, software, and peripherals. The company also offers consulting, planning, and implementation services. **Positions advertised include:** Program Director. **Corporate headquarters location:** Rye Brook NY. **Other U.S. locations:** Nationwide. **International locations:** Worldwide.

SIEMENS BUSINESS SERVICES
200 Wheeler Road, Burlington MA 01803. 781/273-0480. **Fax:** 781/313-4231. **Contact:** Human Resources. **World Wide Web address:** http://www.sbs-usa.siemens.com. **Description:** A manufacturer of computer systems, software, and peripherals. The company also offers consulting, planning, and implementation services. **Corporate headquarters location:** Rye Brook NY. **Other U.S. locations:** Nationwide. **International locations:** Worldwide.

SKY COMPUTERS INC.
27 Industrial Avenue, Chelmsford MA 01824. 978/250-1920. **Fax:** 978/250-0959. **Contact:** Human Resources Department. **E-mail address:** resumes@skycomputers.com. **World Wide Web address:** http://www.skycomputers.com. **Description:** Manufactures high-speed processing computer components including compilers, daughterboards, and accelerators.

SMART MODULAR TECHNOLOGIES, INC.
7 Lopez Road, Wilmington MA 01887. 978/988-8848. **Contact:** Human Resources. **World Wide Web address:** http://www.smartm.com. **Description:** Designs, manufactures, and sells personal computer cards used in portable computers and industrial applications and font cartridges used in laser printers. The PC cards enhance the utility of portable computers and electronic equipment by adding memory, data/fax capabilities, and custom applications. The company's laser printer font cartridges broaden the capabilities of laser printers with applications in desktop publishing, word processing, and spreadsheet preparation. **Corporate headquarters location:** This location.

SOFTECH, INC.
2 Highwood Drive, Tewksbury MA 01876. 978/640-6222. **Fax:** 978/858-0440. **Contact:** Human Resources. **E-mail address:** hr-tewks@softech.com. **World Wide Web address:** http://www.softech.com. **Description:** Manufacturers, markets, and maintains product life-cycle software. Founded in 1969. **Positions advertised include:** Senior Software Engineer. **NOTE:** Apply online.

SPYGLASS INTEGRATION
55 Hayden Avenue, Lexington MA 02421. 781/372-4600. **Contact:** Human Resources. **World Wide Web address:** http://www.spyglassintegration.com. **Description:** Spyglass Integration is a leading provider of software and services to make non-PC devices including TVs, phones, faxes, and PDAs work with the Web. **Positions advertised include:** Software Engineer; Quality Assurance Engineer. **Corporate headquarters location:** Mountain View CA. **Operations at this facility include:** This location is a research center focused on content conversion, collaborative applications, and an HTML engine. **Parent company:** OpenTV. **Listed on:** NASDAQ. **Stock exchange symbol:** OPTV.

STORAGETEK
230 Third Avenue, 3rd Floor, Waltham MA 02451. 781/890-2650. **Fax:** 781/890-9106. **Contact:** Human Resources. **World Wide Web address:** http://www.stortek.com. **Description:** Storage Technology Corporation manufactures high-performance computer information storage and retrieval

systems for mainframe and mid-frame computers and networks. Products include automated cartridge systems, random access subsystems, and fault-tolerant disk arrays. The company also distributes equipment; sells new peripherals, software, and hardware; and offers support services. **Corporate headquarters location:** Louisville CO. **Operations at this facility include:** This location sells computer data storage systems.

STRATUS TECHNOLOGIES
111 Powdermill Road, Maynard MA 01754. 978/461-7000. **Contact:** Human Resources. **World Wide Web address:** http://www.stratus.com. **Description:** Stratus Technologies offers a broad range of computer systems, application solutions, middleware, and professional services for critical online operations. **Corporate headquarters location:** This location. **Subsidiaries include:** Shared Systems Corporation provides software and professional services to the financial services, retail, and health care industries. SoftCom Systems, Inc. provides data communications middleware and related professional services that bridge the gap between open distributed systems and legacy mainframe and midrange systems used for online applications. Isis Distributed Systems, Inc. develops advanced messaging middleware products that enable businesses to develop reliable, high-performance distributed computing applications involving networked desktop computers and shared systems.

STREAM INTERNATIONAL
85 Dan Road, Canton MA 02021. 781/575-6800. **Contact:** Human Resources. **World Wide Web address:** http://www.stream.com. **Description:** Resells computer software and offers support services. **Other locations:** Beaverton Oregon, Watertown New York.

SUN MICROSYSTEMS, INC.
One Network Drive, Burlington MA 01803. 978/442-6200. **Contact:** Human Resources. **World Wide Web address:** http://www.sun.com. **Description:** Produces high-performance computer systems, workstations, servers, CPUs, peripherals, and operating system software. The company developed its own microprocessor called SPARC. **Positions advertised include:** Programming Analyst; Web Design Administration; Mission Critical Technical Support; Technical Training Development & Delivery; Customer Services; Application Development; GUI Design; Test Engineer; Product Engineer; Product Management. **Corporate headquarters location:** Palo Alto CA. **Subsidiaries include:** Forte Software Inc. manufactures enterprise application integration software. **Listed on:** NASDAQ. **Stock exchange symbol:** SUNW.

SYBASE, INC.
561 Virginia Road, Concord MA 01742. 978/287-1500. **Fax:** 978/369-3175. **Contact:** Human Resources. **World Wide Web address:** http://www.sybase.com. **Description:** Develops, markets, and supports a full line of relational database management software products and services for integrated, enterprisewide information management systems. Founded in 1984. **Positions advertised include:** Software Engineer. **Special programs:** Internships; Co-ops. **Corporate headquarters location:** Emeryville CA. **Other U.S. locations:** Nationwide. **Operations at this facility include:** Divisional Headquarters. **Listed on:** NASDAQ. **Stock exchange symbol:** SYBS. **President/CEO:** Michael Kietzman. **Annual sales/revenues:** More than $100 million. **Number of employees at this location:** 800. **Number of employees worldwide:** 5,600.

SYSTEMS ENGINEERING, INC.
657 Main Street, Waltham MA 02451-0602. 781/736-9100. **Fax:** 781/736-6969. **Contact:** Human Resources. **E-mail address:** info@sengi.com. **World Wide Web address:** http://www.sengi.com. **Description:** A computer consulting firm. **Positions advertised include:** Microsoft Software Designer/Developer; Sales Professional.

SYSTEMSOFT CORPORATION
275 Grove Street, Suite 1-300, Newton MA 02466-2273. 617/614-4315. **Fax:** 508/651-4138. **Contact:** Recruiter. **World Wide Web address:** http://www.systemsoft.com. **Description:** Supplies PCMCIA (Personal Computer Memory Card International Association) and other system-level software to the rapidly growing market of mobile computers, comprised of laptops, notebooks, subnotebooks, and personal computing devices. System-level software provides both a connectivity layer, which facilitates the addition, configuration, and use of peripheral devices; and a hardware adaptation layer including the communication link between a computer operating system and hardware. **Corporate headquarters location:** This location. **Parent company:** Rocket Software. **Number of employees nationwide:** 250.

TAXWARE INTERNATIONAL, INC.
27 Congress Street, Salem MA 01970. 978/741-0101. **Contact:** Lisa Burns, Human Resources Manager. **World Wide Web address:** http://www.taxware.com. **Description:** Develops a line of tax software. **Positions advertised include:** Business Development Director Systems Analyst; Marketing Director; Ohio Regional Sales Manager; Telemarketer; New England Regional Sales Manager; Database Administrator; Software Engineer; Research Lead Tax Counsel.

TECHNICAL COMMUNICATIONS CORPORATION (TCC)
100 Domino Drive, Concord MA 01742. 978/287-5100. **Fax:** 978/287-4475. **Contact:** Personnel. **E-mail address:** tccjobs@tccsecure.com. **World Wide Web address:** http://www.tccsecure.com. **Description:** Technical Communications Corporation designs, manufactures, and sells communications security devices and systems. Products include the Cipher family of encryption devices, which protect computer terminals with an encryption key that needs to be changed on a regular basis; and KEYNET key management system, which is an advanced system that permits geographically dispersed data networks to be managed economically and safely from a single secured site. The KEYNET system provides an electronic courier to distribute the keys automatically, securely, cost effectively, and invisibly. KEYNET protects and manages the sensitive data traveling between U.S. government agencies on government networks. **Positions advertised include:** Embedded Software Engineer. **Corporate headquarters location:** This location. **Annual sales/revenues:** $11 - $20 million. **Number of employees at this location:** 65.

TELCO SYSTEMS
2 Hampshire Street, Suite 3A, Foxboro MA 02035-2897. 781/551-0300. **Contact:** Human Resources. **World Wide Web address:** http://www.telco.com. **Description:** Develops, manufactures, and markets fiber-optic transmission products, customer premises network access products, and LAN/WAN internetworking products. Applications include voice, data, and video communication networks. Primary customers are independent telephone companies, resellers, competitive access providers, interexchange carriers, and corporate end users. **Positions advertised include:** Design Engineer; Verification Engineer; Automotive Design Engineer; Commercial Manager;

Country Manager; Customer Support Engineer; Database Software Engineer; Marketing Communication Director; Elearning Developer; Financial Analyst; GUI Software Developer. **Corporate headquarters location:** This location.

3COM CORPORATION
350 Campus Drive, Marlborough MA 01752. 508/323-5000. **Contact:** Human Resources. **World Wide Web address:** http://www.3com.com. **Description:** 3Com is a *Fortune* 500 company delivering global data networking solutions to organizations around the world. 3Com designs, manufactures, markets, and supports a broad range of ISO 9000-compliant global data networking solutions including routers, hubs, remote access servers, switches, and adapters for Ethernet, Token Ring, and high-speed networks. These products enable computers to communicate at high speeds and share resources including printers, disk drives, modems, and minicomputers. **Corporate headquarters location:** This location. **Listed on:** NASDAQ. **Stock exchange symbol:** COMS. **Annual sales/revenues:** More than $100 million. **Number of employees worldwide:** 1,800.

3M TOUCH SYSTEMS
501 Griffin Brook Park Drive, Methuen MA 01844. 978/659-9000. **Fax:** 978/659-9100. **Contact:** Human Resources Manager. **World Wide Web address:** http://www.3mtouch.com. **Description:** 3M Touch Systems is a manufacturer of touch-screen systems. Products are used in a broad range of applications including point-of-sale terminals, self-service kiosks, gaming machines, industrial systems, ATMs, multimedia applications, and many other computer-based systems. MicroTouch also manufactures and markets TouchPen, a touch- and pen-sensitive digitizer used for pen-based and whiteboarding applications; TouchMate, a pressure-sensitive pad that makes any monitor placed on it touch-sensitive; and ThruGlass, a product that can sense a touch through up to two inches of glass, allowing kiosks to be placed behind store windows for 24-hour access. **Listed on:** New York Stock Exchange. **Stock exchange symbol:** MMM.

TITAN CORPORATION
12 Oak Park Drive, Bedford MA 01730. 781/266-5550. **Contact:** Human Resources. **World Wide Web address:** http://www.titan.com. **Description:** Provides software systems, services, and products to a broad base of customers around the world. The company specializes in language design and programmer productivity tools; digital signal processing tools and application; hardware and system simulation; computer and network security; guidance, navigation, and control; and information systems integration.

TURBINE INC.
60 Glazier Drive, Westwood MA 02090. 781/320-8222. **Fax:** 781/329-5463. **Contact:** Human Resources. **World Wide Web address:** http://www.turbine.com. **Description:** A leading producer and publisher of multiplayer online games. **Other U.S. locations:** Santa Monica CA.

UNISYS CORPORATION
154 Middlesex Turnpike, Burlington MA 01803. 781/238-1300. **Contact:** Human Resources. **World Wide Web address:** http://www.unisys.com. **Description:** Provides information services, technology, and software. Unisys Corporation specializes in developing critical business solutions based on open information networks. The company's Enabling Software Team creates a variety of software projects that facilitate the building of user applications and the management of distributed systems. The company's Platforms Group is responsible for UNIX Operating Systems running across a wide range of multiple processor server

platforms including all peripheral and communication drivers. The Unisys Commercial Parallel Processing Team develops microkernel-based operating systems, I/O device drivers, ATM hardware, diagnostics, and system architectures. The System Management Group is in charge of the overall management of development programs for UNIX desktop and entry-server products. **Positions advertised include:** System Architect. **Corporate headquarters location:** Blue Bell PA. **Other U.S. locations:** Nationwide. **Listed on:** New York Stock Exchange. **Stock exchange symbol:** UIS.

VIRYANET
2 Willow Street, Southborough MA 01745. 508/490-8600. **Contact:** Human Resources Department. **E-mail address:** jobs@viryanet.com. **World Wide Web address:** http://www.viryanet.com. **Description:** Develops field management system software for large organizations. **Positions advertised include:** Sales; Pre Sales; Sales Engineering; Product Management; Project Management; Software Engineer; Product Marketer.

WEBHIRE, INC.
91 Hartwell Avenue, Lexington MA 02421. 781/869-5000. **Fax:** 781/869-5050. **Contact:** Human Resources. **World Wide Web address:** http://www.webhire.com. **Description:** Manufactures and sells software that sorts and ranks resumes by criteria selected by the resume screener. **Positions advertised include:** Staff Accountant; Strategic Process Consultant; Vice President Client Services & Operations; Lead Development Representative. **Corporate headquarters location:** This location. **Listed on:** Privately held.

XYVISION ENTERPRISE SOLUTIONS, INC.
30 New Crossing Road, Reading MA 01867. 781/756-4400. **Fax:** 781/756-4330. **Contact:** Diane Lambas, Human Resources. **World Wide Web address:** http://www.xyvision.com. **Description:** Develops and supports software for document management, publishing, and prepress applications worldwide. The company combines its software with standard computer hardware, selected third-party software, and support services to create integrated systems that improve productivity and strategic position. **Corporate headquarters location:** This location.

YANTRA
One Park West, Tewksbury MA 01876. 978/513-6000. Toll-free phone: 888/292-6872. **Fax:** 978/513-6006. **Contact:** Human Resources. **E-mail address:** Human_Resources@yantra.com. **World Wide Web address:** http://www.yantra.com. **Description:** Yantra provides software for fulfillment solutions for the retail, wholesale distribution, logistics, communications and manufacturing industries. **Positions advertised include:** Software Architect.

ZOOM TELEPHONICS INC.
207 South Street, Boston MA 02111. 617/423-1072. **Fax:** 617/423-2836. **Contact:** Karen Player, Director of Human Resources. **E-mail address:** hr@zoom.com. **World Wide Web address:** http://www.zoomtel.com. **Description:** Designs, produces, and markets internal, external, and PCMCIA modems and fax modems. **Positions advertised include:** Accountant/Auditor; Design Engineer; Industrial Engineer; Mechanical Engineer; MIS Specialist; Software Engineer; Technical Writer/Editor. **Corporate headquarters location:** This location. **Listed on:** NASDAQ. **Stock exchange symbol:** ZOOM. **Annual sales/revenues:** $51 - $100 million. **Number of employees at this location:** 320.

EDUCATIONAL SERVICES

You can expect to find the following types of companies in this section:
Business/Secretarial/Data Processing Schools •
Colleges/Universities/Professional Schools • Community Colleges/Technical Schools/Vocational Schools • Elementary and Secondary Schools • Preschool and Child Daycare Services

---

AMERICAN INTERNATIONAL COLLEGE
1000 State Street, Springfield MA 01109. 413/737-7000. **Contact:** Human Resources. **World Wide Web address:** http://www.aic.edu. **Description:** A private, independent, coeducational college with approximately 1,200 undergraduate and 800 graduate and part-time students. The college offers more than 35 majors within the schools of Arts and Sciences, Business Administration, Psychology and Education, and Health Sciences. **Positions advertised include:** Non Credit Program Manager; Student Activities Director; Political Science Assistant Professor.

ANNA MARIA COLLEGE
50 Sunset Lane, Paxton MA 01612-1198. 508/849-3398. **Toll-free phone:** 800/344-4586. **Fax:** 508/849-3319. **Contact:** Human Resources. **E-mail address:** ldriscoll@annamaria.edu. **World Wide Web address:** http://www.annamaria.edu. **Description:** A nonprofit, private, liberal arts college for women offering both undergraduate and graduate degrees. Founded in 1947. **NOTE:** Entry-level positions and part-time jobs are offered. **Special programs:** Internships; Summer Jobs. **Office hours:** Monday - Friday, 8:30 a.m. - 4:30 p.m. **President:** William McGarry. **Facilities Manager:** Paul Chenevert. **Information Systems Manager:** John Price. **Purchasing Manager:** Susan Lynch. **Number of employees at this location:** 165.

ASSUMPTION COLLEGE
P.O. Box 15005, Worcester MA 01615-0005. 508/767-7000. **Fax:** 508/756-1780. **Contact:** Human Resources. **E-mail address:** resumes@assumption.edu. **World Wide Web address:** http://www.assumption.edu. **Description:** A Catholic college with an undergraduate enrollment of approximately 1,600 students. Approximately 1,200 students are enrolled in graduate and continuing education programs. The college also offers a Center for Continuing and Professional Education, which grants associate's and bachelor's degrees on a part-time basis; The French Institute, an academic research facility and a center for French cultural activities; and the Institute for Social and Rehabilitation Services. Founded in 1904. **Positions advertised include:** Annual Giving Director; Graduate Assistant for Student Activities; Resident Director; Area Coordinator; Assistant Director of Athletics for Sports Medicine. **Corporate headquarters location:** This location.

BABSON COLLEGE
Nichols Hall, Babson Park MA 02457. 781/239-4121. **Contact:** Human Resources. **E-mail address:** jobs@babson.edu. **World Wide Web address:** http://www.babson.edu. **Description:** A four-year business college with an enrollment of approximately 1,700 undergraduate students and 1,730 graduate students. **Positions advertised include:** Undergraduate Student Accounts

Coordinator; Financial Accounting Coordinator; Corporate Outreach Manager; Reserve Librarian.

BAY STATE SCHOOL OF TECHNOLOGY
225 Turnpike Street, Canton MA 02021. 781/828-3434. **Toll-free phone:** 888/828-3434. **Fax:** 781/575-0089. **Contact:** Human Resources. **E-mail address:** bssanet@ultranet.com. **World Wide Web address:** http://users.rcn.com/bssanet. **Description:** A technical institute offering programs in electronics, HVAC, and computers. **Positions advertised include:** Electronics Instructor; Major Appliance Instructor.

BECKER COLLEGE
61 Sever Street, Box 15071, Worcester MA 01609-2195. 508/791-9241. **Toll-free phone:** 877/5BECKER. **Fax:** 508/849-5275. **Contact:** Kathy Garvey, Director of Human Resources. **E-mail address:** kgarvey@becker.edu. **World Wide Web address:** http://www.beckercollege.com. **Description:** Offers a variety of associate's and bachelor's degrees, and certificate programs in business, law, computers, health, education, and social sciences. **Positions advertised include:** Nursing Faculty; Library Supervisor; Adjunct Faculty.

BENTLEY COLLEGE
175 Forest Street, Waltham MA 02452-4705. 781/891-3427. **Fax:** 781/891-2494. **Contact:** Joseph Salvucci, Senior Human Resources Business Partner. **World Wide Web address:** http://www.bentley.edu. **Description:** A business college offering undergraduate and graduate programs, as well as professional development certificates. The college offers associate's, bachelor's, and master's (including MBAs) degrees. **Positions advertised include:** Associate Director of Corporate Relations; Communication Designer; Assistant Director of Development; Receptionist; Campus Police Officer; Dispatcher; Records Coordinator; Work Order Control Assistant; Behavioral & Political Sciences Faculty; CIS Faculty; English Faculty; History Faculty; International Studies Faculty; Media Studies Faculty; Philosophy Faculty.

BERKLEE COLLEGE OF MUSIC
1140 Boylston Street, Boston MA 02215. 617/266-1400. **Fax:** 617/247-0166. **Contact:** Employee Relations Manager. **World Wide Web address:** http://www.berklee.edu. **Description:** An independent music college offering four-year programs of study in composition, film scoring, music business/management, music education, music production and engineering, music synthesis, music therapy, and performance. The college enrolls 3,000 students. **Positions advertised include:** Assistant Chair; Stage Manager; Assistant Vice President for Berklee Media; Course Developer; Continuing Education Registrar; Lab Monitor; Harmony Department Chair; Front Desk Supervisor. **Corporate headquarters location:** This location. **Number of employees at this location:** 170.

BOSTON COLLEGE
140 Commonwealth Avenue, More Hall, Room 315, Chestnut Hill MA 02467. 617/552-3330. **Contact:** Human Resources. **World Wide Web address:** http://www.bc.edu/. **Description:** A private, four-year, Jesuit college offering bachelor's and master's degree programs. **Positions advertised include:** Administrative Secretary; Administrative Coordinator; General Service Worker; Development Secretary; Staff Assistant; Research Director; Sales Assistant; Second Cook; Digital Media Producer; Associate Dean; Gate Attendant; Classroom Technology Specialist.

BOSTON UNIVERSITY

25 Buick Street, Boston MA 02215. 617/353-2380. **Contact:** Human Resources. **World Wide Web address:** http://www.bu.edu/. **Description:** A private, four-year university offering both undergraduate and graduate degrees. **Positions advertised include:** Administrative Assistant; Patient Coordinator; Research Administrative Assistant; Data Technician; Admissions Officer; Clinical Operations Manager; Program Manager; Research Administrator; Community Liaison; Project Coordinator; Data Manager; Executive Secretary; Program Coordinator. **Corporate headquarters location:** This location.

BRANDEIS UNIVERSITY

Mail Stop 118, P.O. Box 9110, Waltham MA 02454-9110. 781/736-4473. **Fax:** 781/736-4466. **Contact:** Employment Administrator. **World Wide Web address:** http://www.brandeis.edu. **Description:** A four-year university offering both undergraduate and graduate programs of study. **Positions advertised include:** Assistant Controller; Executive Director of Intellectual Properties; Director of Athletics; Advancement Services Director; Research Analyst; Lab Coordinator; Lab Technician; Administrative Assistant; Cashier; University Police Officer. **Corporate headquarters location:** This location. **Number of employees at this location:** 1,300.

BRIDGEWATER STATE COLLEGE

Boyden Hall, Room 103, Offices of Human Resources, Bridgewater MA 02325. 508/697-1324. **Fax:** 508/531-1725. **Contact:** Human Resources. **E-mail address:** humres@bridgew.edu. **World Wide Web address:** http://www.bridgew.edu. **Description:** A four-year state college offering a variety of undergraduate and graduate degree programs. **Positions advertised include:** Vice President Student Affairs; Head Women's Tennis Coach; Bookkeeper; Clerk. **Special programs:** Internships. **Number of employees at this location:** 900.

CAMBRIDGE COLLEGE

1000 Massachusetts Avenue, Cambridge MA 02138. 617/873-0100. **Toll-free phone:** 888/868-1002. **Contact:** Human Resources. **World Wide Web address:** http://www.cambridgecollege.edu. **Description:** A college offering bachelor's and master's degrees for adult psychology students.

CAPE COD COMMUNITY COLLEGE

2240 Iyanough Road, West Barnstable MA 02668. 508/362-2131. **Toll-free phone:** 877/846-3672. **Fax:** 508/362-3988. **Contact:** Human Resources. **E-mail address:** info@capecod.mass.edu. **World Wide Web address:** http:///www.capecod.mass.edu. **Description:** A two-year college offering associate degrees. **Positions advertised include:** Program Assistant; Special Program Coordinator; Part Time Faculty; Associate Academic Dean.

CATHOLIC CHARITIES
EL CENTRO DEL CARDENAL

76 Union Park Street, Boston MA 02118. 617/542-9292. **Contact:** Human Resources. **Description:** A social service agency. Services include career counseling, alternative education, immigration refugee services and relief, family guidance, shelter and ministry programs, substance abuse services, and English-as-a-Second-Language (ESL) programs.

CLARK UNIVERSITY

950 Main Street, Worcester MA 01610. 508/793-7294. **Fax:** 508/793-8809. **Contact:** Human Resources Department. **E-mail address:**

resumes@clarku.edu. **World Wide Web address:** http://www.clarku.edu. **Description:** A four-year research university offering bachelor's, master's, and doctoral degrees. The student body consists of approximately 2,200 graduate and undergraduate students. During the summer the College of Professional and Continuing Education (C.O.P.A.C.E.) program offers select classes for credit or personal enrichment. **NOTE:** Entry-level positions and part-time jobs are offered. **Positions advertised include:** Assistant Director of Admissions; Office Assistant; Assistant Director; Area Coordinator; Director of Major Gifts. **Office hours:** Monday - Friday, 8:30 a.m. - 4:30 p.m. **Other area locations:** Framingham MA.

CLARK UNIVERSITY
COMPUTER CAREER INSTITUTE
10 California Avenue, Framingham MA 01701. 508/620-5904. **Toll-free phone:** 800/568-1776. **Fax:** 508/875-7285. **Contact:** Human Resources. **Description:** Offers a variety of computer-related courses designed to help people reentering the workforce. Certificates are awarded at the end of 9 to 12 week daytime class sessions, or 6 to 7 month evening class sessions.

CURRY COLLEGE
1071 Blue Hill Avenue, Milton MA 02186. 617/333-0500. **Contact:** Human Resources. **World Wide Web address:** http://www.curry.edu. **Description:** A four-year liberal arts college with programs for undergraduate and graduate students. **Positions advertised include:** Graduate Education Faculty; Assistant Director Financial Aide; Enrollment Representative; Assistant Director Admissions; Public Safety Officer

EMERSON COLLEGE
120 Boylston Street, Boston MA 02116. 617/824-8500. **Contact:** Human Resources. **World Wide Web address:** http://www.emerson.edu. **E-mail address:** employment@emerson.edu. **Description:** A four-year communications college offering both undergraduate and graduate degrees to approximately 2,000 students. **Positions advertised include:** Associate Vice President; College Counsel; Assistant Director; Head Women's Soccer Coach; Social Worker; Education Technologist; Loading Dock Supervisor; Public Safety Officer; Journalism Technology Manager; Student Service Advisor; Multi-cultural Student Affairs Director. **Special programs:** Internships. **Corporate headquarters location:** This location. **Operations at this facility include:** Administration. **Number of employees at this location:** 350.

EMMANUEL COLLEGE
400 The Fenway, Boston MA 02115. 617/735-9991. **Fax:** 617/735-9877. **Contact:** Human Resources. **E-mail address:** jobs@emaunuel.edu. **World Wide Web address:** http://www.emmanuel.edu. **Description:** A four-year undergraduate college. **Positions advertised include:** Site Coordinator; Director of the Annual Fund; Assistant Director of Corporate; Development Assistant; Web Designer; Graphic Designer; Assistant Professor.

FISHER COLLEGE
118 Beacon Street, Boston MA 02116. 617/536-4647. **Contact:** Human Resources. **World Wide Web address:** http://www.fisher.edu. **Description:** A private junior college. **Positions advertised include:** Administrative Assistant; Associate Registrar; Dean of Student Affairs; Campus Safety Officer; Director for Annual Giving. **Other in-state locations:** Fall River; New Bedford; Attleboro Falls.

FITCHBURG STATE COLLEGE

160 Pearl Street, Fitchburg MA 01420. 978/345-2151. **Contact:** Human Resources. **E-mail address:** resumes@fsc.edu. **World Wide Web address:** http://www.fsc.edu. **Description:** A state college offering bachelor's and master's degrees. **Positions advertised include:** Assistant Professor, Special Education; Assistant/Associate Professor, Criminal Justice; Assistant Professor, Industrial Technology.

FRAMINGHAM STATE COLLEGE

100 State Street, Framingham MA 01701-9101. 508/626-4530. **Fax:** 508/626-4592. **Contact:** Human Resources. **World Wide Web address:** http://www.framingham.edu. **Description:** Founded as the first public teacher's college in the country, Framingham State has grown to include 28 majors in undergraduate, graduate, and continuing education programs with an emphasis on business administration, and elementary and early childhood education. Framingham State's nationally recognized faculty is involved in many community and professional organizations. Learning resources include an advising center, the MetroWest Economic Research Center, modern computer facilities, and a planetarium. Founded in 1839. **Positions advertised include:** Director of Health Services; Distance Education Program Clerical; Office of Residential Life Maintainer; Office of Residential Life Trade Worker; Steam Firemen; Skilled Laborer; HVAC Mechanic; Communications Dispatcher.

GORDON COLLEGE

255 Grapevine Road, Wenham MA 01984. 978/927-2300. **Contact:** Human Resources. **World Wide Web address:** http://www.gordon.edu. **Description:** A four-year liberal arts college offering Bachelor of Science, Bachelor of Arts, Bachelor of Music, and Master of Education degrees. **Positions advertised include:** Head Women's Soccer Coach; Director of Communications; Public Safety Officer.

HARVARD UNIVERSITY

11 Holyoke Street, Harvard Square, Cambridge MA 02138. 617/495-2771. **Contact:** Personnel. **World Wide Web address:** http://www.hr.harvard.edu/employment. **Description:** A private, four-year, Ivy League university. Harvard University collaborates with nearby Radcliffe College, allowing graduate and undergraduate students to take certain classes at Radcliffe and vice versa. **Positions advertised include:** Special Assistant to the President; Facility Manager; Payroll Accountant; Staff Assistant. **NOTE:** Harvard University posts listings for all support and professional job openings. Please check these listings in the employment office or on Harvard University's website and respond directly to the department that is hiring. **Office hours:** Monday, Tuesday, Wednesday, Friday, 11:00 a.m. - 4:00 p.m.; Thursday, 8:30 a.m. - 6:00 p.m.

HEBREW COLLEGE

160 Herrick Street, Newton Centre MA 02459. 617/559-8600. **Toll-free phone:** 800/866-4814. **Fax:** 617/559-8601. **Contact:** Human Resources Department. **E-mail address:** hr@hebrewcollege.edu. **World Wide Web address:** http://www.hebrewcollege.edu. **Description:** A college offering courses in the Hebrew language and literature, Rabbinics, and Jewish music and culture. The college offers courses in cooperation with Boston University, Northeastern University, Simmons College, Boston College, Brandeis University, and University of Massachusetts Boston. **Positions advertised include:** Vice President of Institutional Achievement; Database Depart Writer.

COLLEGE OF THE HOLY CROSS
One College Street, Worcester MA 01610. 508/793-3756. **Fax:** 508/793-3575. **Contact:** Director of Personnel. **E-mail address:** resumes@holycross.edu. **World Wide Web address:** http://www.holycross.edu. **Description:** A private, four-year college offering bachelor's and master's degree programs. **Positions advertised include:** Dining Room Manager; Assistant Director; Community Development Coordinator; Applications Administrator; Vice President Administrative & Finance. **Special programs:** Internships. **Operations at this facility include:** Administration; Sales; Service. **Number of employees at this location:** 800.

KATHARINE GIBBS SCHOOL
126 Newbury Street, Boston MA 02116. 617/578-7100. **Toll-free phone:** 800/6SK-ILLS. **Contact:** Human Resources. **World Wide Web address:** http://www.katharinegibbs.com. **Description:** One of the nation's foremost business instruction schools. Founded in 1911. **Other U.S. locations:** Nationwide.

LESLEY UNIVERSITY
29 Everett Street, Cambridge MA 02138-2890. 617/349-8787. **Toll-free phone:** 800/999-1959. **Contact:** Maryanne Gallagher, Associate Director of Human Resources. **World Wide Web address:** http://www.lesley.edu. **Description:** A private, four-year university offering an undergraduate liberal arts program and a variety of graduate and doctoral degree programs including arts, education, management, and social sciences. **Positions advertised include:** Assistant Director of Financial Aide; Assistant Professor of Mathematics; Conference Assistant; Administrative Assistant; Director of Health Services; Certification Officer; Graphic Design Faculty; Customer Care Coordinator; Administrative Assistant. **Listed on:** Privately held. **Number of employees at this location:** 400. **Number of employees nationwide:** 450.

MIT (MASSACHUSETTS INSTITUTE OF TECHNOLOGY)
400 Main Street, 2nd Floor, Cambridge MA 02142. 617/253-4251. **Contact:** Human Resources. **World Wide Web address:** http://web.mit.edu/personnel. **Description:** A private, four-year academic and research institution with an enrollment of approximately 4,300 undergraduate students and 5,600 graduate students. **Positions advertised include:** Administrative Assistant; Associate Counsel; Chief Radiological Technician; Circulation Assistant; Computational Biologist; Departmental Liaison; Mechanic; Member Relations Representative; Post Doctoral Associate; Research Scientist; Software Engineer; Staff Accountant; Technical Assistant. **Office hours:** Monday - Friday, 9:00 a.m. - 5:00 p.m. **NOTE:** Send resumes to P.O. Box 391229, Cambridge MA 02139.

MASSACHUSETTS COLLEGE OF ART
621 Huntington Avenue, Boston MA 02115. 617/232-1555. **Fax:** 617/879-7911. **Contact:** Human Resources. **World Wide Web address:** http://www.massart.edu. **Description:** An art school offering multimedia courses in a variety of disciplines including photography and painting.

MASSASOIT COMMUNITY COLLEGE
One Massasoit Boulevard, Brockton MA 02302. 508/588-9100. **Toll-free phone:** 800/CAR-EERS. **Contact:** Personnel. **World Wide Web address:** http://www.massasoit.mass.edu. **Description:** A community college offering a variety of two-year programs. **Other area locations:** Canton MA, **NOTE:** Call 781/821-2222 for Canton Campus.

MOUNT HOLYOKE COLLEGE
50 College Street, South Hadley MA 01075. **Contact:** Human Resources. **World Wide Web address:** http://www.mtholyoke.edu. **Description:** A private, four-year college offering a variety of programs for undergraduate and graduate students. **Positions advertised include:** Director of Administrative Computing; Public Safety Officer; Director of Financial Assistance; Class Dean; Administrative Assistant; Coordinator of Educational Opportunities Abroad; Academic Computer Support Specialist; Director of Residential Life; Counseling Service Postdoctoral Clinician; Research Assistant in Educational Psychology; Laboratory Director Introductory Physics; Coordinator of Multicultural Affairs; Director of Equestrian Center; Payroll Specialist.

NATIONAL EVALUATION SYSTEMS
30 Gatehouse Road, Amherst MA 01002. 413/256-0444. **Contact:** Personnel Director. **E-mail address:** personnel@nesinc.com. **World Wide Web address:** http://www.nesinc.com. **Description:** A contract-based company providing educational products and services in a variety of areas including professional licensing and certification testing programs, large-scale pupil assessment, and print-based educational materials. Clients include state departments of education and professional licensing boards. **Positions advertised include:** Project Director; Statistical Programmer/Analyst; Project Assistant. **Corporate headquarters location:** This location. **Other U.S. locations:** Sacramento CA; Austin TX. **Operations at this facility include:** Administration; Research and Development; Service.

NEW ENGLAND COLLEGE OF FINANCE
One Lincoln Plaza, 89 South Street, Boston MA 02111. 617/951-2350. **Fax:** 617/951-2533. **Contact:** Personnel. **E-mail address:** info@finance.edu. **World Wide Web address:** http://www.finance.edu. **Description:** A college offering associate's degrees, bachelor's degrees, and certificate courses in the areas of finance, banking, and insurance. Founded in 1909.

NEW ENGLAND CONSERVATORY OF MUSIC
290 Huntington Avenue, Boston MA 02115. 617/585-1230. **Contact:** Human Resources. **World Wide Web address:** http://www.newenglandconservatory.edu. **Description:** A music school. New England Conservatory of Music also operates a preparatory school and offers continuing education classes for students of all levels. **Positions advertised include:** Composition Faculty; Music Theory Faculty; Academic Training; Executive Director of Development; Office Manager; Major Gifts Officer; Technology Support Specialist.

NICHOLS COLLEGE
P.O. Box 5000, Dudley MA 01571-5000. 508/943-2055. **Toll-free phone:** 800/470-3379. **Contact:** Rick Woods, Director of Human Resources. **E-mail address:** rick.woods@nichols.edu. **World Wide Web address:** http://www.nichols.edu. **Description:** A private, coeducational, liberal arts college known for business education with an enrollment of 700 undergraduates. Founded in 1815. **Positions advertised include:** Office Assistant.

NORTHEASTERN UNIVERSITY
360 Huntington Avenue, 250 Columbus Place, Boston MA 02115. 617/373-2230. **Contact:** Human Resources. **World Wide Web address:** http://www.neu.edu. **Description:** A university operating through several colleges and programs including the College of Arts and Science, the Boston Bouve College of Pharmacy and Health Professions, the Graduate School of Business

Administration, a law school, part-time evening programs, and graduate, professional, and continuing education courses. **Positions advertised include:** Spanish Instructor; Math Instructor; Science Instructor; Math SAT Instructor; Decision Making Instructor; Recreational Coordinator; Current Events Instructor; English SAT Instructor; English Instructor; Assistant Residential Director; Administration Coordinator; Grants & Contract Specialist; Carpentry & Lockshop Supervisor. **Corporate headquarters location:** This location. **Other area locations:** Burlington MA; Dedham MA.

QUINCY COLLEGE
34 Coddington Street, Quincy MA 02169. 617/984-1600. **Contact:** Steve McGrath, Human Resources. **E-mail address:** smcgrath@quincycollege.edu. **World Wide Web address:** http://www.quincycollege.edu. **Description:** A two-year commuter college. Quincy College's combined full-time and part-time student enrollment is 5,000.

RADCLIFFE INSTITUTE FOR ADVANCED STUDY
10 Garden Street, Faye House, Room 106, Cambridge MA 02138. 617/495-8608. **Fax:** 617/496-0255. **Contact:** Human Resources. **E-mail address:** info@radcliffe.edu. **World Wide Web address:** http://www.radcliffe.edu. **Description:** A college offering both graduate and undergraduate programs. Radcliffe Institute for Advanced Study was established as a result of the merger of Radcliffe College with Harvard University.

REGIS COLLEGE
Box 4, 235 Wellesley Street, Weston MA 02493. 781/768-7210. **Contact:** Human Resources. **World Wide Web address:** http://www.regiscollege.edu. **Description:** A private liberal arts and sciences college for women. Founded in 1927.

SALEM STATE COLLEGE
352 Lafayette Street, Salem MA 01970. 978/542-6000. **Contact:** Human Resources. **E-mail address:** eo-hr@salemstate.edu. **World Wide Web address:** http://www.salemstate.edu. **Description:** A state college.

SIMMONS COLLEGE
300 The Fenway, Boston MA 02115-5898. 617/521-2000. **Contact:** Human Resources. **World Wide Web address:** http://www.simmons.edu. **Description:** A private, four-year, liberal arts and sciences college for women. The college also offers 12 graduate programs for both men and women. The total graduate enrollment is approximately 2,000.

SINNOTT SCHOOL
210 Winter Street, Suite 204, Weymouth MA 02188. 781/331-6769. **Contact:** Human Resources. **World Wide Web address:** http://www.sinnottschool.com. **Description:** A computer training school offering classes in Microsoft Office and other applications. Clients are both individuals and corporations. The Microsoft Office curriculum includes Windows, NT, Microsoft Word, Excel, Access, and PowerPoint. Classes are held both on-site as well as at corporate locations. Sinnott School offers long-term day courses as well as half- and full-day courses.

STONEHILL COLLEGE
320 Washington Street, Easton MA 02357. 508/565-1000. **Contact:** Human Resources. **E-mail address:** employment_ervices@stonehill.edu. **World Wide Web address:** http://www.stonehill.edu. **Description:** A private, four-year,

Catholic college. Stonehill offers liberal arts programs to approximately 2,000 undergraduate students.

SUFFOLK UNIVERSITY
8 Ashburton Place, Boston MA 02108. 617/573-8415. **Fax:** 617/367-2250. **Contact:** Judy Minardi, Director of Human Resources. **E-mail address:** jobs@suffolk.edu. **World Wide Web address:** http://www.suffolk.edu. **Description:** A four-year university. Suffolk University's Frank Sawyer School of Management offers an Executive MBA program. Suffolk University also houses a law school. **Positions advertised include:** Assistant Director; Leadership Giving Officer.

TUFTS UNIVERSITY
169 Holland Street, Somerville MA 02144. 617/627-3272. **Fax:** 617/627-3725. **Contact:** Human Resources. **World Wide Web address:** http://www.tufts.edu. **Description:** Offers both undergraduate and graduate programs through the schools of arts and sciences; Fletcher School of Law and Diplomacy; medical, dental, and veterinary schools; and a human nutrition research center. **Other area locations:** Boston MA.

UNIVERSITY OF MASSACHUSETTS/AMHERST
167 Whitmore Administration Building, Amherst MA 01003. 413/545-1396. **Contact:** Employment Office. **World Wide Web address:** http://www.umass.edu/humres. **Description:** The main campus of the four-year, state university. **Other U.S. locations:** Boston MA; North Dartmouth MA; Lowell MA.

UNIVERSITY OF MASSACHUSETTS/BOSTON
100 Morrissey Boulevard, Boston MA 02125-3393. 617/287-5150. **Fax:** 617/287-5179. **Contact:** Human Resources. **World Wide Web address:** http://www.umb.edu. **Description:** A campus of the four-year, state university offering approximately 90 fields of study to over 12,000 students. **Other area locations:** Amherst MA; North Dartmouth MA; Lowell MA. **Number of employees at this location:** 1,800.

UNIVERSITY OF MASSACHUSETTS/DARTMOUTH
285 Old Westport Road, North Dartmouth MA 02747-2300. 508/999-8060. **Contact:** Todd Swarts, Director of Human Resources. **World Wide Web address:** http://www.umassd.edu. **Description:** A campus of the four-year, state university offering graduate and undergraduate programs to approximately 6,000 students. **Other area locations:** Amherst MA; Boston MA; Lowell MA.

UNIVERSITY OF MASSACHUSETTS/LOWELL
883 Broadway Street, Room 101, Lowell MA 01854. 978/934-3555. **Contact:** Human Resources. **World Wide Web address:** http://www.uml.edu. **Description:** A campus of the four-year, state university. University of Massachusetts/Lowell offers undergraduate majors in a variety of disciplines including engineering, computer technology, sales, business, sciences, education, health professions, human services, liberal arts, and music. The college also offers post-graduate certificate programs in paralegal studies, electronics technology, packaging, data/telecommunications, technical writing, purchasing management, quality assurance, and wastewater treatment. **NOTE:** Each fall (and sometimes in the spring) UMass/Lowell hosts a business and technology career fair. For more information, visit the UMass/Lowell Career Services Website at http://ocs.uml.edu. **Other area locations:** Amherst MA; Boston MA; North Dartmouth MA.

WELLESLEY COLLEGE
106 Central Street, Wellesley MA 02481. 781/235-0320. **Contact:** Human Resources. **World Wide Web address:** http://www.wellesley.edu. **Description:** A private liberal arts college for women. **Positions advertised include:** Vice President for Finance Treasurer; Director of Admission; Campus Police Office; Science Librarian; Director of International Studies; Residential Director.

WENTWORTH INSTITUTE OF TECHNOLOGY
550 Huntington Avenue, Boston MA 02115-5998. 617/989-4590. **Fax:** 617/989-4195. **Contact:** Anne Gill, Associate Vice President of Human Resources. **World Wide Web address:** http://www.wit.edu. **Description:** A technical university noted for its strengths in engineering, science, technology, and design. Total student enrollment is approximately 3,000. Founded in 1904. **Positions advertised include:** Student Services Representative; Assistant Director of Alumni Relations; Provost; Architecture Faculty; Laboratory Technician; Academic Department Head; Career Planning Coordinator; Co-op Coordinator; Assistant Director of Student Undergraduate Program HVAC B Level Mechanic. **Special programs:** Internships. **Corporate headquarters location:** This location. **Number of employees at this location:** 380.

WHEATON COLLEGE
26 East Main Street, Norton MA 02766. 508/285-7722. **Fax:** 508/286-8262. **Recorded jobline:** 508/286-3547. **Contact:** Barbara Lema. Director of Human Resources. **E-mail address:** hr@wheatoncollege.edu. **World Wide Web address:** http://www.wheatonma.edu. **Description:** A private, coed, four-year college. **Positions advertised include:** Program Coordinator; Communications Officer; Grounds Helper; Writing Teacher; Quantitative Analysis Instructor.

WHEELOCK COLLEGE
200 The Riverway, Boston MA 02215. 617/734-5200. **Fax:** 6177/879-2000. **Contact:** Human Resources. **E-mail address:** opportunities@wheelock.edu. **World Wide Web address:** http://www.wheelock.edu. **Description:** A small liberal arts college offering both graduate and undergraduate courses of study. **Positions advertised include:** Assistant Professor of Human Development; Associate Professor in Juvenile Justice; Department Chair; Head Field Coach; HVAC Maintenance Mechanic.

WORCESTER POLYTECHNIC INSTITUTE
100 Institute Road, Worcester MA 01609. 508/831-5000. **Fax:** 508/831-5715. **Contact:** Human Resources. **E-mail address:** human-resources@wpi.edu. **World Wide Web address:** http://www.wpi.edu. **Description:** A technical college offering both undergraduate and graduate programs. Founded in 1865. **Positions advertised include:** Instructional Technologist; Accounting Manager; Assistant Director of Annual Giving; Web Applications Director; Assistant Football Coach; Magazine Editor.

WORLDTEACH
Center for International Development, Harvard University, 79 JFK Street, Cambridge MA 02138. 617/495-5527. **Toll-free phone:** 800/4TE-ACH0. **Fax:** 617/495-1599. **Contact:** Director of Recruiting. **E-mail address:** info@worldteach.org. **World Wide Web address:** http://www.worldteach.org. **Description:** A nonprofit organization, based at Harvard University, which places volunteers overseas as teachers in developing countries. Volunteers have served in Asia, Africa, Central America, and Central Europe. Volunteers make a commitment of either six months or one year and pay a program fee of

approximately $4,800. Volunteers must have a bachelor's degree, but no previous teaching or foreign language is required. WorldTeach also runs a summer teaching program in China for undergraduate and graduate students. **Positions advertised include:** Ecuador Summer Field Director.

ELECTRONIC/INDUSTRIAL ELECTRICAL EQUIPMENT AND COMPONENTS

You can expect to find the following types of companies in this section:
Electronic Machines and Systems • Semiconductor Manufacturers

ADE CORPORATION
80 Wilson Way, Westwood MA 02090. 781/467-3500. **Fax:** 781/467-0500. **Contact:** Human Resources. **World Wide Web address:** http://www.ade.com. **Description:** Develops and manufactures measurement and automation equipment for the instrumentation, electronics, and semiconductor markets. **Positions advertised include:** Application Engineering Manager. **NOTE:** Entry-level positions are offered. **Special programs:** Internships. **Corporate headquarters location:** This location. **Other area locations:** Newton MA. **Other U.S. locations:** Tuscon AZ. **Operations at this facility include:** Administration; Divisional Headquarters; Manufacturing; Research and Development; Sales; Service. **Listed on:** NASDAQ. **Stock exchange symbol:** ADEX. **Annual sales/revenues:** $51 - $100 million. **Number of employees at this location:** 200. **Number of employees worldwide:** 600.

AEROVOX, INC.
167 John Vertente Boulevard, New Bedford MA 02745-1221. 508/994-9661. **Fax:** 508/995-3000. **Contact:** Human Resources. **E-mail address:** sales@aerovox.com. **World Wide Web address:** http://www.aerovox.com. **Description:** A manufacturer of capacitors for electrical and electronic applications. **Operations at this facility include:** Manufacturing; Research and Development. **Number of employees nationwide:** 1,300.

ALLEGRO MICROSYSTEMS
115 Northeast Cutoff, P.O. Box 15036, Worcester MA 01615. 508/853-5000. **Contact:** Human Resources. **E-mail address:** allegro@rpc.webhire.com. **World Wide Web address:** http://www.allegromicro.com. **Description:** Manufactures mixed-signal integrated circuits. **Positions advertised include:** Design Engineer; Failure Analysis Engineer; Product Design Engineer; Process Technician; Buyer; .NET Programmer; Analyst; Product Applications Engineer; Product Supervisor.

AMERICAN SUPERCONDUCTOR CORPORATION
Two Technology Drive, Westborough MA 01581. 508/836-4200. **Fax:** 508/836-4248. **Contact:** Human Resources. **E-mail address:** resumes@amsuper.com. **World Wide Web address:** http://www.amsuper.com. **Description:** Manufactures flexible high-temperature superconductor wires, wire products, and systems. Products are incorporated in compact, cost-effective electric power and magnet systems such as power transmission cables, motors, generators, transformers, energy storage devices, and magnetic resonance imaging systems. **Positions advertised include:** Chief Engineer. **Corporate headquarters location:** This location. **Other U.S. locations:** Madison WI; Milwaukee WI. **Subsidiaries include:** American Superconductor Europe GmbH, Germany. **Listed on:** NASDAQ. **Stock exchange symbol:** AMSC. **Number of employees nationwide:** 100.

ANALOG DEVICES, INC.
One Technology Way, P.O. Box 9106, Norwood MA 02062-9106. 781/329-4700.
Contact: Human Resources. **World Wide Web address:**
http://www.analog.com. **Description:** Designs, manufactures, and markets a
broad line of high-performance analog, mixed-signal, and digital integrated
circuits (ICs) that address a wide range of real-world signal processing
applications. The company's principal products include system-level ICs and
general purpose, standard linear ICs. Other products include devices
manufactured using assembled product technology such as hybrids, which
combine unpackaged IC chips and other chip-level components in a single
package. Analog Device's system-level ICs are used predominately in
communications and computer applications. The company's largest
communications application is the pan-European GSM (Global System for Mobile
Communications) digital cellular telephone system. **Positions advertised
include:** Corporate US Business Analyst; Human Resources Director; Layout
Engineering Specialist; NT Web Security Project Leader; PC Support Specialist;
Product Development Engineer; Benefits Analyst; Design Engineer;
Development Engineer; Software Engineer. **Corporate headquarters location:**
This location. **Other U.S. locations:** Nationwide. **International locations:**
Worldwide. **Operations at this facility include:** Administration; Manufacturing;
Research and Development. **Listed on:** New York Stock Exchange. **Stock
exchange symbol:** ADI.

ANALOGIC CORPORATION
8 Centennial Drive, Peabody MA 01960. 978/977-3000. **Fax:** 978/977-6810.
Contact: Human Resources. **World Wide Web address:**
http://www.analogic.com. **Description:** Designs, manufactures, and sells a broad
line of high-precision data-conversion and signal-processing equipment. Principal
customers are original equipment manufacturers who incorporate products into
systems for medical, industrial, and telecommunications applications. The
company's products include measurement, display, and control instruments,
consisting of digital panel instruments, digital test instruments, and industrial
digitizing systems; data acquisition and conversion products, consisting of A/D
and D/A converters, supporting modules, data acquisition systems, and
subsystems; and computer-based products, consisting of medical imaging
equipment and array processors. Founded in 1969. **Company slogan:** The
world resource for precision signal technology. **Positions advertised include:**
Corporate US Business Analyst; Human Resource Director; Layout Engineering
Specialist; PC Support Specialist; Product Development Engineer; Benefits
Analyst; Design Engineer; Development Engineer; Software Engineer. **Special
programs:** Co-ops. **Corporate headquarters location:** This location. **Other
U.S. locations:** WI. **Subsidiaries include:** Anatel Communications Corporation;
B-K Medical A/S; Camtronics Medical Systems; International Security Systems;
SKY Computers. **Listed on:** NASDAQ. **Stock exchange symbol:** ALOG.
Annual sales/revenues: More than $100 million. **Number of employees at this
location:** 1,150. **Number of employees nationwide:** 1,400.

ANDOVER CONTROLS CORPORATION
300 Brickstone Square, Andover MA 01810. 978/470-0555. **Fax:** 978/470-0946.
Contact: Human Resources. **World Wide Web address:**
http://www.andovercontrols.com. **Description:** Manufactures building automation
systems. **Positions advertised include:** Project Engineer; Service Technician.
International locations: Worldwide. **Parent company:** Balfour Beatty.

ARK-LES CORPORATION
95 Mill Street, Stoughton MA 02072. 781/297-6000. **Fax:** 781/297-6160. **Contact:** Human Resources. **World Wide Web address:** http://www.ark-les.com. **Description:** ARK-LES manufactures electrical components and switches. **Corporate headquarters location:** This location. **Other area locations:** Stoughton MA (Manufacturing); Gloucester MA. **Other U.S. locations:** Raleigh NC; New Berlin WI. **International locations:** Guandong, China; Juarez, Mexico.

AXCELIS TECHNOLOGIES
108 Cherry Hill Drive, Beverly MA 01915. 978/921-0750. **Contact:** Human Resources. **World Wide Web address:** http://www.axcelis.com. **Description:** Manufactures ion implanters. **Positions advertised include:** Documentation Contest Specialist; Eco Planner; Electronics Engineer; Group Manager Software; Marketing Analyst; Packaging Engineer; Section Coordinator; Tax Accountant; Telecom Analyst. **Corporate headquarters location:** This location. **Other U.S. locations:** Nationwide. **Listed on:** NASDAQ. **Stock exchange symbol:** ACLS. **Number of employees worldwide:** 64,000.

BAE SYSTEMS
2 Forbes Road, Lexington MA 02421-7306. 781/862-6222. **Contact:** Human Resources. **E-mail:** careers@baesystems.com. **World Wide Web address:** http://www.na.baesystems.com. **Description:** A business unit of the Information and Electronic Systems Integration Sector within BAE SYSTEMS North America. They are a major producer of aircraft self-protection systems and tactical surveillance and intelligence systems. Their products are supplied to all branches of the armed forces. BAE SYSTEMS also produces missile and space electronics; infrared imaging; and automated mission planning systems. **Corporate headquarters location:** Bethesda MD. **Other U.S. locations:** Pomona CA; Hudson NH; Nahua NH; Merrimack NH; Yonkers NY; Arlington VA; Manassas VA. **Number of employees nationwide:** 4,400.

BROOKS AUTOMATION, INC.
15 Elizabeth Drive, Chelmsford MA 01824. 978/262-2400. **Contact:** Human Resources. **E-mail address:** hr@brooks-pri.com. **World Wide Web address:** http://www.brooks-pri.com. **Description:** Manufactures robotic arms, wafer disks, vacuum cassette elevators, and other electronic devices. **Positions advertised include:** Accounts Payable Specialist; Product Marketing Manager; Product Manager; Mechanical Engineer; Mechanical Systems Engineer; Quality Engineer; Sales Account Manager; Software Support Engineer; Software Engineer. **Corporate headquarters location:** This location. **Other U.S. locations:** Nationwide. **International locations:** Worldwide. **Subsidiaries include:** AutoSimulations, Inc.; Auto-Soft Corporation; CCS Technology, Inc.; Daifuku Co., Ltd. Business Unit; Domain Manufacturing Corporation; e-Diagnostics; FASTech Integration, Inc.; Hanyon Technology; INFAB; Irvine Optical Company; MiTeX; Progressive Technologies, Inc.; SEMY Engineering Inc.; SimCon Engineering Inc.; Smart Machines; Techware Systems Corporation. **Listed on:** NASDAQ. **Stock exchange symbol:** BRKS.

BURLE ELECTRO-OPTICS
Sturbridge Business Park, P.O. Box 1159, Sturbridge MA 01566-1159. 508/347-4000. **Contact:** Human Resources. **E-mail address:** rabens@burle.com. **World Wide Web address:** http://www.burle.com. **Description:** Manufactures microchannel plates, flexible fiber optics, and amplifiers. **Corporate headquarters location:** Lancaster PA. **International locations:** England; Germany.

CALIPER LIFE SCIENCES

68 Elm Street, Hopkinton MA 01748. 508/435-9500. **Fax:** 508/497-2685. **Contact:** Human Resources. **World Wide Web address:** http://wwwcaliperts.com. **Description:** Designs and manufactures robots and robotic systems for use in laboratories to speed the discovery process in the biotechnological and pharmaceutical industries. Founded in 1981. **NOTE:** Entry-level positions are offered. **Positions advertised include:** Project Manager; Consumables Business Line Manager. **Special programs:** Internships; Co-ops; Summer Jobs. **Office hours:** Monday - Friday, 8:00 a.m. - 5:00 p.m. **Corporate headquarters location:** This location.

CHASE & SONS

19 Highland Avenue, Randolph MA 02368. 781/963-2600. **Contact:** Human Resources. **World Wide Web address:** http://www.chasecorp.com. **Description:** Produces shielding and binding tapes for electronic and telecommunication cables. **Corporate headquarters location:** Bridgewater MA. **Other U.S. locations:** Webster MA. **Parent company:** Chase Corporation is involved in the manufacture of insulating products. The company's divisions produce and market products worldwide to insulated electric, electronic, and telecommunications cable manufacturers, producers of electronic parts, and to contractors involved in the construction of underground gas and oil pipelines and highway and bridge construction and repairs.

CHASE & SONS

Goya Industrial Park, Cudworth Road, Webster MA 01570. 508/949-6006. **Contact:** Human Resources. **World Wide Web address:** http://www.chasecorp.com. **Description:** Produces shielding and binding tapes for electronic and telecommunication cables. **Corporate headquarters location:** Bridgewater MA. **Other U.S. locations:** Randolph MA. **Parent company:** Chase Corporation is involved in the manufacture of insulating products. The company's divisions produce and market products worldwide to insulated electric, electronic, and telecommunications cable manufacturers, producers of electronic parts, and to contractors involved in the construction of underground gas and oil pipelines and highway and bridge construction and repairs.

CHASE CORPORATION

26 Summer Street, Bridgewater MA 02324. 508/279-1789. **Contact:** Human Resources. **World Wide Web address:** http://www.chasecorp.com. **Description:** Manufactures insulating products. **Corporate headquarters location:** This location. **Subsidiaries include:** Chase & Sons produces shielding and binding tapes for electronics and telecommunications cables; Chase Canada manufactures tapes for electronics, telecommunications, and fiber optic cables as well as specialty tapes and laminates for packaging and industrial applications; Fluid Polymers (Pittsburgh PA) provides sealants, adhesives coating, and dielectric materials for fluid purification and other processes; Sunburst EMS (West Bridgewater MA) manufactures electronics; HumiSeal (Woodside NY) provides insulating conformal coatings, potting compounds, and ancillary products for electronic applications; and Royston (Pittsburgh PA) offers insulating and protective mastics, coatings, and tapes for pipelines, highways, and bridges as well as waterproofing membranes for commercial and residential construction. **Number of employees nationwide:** 145.

DATAMARINE INTERNATIONAL, INC.

4 Barlows Landing Road, Pocasset MA 02559-1984. 508/563-7151. **Contact:** Human Resources. **Description:** Manufactures and markets electronics

including ocean depth sounders, and radio and telephone systems for land and ocean applications.

DATEL INC.
11 Cabot Boulevard, Mansfield MA 02048. 508/339-3000. **Contact:** Human Resources. **World Wide Web address:** http://www.datel.com. **Description:** Manufactures electronic components used in data acquisition. **International locations:** England; France; Germany; Japan.

DIEBOLD, INC.
261 Cedar Hill Road, Marlborough MA 01752. 508/480-6400. **Contact:** Personnel. **E-mail:** hrinfo@diebold.com. **World Wide Web address:** http://www.diebold.com. **Description:** Diebold is engaged in the sale, manufacture, installation, and service of automated teller machines, physical and electronic security systems, and software for the financial and commercial industries. Other products include vaults, vault doors, lockers, safes, alarms, video surveillance systems, and data line security systems. Founded in 1859. **NOTE:** Resumes should be sent to: Human Resources, 5995 Mayfair Road, P.O. Box 3077, North Canton OH 44720-8077. **Corporate headquarters location:** North Canton OH. **Operations at this facility include:** This location is a sales office for the company's MedSelect product line. **Listed on:** New York Stock Exchange. **Stock exchange symbol:** DBD.

DOBLE ENGINEERING COMPANY
85 Walnut Street, Watertown MA 02472. 617/926-4900. **Fax:** 617/926-0528. **Contact:** Human Resources. **E-mail address:** hr@doble.com. **World Wide Web address:** http://www.doble.com. **Description:** Manufactures and repairs circuit breakers and test transformers for utility companies.

E INK CORPORATION
733 Concord Avenue, Cambridge MA 02138. 617/499-6000. **Fax:** 617/234-8450. **Contact:** Human Resources. **E-mail address:** jobs@eink.com. **World Wide Web address:** http://www.eink.com. **Description:** A growth-stage company that commercialized the invention of electronic ink. Founded in 1987. **Positions advertised include:** Polymeric Materials Engineer; Device Performance Scientist/Engineer; Chemical Technician; Utility Technician. **International locations:** Japan.

FEI COMPANY
One Corporation Way, Peabody MA 01960. 978/538-6700. **Fax:** 978/531-9648. **Contact:** Human Resources. **World Wide Web address:** http://www.feic.com. **Description:** Designs, develops, manufactures, and markets focused ion and electron beam technology for the semiconductor, thin film head, life science, and material science industries. **Positions advertised include:** Mask Repair Applications Engineer; Fib Systems Engineer. **Corporate headquarters location:** Hillsboro OR. **Other U.S. locations:** Sunnyvale CA. **International locations:** Czech Republic; The Netherlands. **Listed on:** NASDAQ. **Stock exchange symbol:** FEIC. **Number of employees worldwide:** 1,500.

FLIR SYSTEMS
16 Esquire Road, North Billerica MA 01862. 978/901-8000. **Fax:** 978/901-8367. **Contact:** Human Resources. **World Wide Web address:** http://www.flir.com. **Description:** A manufacturer of infrared systems. **Positions advertised include:** Business Development Representative; Customer Service Representative; Administration Assistant; Systems Engineer; Buyer Planner;

Commodity Manager. **Other U.S. locations:** Portland OR. **International locations:** Sweden. **Listed on:** NASDAQ. **Stock exchange symbol:** FLIR.

THE FOXBORO COMPANY

38 Neponset Avenue, Foxboro MA 02035. 508/543-8750. **Contact:** Human Resources. **World Wide Web address:** http://www.foxboro.com. **Description:** Designs, builds, and markets instruments and systems for process management and control. Products include pneumatic and electronic instruments, and analog and digital control systems. The company also offers a range of engineering services, education and training, and post-sales technical support. **Parent company:** Invensys Systems, Inc.

GSI LUMONICS INC.

39 Manning Road, Billerica MA 01821. 978/439-5511. **Contact:** Human Resources. **World Wide Web address:** http://www.gsilumonics.com. **Description:** Produces laser-based, automated manufacturing systems, instrumentation, and components for a wide range of industries. **Positions advertised include;** Internal Audit Director; Principal Development Engineer; Human Resources Representative; Principal Supply Quality Engineer; Customer Support Manager; Financial Reporting Accountant; supply Chain Specialist; Machinist. **Corporate headquarters location:** Kanata, Ontario. **Other U.S. locations:** Wilmington MA. **Listed on:** NASDAQ. **Stock exchange symbol:** GSLI.

GSI LUMONICS INC.

60 Fordham Road, Wilmington MA 01887. 978/661-4300. **Fax:** 978/998-8798. **Contact:** Human Resources. **World Wide Web address:** http://www.gsilumonics.com. **Description:** Produces laser-based, automated manufacturing systems, instrumentation, and components for a wide range of industries. **Positions advertised include:** Manufacturing Technician; Engineering Technician; Principal Hardware Engineer; Technical Support Engineer; Principal Software Engineer; Buyer; Planner; Manufacturing Engineer. **Corporate headquarters location:** Kanata, Ontario. **Other U.S. locations:** Billerica MA. **Listed on:** NASDAQ. **Stock exchange symbol:** GSLI.

GOODRICH CORPORATION

5 Omni Road, Chelmsford MA 01824. 978/250-2325. **Contact:** Human Resources. **World Wide Web address:** http://www.goodrich.com. **Description:** A research and development firm involved in the technologies of optics, electro-optics, and imaging systems. These technologies are applied to the fields of surveillance and reconnaissance, mapping, and remote sensing. **Positions advertised include:** Software Engineer; Field Service Engineer; Facilities Operations Specialist; Manager Facility Maintenance; Electrical Engineer; Mechanical Engineer; Systems Engineer; Hardware Configuration Management Specialist; Quality Engineer. **Corporate headquarters location:** Charlotte NC. **Listed on:** New York Stock Exchange. **Stock exchange symbol:** GR.

HEILIND ELECTRONICS INC.

58 Jonspin Road, Wilmington MA 01887. 978/657-4870. **Fax:** 978/657-7905. **Contact:** Human Resources. **World Wide Web address:** http://www.heilind.com. **Description:** Distributes internal electric components for computer systems and other computer-related products. **Positions advertised include:** Northeast Regional Product Manager. **Other U.S. locations:** Wallingford CT; Orlando FL; Norcross GA; Arlington Heights IL; Eden Prairie MN; Hudson NH; Mountain Lakes NJ; Binghamton NY; Raleigh NC; Highland Heights OH; King of Prussia PA.

HELIX TECHNOLOGY CORPORATION
Mansfield Corporate Center, 9 Hampshire Street, Mansfield MA 02048. 508/337-5500. **Fax:** 508/337-5169. **Contact:** Human Resources. **E-mail address:** careers@helixtechnology.com. **World Wide Web address:** http://www.ctihelix.com. **Description:** Manufactures vacuum technology products for the semiconductor industry. **Positions advertised include:** Global Service Supply Chain Manager; Services Marketing Director; Corporate Accountant; Director of Product Marketing; Quality Systems Manager; Buyer Planner. **Special programs:** Internships; Training; Co-ops. **Corporate headquarters location:** This location. **Other U.S. locations:** Tempe AZ; Santa Clara CA; Longmont CO; Austin TX. **International locations:** France; Germany; Japan; Scotland; Taiwan. **Subsidiaries include:** GPC. **Listed on:** NASDAQ. **Stock exchange symbol:** HELX. **Annual sales/revenues:** More than $100 million. **Number of employees at this location:** 300. **Number of employees worldwide:** 500.

ITT INDUSTRIES CANNON
57 Stanley Avenue, Watertown MA 02472. 617/926-6400. **Contact:** Human Resources. **World Wide Web address:** http://www.ittcannon.com. **Description:** Manufactures switchgear and switchboard apparatus. **Positions advertised include:** E-learning Coordinator. **Corporate headquarters location:** White Plains NY. **Other U.S. locations:** Santa Ana CA: Loveland CO; Cromwell CT; Eden Prairie MN; Newport News VA. **International locations:** Worldwide. **Listed on:** New York Stock Exchange. **Stock exchange symbol:** ITT.

KEVLIN CORPORATION
596 Lowell Street, Methuen MA 01844 978/557-2400. **Contact:** Human Resources. **World Wide Web address:** http://www.kevlin.com. **Description:** Kevlin Corporation designs, manufactures, and sells microwave rotary couplers, connectors, cable assemblies, and microwave components. These products are used in air traffic control radars, satellite communications systems, airborne weather radars, and surveillance radars for drug interdiction. **Positions advertised include:** Contract Administrator; Engineer; Antenna Design Engineer; Microwave Manufacturing Engineer; Assembler; Bonder; Machinist Assistant; Program Manager; Sales Engineer; Test Technician; Antenna Technician.

KOLLMORGEN CORPORATION
347 King Street, Northampton MA 01060. 413/586-2330. **Fax:** 413/586-1324. **Contact:** Human Resources. **Description:** Kollmorgen operates in three business segments: Industrial Drives, Motors and Controls, and Electro-Optical Instruments. Founded in 1916. **NOTE:** Entry-level positions are offered. **Other U.S. locations:** VT. **International locations:** Italy. **Operations at this facility include:** This location designs and supplies advanced submarine periscopes, weapon directors, and military optics for the U.S. armed forces and its allies. Products allow the operator to search, detect, and identify targets anytime during the day or night using thermal imaging, high-resolution TV, lasers, direct-viewing channels, and video tracking and processing technologies. **Annual sales/revenues:** $21 - $50 million. **Number of employees at this location:** 230.

KOPIN CORPORATION
200 John Hancock Road, Taunton MA 02780. 508/824-6696. **Fax:** 508/822-1381. **Contact:** Human Resources. **E-mail address:** info@kopin.com. **World Wide Web address:** http://www.kopin.com. **Description:** Kopin Corporation is a developer of advanced flat-panel display products. The company's products

include compact projectors and head-mounted display systems featuring higher resolution, lighter weight, and greater portability as well as large-screen monitors offering higher definition and streamlined dimensions. Kopin's proprietary wafer engineering has a broad range of computer, entertainment, business product, medical imaging, avionics, and industrial applications. **Positions advertised include:** Process Engineer; Cleanroom Operator; Equipment Maintenance Technician; Test Technician. **Corporate headquarters location:** This location. **Other area locations:** Westborough MA. **Other U.S. locations:** Los Gatos CA. **Listed on:** NASDAQ. **Stock exchange symbol:** KOPN.

KOPIN CORPORATION
125 North Drive, Westborough MA 01581. 508/870-5959. **Fax:** 508/870-0660. **Contact:** Human Resources. **E-mail address:** info@kopin.com. **World Wide Web address:** http://www.kopin.com. **Description:** Kopin Corporation is a developer of advanced flat-panel display products. The company's products include compact projectors and head-mounted display systems featuring higher resolution, lighter weight, and greater portability as well as large-screen monitors offering higher definition and streamlined dimensions. Kopin's proprietary wafer engineering has a broad range of computer, entertainment, business product, medical imaging, avionics, and industrial applications. **Corporate headquarters location:** Taunton MA. **Other U.S. locations:** Los Gatos CA. **Listed on:** NASDAQ. **Stock exchange symbol:** KOPN.

LTX CORPORATION
50 Rosemount Road, Westwood MA 02090. 781/461-1000. **Contact:** Human Resources. **World Wide Web address:** http://www.ltx.com. **Description:** Manufactures and markets testing equipment for semiconductors and electronic assemblies. The company's semiconductor test systems include digital test systems, which test digital ICs such as microprocessors and microcontrollers; linear/mixed signal test systems, which test a wide range of linear and mixed signal ICs; and discrete component test systems. The company also provides applications support for its test systems. Founded in 1976. **Positions advertised include:** Research & Development; Software Engineer; Hardware Engineer; Manufacturing Engineer; Sales Associate; Marketing Representative; Product Manufacturing Representative; Information Services Representative; Finance Accountant. **Corporate headquarters location:** This location. **Other U.S. locations:** AZ; CA; IN; PA; TX. **International locations:** England; France; Germany; Israel; Italy; Japan; Korea; Singapore; Taiwan. **Listed on:** NASDAQ. **Stock exchange symbol:** LTXX.

LUCENT TECHNOLOGIES INC.
1600 Osgood Street, North Andover MA 01845. 978/960-2000. **Contact:** Human Resources. **World Wide Web address:** http://www.lucent.com. **Description:** Manufactures communications products including switching, transmission, fiber-optic cable, wireless systems, and operations systems. **Positions advertised include:** Security Consultant; Project Manager. **Corporate headquarter location:** Murray Hill NJ. **Other U.S. locations:** Nationwide. **Listed on:** New York Stock Exchange. **Stock exchange symbol:** LU.

M/A-COM, INC.
1011 Pawtucket Boulevard, Lowell MA 01854. 978/442-5000. **Contact:** Human Resources. **World Wide Web address:** http://www.macom.com. **Description:** Designs, develops, and manufactures microwave semiconductors and subsystems for commercial wireless, cellular, satellite, and automotive communications, and for government and defense applications. **Positions advertised include:** Electronics Engineer; Accountant; Manufacturing Engineer;

Reliability Engineer. **Corporate headquarters location:** This location. **Other area locations:** Burlington MA. **Other U.S. locations:** San Jose CA; Torrance CA; Harrisburg PA; Lynchburg VA; Roanoke VA. **International locations:** Canada; England; Ireland. **Parent company:** Tyco Electronics.

MKS-ASTEX PRODUCTS
90 Industrial Way, Wilmington MA 01887-4610. 978/284-4000. **Contact:** Human Resources. **World Wide Web address:** http://www.astex.com. **Description:** A manufacturer of systems and components used in the production of advanced semiconductors and chemical vapor deposition (CVD) diamond. ASTeX components are used in a number of semiconductor fabrication steps such as stripping, etching, CVD, and physical vapor deposition. The company's CVD diamond production systems are used to develop and manufacture tool coatings, optics and optical coatings, thermal management substrates for high performance electronics, and bearing seals and wear parts for a variety of applications. ASTeX markets its systems to producers of CVD diamond, while its microwave power generators, plasma sources, and ozone generators and subsystems are marketed to semiconductor capital equipment manufacturers. **Positions advertised include:** Electrical Engineer; Engineer; Employment Relations Manager; Advanced Manufacturing Engineer. **Corporate headquarters location:** Andover MA. **Listed on:** NASDAQ. **Stock exchange symbol:** MKSI.

MICRO NETWORKS INTEGRATED CIRCUIT SYSTEMS
ANDERSEN LABORATORIES
324 Clark Street, Worcester MA 01606. 508/852-5400. **Fax:** 508/853-8296. **Contact:** Human Resources. **E-mail address:** humanresources@mnc,com. **World Wide Web address:** http://www.mnc.com. **Description:** Micro Networks supplies microelectronic circuits to OEMs. These circuits are used for frequency control and data conversion in the information technology field. Founded in 1969. **Positions advertised include:** Applications Engineer. **Corporate headquarters location:** This location. **Other U.S. locations:** Bloomfield CT; Auburn NY. **International locations:** England; The Netherlands. **Subsidiaries include:** Andersen Laboratories (also at this location) manufactures acoustic signal processing products for use in the commercial communications market. **Listed on:** Privately held. **Number of employees at this location:** 95.

MICROSEMI CORPORATION
580 Pleasant Street, Watertown MA 02472-2408. 617/926-0404. **Fax:** 617/924-1235. **Contact:** Human Resources. **World Wide Web address:** http://www.microsemi.com. **Description:** Microsemi Corporation manufactures and markets semiconductors and similar products and provides related services, principally for the military, aerospace, medical, computer, and telecommunications industries. Major products include high-reliability silicon rectifiers and zener diodes; low-leakage and high-voltage diodes; temperature-compensated zener diodes; and a family of subminiature high-power transient suppresser diodes. **Positions advertised include:** Water Process Technician; Water Process Operator; Data Entry Clerk; In Process Inspector. **Corporate headquarters location:** Irvine CA. **Other area locations:** Lawrence MA; Lowell MA; Melrose MA. **Other U.S. locations:** Scottsdale AZ; Carlsbad CA; Garden Grove CA; Los Angeles CA; Broomfield CO; Riveria Beach FL; Montgomery PA. **International locations:** Hong Kong; India; Ireland. **Operations at this facility include:** This location is a manufacturing facility. **Listed on:** NASDAQ. **Stock exchange symbol:** MSCC. **Number of employees at this location:** 315.

MICROSEMI MICROWAVE PRODUCTS

75 Technology Drive, Lowell MA 01851. 978/442-5600. **Contact:** Human Resources. **World Wide Web address:** http://www.microsemi.com. **Description:** Manufactures and markets semiconductors and similar products and provides related services, principally for the military, aerospace, medical, computer, and telecommunications industries. Major products include high-reliability silicon rectifiers and zener diodes; low-leakage and high-voltage diodes; temperature-compensated zener diodes; and a family of subminiature high-power transient suppresser diodes. **Corporate headquarters location:** Irvine CA. **Other area locations:** Lawrence MA; Melrose MA; Watertown MA. **Other U.S. locations:** Scottsdale AZ; Carlsbad CA; Garden Grove CA; Los Angeles CA; Broomfield CO; Riveria Beach FL; Montgomery PA. **International locations:** Hong Kong; India; Ireland. **Listed on:** NASDAQ. **Stock exchange symbol:** MSCC.

MIKRON BOSTOMATIC CORPORATION

150 Hopping Brook Road, Holliston MA, 01746. 508/474-1100. **Fax:** 508/474-1111. **Contact:** Human Resources. **E-mail address:** info@mikronus.com. **World Wide Web address:** http://www.bostomatic.com. **Description:** A manufacturer of vertical and horizontal machining centers; modular machining centers for stand-alone and cellular applications; and CNC controls marketed under the Bostomatic trademark. **International locations:** France; Germany.

MITRE CORPORATION

202 Burlington Road, Bedford MA 01730-1420. 781/271-2000. **Contact:** Human Resources. **World Wide Web address:** http://www.mitre.org. **Description:** An international, nonprofit high-technology electronics and communications firm that produces large-scale command, control, and communications (C3) systems for the U.S. Air Force. **Positions advertised include:** Office Support Staff; Associate Section Leader; Global Positioning Systems Engineer; Database & Data Mining Researcher; Lead Software Systems Engineer; Radar Systems Engineer; Office Support Staff; Database Developer; Information Systems Engineer; Budget Analysis; Sensors System Engineer. **Corporate headquarters location:** This location. **Other U.S. locations:** Ft. Huachuca AZ; Colorado Springs CO; Ft. Monmouth NJ; San Antonio TX; McLean VA. **Operations at this facility include:** Research and Development.

ORBOTECH LTD.

44 Manning Road, Billerica MA 01821. 978/667-6037. **Fax:** 978/667-9969. **Contact:** Human Resources. **E-mail address:** jobsusa@orbotech.com. **World Wide Web address:** http://www.orbotech.com. **Description:** Orbotech, Ltd. designs, develops, manufactures, and services computerized, electro-optical systems for automated inspection and identification of flaws in printed circuit boards, multichip modules, and flat panel displays, and sells CAD/CAM systems for electronic design and preparation of printed circuit board artwork masters and tooling. **Listed on:** NASDAQ. **Stock exchange symbol:** ORBK.

PCD (PRODUCT DEVELOPMENT CONSULTING, INC.)

2 Technology Drive, Centennial Park, Peabody MA 01960. 978/532-8800. **Fax:** 978/532-6800. **Contact:** Human Resources. **E-mail address:** info@amphenolpcd.com. **World Wide Web address:** http://www.pcdinc.com. **Description:** Manufactures electronic connector devices. **Listed on:** NASDAQ. **Stock exchange symbol:** PCDI.

PARLEX CORPORATION
One Parlex Place, Methuen MA 01844. 978/685-4341. **Fax:** 978/685-8809. **Contact:** Joyce Collins, Human Resources. **E-mail address:** flexcircuits@parlex.com. **World Wide Web address:** http://www.parlex.com. **Description:** Manufactures flexible and rigid printed circuits, multilayer boards, flat cable products, and other electronic components. **Positions advertised include:** Regional Sales Engineer; Product Line Manager; Director of Sales & Marketing. **Corporate headquarters location:** This location. **Listed on:** NASDAQ. **Stock exchange symbol:** PRLX.

PLEXUS NPI PLUS
4 Copeland Drive, Ayer MA 01432. 978/784-1500. **Contact:** Human Resources. **World Wide Web address:** http://www.plexus.com. **Description:** Manufactures circuit boards. **Positions advertised include:** Engineer. **Corporate headquarters location:** Neenah WI. **Parent Company:** Plexus Corporation. **Listed on:** NASDAQ. **Stock exchange symbol:** PLXS.

QUADTECH INC.
5 Clock Tower Place, Suite 210 East, Maynard MA 01754. 978/461-2100. **Toll-free phone:** 800/253-1230. **Fax:** 978/461-4295. **Contact:** Human Resources Department. **World Wide Web address:** http://www.quadtechinc.com. **Description:** Engaged in the sale of electronic test equipment. **Positions advertised include:** Applications Engineer; Electronics Technician; Documentation Control Specialist; Customer Service Representative.

RVSI ACUITY CIMATRIX
5 Shawmut Road, Canton MA 02021. 781/821-0830. **Toll-free phone:** 800/646-6664. **Fax:** 781/828-8942. **Contact:** Human Resources. **World Wide Web address:** http://www.rvsi.com. **Description:** RVSI Acuity CiMatrix is a leader in the development of bar code and symbology solutions that automatically capture, analyze, and communicate identification information in industrial, material handling, and manufacturing environments. The company also manufactures machine vision systems, industrial controllers, data entry technicals, and LANs. **Positions advertised include:** Embedded Software Engineer; Applications Engineer; Software Engineer. **Corporate headquarters location:** This location. **Other U.S. locations:** Mission Viejo CA; San Jose CA; West Hartford CT; Roswell GA; Schaumburg IL; Southfield MI; Raleigh NC; Cincinnati OH; Irving TX. **Parent company:** Robotic Vision Systems, Inc. **Listed on:** NASDAQ. **Stock exchange symbol:** ROBV.

RAYTHEON COMPANY
141 Spring Street, Lexington MA 02421. 781/862-6600. **Contact:** Human Resources. **World Wide Web address:** http://www.raytheon.com. **Description:** Raytheon Company is a diversified, international, multi-industry technology-based company ranked among the 100 largest U.S. industrial corporations. Raytheon has facilities in 42 states and the District of Columbia. Overseas facilities and representative offices are located in 34 countries. The company's two business segments include Defense and Commercial Electronics, and Business Aviation and Special Mission Aircraft. **Corporate headquarters location:** This location. **Other U.S. locations:** Nationwide. **International locations:** Worldwide. **Listed on:** New York Stock Exchange. **Stock exchange symbol:** RTN.

RAYTHEON SYSTEMS COMPANY
1001 Boston Post Road, Marlborough MA 01752. 508/490-1000. **Contact:** Human Resources. **World Wide Web address:** http://www.raytheon.com.

Description: Manufactures search, detection, navigation, guidance, aeronautical, and nautical systems and instruments. **Parent company:** Raytheon Company is a diversified, international, multi-industry, technology-based company ranked among the 100 largest U.S. industrial corporations. The company has four business segments: Electronics, Major Appliances, Aircraft Products, and Energy and Environmental. Raytheon has over 100 facilities in the United States.

RAYTHEON TECHNICAL SERVICES
2 Wayside Road, Burlington MA 01801. 781/238-3000. **Contact:** Human Resources. **World Wide Web address:** http://www.raytheon.com. **Description:** Provides electrical engineering services. **Positions advertised include:** Software Engineer; Program Manager; Project Manager; Logistics Engineer; Civil Engineer; ATM Transitional Implementation Manager; Technical Recruiter; Web Project Manager; Support Assistant; Media Production Specialist; Electrical Engineer; Subcontract Administrator. **Corporate headquarters location:** Lexington MA. **Parent company:** Raytheon Company is a diversified, international, multi-industry, technology-based company ranked among the 100 largest U.S. industrial corporations. The company has four business segments: Electronics, Major Appliances, Aircraft Products, and Energy and Environmental. Raytheon has over 100 facilities in the United States. Overseas facilities and representative offices are located in 26 countries, principally in Europe, the Middle East, and the Pacific Rim.

ROCKBESTOS-SURPRENANT CABLE CORPORATION
172 Sterling Street, Clinton MA 01510. 978/365-6331. **Toll-free phone:** 800/444-3792. **Fax:** 978/365-3287. **Contact:** Peter Stephan, Human Resources Manager. **World Wide Web address:** http://www.r-scc.com. **Description:** A major manufacturer of quality-assured, specialty purpose insulated wire and cable products. **Special programs:** Internships. **Office hours:** Monday - Friday, 8:00 a.m. - 5:00 p.m. **Corporate headquarters location:** This location. **Other U.S. locations:** New Haven CT. **Operations at this facility include:** Administration; Manufacturing; Research and Development; Sales. **Listed on:** Privately held. **President:** Fred Schwelm. **Annual sales/revenues:** More than $100 million. **Number of employees at this location:** 300. **Number of employees nationwide:** 600.

ROCKWELL AUTOMATION
ALLEN-BRADLEY COMPANY
2 Executive Drive, Chelmsford MA 01824. 978/441-9500. **Contact:** Human Resources. **World Wide Web address:** http://www.automation.rockwell.com. **Description:** Designs, manufactures, and markets electronic controls and control systems for industrial markets. Principal products are photoelectric controls, inductive proximity controls, sensing products, and mechanical limit switches for the automation of industrial processes. Founded in 1904. **Positions advertised include:** Product Manager; Electrical Engineer. **Corporate headquarters location:** Milwaukee WI. **Other U.S. locations:** Manchester NH. **Parent company:** Rockwell International. **Listed on:** New York Stock Exchange. **Stock exchange symbol:** ROK. **Number of employees at this location:** 115. **Number of employees nationwide:** 900. **Number of employees worldwide:** 26,000.

SATCON TECHNOLOGY CORPORATION
161 First Street, Cambridge MA 02142. 617/661-0540. **Fax:** 617/661-3373. **Contact:** Human Resources. **World Wide Web address:** http://www.satcon.com. **Description:** Designs, develops, manufactures, and

markets active motion control systems. These systems use magnetic forces, coupled with precision sensors and specialized electronics, to control both linear and rotary motion. The company has developed revolutionary technologies for applications that affect large segments of global industries, from ground and air transportation to CFC-free refrigeration and air conditioning systems. **Listed on:** NASDAQ. **Stock exchange symbol:** SATC.

SIPEX CORPORATION
22 Linnell Circle, Billerica MA 01821. 978/667-8700. **Fax:** 978/671-9502. **Contact:** Human Resources. **E-mail address:** maresume@sipex.com. **World Wide Web address:** http://www.sipex.com. **Description:** Manufactures analog integrated circuits, microchips, and semiconductors. **Positions advertised include:** Design Engineer; Product Application Engineer.

SIPPICAN, INC.
7 Barnabas Road, Marion MA 02738. 508/748-1160. **Contact:** Human Resources. **World Wide Web address:** http://www.sippican.com. **Description:** Manufacturers of radar, infrared, and electro-optical expendable countermeasure systems for ships, aircraft, and ground vehicles. **Positions advertised include:** Components Engineer; Purchasing Agents; Security Engineer; Engineer Manager; Program Administrator; Software Engineer; Configuration Manager; Production Control; Electronics Design Engineer.

SKYWORKS SOLUTIONS, INC.
20 Sylvan Road, Woburn MA 01801. 781/935-5150. **Contact:** Human Resources. **World Wide Web address:** http://www.skyworksinc.com. **Description:** A manufacturer of integrated circuits and microwave semiconductor devices including gallium arsenide microwave monolithic integrated circuits; microwave ferrite and other microwave ceramic materials; microwave solid state switches, oscillators, gallium arsenide field effect transistor amplifiers; and millimeter wave components, subsystems, and antennas. **Positions advertised include** Applications Staff Engineer; Electrical Principal Engineer; ESD Quality Engineer; Senior Director Operations; Photolithography Equipment/Process Engineer; Power Amplifier Design Engineer; I/C Layout Designer. **Corporate headquarters location:** This location. **Other U.S. locations:** Irvine CA; Santa Rosa CA; Hillsboro OR; Cedar Rapids IA. **Operations at this facility include:** Administration; Manufacturing; Research and Development; Sales. **Listed on:** NASDAQ. **Stock exchange symbol:** SWKS.

SPIRE CORPORATION
One Patriots Park, Bedford MA 01730-2396. 781/275-6000. **Fax:** 781/275-7470. **Contact:** Human Resources. **E-mail address:** hr@spirecorp.com. **World Wide Web address:** http://www.spirecorp.com. **Description:** Provides products and services to customers in the solar photovoltaics, opto-electronics, and biomedical markets. The company's products include compound semiconductor wafers and devices, photovoltaic manufacturing equipment and production lines, and ion beam-based processing services for medical components. **Positions advertised include:** Production & Inventory Control Coordinator; Biomaterials Coatings Technician; Lead Process Engineer. **Corporate headquarters location:** This location. **Listed on:** NASDAQ. **Stock exchange symbol:** SPIR. **Number of employees at this location:** 150.

TECH/OPS SEVCON, INC.
155 Northboro Road, Southborough MA 01772. 508/281-5500. **Fax:** 508/281-5341. **Contact:** Human Resources. **E-mail address:** hr@sevcon.com. **World Wide Web address:** http://www.sevcon.com. **Description:** A world leader in the

design, manufacture, and marketing of microcomputer-based solid-state controls for electric vehicles. These controllers vary the speed of vehicles, improve performance, and prolong the shift life of batteries. The company's customers include manufacturers of forklift trucks, mining vehicles, airport tractors, aerial lifts, sweepers, and other battery-powered vehicles.

TERADYNE, INC.
321 Harrison Avenue, Boston MA 02118. 617/482-2700. **Contact:** Human Resources. **E-mail address:** jobs@teradyne.com. **World Wide Web address:** http://www.teradyne.com. **Description:** Designs and manufactures a variety of automatic test equipment. **NOTE:** Apply online or e-mail resume. Please refer to the company's Website for instructions about where resumes for each available position should be directed. If no applicable jobs are available, resumes may be directed to this location and will be entered into a searchable database. **Positions advertised include:** Administrative Assistant; Test Development Engineer; Project Manager; Application Engineer; Financial Analyst; Financial Manager; Human Resources Representative; Information Technology Manager; Attorney; Product Manager; Calibration Technologist; Business Analyst. **Corporate headquarters location:** This location. **Listed on**: New York Stock Exchange. **Stock exchange symbol:** TER.

TEXAS INSTRUMENTS, INC.
34 Forest Street, Attleboro MA 02703. 508/236-3800. **Fax:** 508/236-1322. **Contact:** Human Resources. **World Wide Web address:** http://www.ti.com. **Description:** Texas Instruments (TI) is one of the world's largest suppliers of semiconductor products. TI's defense electronics business is a leading supplier of avionics, infrared, and weapons guidance systems to the U.S. Department of Defense and U.S. allies. The company is also a technology leader in high-performance notebook computers and model-based software development tools. TI sensors monitor and regulate pressure and temperature in products ranging from automobiles to air conditioning systems. **Positions advertised include:** Product Marketing Developer; Electro Mechanical Technician. **NOTE:** Apply online. **Corporate headquarters location:** Dallas TX. **Operations at this facility include:** This location manufactures controls and sensors. **Listed on:** New York Stock Exchange. **Stock exchange symbol:** TXN. **Annual sales/revenues:** More than $100 million. **Number of employees at this location:** 4,000. **Number of employees nationwide:** 5,000.

THERMO BLH
75 Shawmut Road, Canton MA 02021. 781/821-2000. **Contact:** Human Resources. **World Wide Web address:** http://www.blh.com. **Description:** An electronics manufacturer that produces strain gauges, transducers, and instrumentation controls. **Corporate headquarters location:** This location. **Operations at this facility include:** Manufacturing.

UNITED ELECTRIC CONTROLS
P.O. Box 9143, Watertown MA 02471. 617/926-1000. **Fax:** 617/926-8076. **Contact:** Human Resources. **World Wide Web address:** http://www.ueonline.com. **Description:** Manufactures temperature control devices for many industries.

VICOR CORPORATION
25 Frontage Street, Andover MA 01810. 978/470-2900. **Fax:** 978/749-7700. **Contact:** Human Resources. **E-mail address:** hr@vicr.com. **World Wide Web address:** http://www.vicr.com. **Description:** Develops, manufactures, and markets components for modular power systems and complete power systems

using a patented, high-frequency, electronic power conversion technology called zero current switching. Components are used in electronic products to convert power from a primary power source into the direct current required by most contemporary electronic circuits. **Positions advertised include:** Front End Manufacturing Engineering Manager; Engineering Aide; Design Engineer; Layout Design Engineer. **Corporate headquarters location:** This location. **Other U.S. locations:** Sunnyvale CA; Lombard IL. **International locations:** France; Gemany; Hong Kong; Italy; Japan; United Kingdom. **Operations at this facility include:** Administration; Manufacturing; Research and Development; Sales; Service. **Listed on:** NASDAQ. **Stock exchange symbol:** VICR. **Number of employees at this location:** 700.

ENVIRONMENTAL & WASTE MANAGEMENT SERVICES

**You can expect to find the following types of companies
in this section:**
Environmental Engineering Firms • Sanitary Services

AMERICAN REF-FUEL
257 Ivory Street, Braintree MA 02184. 781/843-6209. **Contact:** Human Resources. **World Wide Web address:** http://www.ref-fuel.com. **Description:** American Ref-Fuel accepts municipal solid waste from residents and commercial haulers and transfers the waste to an incinerator site in Wareham MA. **NOTE:** Please forward all resumes to Jerry Croufford, Human Resources Manager, 141 Cranberry Highway, Wareham MA 02576-1504. **Positions advertised include:** Operating Technician; Fuel Plant Service Technician. **Corporate headquarters location:** Houston TX. **Operations at this facility include:** This location is a transfer station. **Subsidiaries include:** Duke Energy North America; United American Energy Corp.

BETA GROUP, INC.
1420 Providence Highway, Suite 117, Norwood MA 02062. 781/255-1982. **Contact:** Human Resources. **E-mail address:** tgarro@beta-inc.com. **World Wide Web address:** http://www.beta-inc.com. **Description:** An engineering firm specializing in environmental engineering and site remediation; highway engineering; water/wastewater engineering; and landfill closures. **Positions advertised include:** Civil Transportation Engineer; Structural Engineer; Geographic Information Systems Project Manager.

BLACK & VEATCH
230 Congress Street, Suite 802, Boston MA 02110. 617/451-6900. **Contact:** Human Resources. **World Wide Web address:** http://www.bv.com. **Description:** An environmental/civil engineering and construction firm serving utilities, commerce, and government agencies in more than 40 countries worldwide. Black & Veatch provides a broad range of study, design, construction management, and turnkey capabilities to clients in the water and wastewater fields. The firm is one of the leading authorities on drinking water treatment through the use of activated carbon, ozone, and other state-of-the-art processes. Black & Veatch is also engaged in wastewater treatment work including reclamation and reuse projects and the beneficial use of wastewater residuals. Other services are provided for solid waste recycling and disposal, transportation, and storm water management. In the energy field, Black & Veatch is a leader in providing engineering procurement and construction for electric power plants. The firm's areas of expertise include coal-fueled plants, simple and combined-cycle combustion turbines, fluidized bed combustion, waste-to-energy facilities, hydroelectric plants, and cogeneration facilities. Black & Veatch's capabilities also include nuclear power projects, advanced technology, air quality control, performance monitoring, plant life management, and facilities modification. In addition, Black & Veatch operates in the transmission and distribution field. In the industrial sector, Black & Veatch focuses on projects involving cleanrooms, industrial processes and planning, utility systems, and cogeneration. In addition to engineering, procurement, and construction, Black & Veatch offers a variety of management and financial services including institutional strengthening, privatization, strategic financial planning, and information management. **Positions advertised include:** Communication

Specialist; Document Associate; Civil Engineer; Consultant; Electrical Engineer; Engineering Technician; Associate Estimator; Programming Analyst; Human Resources Division Director; Mechanical Engineer; Planning Specialist; Engineer; Procurement Specialist. **Special programs:** Co-ops. **Corporate headquarters location:** Kansas City MO. **Other U.S. locations:** Nationwide. **International locations:** Worldwide. **Listed on:** Privately held. **Number of employees worldwide:** 10,000.

C.E.A. (CORPORATE ENVIRONMENTAL ADVISORS)
127 Hartwell Street, West Boylston MA 01583. 508/835-8822. **Contact:** Human Resources **Description:** An environmental consulting firm engaged in contract consulting projects.

CH2M HILL
25 New Chardon Street, Suite 500, Boston MA 02114. 617/523-2260. **Fax:** 617/723-9036. **Contact:** Human Resources. **World Wide Web address:** http://www.ch2m.com. **Description:** An environmental engineering company specializing in water and remediation projects. **Positions advertised include:** NEPA Expert; Process Engineer; Air Water Process Project Manager; Construction Manager. **NOTE:** Jobseekers should address resumes to the attention of the manager of the group to which they are applying. Please contact this location for further information. **Corporate headquarters location:** Greenwood Village CO. **Other U.S. locations:** Nationwide. **International locations:** Worldwide.

THE CADMUS GROUP, INC.
57 Water Street, Watertown MA 02472. 617/673-7000. **Contact:** Human Resources. **World Wide Web address:** http://www.cadmusgroup.com. **Description:** An environmental consulting and engineering firm. **Positions advertised include:** Analyst; Environmental Professional; Research Analyst.

CAMP DRESSER & McKEE, INC. (CDM)
One Cambridge Place, 50 Hampshire Street, Cambridge MA 02139. 617/452-6000. **Contact:** Human Resources. **World Wide Web address:** http://www.cdm.com. **Description:** A worldwide provider of environmental engineering, scientific, planning, and management services. The company focuses on professional activities for the management of wastewater, drinking water, water resources, hazardous waste, solid waste, infrastructure, and environmental systems. **Positions advertised include:** Geotechnical Engineer; Environmental Scientist; Environmental Engineer; Instrumentation Control Engineer; O&M Specialist; Marketing Coordinator; Planner; Air Quality Scientist or Engineer; Administrative Assistant. **Special programs:** Internships. **Corporate headquarters location:** This location. **Other U.S. locations:** Nationwide. **International locations:** Worldwide.

CHECKPOINT ENVIRONMENTAL, INC.
12 Linden Street, Hudson MA 01749. 978/562-4300. **Contact:** Personnel. **Description:** An environmental engineering firm specializing in the drilling of small diameter wells.

CLEAN HARBORS, INC.
530 East First Street, South Boston MA 02127. 617/269-5830. **Contact:** Personnel. **World Wide Web address:** http://www.cleanharbors.com. **Description:** Through its subsidiaries, Clean Harbors, Inc. provides comprehensive environmental services in 35 states in the Northeast, Midwest, Central, and Mid-Atlantic regions. Clean Harbors provides a wide range of

hazardous waste management and environmental support services to a diversified customer base from 40 locations. The company's hazardous waste management services include treatment, storage, recycling, transportation, risk analysis, site assessment, laboratory analysis, site closure, and disposal of hazardous materials through environmentally sound methods. Environmental remediation services include emergency response, surface remediation, groundwater restoration, industrial maintenance, and facility decontamination. Customers include nearly 300 *Fortune* 500 companies; regional utilities; oil, pharmaceutical, and chemical companies; small businesses; and the high-tech and biotech industries. **Positions advertised include:** Accountant; Transportation Compliance Manager; Container Business Development Manager; Web Developer; Technician Services Representative; Purchase Order Administrator; Billing Clerk; Credit Request Check; T&D Order Placement Representative; Billing Supervisor; Tech Services. **NOTE:** Interested jobseekers should direct resumes to: Human Resources, 1501 Washington Street, Braintree MA 02184. **Corporate headquarters location:** Braintree MA. **Other area locations:** Kingston MA; Natick MA; North Grafton MA: West Springfield MA; Weymouth MA; Woburn MA. **Other U.S. locations:** Nationwide. **Listed on:** NASDAQ. **Stock exchange symbol:** CLHB. **Number of employees nationwide:** 1,400.

CLEAN HARBORS, INC.
P.O. Box 859048, Braintree MA 02185-9048. 781/849-1800. **Fax:** 781/356-1363. **Contact:** Personnel. **World Wide Web address:** http://www.cleanharbors.com. **Description:** Through its subsidiaries, Clean Harbors, Inc. provides comprehensive environmental services in 35 states in the Northeast, Midwest, Central, and Mid-Atlantic regions. Clean Harbors provides a wide range of hazardous waste management and environmental support services. The company's hazardous waste management services include treatment, storage, recycling, transportation, risk analysis, site assessment, laboratory analysis, site closure, and disposal of hazardous materials through environmentally sound methods. Environmental remediation services include emergency response, surface remediation, groundwater restoration, industrial maintenance, and facility decontamination. Customers include regional utilities; oil, pharmaceutical, and chemical companies; small businesses; and the high-tech and biotech industries. **Positions advertised include:** Accountant; Transportation Compliance Manager; Container Business Development Manager; Web Developer; Technician Services Representative; Purchase Order Administrator; Billing Clerk; Credit Request Check; T&D Order Placement Representative Billing Supervisor; Tech Services. **NOTE:** Interested jobseekers should direct resumes to: Human Resources, 1501 Washington Street, Braintree MA 02184. **Corporate headquarters location:** This location. **Other area locations:** Kingston MA; Natick MA; North Grafton MA: West Springfield MA; Weymouth MA; Woburn MA. **Other U.S. locations:** Nationwide. **Listed on:** NASDAQ. **Stock exchange symbol:** CLHB. **Number of employees nationwide:** 1,400.

COLER & COLANTONIO
101 Accord Park Drive, Norwell MA 02061. 781/982-5400. **Contact:** Human Resources. **World Wide Web address:** http://www.col-col.com. **Description:** A civil and environmental engineering firm. Coler & Colantonio specializes in a variety of engineering projects including pipeline, transportation, and water projects. **Positions advertised include:** Waste Water Treatment Operator; Project Engineer; Drafter; Civil Engineer. **Other area locations:** South Deerfield MA; South Easton MA. **Other U.S. locations:** Houston TX.

CYN ENVIRONMENTAL
P.O. Box 119, Stoughton MA 02072. 781/341-1777. **Toll-free phone:** 800/242-5818. **Fax:** 781/341-6246. **Physical address:** 100 Tosca Drive, Stoughton MA 02072. **Contact:** Chuck Klinger, Human Resources. **E-mail address:** cklinger@cynenv.com. **World Wide Web address:** http://www.cynenv.com. **Description:** Provides hazardous waste removal and remediation. **Positions advertised include:** Environmental Project Manager. **Other area locations:** Wilbraham MA. **Other U.S. locations:** Dover NH; Johnston RI.

DEC-TAM CORPORATION
50 Concord Street, North Reading MA 01864. 978/470-2860. **Contact:** Human Resources. **World Wide Web address:** http://www.dectam.com. **Description:** Provides lead paint and asbestos removal.

DEER ISLAND TREATMENT PLANT
P.O. Box 100, Winthrop MA 02152. 617/846-5800. **Contact:** Human Resources. **Description:** A wastewater treatment facility run by the Massachusetts Water Resources Authority (MWRA).

ENSR INTERNATIONAL
2 Technology Park Drive, Westford MA 01886-3140. 978/589-3000. **Toll-free phone:** 800/722-2440. **Contact:** Human Resources. **World Wide Web address:** http://www.ensr.com. **Description:** An environmental consulting and engineering services firm. Services include pollution prevention, risk assessment, property transfer assessment, environmental permitting, environmental communication, remedial design, and engineering and construction management. ENSR has over 1,000 scientists, engineers, communications professionals, construction managers, regulatory specialists, and health and safety experts nationwide. **Positions advertised include:** Proposal Coordinator; Staff Specialist; Technician; Project Specialist; Engineer; Administrative Assistant; Training Specialist; Project Manager; Program Manager; Fisheries Biologist. **Corporate headquarters location:** This location. **Other U.S. locations:** Nationwide. **International locations:** Worldwide.

EARTHTECH
196 Baker Avenue, Concord MA 01742. 978/371-4000. **Contact:** Human Resources. **World Wide Web address:** http://www.earthtech.com. **Description:** An environmental engineering compliance firm. **Positions advertised include:** Administrative Assistant; Project Professional. **Corporate headquarters location:** Long Beach CA. **Other area locations:** Middleboro MA. **Other U.S. locations:** Nationwide. **International locations:** Worldwide.

ENVIROGEN, INC.
480 Neponset Street, Canton MA 02021. 781/821-5560. **Contact:** Human Resources. **E-mail address:** employment@envirogen.com. **World Wide Web address:** http://www.envirogen.com. **Description:** Provides a variety of environmental services including remediation and engineering. **Corporate headquarters location:** Lawrenceville NJ. **Other U.S. locations:** San Diego CA; St. Charles IL; Lansing MI; Ashwaubenon WI; Onalaska WI; Mosinee WI; Pewaukee WI. **Listed on:** NASDAQ. **Stock exchange symbol:** ENVG.

ENVIRONMENTAL SCIENCE SERVICES, INC.
888 Worcester Street, Suite 240, Wellesley MA 02482. 781/431-0500. **Contact:** Human Resources. **World Wide Web address:** http://www.essgroup.com. **Description:** An environmental consulting and engineering firm offering a variety of services including soil sampling, water sampling, and hazardous materials

services. **Other U.S. locations:** Providence RI. **Positions advertised include:** Environmental Engineer; Engineer; Geologist; Civil Engineer.

ENVIRONMENTAL STRATEGIES CORPORATION

1740 Massachusetts Avenue, Boxborough MA 01719. 978/635-9600. **Contact:** Human Resources. **E-mail address:** envtl-recruit@escva.com. **World Wide Web address:** http://www.envstratcorp.com. **Description:** An environmental engineering firm. **Positions advertised include:** Environmental Engineer; Geologist; Environmental Professional; Environmental Compliance Auditor; Industrial Hygienist Safety Specialist. **Corporate headquarters location:** Reston VA. **Other U.S. locations:** San Jose CA; Denver CO; Minneapolis MN; Somerset NJ; Albany NY; Cazenovia NY; Durham NC; Pittsburgh PA; Houston TX.

FOSTER WHEELER ENVIRONMENTAL CORPORATION

133 Federal Street, 6th Floor, Boston MA 02110. 617/451-1201. **Contact:** Human Resources. **World Wide Web address:** http://www.fwec.com. **Description:** An environmental engineering firm.

FRANKLIN ENVIRONMENTAL SERVICES, INC.

P.O. Box 617, Wrentham MA 02093. 508/384-6151. **Physical address:** 185 Industrial Road, Wrentham MA 02093. **Contact:** Human Resources. **Description:** Engaged in hazardous waste remediation and transportation services. Founded in 1977.

GEI CONSULTANTS, INC.

1021 Main Street, Winchester MA 01890. 781/721-4000. **Contact:** Human Resources. **World Wide Web address:** http://www.geiconsultants.com. **Description:** An environmental and geo-technical engineering firm. **Positions advertised include:** Accounting Assistant; Geotechnical Engineer; Civil Engineer; Drafter; Environmental Engineer; Geologist; Human Resources Generalist; Laboratory & Field Technician; Project Manager; Staff Engineer; Technician. **Corporate headquarters location:** This location. **Other U.S. locations:** Carlsbad CA; Oakland CA; Colchester CT; Englewood CO; Concord NH; St. Louis MO.

GZA GEOENVIRONMENTAL TECHNOLOGIES

One Edgewater Drive, Norwood MA 02062. 781/278-3700. **Contact:** Human Resources. **World Wide Web address:** http://www.gza.com. **Description:** Provides consulting, remediation, and geo-technical services, principally in the Northeast and the Midwest. The company also maintains its own drilling, laboratory, and instrumentation facilities to support environmental and geo-technical activities. Environmental services range from initial assessment and evaluation of contaminated sites to design, construction, and operation of remediation systems. **Corporate headquarters location:** This location. **Other U.S. locations:** CT; ME; MA; MI; NH; NJ; NY; PA; RI; VT; WI. **Subsidiaries include:** Environmental Real Estate Investors, Inc. (EREI); GZA Drilling, Inc. provides drilling services; GZA GeoEnvironmental, Inc. provides environmental consulting and geo-technical services; Soil and Rock Instrumentation Division (SRI). **Number of employees nationwide:** 450.

GANNETT FLEMING

150 Wood Road, Braintree MA 02184. 781/380-7750. **Contact:** Donald B. Nicholas, Human Resources. **E-mail address:** dnicholas@gfnet.com. **World Wide Web address:** http://www.gannettfleming.com. **Description:** An engineering firm offering a wide variety of services including structural, geo-

technical, environmental, hazardous waste, bridge design, and tunnel design. **Positions advertised include:** Environmental Engineer; Resident Engineer. **Other U.S. locations:** Nationwide.

GEOLABS, INC.
45 Johnson Lane, Braintree MA 02184. 781/848-7844. **Toll/free phone:** 800/298-7060. **Fax:** 781/848-7811. **Contact:** Human Resources. **E-mail address:** geolabs@attbi.net. **World Wide Web address:** http://www.geolabs.com. **Description:** Provides analytical environmental testing of soil, ground water, wastewater, and air. Founded in 1995. **NOTE:** Entry-level positions are offered. **Company slogan:** Quick service without sacrificing. **Special programs:** Internships; Training; Co-ops; Summer Jobs. **Office hours:** Monday - Friday, 8:00 a.m. - 5:00 p.m. **Corporate headquarters location:** This location. **Listed on:** Privately held. **President/Owner:** David J. Kahler. **Annual sales/revenues:** Less than $5 million. **Number of employees at this location:** 20.

GEOLOGIC SERVICES CORPORATION
15 Robert Bonazzoli Avenue, Hudson MA 01749. 978/568-8740. **Contact:** Human Resources. **Description:** Provides underground storage tank evaluation services.

GRADIENT CORPORATION
238 Main Street, Cambridge MA 02142. 617/395-5000. **Contact:** Laura Gordon, Human Resources. **E-mail address:** lgordon@gradientcorp.com. **World Wide Web address:** http://www.gradcorp.com. **Description:** An environmental consulting firm. **Positions advertised include:** Technologist; Environmental Engineer. **Other U.S. locations:** Mercer Island WA. **Annual sales/revenues:** $5 - $10 million. **Number of employees at this location:** 50.

GROUNDWATER & ENVIRONMENTAL SERVICES, INC.
364 Littleton Road, Suite 4, Westford MA 01886. 978/392-0090. **Contact:** Human Resources. **World Wide Web address:** http://www.gesonline.com. **Description:** An environmental engineering firm specializing in groundwater and remediation. **Corporate headquarters location:** Wall NJ. **Other U.S. locations:** CT; IL; MD; MI; NJ; NY; OH; PA; TN; VA; WV. **Listed on:** Privately held.

GULF OF MAINE RESEARCH CENTER
204 Lafayette Street, Salem MA 01970. 978/745-6618. **Contact:** Human Resources. **Description:** An environmental consulting firm specializing in a variety of areas including wetlands projects and hazardous waste remediation.

HALEY & ALDRICH INC.
465 Medford Street, Suite 2200, Charlestown MA 02129. 617/886-7300. **Contact:** Human Resources. **E-mail address:** info@haleyaldrich.com. **World Wide Web address:** http://www.haleyaldrich.com. **Description:** An environmental and geotechnical engineering firm. **Positions advertised include:** Geotechnical Engineer; Tunnel Engineer; Structural Engineer; Environmental Scientist; Environmental Engineer; Chemical Engineer; Environmental Health & Safety Specialist; Industrial Hygienist; Geologist; Information Technology Specialist; Scientific Visualization Specialist.

LOCKHEED ENVIRONMENTAL SYSTEMS
175 Cabot Street, Suite 415, Lowell MA 01854. 978/275-9730. **Contact:** Personnel. **Description:** Engaged in contract environmental analysis work for the Environmental Protection Agency (EPA).

MWH
12 Farnsworth Street, Boston MA 02110. 617/338-7100. **Contact:** Human Resources. **World Wide Web address:** http://www.mw.com. **Description:** An environmental engineering firm specializing in water and wastewater projects. **Corporate headquarters location:** Broomfield CO. **Other U.S. locations:** Nationwide.

MWRA (MASSACHUSETTS WATER RESOURCES AUTHORITY)
100 First Avenue, Charlestown Navy Yard, Boston MA 02129. 617/242-6000. **Contact:** Human Resources. **World Wide Web address:** http://www.mwra.com. **Description:** Manages the quality of water throughout Massachusetts, including the cleanup of Boston Harbor and other large projects.

META ENVIRONMENTAL, INC.
49 Clarendon Street, Watertown MA 02472. 617/923-4662. **Fax:** 617/923-4610. **Contact:** Human Resources. **Description:** An environmental engineering firm. This location also houses a research laboratory. **NOTE:** Entry-level positions are offered. **Special programs:** Co-ops. **Corporate headquarters location:** This location. **Listed on:** Privately held. **Annual sales/revenues:** Less than $5 million. **Number of employees at this location:** 15.

METCALF & EDDY, INC.
30 Harvard Mill Square, P.O. Box 4071, Wakefield MA 01880-5371. 781/246-5200. **Fax:** 781/245-6293. **Contact:** Human Resources. **World Wide Web address:** http://www.m-e.com. **Description:** An environmental engineering firm offering professional consulting services for water, wastewater, hazardous waste, and landfills. Metcalf & Eddy, Inc. specializes in design engineering. The firm's projects include wastewater treatment facilities, waterworks projects, industrial and hazardous waste treatment, environmental modeling, and solid waste treatment. **Positions advertised include:** Human Resources Generalist; Production Architect; Librarian; Project Director. **Other U.S. locations:** Nationwide. **Parent company:** AECOM.

NORFOLK RAM GROUP
One Roberts Road, Plymouth MA 02360. 508/822-5500. **Fax:** 508/747-3658. **Contact:** Human Resources. **World Wide Web address:** http://www.norfolkenvironmental.com. **Description:** An environmental and civil engineering firm. **Positions advertised include:** Civil Engineer.

PSG
775 South Street, Holbrook MA 02343. 781/767-3670. **Contact:** Human Resources. **Description:** An environmental engineering firm offering professional consulting services for water, wastewater, hazardous waste, and landfills.

RANSOM ENVIRONMENTAL CONSULTANTS, INC.
Brown's Wharf, Newburyport MA 01950. 978/465-1822. **Fax:** 978/465-2986. **Contact:** Human Resources. **World Wide Web address:** http://www.ransomenv.com. **Description:** An environmental consulting firm specializing in remediation design and environmental risk assessment. **Positions advertised include:** Project Geologist; Project Manager; Engineer Geologist; Manager Engineer. **Corporate headquarters location:** This location. **Other U.S. locations:** Bristol RI.

RIZZO ASSOCIATES, INC.
P.O. Box 9005, One Grant Street, Framingham MA 01701-9005. 508/903-2401.
Fax: 508/903-2000. **Contact:** Human Resources. **E-mail address:**
hr@rizzo.com. **World Wide Web address:** http://www.rizzo.com. **Description:**
An engineering and environmental consulting firm. The company provides
engineering, environmental compliance, hazardous waste management,
transportation, and water/wastewater services. **NOTE:** Entry-level positions and
part-time jobs are offered. **Positions advertised include:** Civil Engineer; Site
Engineer; Engineer. **Special programs:** Internships; Co-ops. **Office hours:**
Monday - Friday, 9:00 a.m. - 5:30 p.m. **Parent company:** Tetra Tech, Inc. **Listed
on:** Privately held. **Annual sales/revenues:** $21 - $50 million.

SEA CONSULTANTS, INC.
485 Massachusetts Avenue, Cambridge MA 02139. 617/497-7800. **Contact:**
Human Resources. **World Wide Web address:** http://www.seacon.com.
Description: A multifunctional engineering firm offering a wide variety of
engineering services including civil, structural, scientific, and environmental
engineering. **Positions advertised include:** Accounts Payable Coordinator.

SHAW ENVIRONMENTAL & INFRASTRUCTURE
88C Elm Street, Hopkinton MA 01748-1656. 508/435-9561. **Contact:** Human
Resources. **World Wide Web address:** http://www.shawgrp.com. **Description:**
Develops advanced technologies for the environmental restoration of
contaminated sites. One of the largest environmental consulting, engineering,
and remediation firms in the world, the company operates 70 locations
worldwide. **Positions advertised include:** Engineer Technician.

TELLUS INSTITUTE
11 Arlington Street, Boston MA 02116. 617/266-5400. **Fax:** 617/266-8303.
Contact: David McAnulty, Human Resources. **E-mail address:**
dmac@tellus.org. **World Wide Web address:** http://www.tellus.org.
Description: An environmental research and consulting agency. Much of the
Tellus Institute's work is under government contract in the fields of energy, gas,
and solid waste. **Corporate headquarters location:** This location.

TETRA TECH, INC.
55 Jonstin Road, Wilmington MA 01887. 978/658-7500. **Contact:** Human
Resources. **World Wide Web address:** http://www.tetratech.com. **Description:**
An environmental engineering firm.

WTE CORPORATION
7 Alfred Circle, Bedford MA 01730. 781/275-6400. **Contact:** Human Resources.
World Wide Web address: http://www.wte.com. **Description:** Recycles plastics
and metals. **Corporate headquarters location:** This location.

WASTE MANAGEMENT, INC.
256 New Lancaster Road, Leominster MA 01453. 978/840-9557. **Contact:**
Human Resources. **World Wide Web address:**
http://www.wastemanagement.com. **Description:** Engaged in hauling trash and
waste.

WESTON & SAMPSON ENGINEERS INC.
5 Centennial Drive, Peabody MA 01960. 978/532-1900. **Toll-free phone:**
800/SAM-PSON. **Fax:** 978/977-0100. **Contact:** Colleen Manning, Human
Resources Manager. **World Wide Web address:** http://www.wseinc.com.
Description: Specializes in infrastructure and environmental engineering. The

company provides services in the areas of water, wastewater, transportation, solid waste, and geo-technical. Founded in 1899. **Positions advertised include:** Construction Inspector; Project Manager; Environmental Scientist; Engineer; Waste Water Treatment Operator; Water Operator.

FABRICATED METAL PRODUCTS AND PRIMARY METALS

You can expect to find the following types of companies in this section:
Aluminum and Copper Foundries • Die-Castings • Iron and Steel Foundries • Steel Works, Blast Furnaces, and Rolling Mills

AUTOMATIC SPECIALTIES, INC.
422 Northboro Road, Marlboro MA 01752. 508/481-2370. **Toll-free phone:** 800/445-2370. **Fax:** 508/485-6276. **Contact:** Human Resources. **Description:** A leading manufacturer of a variety of metal products including wire and strip forms, metal stampings, and welded wire assemblies.

CAMBRIDGE-LEE INDUSTRIES, INC.
500 Lincoln Street, Allston MA 02134. 617/783-3100. **Contact:** Human Resources. **World Wide Web address:** http://www.cambridgelee.com. **Description:** A distributor of copper, brass, and other industrial metals. Founded in 1939. **Subsidiaries include:** IUSA; Reading Tube Corporation.

CANAM STEEL CORPORATION
P.O. Box 1245, Easton MA 02334-1245. 508/238-4500. **Physical address:** 50 Eastman Street, Easton MA 02334. **Fax:** 508/238-8253. **Contact:** Paul Lestrange, Controller. **World Wide Web address:** http://www.canammanac.com. **Description:** A fabricator of structural steel and steel commodities including joists and metal deck. **Corporate headquarters location:** Point of Rocks MD. **Parent company:** Canam Manac Group (Saint George's, Quebec, Canada). **Operations at this facility include:** Administration; Engineering and Design; Sales. **Number of employees at this location:** 50.

DORANCO INC.
200 Gilbert Street, Mansfield MA 02048. 508/261-1200. **Fax:** 508/237-6965. **Contact:** Human Resources. **E-mail address:** info@doranco.com. **World Wide Web address:** http://www.doranco.com. **Description:** A manufacturer of decorative metal parts, primarily for the consumer audio electronics and telecommunications industries. Products include floor stands for speakers and faceplates for audio and computer components as well as nameplates for consumer products ranging from automobiles to household appliances. **Corporate headquarters location:** This location. **Other U.S. locations:** Phoenix AZ; Attleboro Falls MA. **International locations:** South Korea. **Number of employees worldwide:** 200.

EMJ METALS
59 South Street, Hopkinton MA 01748. 508/435-6854. **Toll-free phone:** 800/336-5365. **Fax:** 508/435-2520. **Contact:** Human Resources. **World Wide Web address:** http://www.emjmetals.com. **Description:** A metal services center offering a diverse stock of metal products. Products include various forms of tubing and bars as well as steel and aluminum products. **Corporate headquarters location:** Brea CA. **Other U.S. locations:** Nationwide. **Operations at this facility include:** Manufacturing; Sales; Service. **Number of employees at this location:** 45.

EXTRUSION TECHNOLOGY, INC.
80 Trim Way, Randolph MA 02368. 781/963-7200. **Contact:** Human Resources. **E-mail address:** careers@extrutech.com. **World Wide Web address:** http://www.extrutech.com. **Description:** Manufactures fabricated aluminum extrusions including electronic enclosures and rack systems. **Positions advertised include:** Sales Program Manager; Materials Service Manager; Computer Numerical Control Operator; Lead Mechanical Assembler; Shipper Supervisor; Environmental & Supply Specialist; Customer Support Representative; Junior Accountant; Manager.

KEN-WELD COMPANY, INC.
P.O. Box 15021, Worcester MA 01615-0021. 508/798-8756. **Physical address:** 68 Albany Street, Worcester MA 01604. **Fax:** 508/798-3785. **Contact:** Human Resources. **E-mail address:** kenweld@compuserve.com. **World Wide Web address:** http://www.kenweld.com. **Description:** Engaged in metal fabrication and machining. Founded in 1945.

REED & PRINCE
8 Mohawk Drive, Leominster MA 01453. 508/753-2931. **Fax:** 978/466-6980. **Contact:** Human Resources. **Description:** A manufacturer and packager of metal fasteners and fastening systems including high-precision fittings for use in spacecraft, recessed and slotted screws, nuts, bolts, rivets, and screwdrivers. **Corporate headquarters location:** This location.

SUNCOR STAINLESS
70 Armstrong Road, Plymouth MA 02360. 508/732-9191. **Fax:** 508/732-9798. **Contact:** Human Resources. **E-mail address:** sales@suncorstainless.com. **World Wide Web address:** http://www.suncorstainless.com. **Description:** A stainless steel and titanium products manufacturer. **Other U.S. Locations:** California, Florida & New Mexico. **International location:** Ontario Canada.

VULCAN INDUSTRIES, INC.
P.O. Box 166, 4 Cabot Road, Hudson MA 01749. 978/562-0003. **Fax:** 978/562-0285. **Contact:** Personnel. **E-mail address:** metalman@vulcanindustries.com. **World Wide Web address:** http://www.vulcanindustry.com. **Description:** A leading fabricator of precision sheet metal. **Positions advertised include:** Engineering Associate; Shearing Associate.

FINANCIAL SERVICES

You can expect to find the following types of companies in this section:
Consumer Financing and Credit Agencies • Investment Specialists • Mortgage Bankers and Loan Brokers • Security and Commodity Brokers, Dealers, and Exchanges

---

ACADIAN ASSET MANAGEMENT INC.
10 Post Office Square, 8th Floor, Boston MA 02109. 617/946-3500. **Fax:** 617/946-3501. **Contact:** Human Resources. **World Wide Web address:** http://www.acadian-asset.com. **Description:** A money management firm specializing in international stocks. **Positions advertised include:** Investment Operations Specialist; Portfolio Associate; Database Systems Engineer. **NOTE:** Summer internships available. Search for current positions on website.

ADVEST
100 Federal Street, 29th Floor, Boston MA 02110. 617/348-2200. **Contact:** Human Resources. **World Wide Web address:** http://www.advest.com. **Description:** Provides stock brokerage services. **Positions advertised include:** Financial Analyst.

BEAR, STEARNS & COMPANY, INC.
One Federal Street, 29th Floor, Boston MA 02110. 617/654-2800. **Toll-free phone:** 800/333-2327. **Fax:** 617/654-2329. **Contact:** Human Resources. **World Wide Web address:** http://www.bearstearns.com. **Description:** A leading worldwide investment banking, securities trading, and brokerage firm. The firm's business includes corporate finance, mergers and acquisitions, public finance, institutional equities, fixed income sales and trading, private client services, foreign exchange, future sales and trading, derivatives, and asset management. **Corporate headquarters location:** New York NY. **Other U.S. locations:** Nationwide. **International locations:** Worldwide. **Parent company:** The Bear Stearns Companies Inc. also operates Bear, Stearns Securities Corporation, providing professional and correspondent clearing services, including securities lending; and Custodial Trust Company, providing master trust, custody, and government securities services. **Listed on:** New York Stock Exchange. **Stock exchange symbol:** BSC. **Annual sales/revenues:** More than $100 million. **Number of employees nationwide:** 7,800.

THE BOSTON COMPANY
One Boston Place, Boston MA 02108. 617/722-7000. **Contact:** Human Resources. **World Wide Web address:** http://www.thebostoncompany.com. **Description:** A bank and mutual fund management company. **NOTE:** Please send resumes to: The Boston Company, Human Resources, 135 Santelli Highway, Everett MA 02149. **Special programs:** Internships. **Corporate headquarters location:** Pittsburgh PA. **Other U.S. locations:** CA; DE; MD; PA. **Subsidiaries include:** Boston Safe Deposit & Trust Company (also at this location.) **Parent company:** Mellon Bank Corporation. **Operations at this facility include:** Regional Headquarters. **Listed on:** New York Stock Exchange. **Stock exchange symbol:** MEL. **Number of employees at this location:** 3,000. **Number of employees nationwide:** 3,200.

BOSTON FINANCIAL DATA SERVICES, INC.
2 Heritage Drive, North Quincy MA 02171. 617/483-5000. **Toll-free phone:** 888/772-BFDS. **Contact:** Human Resources. **E-mail address:** jobs@bostonfinancial.com. **World Wide Web address:** http://www.bostonfinancial.com. **Description:** A service agent for State Street Bank & Trust Company specializing in the mutual fund, corporate stock transfer, and insurance services industries. **Positions advertised include:** Mutual Fund Correspondence Specialist; Customer Services Representative; Operations Representative; Audit Specialist. **Special programs:** Internships. **Parent company:** State Street Bank & Trust and DST Systems. **Operations at this facility include:** Administration; Service.

BOSTON 128 COMPANIES, INC.
3 University Office Park, 95 Sawyer Road, Suite 110, Waltham MA 02453. 781/642-0777. **Contact:** Human Resources. **World Wide Web address:** http://www.boston128companies.com. **Description:** A full-service financial company. Boston 128 Companies specializes in deferred compensation plans for corporate and individual clients. **Positions advertised include:** Account Manager; Brokerage Relationship Manager.

BOSTON STOCK EXCHANGE
100 Franklin Street, Boston MA 02110. 617/235-2000. **Fax:** 617/235-2200. **Contact:** Human Resources. **World Wide Web address:** http://www.bostonstock.com. **Description:** A stock exchange. **Positions advertised include:** Sales; Staff Accountant.

CDC IXIS ASSET MANAGEMENT NORTH AMERICA
399 Boylston Street, Boston MA 02116. 617/449-2100. **Contact:** Human Resources. **World Wide Web address:** http://www.cdcixis-amna.com. **Description:** An investment management company. **Parent company:** CDC IXIS Asset Management (France). **Corporate headquarters location:** This location.

CGM FUNDS
P.O. Box 8511, Boston MA 02266 **Physical address:** 222 Berkeley Street, Suite 1013, Boston MA 02116. 617/859-7714. **Toll-free phone:** 800/345-4048. **Fax:** 617/226-1838. **Contact:** Tony Figueiredo, Human Resources. **World Wide Web address:** http://www.cgmfunds.com. **Description:** Manages mutual funds for investors.

CHARLES SCHWAB & CO., INC.
127 Congress Street, Boston MA 02110. **Toll-free phone:** 800/435-4000. **Fax:** 617/210-7418. **Contact:** Branch Manager. **World Wide Web address:** http://www.schwab.com. **Description:** A leading provider of discount brokerage services and no-transaction fee mutual funds. The company provides a wide range of services for individuals, institutions, financial advisors, and retirement plans, and has over 4 million investor accounts. Charles Schwab & Co., Inc. also provides online brokerage services. **Positions advertised include:** Account Representative; Branch Manager. **Corporate headquarters location:** San Francisco CA. **Other U.S. locations:** Nationwide. **Operations at this facility include:** Sales; Service. **Listed on:** New York Stock Exchange. **Stock exchange symbol:** SCH. **Number of employees worldwide:** 10,400.

CHARLES SCHWAB & CO., INC.
Liberty Square, 1220 Iyanough Road, Route 132, Suite G, Hyannis MA 02601. 508/778-5050. **Toll-free phone:** 800/435-4000. **Contact:** Branch Manager.

World Wide Web address: http://www.schwab.com. **Description:** A leading provider of discount brokerage services and no-transaction fee mutual funds. The company provides a wide range of services for individuals, institutions, financial advisors, and retirement plans, and has over 4 million investor accounts. Charles Schwab & Co., Inc. also provides online brokerage services. **Corporate headquarters location:** San Francisco CA. **Stock exchange symbol:** SCH. **Number of employees worldwide:** 10,400.

CHARLES SCHWAB & CO., INC.
1262 Boylston Street, Chestnut Hill MA 02467. **Toll-free phone:** 800/435-4000. **Contact:** Branch Manager. **World Wide Web address:** http://www.schwab.com. **Description:** A leading provider of discount brokerage services and no-transaction fee mutual funds. The company provides a wide range of services for individuals, institutions, financial advisors, and retirement plans, and has over 4 million investor accounts. Charles Schwab & Co., Inc. also provides online brokerage services. **Corporate headquarters location:** San Francisco CA. **Stock exchange symbol:** SCH. **Number of employees worldwide:** 10,400.

CHARLES SCHWAB & CO., INC.
54 Mall Road, Burlington MA 01803. 781/270-7475. **Contact:** Branch Manager. **World Wide Web address:** http://www.schwab.com. **Description:** A leading provider of discount brokerage services and no-transaction fee mutual funds. The company provides a wide range of services for individuals, institutions, financial advisors, and retirement plans, and has over 4 million investor accounts. Charles Schwab & Co., Inc. also provides online brokerage services. **Corporate headquarters location:** San Francisco CA. **Stock exchange symbol:** SCH. **Number of employees worldwide:** 10,400.

CONTRAVISORY RESEARCH & MANAGEMENT CORPORATION
99 Derby Street, Suite 302, Hingham MA 02043. 781/749-3380. **Contact:** Human Resources. **E-mail address:** info@contravisory.com. **World Wide Web address:** http://www.contravisory.com. **Description:** An investment advisory firm whose services include mutual funds.

THE CREDIT NETWORK
59 Howard Street, Framingham MA 01702. 508/875-5266. **Contact:** Human Resources. **World Wide Web address:** http://www.tcnlink.com. **Description:** A credit reporting service catering to the mortgage industry. **Positions advertised include:** National Account Manager.

EATON VANCE CORPORATION
255 State Street, Boston MA 02109. 617/482-8260. **Toll-free phone:** 800/225-6265. **Contact:** Mora O'Brien, Recruiting Manager. **World Wide Web address:** http://www.eatonvance.com. **Description:** An investment firm. **CEO/President:** James Hawkes.

EQUISERVE
150 Royall Street, Canton MA, 02021. 781/575-2508. **Contact:** Human Resources. **World Wide Web address:** http://www.equiserve.com. **Description:** A stock trading transfer agency. **Positions advertised include:** Account Administrator; Accountant; Business Operations Specialist; Business Systems Analyst; Conversion Analyst; Mail Distribution Associate; Processing Associate; Unit Leader, Transfer Operation.

EVERGREEN FUNDS
200 Berkeley Street, Boston MA 02116. 617/338-3200. **Fax:** 617/210-3234. **Contact:** Human Resources. **World Wide Web address:** http://www.evergreenfunds.com. **Description:** A mutual fund and retirement management company. Founded in 1932. **Positions advertised include:** Financial Advisor.

FIDELITY INVESTMENTS
82 Devonshire Street, Boston MA 02109. 617/563-7000. **Fax:** 617/476-4262. **Contact:** Human Resources. **World Wide Web address:** http://www.fidelity.com/employment. **Description:** One of the nation's leading investment counseling and mutual fund/discount brokerage firms. **Positions advertised include:** Quantitative Analyst; Report Developer; Business Analyst; Benefits Specialist; Team Manager; Fund Accounting Manager. **Corporate headquarters location:** This location. **Other U.S. locations:** Nationwide. **International locations:** Worldwide. **Operations at this facility include:** Administration; Regional Headquarters; Research and Development; Sales. **Listed on:** Privately held. **Number of employees at this location:** 9,000.

FIDELITY INVESTMENTS
300 Puritan Way, Mail Zone MM1H, Marlborough MA 01752. 508/787-7000. **Contact:** Human Resources. **World Wide Web address:** http://www.fidelity.com. **Description:** Fidelity Investments is one of the nation's leading investment counseling and mutual fund/discount brokerage firms. **Corporate headquarters location:** Boston MA. **Operations at this facility include:** This location is an investor center. **Number of employees at this location:** 3,500.

FIDELITY INVESTMENTS
300 Granite Street, Suite 102, Braintree MA 02184. **Toll-free phone:** 800/544-9797. **Contact:** Human Resources. **World Wide Web address:** http://www.fidelity.com. **Description:** Fidelity Investments is one of the nation's leading investment counseling and mutual fund/discount brokerage firms. **Positions advertised include:** Benefits Manager; Pension Manager. **Corporate headquarters location:** Boston MA. **Operations at this facility include:** This location is an investor center.

FIDELITY INVESTMENTS
155 Congress Street, Boston MA 02109. **Toll-free phone:** 800/544-9797. **Contact:** Human Resources. **World Wide Web address:** http://www.fidelity.com. **Description:** Fidelity Investments is one of the nation's leading investment counseling and mutual fund/discount brokerage firms. **Corporate headquarters location:** Boston MA. **Operations at this facility include:** This location is an investor center.

FIRST INVESTORS CORPORATION
305 Second Avenue, Waltham MA 02451. 781/890-9201. **Fax:** 781/890-8817. **Contact:** Human Resources. **World Wide Web address:** http://www.firstinvestors.com. **Description:** Offers investment programs, life insurance, retirement planning, and other tax-deferred programs. Founded in 1930. **NOTE:** Entry-level workers begin as Registered Representative/Management Trainees after successfully completing the National Association of Securities Dealers Licensing Course and passing examinations administered by First Investors Corporation. **Corporate headquarters location:** New York NY. **Other U.S. locations:** Nationwide. **Operations at this facility include:** Regional Headquarters.

FREEDOM CAPITAL
One Beacon Street, 5th Floor, Boston MA 02108. 617/725-2300. **Contact:** Human Resources. **Description:** A security brokerage firm.

JEFFERIES & COMPANY, INC.
One Post Office Square, 40th Floor, Boston MA 02109. 617/342-7800. **Contact:** Human Resources. **World Wide Web address:** http://www.jefco.com. **Description:** Engaged in equity, convertible debt, taxable fixed income securities brokerage and trading, and corporate finance. Jefferies is one of the leading national firms engaged in the distribution and trading of blocks of equity securities and conducts such activities primarily in the third market. Founded in 1962. **Corporate headquarters location:** Los Angeles CA. **Other U.S. locations:** San Francisco CA; Stamford CT; Atlanta GA; Chicago IL; New Orleans LA; Jersey City NJ; Short Hills NJ; New York NY; Nashville TN; Dallas TX; Richmond VA. **International locations:** Australia; Hong Kong; London; Paris; Tokyo; Zurich. **Listed on:** New York Stock Exchange. **Stock exchange symbol:** JEF. **Parent company:** Jefferies Group, Inc. is a holding company that, through Jefferies & Company and its three other primary subsidiaries, Investment Technology Group, Inc., Jefferies International Limited, and Jefferies Pacific Limited, is engaged in securities brokerage and trading, corporate finance, and other financial services.

JOHN HANCOCK FINANCIAL SERVICES
John Hancock Place, Box 111, Boston MA 02117. 617/572-4500. **Fax:** 617/572-4539. **Contact:** Human Resources. **E-mail address:** employment@jhancock.com. **World Wide Web address:** http://www.jhancock.com. **Description:** An insurance and financial services firm operating through two divisions: The Retail Sector offers protection and investment products to middle- and upper-income markets; The Investment & Pension Group is involved in bond and corporate finance services as well as in real estate and mortgage loans. Founded in 1862. **NOTE:** Entry-level positions are offered. **Special programs:** Internships; Training. **Corporate headquarters location:** This location. **International locations:** Worldwide. **Annual sales/revenues:** More than $100 million. **Number of employees at this location:** 4,100. **Number of employees nationwide:** 11,000.

MFS INVESTMENT MANAGEMENT
500 Boylston Street, Boston MA 02116. 617/954-5000. **Contact:** Human Resources. **E-mail address:** jobs@mfs.com. **World Wide Web address:** http://www.mfs.com. **Description:** A full-service investment management firm. Founded in 1924. **Positions advertised include:** Divisional Director; Administrative Assistant; Regional Vice President; Regional Sales Representative; Office Associate; Lead RFP Writer; Programmer; Financial Systems Analyst; Corporate Tax Manager; Tax Analyst; Equity Trader; Asset Controller; Fund Administrator; Fund Team Manager. **NOTE:** Entry-level positions are offered. **Corporate headquarters location:** This location. **Other U.S. locations:** Phoenix AZ. **Parent company:** Sun Life Assurance. **Operations at this facility include:** Administration; Research and Development; Sales; Service. **Number of employees at this location:** 1,500.

MERRILL LYNCH
2 Batterymarch Park, Quincy MA 02169. 617/745-5500. **Contact:** Human Resources. **World Wide Web address:** http://www.ml.com. **Description:** One of the largest securities brokerage firms in the United States. Merrill Lynch provides securities, extensive insurance, and real estate and related services. The

company also brokers commodity futures, commodity options, and corporate and municipal securities. In addition, Merrill Lynch is engaged in investment banking activities. **Positions advertised include:** Manager Assistant; Financial Advisor. **Special programs:** Internships. **Office hours:** Monday - Friday, 8:30 a.m. - 5:00 p.m. **Corporate headquarters location:** New York NY. **Other U.S. locations:** Nationwide. **International locations:** Worldwide. **Listed on:** New York Stock Exchange. **Stock exchange symbol:** MER. **President/CEO:** E. Stanley O'Neal. **Annual sales/revenues:** More than $100 million. **Number of employees worldwide:** 63,800.

MORGAN STANLEY DEAN WITTER & COMPANY
125 High Street, 24th Floor, Boston MA 02110. 617/478-6400. **Contact:** Human Resources. **World Wide Web address:** http://www.msdw.com. **Description:** Offers diversified financial services including equities, fixed income securities, commodities, money market instruments, and investment banking services. **Office hours:** Monday - Friday, 8:30 a.m. - 5:00 p.m. **Corporate headquarters location:** New York NY.

MORGAN STANLEY DEAN WITTER & COMPANY
6 Park Avenue, Worcester MA 01605. 508/849-5500. **Contact:** Human Resources. **World Wide Web address:** http://www.msdw.com. **Description:** Offers diversified financial services including equities, fixed income securities, commodities, money market instruments, and investment banking services. **Corporate headquarters location:** New York NY.

NORTHWESTERN MUTUAL FINANCIAL NETWORK
55 William Street Suite 110, Wellesley MA, 02481. 781/237-7070. **Contact:** Steve Tipton, Director of Training & Development. **World Wide Web address:** http://www.nmfn.com. **Description:** A financing network with home offices in Milwaukee WI.

OLD MUTUAL ASSET MANAGERS (U.S.)
200 Clarendon Street, 53rd Floor, Boston MA 02116. 617/369-7300. **Contact:** Lucy Stinson, Human Resources. **World Wide Web address:** http://www.omam.com. **Description:** Provides investment management services primarily to institutional investors through 42 operating firms. **Corporate headquarters location:** This location. **Subsidiaries include:** Acadian Asset Management; Analytic Investment Management; Barrow, Hanley, Mewhinney & Strauss; C.S. McKee & Company; Cambiar Investors; Chicago Asset Management Company; Cooke & Bieler; Dewey Square Investors Corporation; Dwight Asset Management Company; Fiduciary Management Associates; First Pacific Advisors; GSB Investment Management; Hagler, Mastrovita & Hewitt; Hamilton, Allen & Associates; Hanson Investment Management Company; Heitman Financial; Hellman, Jordan Management Company; Investment Counselors of Maryland; Investment Research Company; Murray Johnstone Limited; Nelson, Benson & Zellmer; Newbold's Asset Management; Northern Capital Management; NWQ Investment Management Company; Olympic Capital Management; Pell, Rudman & Co.; Provident Investment Counsel; Regis Retirement Plan Services; Rice, Hall, James & Associates; Rothschild/Pell, Rudman & Co.; Sirach Capital Management; Spectrum Asset Management; Sterling Capital Management Company; Suffolk Capital Management; The Campbell Group; The L&B Group; Thompson, Siegel & Walmsley; Tom Johnson Investment Management; UAM Investment Services. **Number of employees nationwide:** 1,500.

PFPC
101 Federal Street, Boston MA 02110. 617/535-0300. **Contact:** Human Resources. **World Wide Web address:** http://www.pfpc.com. **Description:** Provides a broad range of financial services including accounting, global fund services, retirement services, securities lending services, and fund custody services.

PNC ADVISORS
99 High Street, Oliver Tower, 27th Floor, Boston MA 02110. 617/334-6030. **Contact:** Human Resources. **World Wide Web address:** http://www.pncadvisors. com. **Description:** An investment firm that provides financial planning, customized credit solutions, brokerage services, mutual funds, and customized investment portfolios. **Positions advertised include:** Administrative Assistant. **NOTE:** Apply online. **Parent company:** PNC Bank Corporation (Pittsburgh, PA).

THE PIONEER GROUP, INC.
60 State Street, 19th Floor, Boston MA 02109. 617/742-7825. **Contact:** Human Resources. **World Wide Web address:** http://www.pioneerfunds.com. **Description:** Offers individual investment, institutional investment management, real estate advisory, venture capital, and emerging market services. **Corporate headquarters location:** This location.

PUTNAM INVESTMENTS
One Post Office Square, Boston MA 02109. 617/292-1000. **Contact:** Human Resources. **World Wide Web address:** http://www.putnaminv.com. **Description:** A money management firm. **Positions advertised include:** Business Data Analyst; Strategic Relationship Analyst; Mail Clerk; Investment Reporting Analyst; Portfolio Analyst; Financial Engineer. **Corporate headquarters location:** This location. **Other U.S. locations:** Andover MA; Franklin MA; Quincy MA.

SALOMON SMITH BARNEY
53 State Street, 39th Floor, Boston MA 02109. 617/589-3500. **Contact:** Human Resources. **World Wide Web address:** http://www.salomonsmithbarney.com. **Description:** An international investment banking, market making, and research firm serving corporations, state and local governments, sovereign and provincial governments and their agencies, central banks, and other financial institutions. **Other area locations:** Brockton; Hingham; Pittsfield; Waltham; State Street Boston; Danvers; Hyannis; Springfield; Worcester. **Corporate headquarters location:** New York NY.

SEACOAST CAPITAL PARTNERS
55 Ferncroft Road, Suite 110, Danvers MA 01923-4001. 978/750-1351. **Fax:** 978/750-1301. **Contact:** Human Resources. **World Wide Web address:** http://www.seacoastcapital.com. **Description:** A personal credit institution. **Other U.S. location:** San Francisco CA.

SOVEREIGN BANK
One Harvard Street, Brookline Village MA 02446. 617/232-0467. **Toll-free phone:** 877/768-2265. **Contact:** Human Resources. **World Wide Web address:** http://www.sovereignbank.com. **Description**: A $55 billion financial institution with nearly 600 community banking offices and 1,000 ATMs in Connecticut, Massachusetts, New Hampshire, New Jersey, New York, Pennsylvania, and Rhode Island. **Parent company:** Sovereign Bancorp, Inc. **Listed on:** New York

Stock Exchange. **Stock exchange symbol:** SOV. **Number of employees nationwide:** 9,500.

SOVEREIGN BANK
75 State Street, Boston MA 02109. **Toll-free phone:** 877/768-2265. **Contact:** Human Resources. **World Wide Web address:** http://www.sovereignbank.com. **Description:** A $55 billion financial institution with nearly 600 community banking offices and 1,000 ATMs in Connecticut, Massachusetts, New Hampshire, New Jersey, New York, Pennsylvania, and Rhode Island. **Positions advertised include:** Anti – Money Laundering Analyst; Community Banking Manager; Customer Service Representative; Teller; Deposit Manager; Executive Assistant; Financial Assistant. **Parent company:** Sovereign Bancorp, Inc. **Listed on:** New York Stock Exchange. **Stock exchange symbol:** SOV. **Number of employees nationwide:** 9,500.

STATE STREET CORPORATION
225 Franklin Street, Boston MA 02110. 617/786-3000. **Contact:** Human Resources. **World Wide Web address:** http://www.statestreet.com. **Description:** Provides securities and recordkeeping services to nearly 2,000 mutual funds and manages a large number of tax-exempt assets. State Street is a major manager of international index assets and provides corporate banking services, specialized lending, and international banking services. **Corporate headquarters location:** This location. **Parent company:** State Street Boston Corporation. **Number of employees worldwide:** 17,400.

STATE STREET RESEARCH
One Financial Center, 22nd Floor, Boston MA 02111. 617/482-3920. **Contact:** Human Resources. **World Wide Web address:** http://www.statestreetresearch.com. **Description:** A financial services organization primarily involved in the management of corporate funds.

STOCKCROSS
One Washington Mall, Boston MA 02108. 617/367-5700. **Toll-free phone:** 800/225-6196. **Fax:** 617/367-6399. **Contact:** Human Resources. **E-mail address:** info@stockcross.com. **World Wide Web address:** http://www.stockcross.com. **Description:** A discount stock brokerage.

UBS PAINEWEBBER INC.
100 Federal Street, 27th Floor, Boston MA 02110. 617/261-1000. **Contact:** Human Resources. **World Wide Web address:** http://www.ubspainewebber.com. **Description:** A full-service securities firm with over 300 offices nationwide. Services include investment banking, asset management, merger and acquisition consulting, municipal securities underwriting, estate planning, retirement programs, and transaction management. Clients include corporations, governments, institutions, and individuals. Founded in 1879. **Corporate headquarters location:** New York NY. **Other U.S. locations:** Nationwide. **Listed on:** New York Stock Exchange. **Stock exchange symbol:** UBS. **Annual sales/revenues:** More than $100 million.

UBS PAINEWEBBER INC.
265 Franklin Street, Boston MA 02110. 617/439-8000. **Contact:** Human Resources. **World Wide Web address:** http://www.ubspainewebber.com. **Description:** A full-service securities firm with over 300 offices nationwide. Services include investment banking, asset management, merger and acquisition consulting, municipal securities underwriting, estate planning, retirement programs, and transaction management. Clients include corporations,

governments, institutions, and individuals. Founded in 1879. **Corporate headquarters location:** New York NY. **Other U.S. locations:** Nationwide. **Listed on:** New York Stock Exchange. **Stock exchange symbol:** UBS. **Annual sales/revenues:** More than $100 million.

ZURICH SCUDDER INVESTMENTS
2 International Place, Boston MA 02110. 617/295-1000. **Contact:** Human Resources. **World Wide Web address:** www.scudder.com. **Description:** An investment firm.

FOOD AND BEVERAGES/AGRICULTURE

**You can expect to find the following types of companies
in this section:**
Crop Services and Farm Supplies • Dairy Farms • Food
Manufacturers/Processors and Agricultural Producers • Tobacco Products

ASLANIS SEAFOODS
10 Granite Street, Quincy MA 02169. 617/479-0500. **Contact:** Personnel. **World Wide Web address:** http://www.aslanis.com. **Description:** A wholesale processor and packager of seafood.

BAKER COMMODITIES INC.
P.O. Box 132, North Billerica MA 01862-0132. 978/454-8811. **Physical address:** 134 Billerica Avenue, North Billerica MA 01862. **Contact:** Human Resources. **Description:** Processes grease, tallow, and bone meal.

BAY STATE MILLING COMPANY
100 Congress Street, Quincy MA 02169. 617/328-4400. **Toll-free phone:** 800/553-5687. **Fax:** 617/479-8910. **Contact:** Human Resources. **E-mail address:** info@bsm.com. **World Wide Web address:** http://www.baystatemilling.com. **Description:** A flour milling company with nationwide manufacturing facilities. **Corporate headquarters location:** This location. **Other U.S. locations:** Tolleson AZ; Platteville CO; Indiantown FL; Minneapolis MN; Winona MN; Clifton NJ; Mooresville NC.

COCA-COLA BOTTLING COMPANY OF CAPE COD
P.O. Box 779, Sandwich MA 02563-0779. 508/888-0001. **Contact:** Human Resources. **World Wide Web address:** http://www.cocacola.com. **Description:** A bottling plant for Coca-Cola, one of the world's largest soft drink makers. Brand names include Coca-Cola, Diet Coke, Coca-Cola light (international), Sprite, Diet Sprite, Mr. PiBB, Mello Yello, Fanta, TAB, Fresca, Fruitopia, Powerade, and Minute Maid. **Parent company:** The Coca-Cola Company owns 100 supporting brands around the world including Aquarius, Hi-C, Georgia (canned coffee, sold in Japan), Thums Up & Limca (India), Sparletta Brands (South Africa), Nestea (distributed by Coca-Cola Enterprises Inc.), and Seiryusabo (Japan). The Coca-Cola Company has owning interest in many bottlers including 44 percent of Coca-Cola Enterprises Inc., as well as Coca-Cola Foods, the world's largest seller of juice and juice-related products under brands such as FiveAlive, Hi-C, Bright & Early, and Bacardi.

COCA-COLA BOTTLING COMPANY OF NEW ENGLAND
9 B Street, Needham Heights MA 02494. 781/449-4300. **Contact:** Human Resources. **World Wide Web address:** http://www.cocacola.com. **Description:** A bottling plant for Coca-Cola, one of the world's largest soft drink makers. Brand names include Coca-Cola, Diet Coke, Coca-Cola light (international), Sprite, Diet Sprite, Mr. PiBB, Mello Yello, Fanta, TAB, Fresca, Fruitopia, Powerade, and Minute Maid. **Corporate headquarters location:** Atlanta GA. **Parent company:** The Coca-Cola Company owns 100 supporting brands around the world including Aquarius, Hi-C, Georgia (canned coffee, sold in Japan), Thums Up & Limca (India), Sparletta Brands (South Africa), Nestea (distributed by Coca-Cola Enterprises Inc.), and Seiryusabo (Japan). The Coca-Cola Company has owning interest in many bottlers including 44 percent of Coca-Cola Enterprises Inc., as

well as Coca-Cola Foods, the world's largest seller of juice and juice-related products under brands such as FiveAlive, Hi-C, Bright & Early, and Bacardi.

GARELICK FARMS
626 Lynnway, Lynn MA 01905. 781/599-1300. **Fax:** 781/595-9862. **Contact:** Human Resources. **Description:** A manufacturer and distributor of dairy and related food items. **Other area locations:** Franklin MA. **Number of employees nationwide:** 15,000.

GORTON'S, INC.
128 Rogers Street, Gloucester MA 01930-6019. 978/283-3000. **Contact:** Personnel. **E-mail:** careers@gortons.com. **World Wide Web address:** http://www.gortons.com. **Description:** Processes frozen and canned seafood products. Founded in 1849. **Positions advertised include:** Project Engineer; Financial Management Associate. **Special programs:** Internships. **Corporate headquarters location:** This location. **Operations at this facility include:** Administration; Manufacturing; Research and Development; Sales. **Number of employees at this location:** 1,000.

H.P. HOOD INC.
90 Everett Avenue, Chelsea MA 02150. 617/887-3000. **Contact:** Employment Manager. **World Wide Web address:** http://www.hphood.com. **Description:** One of New England's largest food products firms, engaged in the processing and distribution of dairy products. **Positions advertised include:** Assistant Marketing Manager; Claims Manager; Retail Area Manager; Sales Manager. **Corporate headquarters location:** This location. **Operations at this facility include:** Administration; Manufacturing; Research and Development; Service. **Other U.S. locations:** Suffield CT; Portland ME; Agawam MA; Oneida NY; Vernon NY; Barre VT; Winchester VA.

OCEAN SPRAY CRANBERRIES, INC.
One Ocean Spray Drive, Lakeville MA 02349. 508/946-1000. **Contact:** Human Resources. **World Wide Web address:** http://www.oceanspray.com. **Description:** A food processor engaged in the packaging, processing, and marketing of fresh cranberries, cranberry sauces, and fruit juices. **Positions advertised include:** Business Development Manager; Customer Development Coordinator; Deduction Collection Analyst; Manager of Consumer Insights; Manager of Internal Audits; Manager of Unsaleables; Financial Analyst; Sensory Scientist. **Corporate headquarters location:** This location. **Other area locations:** Middleborough MA. **Other U.S. locations:** Vero Beach FL; Bordenton NJ; Sulphur Springs TX; Markham WA; Kenosha WI.

OPTA FOOD INGREDIENTS, INC.
25 Wiggins Avenue, Bedford MA 01730. 781/276-5100. **Toll-free phone:** 800/353-OPTA. **Contact:** Human Resources. **World Wide Web address:** http://www.opta-food.com. **Description:** Develops food ingredients including fiber-based texturizers, starch-based texturizers, and protein-based coatings. These products improve the nutrition, texture, and taste of food products and are targeted at the baking, dairy, and meat industries. Founded in 1991. **Positions advertised include:** Technical Support Representative. **Corporate headquarters location:** This location. **Other U.S. locations:** Galesburg IL; Louisville KY. **Listed on:** NASDAQ. **Stock exchange symbol:** OPTS. **President/CEO:** Arthur McEvily, Ph.D. **Annual sales/revenues:** $11 - $20 million. **Number of employees at this location:** 40. **Number of employees nationwide:** 80.

PEPSI-COLA BOTTLING COMPANY
261 Neck Road, Haverhill MA 01835. 978/521-3923. **Contact:** Human Resources. **World Wide Web address:** http://www.pepsico.com. **Description:** An independent franchise that is a bottling facility for the international soft drink company.

PEPSI-COLA BOTTLING COMPANY
111 Eames Street, Wilmington MA 01887. 978/657-8022. **Fax:** 978/658-9647. **Contact:** Human Resources. **World Wide Web address:** http://www.pepsico.com. **Description:** A bottling facility and a division of the international soft drink manufacturer. **Parent company:** PepsiCo, Inc. (Purchase NY) consists of Frito-Lay Company, Pepsi-Cola Company, and Tropicana Products, Inc. **Listed on:** New York Stock Exchange. **Stock exchange symbol:** PBG.

PEPSI-COLA BOTTLING COMPANY
130 Western Avenue, Allston MA 02134. 617/254-2400. **Contact:** Human Resources. **World Wide Web address:** http://www.pepsico.com. **Description:** A bottling facility and a division of the international soft drink manufacturer. **Parent company:** PepsiCo, Inc. (Purchase NY) consists of Frito-Lay Company, Pepsi-Cola Company, and Tropicana Products, Inc. **Listed on:** New York Stock Exchange. **Stock exchange symbol:** PBG.

PEPSI-COLA BOTTLING COMPANY
620 Myles Standish Boulevard, Taunton MA 02780. 508/823-1500. **Contact:** Human Resources. **World Wide Web address:** http://www.pepsico.com. **Description:** A bottling facility and a division of the international soft drink manufacturer. **Parent company:** PepsiCo, Inc. (Purchase NY) consists of Frito-Lay Company, Pepsi-Cola Company, and Tropicana Products, Inc. **Listed on:** New York Stock Exchange. **Stock exchange symbol:** PBG.

U.S. FOODSERVICE
201 Beacham Street, Everett MA 02149. 617/389-3300. **Toll-free phone:** 800/732-3350. **Fax:** 617/381-6929. **Contact:** Human Resources. **World Wide Web address:** http://www.usfoodservice.com. **Description:** Distributes food products, fresh meats, dairy products, and cleaning supplies to restaurants and other institutional food service establishments. **Corporate headquarters location:** Columbia MD.

U.S. FOODSERVICE
CONTRACT AND DESIGN DIVISION
8 Carnegie Row, Norwood MA 02062. 781/551-3145. **Toll-free phone:** 888/374-8774. **Fax:** 781/551-3294. **Contact:** Human Resources. **World Wide Web address:** http://www.usfoodservice.com. **Description:** The Contract and Design Division installs and designs commercial kitchens, dining areas, and hotel/motel rooms. It is also a national distributor of kitchen, hotel, and restaurant equipment. Overall, U.S. Foodservice distributes food products, fresh meats, dairy products, and cleaning supplies to restaurants and other institutional food service establishments. **NOTE:** Entry-level positions and part-time jobs are offered. **Corporate headquarters location:** Columbia MD. **Number of employees at this location:** 30. **Number of employees worldwide:** 14,000.

UNITED LIQUORS LTD.
One United Drive, West Bridgewater MA 02379. 617/323-0500. **Contact:** Human Resources. **E-mail address:** hr@unitedliqours.com. **World Wide Web address:** http://www.unitedliquors.com. **Description:** A beverage wholesaler. **Corporate**

headquarters location: This location. **Operations at this facility include:** Administration; Sales; Service. **Listed on:** Privately held. **Number of employees at this location:** 750.

THE WEETABIX COMPANY, INC.
20 Cameron Street, Clinton MA 01510. 978/368-0991. **Contact:** Human Resources. **World Wide Web address:** http://www.weetabix.com. **Description:** A cereal manufacturer. **Corporate headquarters location:** This location. **Operations at this facility include:** Administration; Manufacturing; Research and Development; Sales; Service.

WELCH FOODS, INC.
3 Concord Farm, 575 Virginia Road, Concord MA 01742. 978/371-1000. **Contact:** Human Resources. **World Wide Web address:** http://www.welchs.com. **Description:** Produces canned fruits, vegetables, and preserves.

GOVERNMENT

You can expect to find the following types of companies in this section:
Courts • Executive, Legislative, and General Government • Public Agencies (Firefighters, Military, Police) • United States Postal Service

---

THE BETTER BUSINESS BUREAU, INC.
235 Central Street, Suite 1, Natick MA 01760. 508/652-4800. **Fax:** 508/652-4833. **Contact:** Human Resources. **World Wide Web address:** http://www.bosbbb.org. **Description:** The Better Business Bureau provides information to consumers and businesses about companies so that they are better informed before entering into a business relationship. **Special programs:** Internships. **Operations at this facility include:** This office is the regional headquarters serving eastern Massachusetts, Maine, and Vermont.

BOSTON POLICE DEPARTMENT
One Schroeder Plaza, Boston MA 02120. 617/343-4200. **Contact:** Human Resources. **World Wide Web address:** http://www.ci.boston.ma.us/police/default.asp. **Description:** This location serves as the headquarters for Boston's police department.

BOSTON PUBLIC WORKS DEPARTMENT
One City Hall Plaza Room 714, Boston MA 02118. 617/635-4900. **Fax:** 617/635-7499. **Contact:** Human Resources. **World Wide Web address:** http://www.cityofboston.gov/publicworks. **Description:** Performs street repairs, snow plowing, street light replacement, trash pickup, and recycling services for the city of Boston.

DEFENSE CONTRACT MANAGEMENT DISTRICT EAST
10 Causeway Street, Boston MA 02222. 617/565-6850. **Contact:** Human Resources. **Description:** The defense contract management center for the Northeast.

GREATER BOSTON CHAMBER OF COMMERCE
75 State Street, 2nd Floor, Boston MA 02109. 617/227-4500. **Contact:** Human Resources. **World Wide Web address:** http://www.gbcc.org. **Description:** Attracts and promotes businesses in the greater Boston area.

HANSCOM AIR FORCE BASE
20 Schilling Circle, Building 1305, Hanscom MA 01731-2135. 781/377-2280. **Contact:** Personnel. **World Wide Web address:** http://www.hanscom.af.mil. **Description:** An Air Force base. This location also offers seasonal hiring. **NOTE:** Entry-level positions and part-time jobs are offered. **Special programs:** Training; Co-ops; Summer Jobs. **Number of employees at this location:** 2,200.

MASSACHUSETTS ATTORNEY GENERAL'S OFFICE
One Ashburton Place, Boston MA 02108. 617/727-2200. **Contact:** Human Resources. **World Wide Web address:** http://www.ago.state.ma.us. **Description:** Provides legal services for all state entities and represents the state in legal cases.

MASSACHUSETTS DEPARTMENT OF BUSINESS AND TECHNOLOGY

One Ashburton Place, Room 2101, Boston MA 02108. 617/727-8380. **Fax:** 617/727-4426. **Contact:** Personnel. **E-mail address:** econ@state.ma.us. **World Wide Web address:** http://www.state.ma.us/econ. **Description:** Dedicated to improving the job market and long-term economic growth of the state. **Director:** Carolyn E. Boviard.

MASSACHUSETTS DEPARTMENT OF ENVIRONMENTAL MANAGEMENT BUREAU OF RECREATION

251 Causeway Street, Boston MA 02114. 617/626-1250. **Contact:** Human Resources. **World Wide Web address:** http://www.state.ma.us/dem. **Description:** Responsible for the maintenance and improvement of Massachusetts state parks and reservations. The department also offers a variety of educational programs.

MASSACHUSETTS DEPARTMENT OF INDUSTRIAL ACCIDENTS

600 Washington Street, 7th Floor, Boston MA 02111. 617/727-4900. **Toll-free phone:** 800/323-3249. **Contact:** Human Resources. **World Wide Web address:** http://www.state.ma.us/dia. **Description:** Responsible for the administration and management of workers' compensation claims. The Department of Industrial Accidents is part of the Massachusetts Department of Labor and Workforce Development.

MASSACHUSETTS DEPARTMENT OF MENTAL RETARDATION

500 Harrison Avenue, Boston MA 02118. 617/727-5608. **Fax:** 617/624-7577. **Contact:** Human Resources. **World Wide Web address:** http://www.dmr.state.ma.us. **Description:** The Department of Mental Retardation provides support and services to Massachusetts residents with mental retardation. Services include assistance with transportation, job placement, and treatment. **Operations at this facility include:** This location houses the administrative offices of the Department of Mental Retardation.

MASSACHUSETTS DEPARTMENT OF PUBLIC HEALTH

250 Washington Street, 1st Floor, Boston MA 02108-4619. 617/624-5700. **Contact:** Human Resources. **World Wide Web address:** http://www.state.ma.us/dph. **Description:** Responsible for ensuring quality health care and safe living conditions to the people of Massachusetts.

MASSACHUSETTS DEPARTMENT OF REVENUE

51 Sleeper Street, Boston MA 02210. 617/626-3400. **Contact:** Human Resources. **World Wide Web address:** http://www.dor.state.ma.us. **Description:** Massachusetts Department of Revenue processes all Massachusetts residents' income tax returns and provides tax forms, state tax information, and tax publications.

MASSACHUSETTS DEPARTMENT OF TELECOMMUNICATIONS AND ENERGY

One South Station, Boston MA 02110. 617/305-3500. **Contact:** Human Resources. **World Wide Web address:** http://www.mass.gov/dte. **Description:** A regulatory agency for utility companies in the state.

MASSACHUSETTS HIGHWAY DEPARTMENT

10 Park Plaza, Room 3510, Boston MA 02116-3973. 617/973-7500. **Contact:** Human Resources. **World Wide Web address:** http://www.state.ma.us/mhd. **Description:** Provides highway maintenance and repair services as part of the Public Works Department.

MASSACHUSETTS OFFICE OF TRAVEL AND TOURISM
State Transportation Building, 10 Park Plaza, Suite 4510, Boston MA 02116. 617/973-8500. **Toll-free phone:** 800/227-MASS. **Contact:** Director of Operations. **World Wide Web address:** http://www.mass-vacation.com. **Description:** Promotes the state of Massachusetts as a vacation destination. **Special programs:** Internships. **Office hours:** Monday - Friday, 8:45 a.m. - 5:00 p.m. **Number of employees at this location:** 30.

MASSACHUSETTS TRADE OFFICE
State Transportation Building, 10 Park Plaza, Suite 3720, Boston MA 02116. 617/367-1830. **Contact:** Personnel. **World Wide Web address:** http://www.state.ma.us/moiti. **Description:** Assists local businesses in their dealings with international companies. Services include export counseling and trade seminars. Founded in 1983.

MERRIMACK VALLEY CHAMBER OF COMMERCE
264 Essex Street, Lawrence MA 01840. 978/686-0900. **Fax:** 978/794-9953. **Contact:** Personnel. **World Wide Web address:** http://www.merrimackvalleychamber.com. **Description:** Attracts and promotes businesses in the Merrimack Valley area.

SALEM CHAMBER OF COMMERCE
63 Wharf Street, Salem MA 01970. 978/744-0004. **Fax:** 978/745-3855. **Contact:** Denise Flynn, Executive Director. **E-mail address:** scc@salem-chamber.org. **World Wide Web address:** http://www.salem-chamber.org. **Description:** Attracts and promotes businesses in the city of Salem.

U.S. ENVIRONMENTAL PROTECTION AGENCY (EPA)
One Congress Street, Boston MA 02114-2023. 617/918-1111. **Contact:** Human Resources. **World Wide Web address:** http://www.epa.gov. **Description:** The EPA is dedicated to improving and preserving the quality of the environment, both nationally and globally, and protecting human health and the productivity of natural resources. The agency is committed to ensuring that federal environmental laws are implemented and enforced effectively; U.S. policy, both foreign and domestic, encourages the integration of economic development and environmental protection so that economic growth can be sustained over the long term; and public and private decisions affecting energy, transportation, agriculture, industry, international trade, and natural resources fully integrate considerations of environmental quality. Founded in 1970. **Special programs:** Internships. **Corporate headquarters location:** Washington DC. **Other U.S. locations:** San Francisco CA; Denver CO; Atlanta GA; Chicago IL; Kansas City KS; New York NY; Philadelphia PA; Dallas TX; Seattle WA. **Number of employees nationwide:** 19,000.

U.S. FISH AND WILDLIFE SERVICE
300 Westgate Center Drive, Hadley MA 01035. 413/253-8200. **Contact:** Human Resources. **World Wide Web address:** http://www.fws.gov. **Description:** Protects fish and wildlife in national parks and recreation areas. **Corporate headquarters location:** Washington DC.

U.S. FOOD AND DRUG ADMINISTRATION (FDA)
NORTHEAST REGION/BOSTON DISTRICT
One Montvale Avenue, 4th Floor, Stoneham MA 02180. 781/279-1675. **Contact:** Human Resources. **World Wide Web address:** http://www.fda.gov. **Description:** Monitors the manufacture, import, transport, storage, and sale of consumer products. Responsibilities include checking wharves for imports of

food, drugs, cosmetics, medical devices, and radiation emitting products. **Other area locations:** Winchester MA.

U.S. HEALTH AND HUMAN SERVICES
JFK Federal Building, Room 2100, Boston MA 02203. 617/565-1500. **World Wide Web address:** http://www.os.dhhs.gov. **Description:** A government health and human services facility.

U.S. POSTAL SERVICE
59 West Dedham Street, Boston MA 02118. **Toll-free phone:** 800/275-8777. **Contact:** Human Resources. **World Wide Web address:** http://www.usps.com. **Description:** A post office.

HEALTH CARE SERVICES, EQUIPMENT, AND PRODUCTS

You can expect to find the following types of companies in this section:
Dental Labs and Equipment • Home Health Care Agencies • Hospitals and Medical Centers • Medical Equipment Manufacturers and Wholesalers • Offices and Clinics of Health Practitioners • Residential Treatment Centers/Nursing Homes • Veterinary Services

---

ABBOTT LABORATORIES
4A Crosby Drive, Bedford MA 01730. 781/276-6000. **Contact:** Human Resources. **World Wide Web address:** http://www.abbott.com. **Description:** Develops, manufactures, and markets blood-glucose monitoring systems that enable diabetics to manage their disease more effectively. **Positions advertised include:** Site Director; Engineer; Program Coordinator; Scientist; Material Handler; Label Editor. **Corporate headquarters location:** Abbott Park IL. **Other U.S. locations:** Nationwide. **International locations:** Worldwide.

ABIOMED, INC.
22 Cherry Hill Drive, Danvers MA 01923. 978/777-5410. **Fax:** 978/777-8411. **Contact:** Human Resources. **E-mail address:** staffing@abiomed.com. **World Wide Web address:** http://www.abiomed.com. **Description:** Develops, manufactures, and markets cardiovascular, medical, and dental products. The company is also engaged in the research and development of heart support systems. **Positions advertised include:** Clinical Manager, Field Operations; Clinical Research Manager; Product Manager; Scientist. **Corporate headquarters location:** This location. **Subsidiaries include:** Abiodent; Abiomed B.V., Abiomed Cardiovascular; Abiomed R&D. **Operations at this facility include:** Administration; Manufacturing; Research and Development; Sales; Service. **Listed on:** NASDAQ. **Stock exchange symbol:** ABMD. **Number of employees at this location:** 140. **Number of employees nationwide:** 170.

ACTON MEDICAL ASSOCIATES, PC
321 Main Street, Acton MA 01720. 978/263-1425. **Fax:** 978/263-1562. **Contact:** Human Resources. **E-mail address:** hr@actonmedical.com. **World Wide Web address:** http://www.actonmedical.com. **Description:** Offices of a primary care medical group that include laboratory and X-ray facilities. Founded in 1958. **NOTE:** Entry-level positions are offered. **Positions advertised include:** Medical Technologist; PA Diabetes Management; Phlebotomist; Registered Nurse; Licensed Practical Nurse; Internal Medicine. **Special programs:** Internships; Summer Jobs. **Listed on:** Privately held. **Number of employees at this location:** 170.

ALL CARE VISITING NURSE ASSOCIATION
16 City Hall Square, Lynn MA 01901. 781/598-2454. **Toll-free phone:** 800/287-2454. **Fax:** 781/586-1636. **Contact:** Ray Felice, Human Resources Representative. **E-mail address:** professional@allcarevna.org. **World Wide Web address:** http://www.allcarevna.org. **Description:** A nonprofit, certified, home health care agency. The agency's services include HIV/AIDS, mental health, pediatric, oncology, rehab nursing, home nursing, and paraprofessional care. **NOTE:** Entry-level positions and second and third shifts are offered.

Company slogan: A tradition of caring. **Positions advertised include:** Community Health Nurse; Physical Therapist. **Special programs:** Training; Summer Jobs. **Office hours:** Monday - Friday, 8:00 a.m. - 5:00 p.m. **Corporate headquarters location:** This location. **Subsidiaries include:** All Care Resources provides private-duty nurses and companion care to the elderly. **Number of employees nationwide:** 650.

ALLIANCE IMAGING
600 Federal Street, Andover MA 01810. 978/658-5357. **Contact:** Human Resources. **World Wide Web address:** http://www.allianceimaging.com. **Description:** Alliance Imaging provides magnetic resonance imaging systems and services. The company schedules and screens patients; maintains medical and administrative records; and operates both mobile and fixed MRI systems. **Positions advertised include:** Medical Records Clerk; Scheduling Coordinator. **NOTE:** Search and apply for jobs online. **Corporate headquarters location:** Anaheim CA. **Other U.S. locations:** Nationwide. **Listed on:** New York Stock Exchange. **Stock exchange symbol:** AIQ.

AMERICAN MEDICAL RESPONSE (AMR)
4 Tech Circle, P.O. Box 3720, Natick MA 01760. 508/650-5600. **Toll-free phone:** 800/950-9266. **Fax:** 508/650-5656. **Contact:** Human Resources. **E-mail address:** snorton@amr-ems.com. **World Wide Web address:** http://www.amr-inc.com. **Description:** Provides emergency medical transportation. **Other U.S. locations:** Nationwide.

ANGELL MEMORIAL ANIMAL HOSPITAL
350 South Huntington Avenue, Boston MA 02130. 617/522-7400. **Fax:** 617/989-1601. **Contact:** Recruiter/Trainer. **E-mail address:** recruiter@mspca.org. **World Wide Web address:** http://www.angell.org. **Description:** A veterinary hospital that offers general medical care as well as specialized services including heart catheterization facilities, kidney transplant procedures, and radiology treatments. **Parent company:** Massachusetts Society for the Prevention of Cruelty to Animals (MSPCA).

THE ANIMAL CARE CENTER
678 Brookline Avenue, Brookline MA 02445. 617/277-2030. **E-mail address:** careers@healthypet.org. **World Wide Web address:** http://www.healthypet.org. **Contact:** Human Resources. **Description:** An animal hospital providing medical and surgical services. The Animal Care Center also runs a pet adoption service for the city of Boston.

ANIMED PET HOSPITAL
918 Providence Highway, Dedham MA 02026. 781/329-5333. **Contact:** Human Resources. **Description:** A full-service pet hospital.

ARBOUR SENIOR CARE & COUNSELING SERVICES
100 Ledgewood Place, Suite 202, Rockland MA 02370. 781/871-6550. **Contact:** Human Resources. **Description:** Provides behavioral health services delivered by mobile multidisciplinary teams of clinicians at outpatient service sites. The company offers therapeutic, psychiatric, neurological, and diagnostic imaging services. **Corporate headquarters location:** This location. **Number of employees at this location:** 100.

ARROW INTERNATIONAL, INC.
9 Plymouth Street, Everett MA 02149. 617/389-6400. **Contact:** Human Resources. **E-mail address:** staffing.manager@arrowintl.com. **World Wide Web**

address: http://www.arrowintl.com. **Description:** Arrow International develops, manufactures, and markets central vascular access catheterization products. The company's products are also used for patient monitoring, diagnosis, pain management, and treating patients with heart and vascular disease. **Corporate headquarters location:** Reading PA. **Operations at this facility include:** This location manufactures intra-aortic balloons. **Listed on:** NASDAQ. **Stock exchange symbol:** ARRO.

ATHOL MEMORIAL HOSPITAL
2033 Main Street, Athol MA 01331. 978/249-3511. **Fax:** 978/249-5658. **E-mail address:** eamparo@atholhospital.org. **Contact:** Human Resources. **World Wide Web address:** http://www.atholhospital.org. **Description:** An acute care hospital. **Positions advertised include:** MLT; Respiratory Therapist; Physical Therapist.

BETH ISRAEL DEACONESS MEDICAL CENTER
330 Brookline Avenue, Boston MA 02215. 617/667-8000. **Contact:** Human Resources. **World Wide Web address:** http://www.bidmc.harvard.edu. **Description:** A hospital that also supports a network of primary care physicians. **NOTE:** Applicants should send resumes to The Talent Bank at: CareGroup, 21 Autumn Street, Boston MA 02215. **Positions advertised include:** Procurement Manager; Food Service Worker; Director of Human Resources Information Systems; Ultrasonographer; Clinical Research Coordinator; Research Student; Customer Service Representative; Administrative Assistant; Financial Analyst; Materials Handler.

BEVERLY HOSPITAL
85 Herrick Street, Beverly MA 01915. 978/922-3000. **Contact:** Human Resources. **World Wide Web address:** http://www.nhs-healthlink.org. **Description:** A hospital. Beverly Hospital is part of the Northeast Health System. **Positions advertised include:** Access Representative; Administrative Associate; Admissions Registered Nurse; Clinical Associates; Coder; Data Manager; Employment Manager; Executive Assistant; Human Resources Clerk; Lab Associate; Registered Nurse; Security Guard.

BOSTON MEDICAL CENTER
88 East Newton Street, Boston MA 02118. 617/638-8585. **Fax:** 617/638-8577. **Contact:** Human Resources. **World Wide Web address:** http://www.bmc.org. **Description:** A private, nonprofit, 277-bed hospital. The center provides a full range of medical services and offers specialty care units that include psychiatric care, coronary care, metabolic care, medical intensive care, surgical intensive care, the Northeast Regional Center for Brain Injury, the New England Regional Spinal Cord Injury Center, the Breast Health Center, the Cancer Center, the Center for Minimal Access Surgery, the Center for Lung Disease, the Voice Center, the Wald Neurological Unit, the New England Male Reproductive Center, and the University Continence Center. As a major teaching hospital, Boston Medical Center ENC specializes in heart care, the neurosciences, emergency medicine and critical care, elderly care, cancer care, and women's health. The center serves approximately 10,000 admissions and 153,000 outpatient and emergency visits annually. Founded in 1855. **NOTE:** Please send resumes to: Human Resources Department, 88 East Newton Street, Boston MA 02118. **Positions advertised include:** Medical Staff Assistant; Medical Technologist; Radiology Technologist; Respiratory Therapist; Certified Nurses Assistant; Nurse Manager; Registered Nurse; Unit Coordinator; Accounts Receivable Clerk; Administrative Assistant; Administrative Coordinator; Billing Assistant; Patient Access Representative; Research Assistant; Medical Staff Assistant; Residency Coordinator; Payment Processor; General Cleaner; Dietary Aide; Central

Processing Technician; Lab Support Technician; Clinical Pharmacist; Budget Manager; Dietician; Record Assistant; Team Leader.

BOSTON PUBLIC HEALTH COMMISSION

1010 Massachusetts Avenue, 6th Floor, Boston MA 02118. 617/534-5395. **Fax:** 617/534-2418. **Contact:** Patty Hall, Staffing Specialist. **E-mail address:** patty_hall@bphc.org. **World Wide Web address:** http://www.bphc.org. **Description:** A nonprofit agency whose mission is to protect, preserve, and promote the well-being of all Boston residents. Boston Public Health Commission provides community-based public health programs including tobacco control, domestic violence prevention, environmental health, communicable disease awareness, maternal/child health, addictions services, homeless services, and AIDS services. **NOTE:** All positions with Boston Public Health Commission require residency in the city of Boston or a willingness to move to Boston if hired. Entry-level positions and second and third shifts are offered. **Positions advertised include:** Research Assistant; Administrative Assistant; Project Manager; Head Administrative Clerk; Project Manager; Administrative Assistant; Social Worker; Program Coordinator; Counselor; Staffing Coordinator; Resource Clerk; Medical Director; Custodian; Data Analyst. **Number of employees at this location:** 1,100.

BOSTON SCIENTIFIC CORPORATION

480 Pleasant Street, Watertown MA 02172. 617/972-4000. **Contact:** Human Resources. **World Wide Web address:** http://www.bostonscientific.com. **Description:** Boston Scientific Corporation is a worldwide developer, manufacturer, and marketer of medical devices used in a broad range of interventional medical procedures including cardiology, gastroenterology, pulmonary medicine, and vascular surgery. **Positions advertised include:** R&D Engineer; Project Manager; APO Supply Planning Manager. **Corporate headquarters location:** Natick MA. **Other area locations:** Quincy MA. **Other U.S. locations:** CA; FL; IN; MN; NJ; NY. **International locations:** Argentina; Brazil; Mexico; Uruguay; Venezuela. **Operations at this facility include:** This location manufactures balloon catheters used in surgery. **Listed on:** New York Stock Exchange. **Stock exchange symbol:** BSX. **Number of employees at this location:** 1,200.

BOSTON SCIENTIFIC CORPORATION

One Boston Scientific Place, Natick MA 01760-1537. 508/650-8000. **Contact:** Human Resources. **World Wide Web address:** http://www.bostonscientific.com. **Description:** A worldwide developer, manufacturer, and marketer of medical devices used in a broad range of interventional procedures including cardiology, gastroenterology, pulmonary medicine, and vascular surgery. **Positions advertised include:** Research Director; Human Resources Manager; Database Administrator; Software Quality Assurance Specialist; Clinical Data Specialist; Principal Engineer; Safety Coordinator; Project Manager; Administrative Assistant; Clinical Counsel; Strategic Sourcing Manager; Associate Scientist; Medical Research Associate; Tax Analyst; Benefits Analyst; Quality Engineer; Human Resource Process Analyst; Database Specialist; Quality Engineer; Assistant Medical Director; Product Manager; Marketing Communication Specialist; Product Manager. **Corporate headquarters location:** This location. **Other area locations:** Quincy MA. **Other U.S. locations:** CA; FL; IN; MN; NJ; NY. **International locations:** Argentina; Brazil; Mexico; Uruguay; Venezuela. **Listed on:** New York Stock Exchange. **Stock exchange symbol:** BSX.

BRIGHAM & WOMEN'S HOSPITAL
75 Francis Street, Boston MA 02115. 617/732-5790. **Fax:** 617/277-1263. **Contact:** Human Resources. **World Wide Web address:** http://www.brighamandwomens.org. **Description:** A 750-bed, nonprofit hospital. Brigham & Women's houses one of New England's largest birthing centers and a regional center for high-risk obstetrics and neonatology. The hospital is nationally recognized for its transplant programs; joint replacement and orthopedic surgery; and the treatment of arthritis, rheumatic disorders, and cardiovascular disease. **Positions advertised include:** Access Facilitator; Administrative Secretary; Admitting Officer; Nurse Manager; Licensed Practical Nurse; Clinical Dietician; Coding Specialist; Data Coordinator; Environmental Services Aide; Exercise Psychologist; Programmer Analyst; Medical Technologist; Nurse Practitioner; Personal Care Assistant; Processing Technician; Research Assistant; Registered Nurse; Social Worker; Unit Coordinator. **Parent company:** Partners HealthCare System Inc. **Number of employees at this location:** 8,500.

BROCKTON HOSPITAL
680 Centre Street, Brockton MA 02302. 508/941-7000. **Fax:** 508/941-6204. **Contact:** Human Resources. **World Wide Web address:** http://www.brocktonhospital.com. **Description:** A 250-bed, acute care hospital. **Positions advertised include:** Case Manager; Centralized Scheduler; Certified Nurses Assistant; Clerk; Clinical Care Assistant; Mental Health Worker; Physical Therapist; Registered Nurse; Speech Pathologist; Staff Accountant; Switch Board Operator; Unit Secretary.

CAMBRIDGE HEALTH ALLIANCE
1493 Cambridge Street, Cambridge MA 02139. 617/498-1000. **Contact:** Human Resources. **World Wide Web address:** http://www.challiance.org. **Description:** An alliance made up of Cambridge Hospital, Somerville Hospital, a nursing home and several neighborhood health centers. Cambridge Hospital, also at this location, is a 170-bed, full-service hospital owned by the city of Cambridge and affiliated with Harvard and Tufts Medical Schools. **Positions advertised include:** Administrative Assistant; Applications Analyst; Buyer; Clerk; Cardiac Sonographer; Central Processing Department Technician; Clerk & Typist; Computerized Tomography Technologist; Dental Hygienist; Marketing Specialist; Medical Technician; Medical Assistant; Physical Therapist; Dietary Trainee; Case Management Director; General Data Manager; Hospital Aide.

CANDELA CORPORATION
530 Boston Post Road, Wayland MA 01778. 508/358-7400. **Contact:** Human Resources. **World Wide Web address:** http://www.clzr.com. **Description:** Designs, manufactures, markets, and services lasers for a variety of medical applications. The company also licenses medical products and sells them through its worldwide distribution network. Products include Vbeam, which treats vascular lesions; AlexLAZR, which removes tattoos; and GentleLASE Plus, which removes unwanted hairs and also treats vascular lesions. **Corporate headquarters location:** This location. **Number of employees at this location:** 200.

CAPE COD HOSPITAL
27 Park Street, Hyannis MA 02601. 508/771-1800. **Fax:** 508/790-7964. **Contact:** Personnel. **World Wide Web address:** http://www.capecodhealth.org. **Description:** A nonprofit, 258-bed, general acute care, regional hospital. **Positions advertised include:** Assessment Team Clinician; CAT Scan Technologist; Clinical Dietician; Environmental Service Aide; Food Service

Assistant; Occupational Therapist. **Number of employees at this location:** 1,400.

CATHOLIC MEMORIAL HOME
2446 Highland Avenue, Fall River MA 02720-4599. 508/679-0011. **Contact:** Human Resources. **World Wide Web address:** http://www.dhfo.org. **Description:** A 300-bed nursing home with a unit specializing in caring for those with Alzheimer's disease. **Positions advertised include:** Registered Nurse; Certified Nursing Aide; Licensed Practical Nurse. **Parent company:** Diocesan Health Facilities Office (Fall River MA) operates five nursing homes throughout southeastern Massachusetts.

CHILDREN'S HOSPITAL
333 Longwood Avenue, 2nd Floor, Boston MA 02115. 617/355-7780. **Contact:** Human Resources. **Note:** Please send all resumes to: P.O. Box 549252, Suite 227, Waltham MA 02454-9252. **Fax:** 781/663-3722. **World Wide Web address:** http://www.childrenshospital.org/jobs. **Description:** A full-service pediatric hospital. **Positions advertised include:** Research Technician; Speech Language Pathologist; Application Development Specialist; Staff Nurse; Patient Access Representative; Audiologist; Physician Assistant.

COMMONWEALTH HEMATOLOGY-ONCOLOGY
10 Willard Street, Quincy MA 02169. 617/479-3550. **Contact:** Human Resources. **World Wide Web address:** http://www.chomed.com. **Description:** A private practice outpatient facility specializing in the treatment of cancer and blood disorders. **Other area locations:** Brighton MA; Dorchester MA; Lawrence MA; Malden MA; Milton MA; South Weymouth MA.

COMMUNITY HEALTHLINK
72 Jaques Avenue, Worcester MA 01610. 508/860-1000. **Contact:** Human Resources. **World Wide Web address:** http://www.umassmemorial.org. **Description:** A multifaceted community service center whose programs include substance abuse treatment, outpatient services, geriatric services, medical day treatment, and services for the homeless. Community Healthlink is a member of the UMass Memorial Behavioral Health System.

CORE, INC.
88 Black Falcon Avenue, Suite 353, Boston MA 02210-2414. 617/375-7700. **Fax:** 617/375-7777. **Contact:** Human Resources. **World Wide Web address:** http://www.coreinc.com. **Description:** A national provider of physician-intensive, specialty-matched, health care utilization management programs. Health care utilization management is a system of reviewing, evaluating, and monitoring the medical necessity and appropriateness of health care services prescribed for participants in health care plans. Services include independent physician review, behavioral health review, medical resource management, comprehensive case management, rehabilitation review, and disability review. **Corporate headquarters location:** Portland ME. **Parent company:** Fortis, Inc. **Number of employees at this location:** 180.

DANA FARBER CANCER INSTITUTE
44 Binney Street, Boston MA 02115. 617/732-3000. **Contact:** Human Resources. **World Wide Web address:** http://www.dfci.havard.edu. **Description:** A cancer research institute and hospital. **Positions advertised include:** Administrative Assistant; Administrative Specialist; Lab Systems Coordinator; Office Support Specialist; Child Life Specialist; Clinic Assistant; Facilitator; Level II Pharmacist; New Patient Coordinator; Human Resources

Specialist; Program Administrator; Clinical Research Audit manager; Intranet Specialist; Health Educator; Intervention Coordinator; Survey Assistant; Research Associate; Research Fellow; Credit Collection Officer; Statistician; Transcription Assistant; Application Analyst; Research Scientist; Nurse Practitioner; Registered Nurse; Research Nurse; Social Worker.

DAVOL INC.

160 New Boston Street, Woburn MA 01801. 781/932-5900. **Fax:** 781/932-4125. **Contact:** Human Resources. **E-mail address:** arlene.andreozzi.@crbard.com. **World Wide Web address:** http://www.davol.com. **Description:** Develops, manufactures, and markets specialty medical products for use in surgical and nonsurgical procedures. Davol specializes in products relating to hernia repair, laparascopy, and orthopedics. **Positions advertised include:** Product Manager; Cost Supervisor; Manufacturing Engineer. **Corporate headquarters location:** Cranston RI. **Parent company:** C.R. Bard, Inc. **Number of employees at this location:** 45.

DEPUY ACROMED

325 Paramount Drive, Raynham MA 02767. 508/880-8100. **Toll-free phone:** 800/227-6633. **Contact:** Personnel. **E-mail address:** careers_acromed@dpyus.jnj.com. **World Wide Web address:** http://www.depuyacromed.com. **Description:** Manufactures and supplies a broad line of surgical products including instruments, equipment, implants, surgical disposables, and electronic pain control stimulators and electrodes. **Positions advertised include:** Product Director; Clinical Research Manager; Clinical Research Associate; Corporate Account Manager; Senior Scientist. **Subsidiaries include:** DePuy International Ltd. (England). **Parent company:** Johnson & Johnson.

DIELECTRICS INDUSTRIES, INC.

300 Burnett Road, Chicopee MA 01020. 413/594-8111. **Toll-free phone:** 800/472-7286. **Fax:** 413/594-2343. **Contact:** Personnel. **World Wide Web address:** http://www.dielectrics.com. **Description:** As the medical division of Dielectrics Industries, DMC designs and fabricates a variety of sophisticated medical devices for the laparoscopic, orthopedic, and blood fluid delivery markets. Overall, Dielectrics Industries is a leading designer, developer, fabricator, and supplier of air cell and other bladder technologies. Markets served include medical, aerospace, automotive, recreational, and industrial. Products include laparoscopic surgical devices, inflatable vests, in-line skate inserts, and lumbar support systems. **Corporate headquarters location:** This location.

DIOCESAN HEALTH FACILITIES

368 North Main Street, Fall River MA 02720. 508/679-8154. **Contact:** Human Resources. **World Wide Web address:** http://www.dhfo.org. **Description:** Operates nonprofit nursing homes including Catholic Memorial Home (Fall River MA), Our Lady's Haven (Fairhaven MA), Madonna Manor (North Attleboro MA), Sacred Heart (New Bedford MA), and Marian Manor (Taunton MA). **Corporate headquarters location:** This location.

DIVERSIFIED VISITING NURSE ASSOCIATION (DVNA)

316 Nichols Road, Fitchburg MA 01420. 978/342-6013. **Contact:** Human Resources. **Description:** Provides home care to residents of north central Massachusetts and south central New Hampshire. Nursing care services include antibiotic and nutritional infusions, wound care, cardiac care, and care of ventilator patients. Rehabilitation services include physical, occupational, and speech therapy. **Corporate headquarters location:** Leominster MA. **Parent**

company: HealthAlliance also operates a number of other subsidiaries, which include Burbank Hospital; Diversified Medical Equipment Services; Leominster Hospital; Fairlawn Nursing Home; The Highlands; and Coordinated Primary Care.

EAST BOSTON NEIGHBORHOOD HEALTH CENTER
10 Gove Street, East Boston MA 02128. 617/569-5800. **Contact:** Human Resources. **Description:** A community health clinic supporting area urgent care, home care, and physician services.

EAST CAMBRIDGE NEIGHBORHOOD HEALTH CENTER
163 Gore Street, Cambridge MA 02141. 617/665-3000. **Contact:** Human Resources. **Description:** A community-based clinic offering general care on an outpatient basis. **Parent company:** Cambridge Hospital is a 170-bed, full-service hospital owned by the city of Cambridge and affiliated with Harvard and Tufts Medical Schools.

EASTWOOD CARE CENTER
1007 East Street, Dedham MA 02026. 781/329-1520. **Contact:** Human Resources. **Description:** A 145-bed medical center focusing on long-term care and rehabilitation.

EPIX MEDICAL INC.
71 Rogers Street, Cambridge MA 02142. 617/250-6000. **Fax:** 617/250-6041. **Contact:** Human Resources. **E-mail address:** careers@epixmed.com. **World Wide Web address:** http://www.epixmed.com. **Description:** Engaged in the development of advanced imaging agents. The company's initial products in development are for magnetic resonance imaging. **Positions advertised include:** Biophysics Intern; Synthetic Organic Chemist; Director of Pharmacology. **Corporate headquarters location:** This location. **Operations at this facility include:** Administration; Research and Development. **Listed on:** NASDAQ. **Stock exchange symbol:** EPIX. **Number of employees at this location:** 30.

FAIRLAWN NURSING HOME
370 West Street, Leominster MA 01453. 978/537-0771. **Fax:** 978/534-0824. **Contact:** Human Resources. **Description:** Offers long-term care services to the elderly and other adults who need 24-hour nursing and personal care. **Parent company:** HealthAlliance operates a number of other subsidiaries, which include Burbank Hospital, Coordinated Primary Care, Diversified Medical Equipment Services, Diversified Visiting Nurse Association, The Highlands, and Leominster Hospital.

FAULKNER HOSPITAL
1153 Centre Street, Boston MA 02130. 617/522-5800. **Recorded jobline:** 617/983-7426. **Contact:** Human Resources Department. **World Wide Web address:** http://www.faulknerhospital.org. **Description:** A hospital. **Positions advertised include:** Registration Office; Community Benefits Associate; Health Information Systems; Receptionist; Rehab Services; Switch Board Operator; Safety Security Shift Operator; Security Officer.

FRANCISCAN CHILDREN'S HOSPITAL AND REHABILITATION CENTER
30 Warren Street, Brighton MA 02135. 617/254-3800. **Contact:** Human Resources. **E-mail address:** aeponte@fchrc.org. **World Wide Web address:** http://www.fchrc.org. **Description:** A hospital and rehabilitation center for children. The hospital also operates the Kennedy Day School for children with

special needs. **Positions advertised include:** Certified Nurses Assistant; Care Manager; Home Health Registered Nurse; Nurse Practitioner; Registered Nurse; Family Therapist; Mental Health Specialist; Psychologist; Impatient Clinical Supervisor; Respiratory Therapist; Teaching Assistant; Fiscal Administrative Coordinator; Registration Manager; Admissions Clerk; Dental Assistant; Pediatric Dietician; Van Driver.

FRESENIUS MEDICAL CARE NORTH AMERICA
2 Ledgemont Center, 95 Hayden Avenue, Lexington MA 02420. 781/402-9000. **Toll-free phone:** 800/662-1237. **Fax:** 781/402-9005. **Contact:** Human Resources. **E-mail address:** resumes@fmc-na.com. **World Wide Web address:** http://www.fmcna.com. **Description:** One of the nation's leading manufacturers and distributors of renal dialysis products and services. The company also provides dialysis treatment, diagnostic testing, blood testing, and home health programs. Fresenius Medical Care's dialysis services include outpatient hemodialysis, peritoneal dialysis, and support for home dialysis patients. **Positions advertised include:** Financial Analyst; Staff Auditor; Secretary; Switchboard Operator; Clinical Quality Manager; Documentation Coordinator; Real Estate Specialist; Treasury Analyst; Employment Coordinator; Human Resources Secretary; Research Assistant; Benefits Analyst; Legal Secretary; Regulatory Affairs Specialist; Clinical Applications Programmer; Manager NT Services; Manager or Desktop PC; Network Security; Specialist; Program Analyst. **Special programs:** Co-ops. **Corporate headquarters location:** This location. **Parent company:** Fresenius Medical Care AG (Germany) **Listed on:** New York Stock Exchange. **Stock exchange symbol:** FMS. **Number of employees at this location:** 600. **Number of employees nationwide:** 21,000. **Number of employees worldwide:** 24,000.

FRESH POND ANIMAL HOSPITAL
15 Flanders Road, Belmont MA 02478. 617/484-1555. **Fax:** 617/484-2509. **Contact:** Human Resources. **World Wide Web address:** http://www.fpah.com. **Description:** An animal hospital offering surgical, dental, and medical services.

DR. SOLOMON CARTER FULLER MENTAL HEALTH CENTER
85 East Newton Street, Boston MA 02118. 617/626-8700. **Contact:** Human Resources. **Description:** A psychiatric hospital.

GAMBRO HEALTHCARE
660 Harrison Avenue, Boston MA 02118. 617/859-7000. **Contact:** Human Resources. **World Wide Web address:** http://www.usa-gambro.com. **Description:** Provides renal dialysis services to patients suffering from chronic kidney failure, primarily in its freestanding outpatient dialysis centers. The company also provides dialysis in patients' homes or at hospitals on a contractual basis; urine and blood testing at its centers; and independent physicians at its clinical labs. **Positions advertised include:** Center Director; Clinical Nurse Manager; Registered Nurse; Patient Care Technician. **Number of employees nationwide:** 1,240.

HAEMONETICS CORPORATION
400 Wood Road, Braintree MA 02184. 781/848-7100. **Toll-free phone:** 800/225-5242. **Fax:** 781/848-9959. **Contact:** Human Resources. **World Wide Web address:** http://www.haemonetics.com. **Description:** Designs, manufactures, markets, and services blood processing systems and related sterile, disposable items used for the processing of human blood for transfusion and other therapeutic medical purposes. The company sells its products to blood banks, hospitals, and commercial plasma centers. **Positions advertised include:**

Contract Agent; Supply Chain Integration Manager; Project Manager; Planning Analyst. **Corporate headquarters location:** This location. **Other U.S. locations:** Leetsdale PA; Union SC. **Operations at this facility include:** Administration; Divisional Headquarters; Manufacturing; Research and Development; Sales; Service. **Listed on:** New York Stock Exchange. **Stock exchange symbol:** HAE. **Number of employees at this location:** 700. **Number of employees nationwide:** 1,000.

HAMMERSMITH HOUSE NURSING CARE CENTER
73 Chestnut Street, Saugus MA 01906. 781/233-8123. **Fax:** 781/231-2918. **Contact:** Human Resources. **Description:** A 103-bed nursing home and rehabilitation center. Hammersmith House also operates a 47-bed special care unit for Alzheimer's patients. **Positions advertised include:** Certified Nurses Aide; Licensed Practical Nurse.

HARVARD PILGRIM HEALTHCARE
1600 Crowne Colony Park, Quincy MA 02169. 617-745-1001. **Contact:** Human Resources. **World Wide Web address:** http://www.harvardpilgrim.org. **Description:** The oldest non-profit healthcare available in New England. **Positions advertised include:** Nurse Care Manager; Account Services Coordinator; Clinical Trainer; Account Services Manager. **NOTE:** Apply online.

HEALTHALLIANCE/BURBANK HOSPITAL
275 Nichols Road, Fitchburg MA 01420. 978/343-5000. **Contact:** Human Resources. **World Wide Web address:** http://www.healthalliance.com. **Description:** An acute care medical facility. The hospital provides inpatient and outpatient services including medical, surgical, and subspecialty care, as well as same-day surgery and 24-hour emergency coverage. The hospital also offers a psychiatric center, speech and hearing center, and regional trauma center. A 25-bed inpatient rehabilitation center affiliated with the Spaulding Rehabilitation Hospital in Boston is also at this location. The center offers a rehabilitation program for patients who have suffered from strokes and patients with arthritis, amputations, neurological disorders, orthopedic conditions, spinal cord injuries, brain injuries, and complex medical conditions. **Corporate headquarters location:** Leominster MA. **Subsidiaries include:** Coordinated Primary Care; Diversified Medical Equipment Services; Diversified Visiting Nurse Association; Fairlawn Nursing Home; The Highlands; and Leominster Hospital.

HEALTHALLIANCE/LEOMINSTER HOSPITAL
60 Hospital Road, Leominster MA 01453. 978/466-2000. **Fax:** 978/466-2189. **Contact:** Human Resources. **World Wide Web address:** http://www.healthalliance.com. **Description:** An acute care medical facility. The hospital provides inpatient and outpatient services including medical, surgical, and subspecialty care, as well as same-day surgery and 24-hour emergency coverage. The hospital also offers the Center for Cancer Care and Blood Disorders, diagnostic services including mobile MRIs, cardiac catheterization labs, and a diagnostic lab for the diagnostic study of sleep disorders. **NOTE:** Entry-level positions are offered. **Positions advertised include:** Certified Nurses Aide; Certified Occupational Therapy Assistant; Clinical Lab Technician; Computer Operator; Computer Programmer; EEG Technologist; EKG Technician; Home Health Aide; Licensed Practical Nurse; Medical Records Technician; Network/Systems Administrator; Nuclear Medicine Technologist; Occupational Therapist; Physical Therapist; Physical Therapy Assistant; Radiological Technologist; Recreational Therapist; Registered Nurse; Respiratory Therapist; Social Worker; Speech-Language Pathologist. **Operations at this facility include:** Administration; Service. **Annual**

sales/revenues: More than $100 million. **Number of employees at this location:** 750. **Number of employees nationwide:** 2,000.

HEALTHALLIANCE/THE HIGHLANDS
335 Nichols Road, Fitchburg MA 01420. 978/343-4411. **Contact:** Human Resources. **World Wide Web address:** http://www.healthalliance.com. **Description:** Offers subacute and long-term care in a residential setting for adults. One unit is devoted to people with Alzheimer's disease. The subacute care unit helps people complete the transition from a hospital or a rehabilitation facility to their home following surgery, accident, or illness. A long-term care unit provides nursing and personal care for residents who need full-time care. HealthAlliance/The Highlands also provides an adult daycare health center. **NOTE:** Entry-level positions are offered. **Positions advertised include:** Accountant/Auditor; Dietician/Nutritionist; Health Services Manager; Licensed Practical Nurse; Occupational Therapist; Physical Therapist; Registered Nurse; Social Worker. **Special programs:** Training. **Corporate headquarters location:** Leominster MA. **Subsidiaries include:** Burbank Hospital; Coordinated Primary Care; Diversified Medical Equipment Services; Diversified Visiting Nurse Association; Fairlawn Nursing Home; Leominster Hospital. **Operations at this facility include:** Service. **Annual sales/revenues:** $5 - $10 million.

HEALTHSOUTH BRAINTREE HOSPITAL
P.O. Box 859020, Braintree MA 02185-9020. 781/848-5353. **Physical address:** 250 Pond Street, Braintree MA 02184. **Contact:** Human Resources. **World Wide Web address:** http://www.healthsouth.com. **Description:** A rehabilitation hospital. Founded in 1984. **Other U.S. locations:** Nationwide. **Listed on:** New York Stock Exchange. **Stock exchange symbol:** HRC.

HOLOGIC INC.
35 Crosby Drive, Bedford MA 01730. 781/999-7300. **Fax:** 781/275-7090. **Contact:** Human Resources. **E-mail address:** hr@hologic.com. **World Wide Web address:** http://www.hologic.com. **Description:** Manufactures quantitative digital radiography X-ray bone densitometers that are used for the precise measurement of bone density to assist in the diagnosis and monitoring of metabolic bone diseases. **Positions advertised include:** Application Support Specialist; Regulatory Affairs Manager. **Corporate headquarters location:** This location. **Other area location:** Littleton MA. **Other U.S. locations:** Danbury CT; Newark DE. **International locations:** Belgium; France. **Listed on:** NASDAQ. **Stock exchange symbol:** HOLX.

HOLYOKE HOSPITAL, INC.
575 Beech Street, Holyoke MA 01040. 413/534-2547. **Fax:** 413/534-2635. **Recorded jobline:** 413/534-2639. **Contact:** Anne Barrett, Human Resources Administrator. **World Wide Web address:** http://www.holyokehealth.com. **Description:** A 225-bed, acute care, community hospital that serves an aggregate population of 145,000 and admits nearly 7,000 patients annually. **Positions advertised include:** Audiologists; Head Research Processor; Medical Transcriber; Nursing Division; Radiological Technology; Speech Pathologist. **Number of employees at this location:** 1,000.

HOME HEALTH AND CHILDCARE SERVICES
P.O. Box 640, Brockton MA 02303-0640. 508/588-6070. **Fax:** 508/587-3560. **Physical address:** 15 Jonathan Drive, Brockton MA 02301. **Contact:** Human Resources. **E-mail address:** ccrr@hhcc.org. **World Wide Web address:** http://www.hhcc.org. **Description:** A private, nonprofit family care services agency providing in-home health care for the elderly and childcare services.

HORIZON GROUP
7232 Garden Street, Needham MA 02492. 781/444-4141. **Contact:** Human Resources. **Description:** Acquires and operates long-term care facilities throughout the United States; provides health care services such as nursing care, rehabilitation, and other therapies; provides institutional pharmacy services; provides specialty care to Alzheimer's patients; and offers subacute care. Horizon Group operates approximately 280 facilities in 25 states.

HUMAN SERVICE OPTIONS, INC.
35 Braintree Hill Park, Suite 307, Braintree MA 02184. 781/356-0710. **Fax:** 781/356-0748. **Contact:** Human Resources. **Description:** A home health care agency that provides staffing to schools, group homes, and workshops. The firm also provides a home health service for elderly and homebound individuals, and community residences for adults with developmental disabilities.

INSTRUMENTATION LABORATORY
101 Hartwell Avenue, Lexington MA 02421. 781/861-0710. **Contact:** Human Resources. **World Wide Web address:** http://www.ilww.com. **Description:** Manufactures medical instruments used in blood gas analysis. **Positions advertised include:** Administrative Support; Marketing Product Specialist; Principal Software Engineer.

INTERNATIONAL EQUIPMENT COMPANY
300 Second Avenue, Needham Heights MA 02494-2811. 781/449-8060. **Fax:** 781/453-3381. **Contact:** Manager of Human Resources. **World Wide Web address:** http://www.labcentrifuge.com. **Description:** Manufactures and distributes laboratory equipment including centrifuges and cryostats. **Parent company:** Thermo Electron. **Operations at this facility include:** Administration; Manufacturing; Research and Development; Sales; Service. **Number of employees at this location:** 175.

INVACARE SUPPLY GROUP
75 October Hill Road, Holliston MA 01746. 508/429-1000. **Fax:** 508/429-6669. **Contact:** Human Resources. **Description:** A wholesale distributor of medical supplies including ostomy dressings, wound care products, respiratory products, and enteral feeding products. **NOTE:** Entry-level positions and part-time jobs are offered. **Positions advertised include:** Account Representative; Consumer Services Representative; Distribution Center Associate. **Special programs:** Training; Summer Jobs. **Office hours:** Monday - Friday, 8:00 a.m. - 5:30 p.m. **Corporate headquarters location:** Elyria OH. **Parent company:** Invacare Corporation. **Listed on:** New York Stock Exchange. **Stock exchange symbol:** IVC. **Number of employees at this location:** 100.

LAHEY AT ARLINGTON MEDICAL CENTER
Hospital Road, Arlington MA 02474. 781/646-1500. **Contact:** Human Resources. **World Wide Web address:** http://www.lahey.org. **Description:** Part of the Lahey Clinic's network of health care services. This location provides emergency, acute, transitional, subacute, and intensive care. **Positions advertised include:** Clinical Nurse; Medical Office Secretary; Physician.

LAWRENCE MEMORIAL HOSPITAL
170 Governors Avenue, Medford MA 02155. 781/306-6000. **Fax:** 781/306-6573. **Contact:** Human Resources. **World Wide Web address:** http://www.lmh.org. **Description:** A hospital that serves as a teaching facility for Tufts University School of Medicine. **Positions advertised include:** Registered Nurse; Clinical

Associate; Licensed Practical Nurse; Clinical Nurse Educator; Medical Transcriptionist; Application Analyst; Desktop Technician; Director; Registered Respiratory Therapist. **Parent company:** Hallmark Health.

LIFELINE SYSTEMS, INC.
111 Lawrence Street, Framingham MA 01702-8156. 508/988-1000. **Fax:** 508/988-1384. **Contact:** Personnel. **World Wide Web address:** http://www.lifelinesys.com. **Description:** Manufactures personal emergency response systems and provides monitoring and related services. The company's services consist of 24-hour, at-home assistance and personalized support for elderly and physically challenged individuals. The company's principal product is LIFELINE, which consists of equipment manufactured by the company combined with a monitoring service. The equipment includes a personal help button, worn or carried by the individual subscriber, and a communicator that connects to the phone line in the subscriber's home. **Positions advertised include:** Marketing Communications Manager; Personal Response Associate; Inside Sales Account; Customer & Referral Sales Manager; Employment Manager; Equipment Product Manager. **Corporate headquarters location:** This location. **Subsidiaries include:** Lifeline Systems Canada. **Listed on:** NASDAQ. **Stock exchange symbol:** LIFE. **Number of employees at this location:** 735.

ERICH LINDEMANN MENTAL HEALTH CENTER
25 Staniford Street, Boston MA 02114. 617/626-8000. **Contact:** Human Resources. **Description:** A residential mental health center. **Number of employees at this location:** 300.

LOWELL GENERAL HOSPITAL INC.
295 Varnum Avenue, Lowell MA 01854. 978/937-6000. **Contact:** Human Resources. **World Wide Web address:** http://www.lowellgeneral.org. **Description:** A 200-bed hospital that offers a variety of specialized services including the Special Care Nursery, the Cancer Center, and the Children's Place. **Positions advertised include:** 2nd Cook; ACR Mechanic; Clinical Manager; CT Technician; Development Assistant; Endoscopy Coordinator; Financial Specialist; Medical Technologist; Registered Nurse.

LUXTEC CORPORATION
99 Hartwell Street, West Boylston MA 01583. 508/856-9454. **Toll-free phone:** 800/325-8966. **Contact:** Human Resources. **World Wide Web address:** http://www.luxtec.com. **Description:** Designs, develops, manufactures, and markets illumination and vision products utilizing fiber-optic technology for the medical and dental industries. These products are designed to produce high-quality light delivered directly to the operative site. Products include fiber-optic headlights and headlight television camera systems for audio/video recordings of surgical procedures; light sources; cables; retractors; loupes; surgical telescopes; and other custom-made surgical specialty instruments. **Corporate headquarters location:** This location. **Subsidiaries include:** Cathtec, Inc.; Fiber Imaging Technologies, Inc.; Luxtec Fiber Optics B.V. **Parent company:** PrimeSource Healthcare (Tuscon AZ). **Number of employees nationwide:** 50.

THE MARINO CENTER FOR PROGRESSIVE HEALTH
2500 Massachusetts Avenue, Cambridge MA 02140. 617/661-6225. **Fax:** 617/492-2002. **Contact:** Human Resources. **E-mail address:** contact@marinocenter.org. **World Wide Web address:** http://www.marinocenter.org. **Description:** A medical center with a full-service health store specializing in family medicine, acupuncture, health education, prevention programs, and complementary therapies. The Marino Center for

Progressive Health includes: The Center for Men's Health is devoted to diagnosing and treating sexual dysfunction, prostate disease, and incontinence; The Center for Women's Health is devoted to gynecological care, birth control, sexually transmitted diseases, PMS, menstrual disorders, and menopause; The UroCare Clinic is devoted to addressing the needs of women with urinary incontinence. Also provided are classes, therapy groups, workshops, and free lectures. Areas of specialization include general medicine, psychology, psychotherapy, stress-reduction, urology, neurology, chiropractic, acupuncture, traditional Chinese medicine, nutrition, massage therapy, infusion therapy, chelation therapy, biofeedback, coping with cancer, yoga, meditation, and fitness. **Positions advertised include:** Primary Care Physician; Nurse Practitioner; Physicians Assistant. **Other area locations:** Dedham MA; Wellesley MA.

MASSACHUSETTS GENERAL HOSPITAL
55 Fruit Street, Boston MA 02114. 617/726-2000. **Fax:** 617/724-2266. **Contact:** Human Resources. **World Wide Web address:** http://www.mgh.harvard.edu. **Description:** An 820-bed, nonprofit, teaching hospital. As part of the Harvard Medical School, MGH offers diagnostic and therapeutic care in virtually every specialty of medicine. This location also hires seasonally. **NOTE:** Please direct resumes to Partners HealthCare System Inc., Human Resources, 101 Merrimac Street, 5th Floor, Boston MA 02114. 617/726-2210. Entry-level positions are offered. **Positions advertised include:** Administrative Assistant; Admissions Coordinator; Admissions Interviewer; Beautician. **Special programs:** Internships; Training; Co-ops; Summer Jobs. **Office hours:** Monday - Friday, 8:30 a.m. - 4:30 p.m. **Parent company:** Partners HealthCare System Inc. **Operations at this facility include:** Administration; Research and Development; Service. **Number of employees at this location:** 10,000.

MASSACHUSETTS HOSPITAL ASSOCIATION
5 New England Executive Park, Burlington MA 01803. 781/272-8000. **Contact:** Lisa Bales, Human Resources. **World Wide Web address:** http://www.mhalink.org. **World Wide Web address:** http://www.mhalink.org. **Description:** A trade association for professionals in the hospital industry, providing such services as continuing education and information on new developments within the industry.

MEDSOURCE TECHNOLOGIES
150 California Street, Newton MA 02458. 617/964-9100. **Fax:** 617/964-2660. **Contact:** Human Resources. **World Wide Web address:** http://www.medsourcetech.com. **Description:** Designs and manufactures disposable medical devices such as endoscopic catheters, safety needles, balloon catheters, ligation devices, and laser delivery devices. **NOTE:** Entry-level positions are offered. **Positions advertised include:** Design Engineer. **Special programs:** Internships; Training. **Corporate headquarters:** Minneapolis MN. **Other U.S. locations:** Nationwide. **Listed on:** Privately held. **Annual sales/revenues:** $11 - $20 million. **Number of employees at this location:** 120.

THE MEDSTAT GROUP
125 Cambridge Park Drive, Cambridge MA 02140. 617/576-3237. **Contact:** Human Resources. **E-mail address:** recruiting@medstat.com. **World Wide Web address:** http://www.medstat.com. **Description:** Provides information that helps manage the purchasing and administration of health benefits and services. **Positions advertised include:** Senior Consultant. **Corporate headquarters location:** Ann Harbor MI. **Parent Company:** Thompson Financial.

MEDTRONIC/AVE
37A Cherry Hill Drive, Danvers MA 01923. 978/777-0042. **Contact:** Human Resources Department. **World Wide Web address:** http://www.medtronic.com. **Description:** Manufactures a line of minimally invasive devices for use in treating patients with coronary artery and peripheral vascular disease. **Positions advertised include:** Packaging Engineer; Manufacturing Engineer; RaD Engineer; Production Scheduler; Supplier Quality Manager. **Corporate headquarters location:** Minneapolis MN. **Listed on:** New York Stock Exchange. **Stock exchange symbol:** MDT.

MILTON HOSPITAL
92 Highland Street, Milton MA 02186. 617/696-4600. **Fax:** 617/698-4730. **Contact:** Human Resources. **E-mail address:** humanresources@miltonhospital.org. **World Wide Web address:** http://www.miltonhospital.org. **Description:** A general hospital. Milton Hospital offers free health screenings, support groups, and lectures for the public, as well as free vaccinations for public safety workers. **Positions advertised include:** Admitting Representative; Care Manager; Environmental Services Assistant; Human Resources Manager; PP&D Supervisor; Medical Technician; Records Clerk; Dietary Aide; Secretary; Pharmacist; Radiological Technician; CT Technician; Ultrasound Technician; Physical Therapist; Registered Nurse; Licensed Practical Nurse; Nurse Assistant; Ward Clerk; Nurse Manager. **Special programs:** Internships.

MITEK PRODUCTS
60 Glacier Drive, Westwood MA 02090. 781/251-2700. **Toll-free phone:** 800/35M-ITEK. **Fax:** 781/278-9578. **Contact:** Human Resources. **World Wide Web address:** http://www.mitek.com. **Description:** Develops, manufactures, and markets minimally-invasive proprietary surgical implants that facilitate the reattachment of damaged tendons, ligaments, and other soft tissue to bones. These devices reduce tissue trauma, speed patient recovery, and shorten operating time. Primary products consist of a line of suture anchors utilizing nitinol, a highly elastic nickel titanium alloy, as well as related surgical instruments such as drill guides and inserters. **NOTE:** Second and third shifts are offered. All mail should be sent to: Human Resources, 249 Vanderbilt Avenue, Norwood MA 02062. **Corporate headquarters location:** This location. **Parent company:** Ethicon, Inc. **Number of employees at this location:** 275.

NATIONAL DENTEX CORPORATION
526 Boston Post Road, Suite 207, Wayland MA 01778. 508/358-4422. **Contact:** Human Resources. **World Wide Web address:** http://www.nationaldentex.com. **Description:** National Dentex Corporation is one of the largest operators of dental laboratories in the United States. These dental laboratories provide a full range of custom-made dental prosthetic appliances, divided into three main groups: restorative products including crowns and bridges; reconstructive products including partial and full dentures; and cosmetic products including porcelain veneers and ceramic crowns. **Positions advertised include:** Dental Lab Trainee; Maintenance; Janitorial Associate; Driver; Office Representative; Scheduler Associate; Department Manager; Shipping & Receiving Clerk; Skilled Technician; Corporate Support Specialist. **Corporate headquarters location:** This location. **Other U.S. locations:** Nationwide. **Subsidiaries include:** Dodd Dental Laboratories; H&O Associated Dental Laboratories; H&O Eliason; Lakeland Dental; Massachusetts Dental Associates. **Listed on:** NASDAQ. **Stock exchange symbol:** NADX.

NEW ENGLAND BAPTIST HOSPITAL

125 Parker Hill Avenue, Boston MA 02120. 617/754-5800. **Contact:** Human Resources. **World Wide Web address:** http://www.nebh.org. **Description:** A 150-bed, surgical hospital providing specialty services in cardiology, sports medicine, occupational medicine, and musculoskeletal care. Founded in 1893. **Positions advertised include:** Administrative Assistant; Central Support Operator; Coding Supervisor; File Clerk; Registered Nurse; Groundskeeper; Head Therapist; Quality Manager; Nurse Assistant; Unit Aide; Unit Secretary.

NEW ENGLAND MEDICAL CENTER

750 Washington Street, New England Medical Center #795, Boston MA 02111. 617/636-5666. **Fax:** 617/636-4658. **Contact:** Human Resources. **World Wide Web address:** http://www.nemc.org. **Description:** New England Medical Center is the major teaching hospital for Tufts University Medical School. One branch of the New England Medical Center is the Floating Hospital for Children, which provides treatment for children suffering from various kinds of cancer, leukemia, and arthritis. **Positions advertised include:** Administrative Assistant; Admitting Representative; Assistant Nurse Manager; Business Operations Manager; Clinical Nutritionist; Clinical Pharmacist; Clinical Research Coordinator; Coder; CT Scanner; Lab Technologist; Medical Assistant; Nursing Technologist; Physical Therapist. **Operations at this facility include:** Administration. **Number of employees at this location:** 6,000.

NEW ENGLAND SINAI HOSPITAL AND REHABILITATION CENTER

150 York Street, Stoughton MA 02072. 781/344-0600. **Contact:** Human Resources. **Description:** A hospital and rehabilitation center providing a variety of services including physical therapy, occupational therapy, and pulmonary rehabilitation, as well as special areas dealing specifically with back, feet, vision, and speech problems.

NEWTON-WELLESLEY HOSPITAL

2014 Washington Street, Newton MA 02462. 617/243-6000. **Fax:** 617/243-6876. **Contact:** Human Resources. **World Wide Web address:** http://www.nwh.org. **Description:** A hospital serving as a teaching facility for Tufts School of Medicine. **Positions advertised include:** Administrative Assistant; Assistant Cook; CT Technologist; Clinical Social Worker; Executive Assistant; Food Service Worker; Human Resources Coordinator; Image Service Representative; Medical Lab Assistant; Pharmacist; Registered Nurse; Ultrasound Technologist; Unit Coordinator

NORTH SHORE MEDICAL CENTER
SALEM HOSPITAL

81 Highland Avenue, Salem MA 01970. 978/741-1200. **Recorded jobline:** 978/741-1215x4365. **Contact:** Personnel. **World Wide Web address:** http://www.partners.org. **Description:** Salem Hospital is a 322-bed teaching hospital that operates as part of North Shore Medical Center. North Shore Medical Center is a nonprofit health care system consisting of several hospitals and health organizations. Services range from primary, emergency/trauma, and advanced levels of acute care to rehabilitation and long-term care. A program of ambulatory health care includes walk-in medical centers and one of the region's largest occupational and preventative health companies. North Shore Medical Center's facilities include Salem Hospital; Shaughnessy-Kaplan Rehabilitation Hospital, a 160-bed rehabilitation facility; North Shore Children's Hospital, one of only four pediatric hospitals in the state; Work Venture, a comprehensive industrial rehabilitation program geared toward returning injured workers to their jobs; and the Visiting Nurse Association of Greater Salem, consisting of various

private duty services. **Positions advertised include:** Clinical Lab Technician; Dietician/Nutritionist; Medical Records Technician; Nuclear Medicine Technologist; Occupational Therapist; Pharmacist; Physical Therapist; Physician; Registered Nurse. **Parent company:** Partners HealthCare System Inc. **Number of employees at this location:** 3,000.

NOVA BIOMEDICAL
200 Prospect Street, Waltham MA 02454. 781/647-3700. **Fax:** 781/899-6259. **Contact:** Human Resources. **E-mail address:** hr@novabio.com. **World Wide Web address:** http://www.novamanufacturing.com. **Description:** Develops and manufactures blood analyzers. **Positions advertised include:** Program Manager; Clinical Applications Training Specialist; Inside Sales Representative; Regional Sales Representative; Clinical Product Specialist; Operator.

OLYMPUS SPECIALTY HOSPITAL
2001 Washington Street, Braintree MA 02184. 781/848-2600. **Contact:** Human Resources. **Description:** A hospital specializing in the treatment of respiratory diseases.

PLC MEDICAL SYSTEMS, INC.
10 Forge Park, Franklin MA 02038. 508/541-8800. **Fax:** 781/326-6048. **Contact:** Jeanne Watkins, Personnel. **E-mail address:** kpapa@insightperformance.com. **World Wide Web address:** http://www.plcmed.com. **Description:** Develops cardiovascular products used to perform transmocardia revascularization (TMR). **Positions advertised include:** Quality Engineer; Principal Engineer. **Corporate headquarters location:** This location. **Parent company:** PLC Systems Inc. **Listed on:** American Stock Exchange. **Stock exchange symbol:** PLC.

PALOMAR MEDICAL TECHNOLOGIES, INC.
82 Cambridge Street, Burlington MA 01803. 781/993-2300. **Fax:** 781/993-2330. **Contact:** Human Resources. **E-mail address:** hr@palmed.com. **World Wide Web address:** http://www.palmed.com. **Description:** Palomar Medical Technologies designs, manufactures, and markets lasers, delivery systems, and related disposable products for use in medical and surgical procedures. The company operates in two business segments. The Medical Product segment develops and manufactures pulsed dye and diode medical lasers for use in clinical trials and is engaged in the research and development of additional medical and surgical products. The Electronic Products segment manufactures high-density, flexible, electronic circuitry for use in industrial, military, and medical devices. **Positions advertised include:** Clinical Research Manager; Accounting Manager; Programming Specialist; Optical Assembler; Laser Technician. **NOTE:** This company also has distribution opportunities. **Corporate headquarters location:** This location. **Listed on:** NASDAQ. **Stock exchange symbol:** PMTI.

PHILIPS ANALYTICAL
12 Michigan Drive, Natick MA 01760. 508/647-1100. **Contact:** Human Resources. **World Wide Web address:** http://www.philips.com. **Description:** Sells and services analytical X-ray systems. **Positions advertised include:** Applications Engineer; Application Group Leader; Assembly Technician; Technology Group Leader. **Corporate headquarters location:** New York NY. **Other U.S. locations:** Tempe AZ; Fremont CA; Alpharetta GA; Roselle IL; Columbia MD; Bellaire TX. **Parent company:** Philips Electronics North America, one of the larger industrial companies in the United States, is a multimarket manufacturing organization with nationwide locations and various subsidiaries. Philips concentrates its efforts primarily in the fields of consumer electronics,

consumer products, electrical and electronics components, and professional equipment.

PHILIPS MEDICAL SYSTEMS

3000 Minuteman Road, Andover MA 01810. 978/687-1501. **Contact:** Human Resources. **World Wide Web address:** http://www.medical.phillips.com. **Description:** Produces stethoscopes, electrolytes, and disposable ECG monitoring electrodes for adults and infants, as well as blood-pressure transducers and disposable transducer domes, chart papers, and disposable pressure kits.

PIONEER BEHAVIORAL HEALTH

200 Lake Street, Suite 102, Peabody MA 01960. 978/536-2777. **Toll-free phone:** 800/543-2447. **Fax:** 978/536-2677. **Contact:** Human Resources. **E-mail address:** info@phc-inc.com. **World Wide Web address:** http://www.phc-inc.com. **Description:** Operates a variety of mental health, chemical dependency, and dual diagnosis programs throughout the country that provide inpatient and outpatient services, partial hospitalization, residential care, aftercare, and employee assistance programs. Founded in 1976. **Subsidiaries include:** Behavioral Stress Center (Elmhurst NY); Harbor Oaks Hospital (New Baltimore MI); Harmony Healthcare (Las Vegas NV); Highland Ridge Hospital (Salt Lake City UT); Mount Regis Center (Salem VA); Pioneer Counseling Centers of Michigan (Farmington Hills MI); Pioneer Counseling of Virginia (Salem VA); Pioneer Development & Support Services (Salt Lake City UT). **President/CEO:** Bruce A. Shear. **Number of employees at this location:** 300.

POLYMEDICA CORPORATION

11 State Street, Woburn MA 01801. 781/933-2020. **Fax:** 781/933-7992. **Contact:** Human Resources. **World Wide Web address:** http://www.polymedica.com. **Description:** A leading provider of targeted medical products and services focusing primarily on the diabetes and consumer health care markets. Founded in 1988. **Special programs:** Co-ops. **Corporate headquarters location:** This location. **Other U.S. locations:** Golden CO; Palm City FL. **Subsidiaries include:** Liberty Medical Supply is one of the largest direct-mail distributors of diabetes supplies covered by Medicare. Liberty distributes more than 200,000 diabetes products to over 70,000 customers. PolyMedica Healthcare, Inc. holds leading positions in the urinary health and over-the-counter medical device markets by distributing a broad range of products to food, drug, and mass retailers nationwide. PolyMedica Pharmaceuticals (USA), Inc. manufactures, distributes, and markets prescription urological and suppository products. **Listed on:** NASDAQ. **Stock exchange symbol:** PLMD. **CEO:** Steven J. Lee. **Annual sales/revenues:** More than $100 million. **Number of employees at this location:** 30. **Number of employees nationwide:** 345.

PRECISION OPTICS CORPORATION

22 East Broadway, Gardner MA 01440. 978/630-1800. **Fax:** 978/630-1487. **Contact:** Human Resources. **E-mail address:** info@poci.com. **World Wide Web address:** http://www.poci.com. **Description:** Designs, develops, manufactures, and sells specialized optical systems and components and optical thin film coatings. The products and services are used in the medical and advanced optical systems industries. Medical products include endoscopes and image couplers, beamsplitters, and adapters that are used as accessories to endoscopes. Advanced optical design and developmental services provide advanced lens design, image analysis, optical system design, structural design and analysis, prototype production and evaluation, optics testing, and optical

system assembly. **Corporate headquarters location:** This location. **Listed on:** NASDAQ. **Stock exchange symbol:** POCI.

QUINCY MEDICAL CENTER
114 Whitwell Street, Quincy MA 02169. 617/773-6100. **Contact:** Human Resources. **World Wide Web address:** http://www.quincymc.com. **Description:** A hospital offering a variety of services including a 24-hour emergency room, surgery, OB/GYN services, radiology, and a center for women's health. **Positions advertised include:** Cafeteria Helper; CT Technologist; Occupational Therapist; Physical Therapist; Radiological Therapist; Registered Nurse; Respiratory Therapist; Security Officer; Ultrasonographer.

RIVERSIDE HEALTH CENTER
205 Western Avenue, Cambridge MA 02139. 617/498-1109. **Contact:** Human Resources. **Description:** An outpatient clinic providing services that include general medical care for adults, prenatal, family planning, nutrition, psychiatric treatment, and pediatric care. **Parent company:** Cambridge Hospital is a 170-bed, full-service hospital owned by the city of Cambridge and affiliated with Harvard and Tufts Medical Schools.

ST. ELIZABETH'S MEDICAL CENTER
736 Cambridge Street, Brighton MA 02135. 617/789-3000. **Contact:** Human Resources. **World Wide Web address:** http://www.semc.org. **Description:** A hospital. **Positions advertised include:** Nursing Administration; Administrative Assistant; Ambulatory Scheduling Coordinator; Benefits Manager; Billing Coordinator; Care Manager; Counselor; Dietician; Housekeeper; Licensed Practical Nurse; Medical Technician; Nursing Assistant; Secretary; Registered Nurse.

SOLDIERS' HOME
110 Cherry Street, Holyoke MA 01040. 413/532-9475. **Contact:** Human Resources. **Description:** A hospital and nursing home for veterans offering both inpatient and outpatient care.

SONAMED CORPORATION
1250 Main Street, Waltham MA 02451. 781/899-6499. **Fax:** 781/899-8318. **Contact:** Human Resources. **E-mail address:** sonamed@sonamed.com. **World Wide Web address:** http://www.sonamed.com. **Description:** Sells equipment for detecting long-term hearing problems in infants. **Positions advertised include:** Sales and Marketing Representative.

SPAULDING REHABILITATION HOSPITAL
125 Nashua Street, Boston MA 02114. 617/720-6400. **Contact:** Human Resources. **World Wide Web address:** http://spauldingrehab.org. **Description:** A 296-bed, rehabilitation hospital. Spaulding is one of the largest rehabilitation facilities nationwide. **Positions advertised include:** Case Manager; Clinical Director; Liaison Representative; Registered Nurse; Nurse Practitioner; Occupational Therapist; Paramedic; Speech Pathologist; Physical Therapist.

TLC STAFF BUILDERS HOME HEALTH
175 Cabot Street, Suite 100, Lowell MA 01853. 978/458-4357. **Toll-free phone:** 800/698-1535. **Contact:** Human Resources. **World Wide Web address:** http://www.tlcathome.com. **Description:** A home health care agency. **Positions advertised include:** Assistant Director of Clinical Services; General Manager; Home Care Nurse; Home Health Aide. **Corporate headquarters location:** Lake

Success NY. **Other U.S. locations:** Nationwide. **Number of employees nationwide:** 20,000.

TNCO, INC.
15 Colebrook Boulevard, Whitman MA 02382. 781/447-6661. **Fax:** 781/447-2132. **Contact:** Human Resources. **E-mail address:** info@tnco-inc.com. **World Wide Web address:** http://www.tnco-inc.com. **Description:** Manufactures surgical instruments. Founded in 1964. **NOTE:** Part-time jobs are offered. **Company slogan:** Passion for precision. **Special programs:** Co-ops. **Office hours:** Monday - Friday, 7:00 a.m. - 3:30 p.m. **Corporate headquarters location:** This location. **Listed on:** Privately held. **Annual sales/revenues:** $5 - $10 million. **Number of employees at this location:** 65.

TUFTS NEW ENGLAND VETERINARY MEDICAL CENTER
200 Westborough Road, North Grafton MA 01536. 508/839-5395. **Contact:** Human Resources. **World Wide Web address:** http://www.tufts.edu/vet. **Description:** An animal hospital that offers a broad range of services including cardiology, dermatology, neurology, nutrition, oncology, and surgical procedures.

TYCO HEALTHCARE KENDALL
15 Hampshire Street, Mansfield MA 02048. 508/261-8000. **Toll-free phone:** 800/962-9888. **Fax:** 508/261-8105. **Contact:** Human Resources. **E-mail address:** jobs@kendallhq.com. **World Wide Web address:** http://www.kendallhq.com. **Description:** Manufactures and markets disposable medical supplies and adhesives for general medical and industrial uses. The company sells its products to hospitals and to alternative health care facilities worldwide, and also markets products to pharmacies and retail outlets. Products include wound care, vascular therapy, urological care, incontinence care, anesthetic care, and adhesives and tapes. Founded in 1903. **NOTE:** Entry-level positions are offered. **Positions advertised include:** Accountant; Associate General Counsel; Patent & Trademarks Attorney; Customer Accounts Representative; Marketing Director. **Special programs:** Internships; Co-ops. **Corporate headquarters location:** This location. **Other U.S. locations:** Nationwide. **International locations:** Worldwide. **Parent company:** Tyco International Inc. **Listed on:** New York Stock Exchange. **Stock exchange symbol:** TYC. **CEO/Chairman:** L. Dennis Kozlowski. **Annual sales/revenues:** More than $100 million. **Number of employees at this location:** 600. **Number of employees nationwide:** 5,000. **Number of employees worldwide:** 19,000.

U.S. DEPARTMENT OF VETERANS AFFAIRS
BROCKTON VETERANS ADMINISTRATION MEDICAL CENTER
940 Belmont Street, Building 1, Brockton MA 02301. 508/583-4500. **Contact:** Craig Polucha, Human Resources Manager. **World Wide Web address:** http://www.va.gov. **Description:** A medical center operated by the U.S. Department of Veterans Affairs. From 54 hospitals in 1930, the VA health care system has grown to include 171 medical centers; more than 364 outpatient, community, and outreach clinics; 130 nursing home care units; and 37 domiciliaries. The VA operates at least one medical center in each of the 48 contiguous states, Puerto Rico, and the District of Columbia. With approximately 76,000 medical center beds, the VA treats nearly 1 million patients in VA hospitals; 75,000 in nursing home care units; and 25,000 in domiciliaries. The VA's outpatient clinics register approximately 24 million visits per year.

U.S. DEPARTMENT OF VETERANS AFFAIRS
EDITH NOURSE ROGERS MEMORIAL VETERANS HOSPITAL
200 Springs Road, Bedford MA 01730-1114. 781/687-2490. **Contact:** Human Resources. **World Wide Web address:** http://www.visn1.med.va.gov/bedford. **Description:** A medical center operated by the U.S. Department of Veterans Affairs. From 54 hospitals in 1930, the VA health care system has grown to include 171 medical centers; more than 364 outpatient, community, and outreach clinics; 130 nursing home care units; and 37 domiciliaries. VA operates at least one medical center in each of the 48 contiguous states, Puerto Rico, and the District of Columbia. With approximately 76,000 medical center beds, VA treats nearly one million patients in VA hospitals; 75,000 in nursing home care units; and 25,000 in domiciliaries. VA's outpatient clinics register approximately 24 million visits per year.

VCA SOUTH SHORE ANIMAL HOSPITAL
595 Columbian Street, South Weymouth MA 02190. 781/337-6622. **Contact:** Human Resources. **World Wide Web address:** http://www.vca.com. **Description:** A full-service pet hospital providing medical, nursing, and surgical services.

VISION-SCIENCES INC.
9 Strathmore Road, Natick MA 01760. 508/650-9971. **Fax:** 508/650-9976. **Contact:** Human Resources. **E-mail address:** info@visionsciences.com. **World Wide Web address:** http://www.visionsciences.com. **Description:** Manufactures a flexible endoscopy system that utilizes single-use protective sheaths designed to reduce reprocessing time and infection concerns. Founded in 1990. **NOTE:** Entry-level positions are offered. **Office hours:** Monday - Friday, 8:00 a.m. - 5:00 p.m. **Corporate headquarters location:** This location. **Other U.S. locations:** Orangeburg NY. **International locations:** Israel. **Listed on:** NASDAQ. **Stock exchange symbol:** VSCI. **President/CEO:** Katsumi Oneda. **Annual sales/revenues:** $5 - $10 million. **Number of employees at this location:** 35. **Number of employees nationwide:** 70.

WAYSIDE YOUTH & FAMILY SUPPORT NETWORK
118 Central Street, Waltham MA 02453. 781/891-0555. **Toll-free phone:** 800/564-4010. **Fax:** 781/647-1432. **Contact:** Human Resources Director. **E-mail address:** wayside_info@waysideyouth.org. **World Wide Web address:** http://www.waysideyouth.org. **Description:** A childcare center and children's mental health clinic. **Positions advertised include:** Classroom Behavioral Assistant; Overnight Counselor; Case Manager; Clinician; Floating Counselor; Day Counselor; Shift Supervisor.

WINCHESTER HOSPITAL
41 Highland Avenue, Winchester MA 01890. 781/729-9000. **Fax:** 781/756-2908. **Contact:** Personnel. **World Wide Web address:** http://www.winchesterhospital.org. **Description:** A community hospital offering a variety of medical services including emergency, pediatrics, surgery, maternity, intensive care, and telemetry. Winchester Hospital also supports wellness and home health care programs. **Positions advertised include:** Accountant; Administrative Assistant; Billing Representative; Cat Scan Technologist; Child Life Coordinator; Clinical Associate; Diet Technician; Message Therapist; Medical Records Clerk; MRI Technologist; Patient Registrar; Radiology Technologist; Registered Nurse; Sleep Lab Technician; Team leader; Ultrasound Technologist.

THE WINDHOVER VETERINARY CENTER
944-A Main Street, Walpole MA 02081. 508/668-4520. **Contact:** Human Resources. **World Wide Web address:** http://www.windhovervet.com. **Description:** A veterinary center providing basic care for small pets with an emphasis on treating birds.

WINDSOR STREET HEALTH CENTER
119 Windsor Street, Cambridge MA 02139. 617/665-3600. **Contact:** Human Resources. **Description:** A community-based health clinic providing general medicine and care. **Parent company:** Cambridge Hospital is a 170-bed, full-service hospital owned by the city of Cambridge and affiliated with Harvard and Tufts Medical Schools.

YOUVILLE HOSPITAL
1575 Cambridge Street, Cambridge MA 02138-4398. 617/876-4344. **Fax:** 617/234-7996. **Contact:** Jack Carrol, Human Resources Director. **World Wide Web address:** http://www.youville.org. **Description:** A nonprofit hospital and nursing home offering rehabilitation and medical care. **Positions advertised include:** Occupational Therapist; Pharmacist; Physical Therapist; Recreational Therapist; Registered Nurse; Respiratory Therapist.

ZOLL MEDICAL CORPORATION
32 Second Avenue, Burlington MA 01803. 781/229-0020. **Contact:** Human Resources. **World Wide Web address:** http://www.zoll.com. **Description:** Designs, manufactures, and markets an integrated line of proprietary, noninvasive, cardiac resuscitation devices and disposable electrodes. **Positions advertised include:** Hospital Territory Manager; Sales Development Specialist; Administrative Assistant; Clinical Nurse Specialist.

Four Seasons

HOTELS AND RESTAURANTS

You can expect to find the following types of companies in this section:
Casinos • Dinner Theaters • Hotel/Motel Operators • Resorts • Restaurants

---

AMERICAN HOSPITALITY CONCEPTS
703 Granite Street, Braintree MA 02184. 781/380-3100. **Contact:** Human Resources. **World Wide Web address:** http://www.ahconcepts.com. **Description:** A restaurant company operating the Ground Round chain of family-oriented restaurants.

ANTHONY'S PIER FOUR
140 Northern Avenue, Boston MA 02210. 617/482-6262. **Contact:** Anthony Athanas, Owner. **E-mail address:** pier4@pier4.com. **World Wide Web address:** http://www.pier4.com. **Description:** A restaurant. **NOTE:** Jobseekers must apply in person at the restaurant.

AU BON PAIN CORPORATION
19 Fid Kennedy Avenue, Boston MA 02210-2497. 617/423-2100. **Contact:** Human Resources. **E-mail address:** kris_broe@aubonpain.com. **World Wide Web address:** http://www.aubonpain.com. **Description:** Owns and operates a chain of 280 French bakery cafes worldwide. **NOTE:** Entry-level positions are offered. **Company slogan:** The French Bakery Cafe. **Positions advertised include:** General Manager; Baker; Customer Service Representative; Catering Call Center Representative; Shift Supervisor; Associate Manager; District Manager. **Special programs:** Internships. **Corporate headquarters location:** This location. **Other U.S. locations:** Nationwide. **Parent company:** Compass plc. **Listed on:** Privately held. **Number of employees nationwide:** 3,500.

BACK BAY RESTAURANT GROUP, INC.
284 Newbury Street, Boston MA 02115. 617/536-2800. **Fax:** 617/236-4175. **Contact:** Human Resources. **E-mail address:** cbradley@bbrginc.com. **World Wide Web address:** http://www.backbayrestaurantgroup.com. **Description:** Owns several Boston-based restaurant chains including Joe's American Bar & Grill, PapaRazzi, Atlantic Fish Company, and Charlie's Saloon. The company also owns a racetrack in New Hampshire. **Special programs:** Internships. **Corporate headquarters location:** This location. **Parent company:** Westwood Group. **Operations at this facility include:** Administration. **Listed on:** NASDAQ. **Number of employees at this location:** 60. **Number of employees nationwide:** 4,500.

BICKFORD'S FAMILY RESTAURANTS
1330 Soldiers Field Road, Boston MA 02135. 617/782-4010. **Contact:** Human Resources. **World Wide Web address:** http://www.bickfordsrestaurants.com. **Description:** Operates the Bickford's Family Restaurants chain in the New England area. **Positions advertised include:** Waiter; Hostess; Utility Person. **Corporate headquarters location:** This location. **Other area locations:** Statewide. **Other U.S. locations:** CT; RI; VT. **Operations at this facility include:** Administration.

BICKFORD'S FAMILY RESTAURANTS
135 Union Street, Braintree MA 02184. 781/848-7045. **Contact:** Manager. **World Wide Web address:** http://www.bickfordsrestaurants.com. **Description:** One location of the restaurant chain. **NOTE:** This location hires for much of the South Shore area outside of Boston. **Positions advertised include:** Waiter; Hostess; Utility Person. **Corporate headquarters location:** Boston MA.

BORDER CAFE
32 Church Street, Cambridge MA 02138. 617/864-6100. **Contact:** Manager. **Description:** A restaurant and bar specializing in Mexican and Cajun food.

BOSTON BEER WORKS
61 Brookline Avenue, Boston MA 02215. 617/536-2337. **Contact:** Manager. **Description:** A restaurant and brewery with a diverse menu serving the area near Fenway Park.

BOSTON CONCESSIONS GROUP INC.
55 Cambridge Parkway, Cambridge MA 02141. 617/499-2700. **Fax:** 617/679-0800. **Contact:** Human Resources. **E-mail address:** joberlander@ bostonconcessionsgroup.com. **World Wide Web address:** http://www.bostonconcessionsgroup.com. **Description:** Provides food services and related products to a wide range of customers. Boston Concessions operates in 15 states. **Corporate headquarters location:** This location.

BOSTON MARRIOTT NEWTON
2345 Commonwealth Avenue, Newton MA 02466. 617/969-1000. **Fax:** 617/630-3578. **Contact:** Human Resources. **World Wide Web address:** http://www.marriott.com. **Description:** A 430-room hotel. **Positions advertised include:** Director of Housekeeping; Night Manager; Business Transient Sales Manager; Marketing Executive. **Special programs:** Internships. **Corporate headquarters location:** Washington DC. **Parent company:** Marriott International. **Operations at this facility include:** Administration; Sales; Service. **Listed on:** New York Stock Exchange. **Stock exchange symbol:** MAR. **Number of employees at this location:** 400.

BOSTON RESTAURANT ASSOCIATES, INC.
999 Broadway, Suite 400, Saugus MA 01906. 781/231-7575. **Fax:** 781/231-3225. **Contact:** Human Resources. **World Wide Web address:** http://www.pizzariaregina.com. **Description:** Boston Restaurant Associates owns and operates a chain of seven pizzerias under the name Pizzeria Regina; two Italian/American, family style restaurants under the name Polcari's North End; and three full-service, Italian restaurants under the names Bel Canto and Cappuccino's.

BRIGHAM'S INC.
30 Mill Street, Arlington MA 02476. 781/648-9000. **Fax:** 781/646-0509. **Contact:** Jessica Olson, Human Resources. **E-mail address:** jolson@brighams.com. **World Wide Web address:** http://www.brighams.com. **Description:** Operates a chain of more than 60 restaurants and ice cream parlors throughout New England, New York, and New Jersey. **Positions advertised include:** Sundae Party Coordinator; On Site Special Events Manager; Special Events Staff. **Corporate headquarters location:** This location. **Operations at this facility include:** Administration; Manufacturing; Regional Headquarters; Sales.

THE CACTUS CLUB
939 Boylston Street, Boston MA 02115. 617/236-0200. **Fax:** 617/236-0419. **Contact:** Manager. **E-mail address:** resumes@bestmarguitas.com. **World Wide Web address:** http://www.cactusclubboston.com. **Description:** A restaurant and bar with a diverse menu including Mexican, South American, and Cuban entrees.

THE COLONNADE HOTEL
120 Huntington Avenue, Boston MA 02116. 617/424-7000. **Fax:** 617/424-1717. **Contact:** Human Resources. **E-mail address:** careers@colonnadehotel.com. **World Wide Web address:** http://www.colonnadehotel.com. **Description:** An independently-owned, luxury hotel featuring dining and on-premise parking facilities. **Positions advertised include:** Banquet Line Cook; Line Cook; Lifeguard; Server; Bell Attendant; Turn Down Attendant.

D'ANGELO SANDWICH SHOPS
49 River Street, Waltham MA 02154. 781/893-0034. **Contact:** Human Resources. **World Wide Web address:** http://www.dangelos.com/. **Description:** One location of a chain of 200 quick-service sandwich shops. **Parent company:** Papa Gino's of America Inc. **Positions advertised include:** Assistant Manager; General Manager; District Manager; Shift Leader; Cashier; Server; Cook.

EAT WELL, INC.
19 North Street, Hingham MA 02043. 781/741-5100. **Contact:** Human Resources. **World Wide Web address:** http://www.eatwellinc.com. **Description:** Operates 13 dining and recreational facilities including Waterworks, a large outdoor bar overlooking the ocean with a volleyball court, pool tables, a TV/bar, a mixed drink bar, concert area and dance floor, and a sit-down food court.

FAIRMONT COPLEY PLAZA HOTEL
138 St. James Avenue, Boston MA 02116. 617/267-5300. **Fax:** 617/859-8836. **Recorded jobline:** 617/867-8500. **Contact:** Human Resources. **E-mail address:** fcphr@aol.com. **World Wide Web address:** http://www.fairmont.com. **Description:** A 376-room, four-star, luxury hotel. Founded in 1907. **Positions advertised include:** Staff Accountant; Banquet Manager; Fairmont Gold Manager; Front Office; Guest Service Manager; Housekeeping; Room Attendant; PT Turn Down Attendant; Refreshment Order Taker; Kitchen Cook. **NOTE:** Entry-level positions and second and third shifts are offered. **Office hours:** Monday - Friday, 8:00 a.m. - 6:00 p.m. **Corporate headquarters location:** San Francisco CA. **Other U.S. locations:** Nationwide. **Parent company:** Fairmont. **Operations at this facility include:** Administration; Sales; Service. **Listed on:** New York Stock Exchange. **Stock exchange symbol:** FHR. **CEO:** Robert Small. **Facilities Manager:** John Unwin. **Number of employees at this location:** 440.

FRIENDLY'S ICE CREAM CORPORATION
1855 Boston Road, Wilbraham MA 01095. 413/543-2400. **Contact:** Human Resources. **World Wide Web address:** http://www.friendlys.com. **Description:** Operates approximately 535 Friendly's restaurants serving hamburgers, sandwiches, salads, and ice cream. **Corporate headquarters location:** This location. **Listed on:** American Stock Exchange. **Stock exchange symbol:** FRN. **Number of employees nationwide:** 35,000.

HARD ROCK CAFE
131 Clarendon Street, Boston MA 02116. 617/353-1400. **Contact:** Manager. **World Wide Web address:** http://www.hardrock.com. **Description:** A casual dining restaurant decorated with rock and roll memorabilia. Hard Rock Cafe

serves American cuisine and operates a gift shop. **Other U.S. locations:** Nationwide. **International locations:** Worldwide.

HOLIDAY INN
55 Ariadne Road, Dedham MA 02026. 781/329-1000. **Contact:** Human Resources. **World Wide Web address:** http://www.holiday-inn.com. **Description:** One location of the hotel chain. **Other U.S. locations:** Nationwide.

HOLIDAY INN LOGAN AIRPORT
225 McClellan Highway, East Boston MA 02128. 617/569-5250. **Contact:** Human Resources. **Description:** Operates a hotel, restaurant, and entertainment facility, primarily for the business traveler.

HYATT REGENCY BOSTON
One Avenue de Lafayette, Boston MA 02111. 617/422-5414. **Fax:** 617/422-5416. **Contact:** Human Resources. **World Wide Web address:** http://www.hyatt.com. **Description:** Operates a 500-room luxury hotel with full convention and dining services. **Positions advertised include:** Customer Service Representative; Services Sales Representative. **Other U.S. locations:** Nationwide.

HYATT REGENCY CAMBRIDGE
575 Memorial Drive, Cambridge MA 02139. 617/492-1234. **Fax:** 617/491-6906. **Contact:** Human Resources. **World Wide Web address:** http://www.hyatt.com. **Description:** A 460-room hotel and function facility. **NOTE:** Entry-level positions and second and third shifts are offered. **Corporate headquarters location:** Chicago IL. **Other U.S. locations:** Nationwide. **International locations:** Worldwide. **Parent company:** Hyatt Hotels Corporation. **Number of employees at this location:** 480. **Number of employees nationwide:** 40,000.

LANTANA
43 Scanlon Drive, Randolph MA 02368. 781/961-4660. **Contact:** Human Resources. **World Wide Web address:** http://www.thelantana.com. **Description:** A restaurant and meeting facility. **NOTE:** Interested jobseekers must apply in person.

LE MERIDIEN BOSTON
250 Franklin Street, Boston MA 02110. 617/451-1900. **Fax:** 617/422-5169. **Recorded jobline:** 617/422-5180. **Contact:** Human Resources. **World Wide Web address:** http://www.lemeridien.com. **Description:** A 326-bed luxury hotel offering extensive conference and banquet facilities. Le Meridien Boston has two restaurants, a seasonal outdoor cafe, a piano bar, nine meeting rooms, a full-service business center, an indoor health club, and a swimming pool. **Positions advertised include:** Cook; On Call Bell Person.

LEGAL SEAFOODS, INC.
1 Seafood Way, Boston MA 02210. 617/783-8084. **Fax:** 617/782-4479. **Contact:** Human Resources. **E-mail address:** careers@legalseafoods.com. **World Wide Web address:** http://www.legalseafoods.com. **Description:** Operates a chain of seafood restaurants. **Special programs:** Internships. **Corporate headquarters location:** This location. **Operations at this facility include:** Administration; Research and Development; Sales.

THE LENOX HOTEL
61 Exeter Street at Boylston Back Bay, Boston MA 02116. 617/536-5300. **Fax:** 617/267-1237. **Contact:** Human Resources. **World Wide Web address:** http://www.lenoxhotel.com. **Description:** A 222-room, full-service hotel.

McDONALD'S CORPORATION
690 Canton Street, Suite 310, Westwood MA 02090. 781/329-1450. **Contact:** Personnel Manager. **World Wide Web address:** http://www.mcdonalds.com. **Description:** McDonald's develops, operates, franchises, and services a worldwide system of restaurants that process, package, and sell a limited menu of fast foods. One of the largest restaurant operations in the United States and one of the largest food service organizations in the world, McDonald's operates more than 30,000 McDonald's restaurants in all 50 states and in 119 countries. **NOTE:** Entry-level positions are offered. **Positions advertised include:** Management Trainee. **Corporate headquarters location:** Oak Brook IL. **Other U.S. locations:** Nationwide. **Operations at this facility include:** This location houses regional management offices for the international fast food chain. **Listed on:** New York Stock Exchange. **Stock exchange symbol:** MCD.

OMNI PARKER HOUSE HOTEL
60 School Street, Boston MA 02108. 617/227-8600. **Fax:** 617/725-1645. **Recorded jobline:** 617/725-1627. **Contact:** Human Resources. **World Wide Web address:** http://www.omnihotels.com. **Description:** A four-star hotel with 550 rooms. **NOTE:** Entry-level positions are offered. **Positions advertised include:** Night Auditor; Housekeeping Manager. **Special programs:** Internships; Summer Jobs. **Corporate headquarters location:** Irving TX. **Other U.S. locations:** Nationwide. **International locations:** Canada; Mexico. **Operations at this facility include:** Service. **Number of employees at this location:** 300.

PAPA GINO'S OF AMERICA INC.
600 Providence Highway, Dedham MA 02026. 781/461-1200. **Toll-free phone:** 800/PAPA-GINO. **Fax:** 781/461-1896. **Contact:** Human Resources. **E-mail address:** hr@papaginos.com. **World Wide Web address:** http://www.papaginos.com. **Description:** Operates an Italian restaurant chain with over 200 restaurants in New England specializing in pizza and pasta. **Positions advertised include:** Restaurant/Food Service Manager. **Operations at this facility include:** Regional Headquarters. **Number of employees nationwide:** 5,500.

ROYAL SONESTA HOTEL
5 Cambridge Parkway, Cambridge MA 02142. 617/491-3600. **Fax:** 617/806-4183. **Contact:** June Oppedisano, Employment Manager. **E-mail address:** joppedisano@sonesta-boston.com. **World Wide Web address:** http://www.sonesta.com. **Description:** Royal Sonesta Hotel offers 400 guest rooms, 15 function rooms, and dining in the Gallery Cafe. **Positions advertised include:** Catering Sales Manager; Shift Engineer; Engineering Office Coordinator; Front Desk Agent. **NOTE:** Entry-level positions are offered. **Corporate headquarters location:** Boston MA. **Other U.S. locations:** Key Biscayne FL; New Orleans LA. **Parent company:** Sonesta International Hotels Corporation. **Operations at this facility include:** Administration; Sales; Service. **Listed on:** NASDAQ. **Stock exchange symbol:** SNSTA. **Number of employees at this location:** 300.

SHERATON COLONIAL HOTEL
One Audubon Road, Wakefield MA 01880. 781/245-9300. **Contact:** Human Resources. **World Wide Web address:** http://www.sheraton.com. **Description:** A full-service hotel complete with restaurant and entertainment facilities, an 18-hole PGA golf course, and a health club. **Corporate headquarters location:** White Plains NY. **Parent company:** Starwood Hotels & Resorts Worldwide, Inc. **Number of employees at this location:** 300.

SHERATON FERNCROFT RESORT
50 Ferncroft Road, Danvers MA 01923. 978/777-2500. **Fax:** 978/750-7959.
Contact: Joanne Sweeney, Human Resources. **World Wide Web address:**
http://www.sheraton.com. **Description:** Operates a 367-room luxury hotel with a
wide range of recreational services including a PGA tour country club, USTA tour
tennis courts, and a full-service health club. **Special programs:** Internships.
Corporate headquarters location: White Plains NY. **Parent company:**
Starwood Hotels & Resorts Worldwide, Inc. **Operations at this facility include:**
Sales; Service. **Number of employees at this location:** 300. **Number of
employees nationwide:** 5,000.

SODEXHO
45 Hayden Avenue, Lexington MA 02420. 781/372-6000. **Contact:** Human
Resources. **World Wide Web address:** http://www.sodexhousa.com.
Description: A contract service management company that provides food
services to health care facilities, schools and colleges, and corporate dining
areas. **Number of employees at this location:** 200. **Number of employees
nationwide:** 6,350.

SONESTA INTERNATIONAL HOTELS CORPORATION
116 Huntington Avenue, Boston MA 02116. 617/421-5400. **Fax:** 617/421-5402.
Contact: Human Resources. **World Wide Web address:**
http://www.sonesta.com. **Description:** Operates hotels including the Royal
Sonesta Hotels in Cambridge MA and New Orleans LA. **Corporate
headquarters location:** This location. **Listed on:** NASDAQ. **Stock exchange
symbol:** SNSTA.

TAGE INN CORPORATION
131 River Road, Andover MA 01810. 978/683-0232. **Fax:** 978/687-2454.
Contact: Human Resources. **World Wide Web address:**
http://www.tageinn.com. **Description:** Operates three hotels in the Greater
Boston area. **Corporate headquarters location:** This location. **Other area
locations:** Boston/Somerville MA; Milford MA.

UNO RESTAURANT CORPORATION
100 Charles Park Road, Boston MA 02132. 617/323-9200. **Fax:** 617/469-3949.
Contact: Human Resources. **E-mail address:** resume@unos.com. **World Wide
Web address:** http://www.pizzeriauno.com. **Description:** Uno Restaurant
Corporation operates and franchises a chain of casual dining, full-service
restaurants under the name Pizzeria Uno. **NOTE:** Entry-level positions are
offered. **Positions advertised include:** Restaurant/Food Service Manager.
Special programs: Training. **Corporate headquarters location:** This location.
Other area locations: Statewide. **Other U.S. locations:** Nationwide.
Operations at this facility include: Administration. **Listed on:** New York Stock
Exchange. **Stock exchange symbol:** UNORST. **Annual sales/revenues:** More
than $100 million. **Number of employees at this location:** 100. **Number of
employees nationwide:** 5,000.

WESTIN WALTHAM-BOSTON
70 Third Avenue, Waltham MA 02451. 781/290-5600. **Fax:** 781/290-5626.
Contact: Director of Human Resources. **World Wide Web address:**
http://www.starwood.com. **Description:** A Four Star/Four Diamond, 346-room
hotel. **Positions advertised include:** Assistant Controller; Director of Group
Sales. **NOTE:** Entry-level positions, part-time jobs, and second and third shifts
are offered. **Special programs:** Internships. **Office hours:** Monday - Friday,
9:00 a.m. - 5:00 p.m. **Corporate headquarters location:** White Plains NY.

Other area locations: Boston MA; Cambridge MA; Providence RI. **Parent company:** Starwood Hotels and Resorts. **Listed on:** New York Stock Exchange. **Stock exchange symbol:** HOT. **CEO:** Barry Sternlicht. **Number of employees at this location:** 250. **Number of employees nationwide:** 80,000. **Number of employees worldwide:** 135,000.

INSURANCE

**You can expect to find the following types of companies
in this section:**
Commercial and Industrial Property/Casualty Insurers • Health Maintenance
Organizations (HMO's) • Medical/Life Insurance Companies

A-AFFORDABLE AUTO INSURANCE
480 Forest Avenue, Brockton MA 02301. 508/588-4333. **Fax:** 508/588-2958.
Contact: Human Resources. **World Wide Web address:** http://www.a-
affordableinsurance.com. **Description:** Provides automobile insurance and some
commercial insurance policies.

ALLMERICA FINANCIAL
440 Lincoln Street, Worcester MA 01653. 508/855-1000. **Fax:** 508/853-5351.
Contact: Human Resources. **World Wide Web address:**
http://www.allmerica.com. **Description:** A major provider of insurance and
financial services and products. Allmerica Financial operates through two
business groups, asset accumulation and risk management. The asset
accumulation group is comprised of Allmerica Financial Services, which provides
insurance and retirement plans to individuals and businesses, and Allmerica
Asset Management Inc., which provides investment management services to
businesses. As part of the risk management group, Hanover Insurance and
Citizens Insurance provide property and casualty insurance to individuals and
businesses. The other subsidiaries that operate as part of the risk management
group are Sterling Risk Management Services and Citizens Management, both of
which offer claims services and benefits administration services. Founded in
1844. **NOTE:** Entry-level positions are offered. **Positions advertised include:**
Shipper Receiver; Service Support Manager; Administrative Assistant; Business
Analyst; Inside Adjuster; Program Manager; CAD Administrative Assistant;
Researcher; Actuarial Trainee; Inside Property Adjuster; Business Analyst;
Accountant; Program Underwriting Manager. **Special programs:** Internships;
Training; Summer Jobs. **Office hours:** Monday - Friday, 8:00 a.m. - 5:00 p.m.
Corporate headquarters location: This location. **Other U.S. locations:**
Nationwide. **Listed on:** New York Stock Exchange. **Stock exchange symbol:**
AFC. **President/CEO:** John O'Brien. **Annual sales/revenues:** More than $100
million. **Number of employees at this location:** 2,900. **Number of employees
nationwide:** 6,000.

BAYSTATE FINANCIAL SERVICES
699 Boylston Street One Exeter Plaza, Suite 1400, Boston MA 02116. 617/585-
4500. **Contact:** Human Resources. **World Wide Web address:**
http://www.baystatefinancial.com. **Description:** A life insurance company.

BERKSHIRE LIFE INSURANCE COMPANY
700 South Street, Pittsfield MA 01201. 413/499-4321. **Contact:** Human
Resources. **E-mail address:** carreers@theberkshire.com. **World Wide Web
address:** http://www.theberkshire.com. **Description:** Offers a wide range of life
insurance and insured pension plans.

BLUE CROSS AND BLUE SHIELD OF MASSACHUSETTS
100 Summer Street, Boston MA 02110. 617/832-5000. **Toll-free phone:**
800/262-BLUE. **Contact:** Human Resources. **World Wide Web address:**

http://www.bcbsma.com. **Description:** A nonprofit health care insurance organization providing managed health care plans to both individuals and groups. Blue Cross and Blue Shield offers Point-of-Service, individual health, PPO, and HMO plans, as well as life, dental, vision, and disability insurance. **Positions advertised include:** Office Administrator; Medical Analyst; Data Architect; Cost Accounting Analyst; Administrative Assistant; Reimbursement Analyst; Project Manager; Secretary; Web Support Analyst; Network Infrastructure Manager; Dental Director; Underwriting Consultant. **Operations at this facility include:** Administration; Sales; Service.

BOSTON MUTUAL LIFE INSURANCE COMPANY
120 Royall Street, Canton MA 02021. 781/828-7000. **Toll-free phone:** 800/669-2668x372. **Fax:** 781/770-0975. **Contact:** Human Resources. **E-mail address:** hr@bostonmutual.com. **World Wide Web address:** http://www.bostonmutual.com. **Description:** Provides life insurance. **Positions advertised include:** Actuarial Assistant; Telephone Representative. **NOTE:** Apply in person Monday – Friday 8:00 a.m. – 3:00 p.m. **Corporate headquarters location:** This location. **Operations at this facility include:** Administration; Sales; Service. **Number of employees at this location:** 300. **Number of employees nationwide:** 500.

BREWER & LORD LLP
P.O. Box 9146, Norwell MA 02061-9146. 781/792-3200. **Physical address:** 600 Longwater Drive, Norwell MA 02061. **Fax:** 781/792-3434. **Contact:** Human Resources. **World Wide Web address:** http://www.brewerlord.com. **Description:** One of the largest insurance agencies in New England, providing commercial and personal lines of insurance. **Positions advertised include:** Accounting Manager; Assistant Account Representative; Marketing Representative; Account Manager; Account Representative; Regional Account Representative. **Other area locations:** Abington MA; Acton MA; Cambridge MA; Danvers MA; Falmouth MA; Framingham MA; Lexington MA; Marshfield MA. **Other U.S. locations:** Providence RI.

COMMERCE INSURANCE COMPANY
211 Main Street, Webster MA 01570. 508/943-9000. **Toll-free phone:** 800/922-8276. **Fax:** 508/949-4921. **Contact:** Carolyn Burke, Human Resources. **World Wide Web address:** http://www.commerceinsurance.com. **Description:** Underwrites personal and commercial property and casualty insurance such as motor vehicle insurance covering personal automobiles; offers homeowners inland/marine, fire, general liability, and commercial multiperil insurance; and provides residential and commercial mortgage loans. Founded in 1972. **NOTE:** Fill out online application. **Positions advertised include:** Physical Damage Coordinator; D/L Auto Service Supervisor; Material Damage Appraiser; SIU Adjuster; Litigation Consultant; Mail Clerk; File Clerk; Underwriter Specialist; Property Services Supervisor; Data Entry Specialist; Programmer Analyst; Cash Analyst; General Claims Representative. **Special programs:** Training. **Corporate headquarters location:** This location. **Subsidiaries include:** American Commerce Insurance Company (Columbus OH); Commerce West Insurance Company (Pleasanton CA); Bay Finance (Webster MA). **Listed on:** New York Stock Exchange. **Stock exchange symbol:** CGI. **Annual sales/revenues:** More than $100 million. **Number of employees at this location:** 1,300.

CONCENTRA MANAGED CARE SERVICES
130 Second Avenue, Waltham MA 02451. 781/290-5350. **Contact:** Human Resources. **World Wide Web address:** http://www.concentramc.com.

Description: A full-service cost containment company that focuses on workers' compensation costs, and offers various consulting services. **Positions advertised include:** .NET Developer; Business Analyst; Quality Assurance Analyst; Business Report Analyst; Customer Service Representative; Operation Business Analyst; Pricing Analyst; Release Support Engineer; Vice President of Sales. **Other U.S. locations:** Nationwide.

JAMES GORMAN INSURANCE
One Exeter Plaza, 3rd Floor, Boston MA 02116. 617/266-4100. **Contact:** Jim Gorman, President. **Description:** Specializes in insurance and risk management services.

LAWYERS TITLE INSURANCE CORPORATION
77 Franklin Street, 7th Floor, Boston MA 02110. 617/619-4500. **Contact:** Human Resources. **World Wide Web address:** http://www.landam.com. **Description:** Lawyers Title Insurance Corporation provides title insurance and other real estate-related services on commercial and residential transactions in the United States, Canada, the Bahamas, Puerto Rico, and the U.S. Virgin Islands. Lawyers Title Insurance Corporation also provides search and examination services and closing services for a broad-based customer group that includes lenders, developers, real estate brokers, attorneys, and homebuyers. **Corporate headquarters location:** Richmond VA. **Other U.S. locations:** Nationwide. **Operations at this facility include:** This location covers Connecticut, Maine, Massachusetts, New Hampshire, Rhode Island, Vermont, and Canada. **Subsidiaries include:** Datatrace Information Services Company, Inc. (Richmond VA) markets automated public record information for public and private use; Genesis Data Systems, Inc. (Englewood CO) develops and markets computer software tailored specifically to the title industry; Lawyers Title Exchange Company functions as an intermediary for individual and corporate investors interested in pursuing tax-free property exchanges. **Parent company:** LandAmerica Financial Group, Inc. **Listed on:** NASDAQ. **Stock exchange symbol:** LFG.

LIBERTY MUTUAL INSURANCE COMPANY
175 Berkeley Street, Boston MA 02117. 617/357-9500. **Fax:** 617/574-5616. **Contact:** Human Resources. **World Wide Web address:** http://www.libertymutual.com. **Description:** A full-line insurance firm offering life, medical, and business insurance, as well as investment and retirement plans. **Positions advertised include:** Customer Service Representative; Assistant Service Manager. **Special programs:** Internships; Training. **Corporate headquarters location:** This location. **Other U.S. locations:** Nationwide. **International locations:** Worldwide. **Subsidiaries include:** Wausau Insurance Company. **Operations at this facility include:** Administration; Research and Development; Sales; Service. **Annual sales/revenues:** More than $100 million. **Number of employees at this location:** 1,800. **Number of employees nationwide:** 23,000.

LUMBER INSURANCE COMPANIES
One Speen Street, P.O. Box 9165, Framingham MA 01701. 508/872-8111. **Fax:** 508/872-9711. **Contact:** Human Resources Department. **Description:** Provides commercial property and casualty insurance. **Corporate headquarters location:** This location. **Number of employees at this location:** 225. **Number of employees nationwide:** 325.

MASSACHUSETTS MUTUAL LIFE INSURANCE COMPANY

1295 State Street, Springfield MA 01111. 413/788-8411. **Contact:** Human Resources. **World Wide Web address:** http://www.massmutual.com. **Description:** One of the largest insurers in the United States, with over 500 offices nationwide. MassMutual Life Insurance Company provides both individual and group insurance coverage. **Positions advertised include:** Customer Service Representative; Data Management Technician; Internal Sales Manager; Financial Reporting Analyst; Accountant; Relationship Manager. **Special programs:** Internships. **Corporate headquarters location:** This location. **Parent company:** MassMutual Financial Group. **Operations at this facility include:** Administration; Service. **Number of employees nationwide:** 10,000.

MED TAC CORPORATION

P.O. Box 9111, Newtonville MA 02460. 617/244-5333. **Fax:** 617/244-5111. **Contact:** Human Resources. **E-mail address:** hr@medtac.com. **World Wide Web address:** http://www.medtac.com. **Description:** Offers medical and dental insurance. **Positions advertised include:** Claims Manager; Regional Sales Representative.

METLIFE FINANCIAL SERVICES

1601 Trapelo Road, 1st Floor, Waltham MA 02451. 781/672-2800. **Contact:** Human Resources. **World Wide Web address:** http://www.metlife.com. **Description:** MetLife is a financial services company that offers a wide range of individual and group insurance policies including life, annuity, disability, and mutual funds. **Positions advertised include:** Recruiting Selection Consultant; Corporate Compliance Consultant; Systems Consultant; Team Manager; Business Systems Analyst; Marketing Consultant; Communications Director; Recruiting Director; Supervisor; Service Representative; Financial Consultant. **Corporate headquarters location:** New York NY. **Other U.S. locations:** Nationwide. **Operations at this facility include:** This location is a sales and service office. **Number of employees nationwide:** 13,500.

METROPOLITAN LIFE INSURANCE COMPANY

99 High Street, 32nd Floor, Boston MA 02110. 617/338-1300. **Contact:** Human Resources. **World Wide Web address:** http://www.metlife.com. **Description:** Offers a wide range of individual and group insurance policies including life, annuity, disability, and mutual funds. **Corporate headquarters location:** New York NY. **Other U.S. locations:** Nationwide. **Number of employees nationwide:** 13,500.

NEIGHBORHOOD HEALTH PLAN

253 Summer Street, Boston MA 02210. 617/772-5500. **Fax:** 617/478-7198. **Contact:** Alessandra DeVaca, Director of Human Development and Employee Systems. **E-mail:** careers@nhp.com. **World Wide Web address:** http://www.nhp.org. **Description:** A nonprofit HMO serving approximately 46,000 members through 116 community health centers and medical groups across Massachusetts. Founded in 1986. **Company slogan:** Make us part of your plan. **Positions advertised include:** Accountant; Administrative Assistant; Appeals Coordinator; Care Manager; Chief Manager; Chief Actuary; Claims Customer Service Representative; Clinical Outcomes Coordinator; Data Analyst; Healthcare Audit Analyst; Information Technologist Security Manager; Nurse Practitioner; Registered Nurse. **Corporate headquarters location:** This location. **Annual sales/revenues:** More than $100 million. **Number of employees at this location:** 200.

NEW ENGLAND FINANCIAL

501 Boylston Street, Boston MA 02116. 617/578-2000. **Toll-free phone:** 800/627-6806. **Fax:** 617/578-3088. **Contact:** Personnel Department. **World Wide Web address:** http://www.nefn.com. **Description:** Provides a variety of financial services including mutual funds, investment advice, IRAs, 401(k)s, and individual and group health insurance. **Positions advertised include:** Sales Representative.

ONEBEACON INSURANCE

One Beacon Street, Boston MA 02108. 617/725-6000. **Contact:** Human Resources. **World Wide Web address:** http://www.onebeacon.com. **Description:** A carrier of property, casualty, and life insurance. **Positions advertised include:** Underwriting Assistant; Administrative Assistant; Legal Administrator; Financial Analyst; Human Resources Consultant; Inspector; Actuarial Manager. **NOTE:** Apply online. **Corporate headquarters location:** This location.

ST. PAUL FIRE & MARINE INSURANCE COMPANY

P.O. Box 8848, Boston MA 02114. 617/227-7890. **Contact:** Human Resources. **Description:** A multiline insurance company providing fire, extended coverage, inland marine, and workers' compensation insurance. **Corporate headquarters location:** St. Paul MN. **Listed on:** New York Stock Exchange. **Stock exchange symbol:** SPC. **Number of employees at this location:** 60. **Number of employees nationwide:** 11,000.

ST PAUL TRAVELERS

300 Crown Colony Drive, Quincy MA 02169. 617/984-1000. **Contact:** Human Resources. **World Wide Web address:** http://www.stpaultravelers.com. **Description:** Provides commercial property-casualty insurance, personal property-casualty insurance and asset management services. **Positions advertised include:** Risk Control Consultant; Account Executive. **Corporate headquarters location:** St Paul MN. **Other area locations:** Boston MA, Worcester MA.

SUN LIFE ASSURANCE COMPANY OF CANADA

One Sun Life Executive Park, Wellesley Hills MA 02481. 781/237-6030. **Contact:** Human Resources. **World Wide Web address:** http://www.sunlife.com. **Description:** Offers a wide range of life, health, and dental insurance products, as well as a variety of other financial services. **Positions advertised include:** Marketing Consultant; Business Systems Analyst; Investment Analyst; Regional Vice President Individual Insurance; Product Services Administrator; Operations Coordinator; Compensation Director; Customer Service Representative; Underwriting Specialist. **Corporate headquarters location:** Toronto, Canada. **Parent company:** Sun Life Financial Services of Canada Inc. **Operations at this facility include:** Administration; Divisional Headquarters; Regional Headquarters; Service.

TUFTS HEALTH PLAN

333 Wyman Street, P.O. Box 9112, Waltham MA 02154. 781/466-9400. **Contact:** Human Resources. **World Wide Web address:** http://www.tufts-healthplan.com. **Description:** A health maintenance organization offering hospital coverage, doctors in private practice, emergency coverage, and coverage for student dependants. Tufts Health Plan also offers a range of fitness benefits. **Positions advertised include:** Accounts Representative; Administrative Assistant; Appeals Analyst; Application Developer; Application Engineer; Benefits Analyst; Claims Specialist; Computer Operator; Executive

Assistant; Graphic Designer; Inside Sales Representative; Member Relations Associate; Mental Health Services Representative; Notes Developer; Project Manager; Registered Nurse; Resource Specialist. **Corporate headquarters location:** This location. **Other U.S. locations:** NH.

UNUMPROVIDENT
18 Chestnut Street, Worcester MA 01608. 508/799-4441. **Contact:** Human Resources. **World Wide Web address:** http://www.unumprovident.com. **Description:** A life insurance carrier with a broad range of group and individual coverages. **Positions advertised include:** Disability Claims Examiner; Orthopedic Clinic Consultant; Clinical Consultant; Registered Nurse. **Corporate headquarters:** Chattanooga TN. **Listed on:** New York Stock Exchange. **Stock exchange symbol:** UNM.

LEGAL SERVICES

You can expect to find the following types of companies in this section:
Law Firms • Legal Service Agencies

ALTMAN & ALTMAN
675 Massachusetts Avenue, 11th Floor, Cambridge MA 02139. 617/492-3000. **Contact:** Human Resources. **Description:** A law firm specializing in personal injury, divorce and family, and criminal defense law.

BOWDITCH & DEWEY
P.O. Box 15156, Worcester MA 01615-0156. 508/791-3511. **Fax:** 508/929-3195. **Physical address:** 311 Main Street, Worcester MA 01615. **Contact:** Human Resources. **E-mail address:** recruiting@bowditch.com. **World Wide Web address:** http://www.bowditch.com. **Description:** A 50-attorney law firm practicing a variety of law disciplines including environmental, labor, real estate, and litigation. **Other area locations:** Framingham MA.

BROWN, RUDNICK, FREED & GESMER
One Financial Center, Boston MA 02111. 617/330-9000. **Contact:** Human Resources. **World Wide Web address:** http://www.brownrudnick.com. **Description:** A 150-attorney law firm specializing in a variety of legal disciplines including bankruptcy, corporate, international, tax, government, and estate law. **Positions advertised include:** Audio Visual Specialist; Support Specialist; Financial Analyst; Intellectual Property & Litigation Partner. **Corporate headquarters location:** This location. **Other U.S. locations:** Hartford CT; Providence RI. **International locations:** London, England. **Number of employees at this location:** 300.

BULKLEY, RICHARDSON AND GELINAS, LLP
1500 Main Street, Suite 2700, Springfield MA 01115-5507. 413/781-2820. **Fax:** 413/785-5060. **Contact:** Michael Burke, Hiring Partner. **World Wide Web address:** http://www.bulkley.com. **Description:** A law firm specializing in a variety of legal disciplines including environmental, employment, health, and intellectual property law. **Other area locations:** Boston MA.

CHOATE, HALL & STEWART
Exchange Place, 53 State Street, Boston MA 02109. 617/227-5020. **Contact:** Human Resources. **World Wide Web address:** http://www.choate.com. **Description:** A law firm whose legal specialties include business, energy and telecommunications, government enforcement and compliance, health care, real estate, and trusts and estates. **Positions advertised include:** Team Leader; Tax Attorney; Bankruptcy Associate; Probate Paralegal.

DAY, BERRY & HOWARD LLP
260 Franklin Street, 21st Floor, Boston MA 02110. 617/345-4600. **Contact:** Human Resources. **E-mail address:** lnotarangelo@dbh.com. **World Wide Web address:** http://www.dbh.com. **Description:** One of New England's largest law firms. Day, Berry & Howard LLP specializes in more than 60 legal disciplines including banking, construction, insurance, torts, and venture capital. **Positions advertised include:** Trust & Estate Paralegal; Paralegal; Associate Employment

Litigator; Attorney. **Other U.S. locations:** Greenwich CT; Hartford CT; Stamford CT; New York NY.

DECHERT
10 Post Office Square South, Boston MA 02109-4603. 617/728-7100. **Fax:** 617/426-6567. **Contact:** Human Resources Department. **World Wide Web address:** http://www.dechert.com. **Description:** A law firm specializing in intellectual property, taxation, and litigation. The firm operates 10 offices throughout the United States and Europe. **Other U.S. locations:** Hartford CT; Washington DC; Princeton NJ; New York NY; Harrisburg PA; Philadelphia PA; Newport RI. **International locations:** Belgium; England; France; Luxembourg.

EDWARDS & ANGELL
101 Federal Street, Boston MA 02110. 617/439-4444. **Contact:** Human Resources. **World Wide Web address:** http://www.ealaw.com. **Description:** A law firm specializing in intellectual property law. **Positions advertised include:** Litigation Legal Secretary; support Staff Supervisor. **Corporate headquarters location:** This location. **Listed on:** Privately held. **Number of employees at this location:** 50.

FISH & RICHARDSON, P.C.
225 Franklin Street, Boston MA 02110-2804. 617/542-5070. **Fax:** 617/542-8906. **Contact:** Betsy Butler, Office Manager. **E-mail address:** work@fr.com. **World Wide Web address:** http://www.fr.com. **Description:** A law firm with various areas of practice including patents, copyrights, and trademarks. **Other U.S. locations:** Redwood City CA; San Diego CA; Wilmington DE; Washington DC; Minneapolis MN; New York NY; Dallas TX.

FOLEY, HOAG & ELIOT, L.L.P.
165 Seaport Boulevard, Boston MA 02210. 617/832-1000. **Contact:** Dina Wreede, Director of Legal Recruiting. **E-mail address:** hiring@foleyhoag,com. **World Wide Web address:** http://www.fhe.com. **Description:** A law firm covering a broad range of practice areas including litigation, labor, business, international, and intellectual property. **Positions advertised include:** Legal Secretary. **Other U.S. locations:** Washington DC.

GOODWIN PROCTER, LLP
53 State Street, Boston MA 02109. 617/570-1000. **Contact:** Human Resources. **World Wide Web address:** http://www.gph.com. **Description:** A general practice law firm. **Corporate headquarters location:** This location. **Other U.S. locations:** Washington DC; Roseland NJ; New York NY.

GOULSTON & STORRS, P.C.
400 Atlantic Avenue, Boston MA 02110-3333. 617/482-1776. **Contact:** Nancy Needle, Recruiting Director. **World Wide Web address:** http://www.goulstorrs.com. **Description:** A law firm with a variety of practice areas including corporate law and litigation. **Other U.S. locations:** Washington DC.

HOLLAND & KNIGHT
10 St. James Avenue, Boston MA 02116. 617/523-2700. **Fax:** 617/523-6850. **Contact:** Hiring Partner. **World Wide Web address:** http://www.hklaw.com. **Description:** A general practice law firm. **Other U.S. locations:** Nationwide. **International locations:** Worldwide.

KIRKPATRICK & LOCKHART LLP
75 State Street, Boston MA 02109. 617/261-3100. **Contact:** Jeffrey King, Hiring Partner. **E-mail address:** bmorrissey@kl.com. **World Wide Web address:** http://www.kl.com. **Description:** A law firm with a broad range of practice areas including international law and intellectual property. **Positions advertised include:** Legal Assistant; Clerk; Legal Secretary; Administration. **Other U.S. locations:** Los Angeles CA; San Francisco CA; Washington DC; Miami FL; Newark NJ; New York NY; Harrisburg PA; Pittsburgh PA; Dallas TX.

LOURIE & CUTLER
60 State Street, Boston MA 02109. 617/742-6720. **Contact:** David Andelman, Esq., Hiring Partner. **Description:** A law firm specializing in estate planning and taxation.

McDERMOTT, WILL & EMERY
28 State Street, Boston MA 02109-1775. 617/535-4000. **Contact:** Human Resources. **World Wide Web address:** http://www.mwe.com. **Description:** A law firm with concentrations in health care, corporate law, and litigation.

MELICK PORTER & SHEA
28 State Street, 22nd Floor, Boston MA 02109-1775. 617/523-6200. **Fax:** 617/523-8130. **Contact:** Human Resources. **E-mail address:** jobs@melicklaw.com. **World Wide Web address:** http://www.melicklaw.com. **Description:** A law firm consisting mainly of defense attorneys. **Positions advertised include:** Associate; Summer Intern; Legal Secretary; Paralegal.

MINTZ, LEVIN, COHN, FERRIS, GLOVSKY & POPEO
One Financial Center, 40th Floor, Boston MA 02111. 617/542-6000. **Contact:** Julie Zammuto, Manager of Attorney Recruiting & Training. **World Wide Web address:** http://www.mintz.com. **Description:** A law firm with a wide range of practice areas including trade regulation, real estate, and technology. **Other U.S. locations:** Los Angeles CA; New Haven CT; Washington DC; New York NY; Reston VA.

MIRICK, O'CONNELL, DEMALLIE & LOUGEE
100 Front Street, 17th Floor, Worcester MA 01608. 508/791-8500. **Fax:** 508/791-8502. **Contact:** Human Resources. **World Wide Web address:** http://www.modl.com. **Description:** A law firm with many areas of practice including intellectual property, banking and commercial lending, labor and employment, and biotechnology. **Other area locations:** Westborough MA; Worcester MA.

NIXON PEABODY LLP
100 Summer Street, Boston MA 02110. 617/345-1280 **Fax:** 866/743-2439. **Contact:** Layla Callahan, Hiring Coordinator. **E-mail address:** ctaylor@nixonpeabody.com. **Wide Web address:** http://www.nixonpeabody.com. **Description:** A law firm covering several areas of practice through its commercial, corporate, estate, litigation, real estate, and syndication groups.

NUTTER, McCLENNEN & FISH, LLP
155 Seaport Boulevard, Boston MA 02210. 617/439-2000. **Fax:** 617/310-9000. **Contact:** Terese M. Cunningham, Human Resources. **E-mail address:** tcunningham@nutter.com. **World Wide Web address:** http://www.nutter.com. **Description:** A law firm offering a variety of legal specialties including litigation,

intellectual property, environmental, labor and employment, and trusts and estates. **Other area locations:** Hyannis MA.

PALMER AND DODGE LLP
111 Huntington Avenue, Boston MA 02199-7613. 617/239-0100. **Contact:** Kathy Von Mehren, Human Resources. **E-mail address:** pdhiring@palmerdodge.com. **World Wide Web address:** http://www.palmerdodge.com. **Description:** A general practice law firm. **Positions advertised include:** Patent Group Associate; Municipal Finance Associate.

PEABODY & ARNOLD LLP
30 Rowes Wharf, Boston MA 02110-3342. 617/951-2100. **Fax:** 617/951-2125.**Contact:** Human Resources. **World Wide Web address:** http://www.peabodyarnold.com. **Description:** A law firm that operates through three legal groups: The Personal Law Group provides tax and estate planning services; The Business Law Group specializes in securities, corporate, banking and finance, and health care; and The Litigation Group specializes in antitrust and trade regulation, employment, environmental, surety, and workers' compensation.

ROBINS, KAPLAN, MILLER & CIRESI LLP
111 Huntington Avenue, Suite 1300, Boston MA 02199-7610. 617/267-2300. **Fax:** 617/267-8288. **Contact:** Human Resources. **World Wide Web address:** http://www.rkmc.com. **Description:** A law firm covering many practice areas including insurance law, business and commercial litigation, and intellectual property law. Founded in 1938. **Corporate headquarters location:** Minneapolis MN. **Other U.S. locations:** Los Angeles CA; San Francisco CA; Washington DC; Atlanta GA; Chicago IL. **Number of employees at this location:** 37. **Number of employees nationwide:** 650.

ROPES & GRAY
One International Place, Boston MA 02110-2624. 617/951-7000. **Contact:** Human Resources. **World Wide Web address:** http://www.ropesgray.com. **Description:** A law firm specializing in corporate law.

SKADDEN, ARPS, SLATE, MEAGHER & FLOM
One Beacon Street, 31st Floor, Boston MA 02108. 617/573-4800. **Fax:** 617/573-4822. **Contact:** Human Resources. **World Wide Web address:** http://www.skadden.com. **Description:** One of the world's largest law firms. Skadden, Arps, Slate, Meagher & Flom specializes in more than 40 practice areas through 21 worldwide offices.

SULLIVAN & WORCESTER
One Post Office Square, Boston MA 02109. 617/338-2800. **Fax:** 617/338-2880. **Contact:** Janet Brussard, Legal Recruiting. **E-mail address:** hrdepartment@sandw.com. **World Wide Web address:** http://www.sandw.com. **Description:** A law firm that practices all areas of law including intellectual property and international law.

WOLF, GREENFIELD & SACKS
Federal Reserve Plaza, 600 Atlantic Avenue, Boston MA 02210. 617/720-3500. **Fax:** 617/720-2441. **Contact:** Sheila LeDuc, Director of Human Resources. **E-mail address:** sleduc@wolfgreenfield.com. **World Wide Web address:** http://www.wolfgreenfield.com. **Description:** A leading intellectual property law firm. Areas of specialization include patent, trademark, and copyright law.

MANUFACTURING: MISCELLANEOUS CONSUMER

**You can expect to find the following types of companies
in this section:**
Art Supplies • Batteries • Cosmetics and Related Products • Household
Appliances and Audio/Video Equipment • Jewelry, Silverware, and Plated Ware •
Miscellaneous Household Furniture and Fixtures • Musical Instruments • Tools •
Toys and Sporting Goods

ACUSHNET COMPANY
333 Bridge Street, Fairhaven MA 02719. 508/979-2000. **Contact:** Human Resources. **World Wide Web address:** http://www.acushnet.com. **Description:** Manufactures a wide range of golf equipment including golf balls, clubs, and shoes. Products are sold under the Titleist, Foot-Joy, Pinnacle, and Cobra brand names. **Positions advertised include:** Interactive Marketing Manager. **Parent company:** Fortune Brands, Inc. **Listed on:** New York Stock Exchange. **Stock exchange symbol:** FO.

AQUA-LEISURE INDUSTRIES
525 Bodwell Street, P.O. Box 239, Avon MA 02322. 508/587-5400. **Contact:** Human Resources. **World Wide Web address:** http://www.aqualeisure.com. **Description:** A manufacturer of water sport products and inflatable water toys and pools.

ARMATRON INTERNATIONAL INC.
15 Highland Avenue, Malden MA 02148. 781/321-2300. **Contact:** Cindie McCue, Human Resources Director. **Description:** Operates through two segments: The Consumer Products segment manufactures and distributes bug killers, chipper/shredders, and leaf-eaters; and The Industrial Products segment imports and sells radios to large automobile manufacturers. **Corporate headquarters location:** This location.

ATARI INC.
50 Dunham Road, Beverly MA 01915. 978/921-3700. **Contact:** Human Resources. **World Wide Web address:** http://www.iatari.com. **Description:** Develops, manufactures, and sells a line of interactive computer and video games and educational materials. **Corporate headquarters location:** New York NY. **Other U.S. locations:** Santa Monica CA; Sunnyvale CA; Beverly MA; Plymouth MN; Bothell WA. **International locations:** Worldwide. **Operations at this facility include:** Administration; Divisional Headquarters; Research and Development; Sales.

ARTHUR BLANK & COMPANY
225 Rivermoor Street, Boston MA 02132. 617/325-9600. **Toll-free phone:** 800/776-7333. **Fax:** 617/327-1235. **Contact:** Human Resources. **E-mail address:** abco@abco.com. **World Wide Web address:** http://www.abco.com. **Description:** Manufactures a wide variety of flat plastic products including calling cards, access cards, and rulers.

BOSE CORPORATION
The Mountain, Framingham MA 01701-9168. 508/766-1099. **Toll-free phone:** 800/999-BOSE. **Contact:** Human Resources. **World Wide Web address:** http://www.bose.com. **Description:** Designs and manufactures audio-related

consumer electronics products including speakers, stereos, and related stereo components. **Positions advertised include:** Program Manager; Administrative Assistant; Channel Marketing Manager; Research Technologist; Mechanical Engineer; DRP Planner; Product Marketing Specialist. **Corporate headquarters location:** This location. **Other U.S. locations:** Yuma AZ; Hillsdale MI; Columbia SC. **International locations:** Canada; Ireland; Mexico. **Operations at this facility include:** Administration; Research and Development.

CHELSEA CLOCK COMPANY
284 Everett Avenue, Chelsea MA 02150. 617/884-0250. **Fax:** 617/884-8639. **Contact:** Human Resources. **World Wide Web address:** http://www.chelseaclock.com. **Description:** Manufactures, sells, and repairs clocks.

FARBERWARE HOME PRODUCTS, INC.
175 McClellan Highway, P.O. Box 9114, East Boston MA 02128. 617/561-2200. **Contact:** Human Resources. **World Wide Web address:** http://www.farberware.com. **Description:** This location houses administrative offices. Overall, Farberware manufactures and sells silverware, flatware, crystal, and water filtration systems. **Corporate headquarters location:** This location.

THE FIRST YEARS
One Kiddie Drive, Avon MA 02322-1171. 508/588-1220. **Contact:** Human Resources. **World Wide Web address:** http://www.thefirstyears.com. **Description:** A leading manufacturer and marketer of products for infants and toddlers. The First Years supplies its products to toy stores, mass merchandising chains, drug stores, grocery chains, and individual retailers worldwide. **Positions advertised include:** Assistant Controller; Associate Business Unit Manager; New Product Manager; Product Development Manager; Project Manager; Insight Manager. **Listed on:** NASDAQ. **Stock exchange symbol:** KIDD.

THE GILLETTE COMPANY
Prudential Tower Building, 40th Floor, Boston MA 02199. 617/421-7000. **Contact:** Personnel Director. **World Wide Web address:** http://www.gillette.com. **Description:** Manufactures consumer products for the personal care market. Products include razors and blades including Trac II, Atra, Sensor, Mach 3, MicroTrac, Daisy, and Platinum Plus; toiletries, cosmetics, and deodorants such as Right Guard, and Dry Idea; hair care products including White Rain and Silkience; skin care and shaving cream products; dental accessories including toothbrushes, toothpaste, rinses, and related items; and Duracell alkaline batteries. **NOTE:** Please check the Website for available positions before applying. **Corporate headquarters location:** This location. **Subsidiaries include:** Braun AG (Germany) manufactures household appliances. **Parent company:** Procter & Gamble. **Listed on:** New York Stock Exchange. **Stock exchange symbol:** G.

HASBRO GAMES
443 Shaker Road, East Longmeadow MA 01028. 413/525-6411. **Contact:** Human Resources. **World Wide Web address:** http://www.hasbro.com. **Description:** Develops, manufactures, and sells a line of games, toys, and educational materials including board and card games; puzzles; skill and action games; electronic games and toys; and activity items. **Other area locations:** Fall River MA; Ludlow MA. **Parent company:** Hasbro, Inc. **Listed on:** New York Stock Exchange. **Stock exchange symbol:** HAS.

HONEYWELL CONSUMER PRODUCTS GROUP

250 Turnpike Road, Southborough MA 01772. 508/490-7000. **Contact:** Human Resources. **World Wide Web address:** http://www.honeywell.com. **Description:** Honeywell is engaged in the research, development, manufacture, and sale of advanced technology products and services in the fields of chemicals, electronics, automation, and controls. The company's major businesses are home and building automation and control, performance polymers and chemicals, industrial automation and control, space and aviation systems, and defense and marine systems. **Corporate headquarters location:** Morristown NJ. **Operations at this facility include:** This location develops, manufactures, and markets a broad range of consumer household products including fans, heaters, humidifiers, vaporizers, and air cleaners. **Listed on:** New York Stock Exchange. **Stock exchange symbol:** HON.

LENOX SAW

301 Chestnut Street, East Longmeadow MA 01028. 413/525-3961. **Contact:** Human Resources. **World Wide Web address:** http://www.lenoxsaw.com. **Description:** A manufacturer of cutting tools and related products. **Corporate headquarters location:** This location. **Listed on:** Privately held. **Number of employees at this location:** 600.

LIGHTOLIER

631 Airport Road, Fall River MA 02720. 508/679-8131. **Fax:** 508/646-3357. **Contact:** Human Resources. **World Wide Web address:** http://www.lightolier.com. **Description:** A manufacturer of lighting fixtures. Founded in 190. **Positions advertised include:** Sourcing Material Analyst; Quotations Analyst. **Special programs:** Training; Co-ops; Summer Jobs. **Corporate headquarters location:** This location. **Other U.S. locations:** Nationwide. **Parent company:** Genlyte Thomas Group. **Operations at this facility include:** Divisional Headquarters; Manufacturing. **Listed on:** NASDAQ. **Stock exchange symbol:** GLYT. **Annual sales/revenues:** More than $100 million. **Number of employees at this location:** 500. **Number of employees nationwide:** 5,000.

NECCO (NEW ENGLAND CONFECTIONERY COMPANY)
HAVILAND CANDY, INC.

135 American Legion Highway, Revere MA, 02151. 617/876-4700. **Fax:** 781/485-4519. **Contact:** Personnel. **E-mail:** njobs@necco.com. **World Wide Web address:** http://www.necco.com. **Description:** NECCO is a manufacturer of a wide variety of candy including NECCO Wafers, Conversation Hearts, and Mary Janes. **Corporate headquarters location:** This location. **Other U.S. locations:** Thibodaux LA; Watertown MA; Pewaukee WI. **Operations at this facility include:** Administration; Manufacturing.

NEW HARBOUR INC.

1 West Street, Fall River MA 02720. 508/678-3202. **Fax:** 508/673-4887. **Contact:** Human Resources. **E-mail address: World Wide Web address:** http://www.newharbour.com. **Description:** A manufacturer of home accessories. **Positions advertised include:** Customer Service Manager; Showroom Manager.

REED & BARTON

144 West Brittania Street, Taunton MA 02780. 508/824-6611. **Toll-free phone:** 800/343-1383. **Contact:** Human Resources. **E-mail address:** information@reedbarton.com. **World Wide Web address:** http://www.reedbarton.com. **Description:** A manufacturer of sterling, silver plate,

pewter, and stainless steel silverware. Reed & Barton also produces a line of jewelry products. **Corporate headquarters location:** This location. **Listed on:** Privately held.

SAUCONY, INC.
P.O. Box 6046, Peabody MA 01961. 978/532-9000. **Fax:** 978/538-3080. **Physical address:** 13 Centennial Drive, Peabody MA 01960. **Fax:** 978/538-3080. **Contact:** Kerry Smith, Director of Human Resources. **World Wide Web address:** http://www.sauconyinc.com. **Description:** Engaged in the design, manufacture, import, export, development, and marketing of a wide range of athletic footwear and recreational products. **Positions advertised include:** Account Development Manager; Technical Product Developer. **Special programs:** Internships. **Corporate headquarters location:** This location. **Other area locations:** Cambridge MA; East Brookfield MA; Fall River MA. **Other U.S. locations:** Bangor ME. **Operations at this facility include:** Administration; Research and Development; Sales; Service. **Listed on:** NASDAQ. **Stock exchange symbol:** SCNYA. **Number of employees at this location:** 140. **Number of employees nationwide:** 415.

SWANK, INC.
6 Hazel Street, Attleboro MA 02703. 508/222-3400. **Contact:** Human Resources. **World Wide Web address:** http://www.swankaccessories.com. **Description:** Manufactures men's and women's jewelry, gift items, and leather products including wallets and key chains.

SYRATECH CORPORATION
175 McClellan Highway, East Boston MA 02128. 617/561-2200. **Fax:** 617/568-1528. **Contact:** Katie Ventura, Human Resources Director. **World Wide Web address:** http://www.syratech.com. **Description:** Manufactures housewares, cookware, and gift items. **NOTE:** Entry-level positions are offered. Use http:///www.monster.com for searching for current job postings for this company. **Special programs:** Internships. **Corporate headquarters location:** This location. **Operations at this facility include:** Administration; Sales. **Listed on:** New York Stock Exchange. **Stock exchange symbol:** SYR. **Annual sales/revenues:** More than $100 million. **Number of employees at this location:** 350. **Number of employees nationwide:** 1,800. **Number of employees worldwide:** 2,300.

THE UNION GROUP
648 Alden Street, P.O. Box 3160, Fall River MA 02722. 508/675-4545. **Fax:** 508/677-0130. **Contact:** Human Resources. **E-mail address:** info@theuniongroup.com. **World Wide Web address:** http://www.theuniongroup.com. **Description:** Manufactures custom loose-leaf ring binders, indexes, software, binder/slipcases, and audio/visual cassette holders. **Subsidiaries include:** Elbe-Cesco; Metropolitan Loose Leaf; Union Bookbinding.

WEBSTER INDUSTRIES
58 Pulaski Street, Peabody MA 01960. 978/532-2000. **Fax:** 978/531-3354. **Contact:** Human Resources. **World Wide Web address:** http://www.websterindustries.com. **Description:** Manufactures a variety of plastic bags including garbage and sandwich bags.

YANKEE CANDLE COMPANY
P.O. Box 110, South Deerfield MA 01373. 413/664-8306. **Fax:** 413/665-0158. **Recorded jobline:** 800/830-6038. **Contact:** Employment Department. **E-mail**

address: jobs@yankeecandle.com. **World Wide Web address:** http://www.yankeecandle.com. **Description:** Manufactures premium scented candles. **Positions advertised include:** Associate Brand Manager; Database Administrator; Business Unit Manager; Electrician; Warehouse Management Systems Specialist.

MANUFACTURING: MISCELLANEOUS INDUSTRIAL

**You can expect to find the following types of companies
in this section:**
Ball and Roller Bearings • Commercial Furniture and Fixtures • Fans, Blowers,
and Purification Equipment • Industrial Machinery and Equipment • Motors and
Generators/Compressors and Engine Parts • Vending Machines

AGFA CORPORATION
200 Ballardvale Street, Wilmington MA 01887. 978/658-5600. **Contact:** Human
Resources. **World Wide Web address:** http://www.agfahome.com. **Description:**
AGFA operates through several divisions: the Photographic Division produces
films, printing papers, cameras, film projectors, lenses, and other related
products used in X-ray and nondestructive testing applications; the Office
Systems Division produces office duplicators and printers, a wide range of
microfiche and microfilm products, and related supplies; and the Magnetic Tape
Division produces professional audio products and amateur videocassette
products. **Corporate headquarters location:** This location. **Other U.S.
locations:** Nationwide. **International locations:** Worldwide. **Operations at this
facility include:** This location manufactures phototypesetting equipment
including fonts, parts, supplies, and output devices.

AMERICAN INK JET CORPORATION
13 Alexander Road, Billerica MA 01821. 978/667-0600. **Fax:** 978/667-0200.
Contact: Human Resources. **E-mail address:** info@amjet.com. **World Wide
Web address:** http://www.amjet.com. **Description:** Manufactures ink, cartridges,
and paper for ink jet printers. American Ink Jet provides retailers with ink jet
supplies for a wide range of printers.

ANDERSON GREENWOOD CROSBY
43 Kendrick Street, Wrentham MA 02093. 508/384-3121. **Contact:** Human
Resources. **World Wide Web address:** http://www.andersongreenwood.com.
Description: Manufacturers and marketers of safety and relief valves for power
generation and petrochemical industries. **Parent Company:** Tyco International.

HH ARNOLD COMPANY
529 Liberty Street, Rockland MA 02370. 781/878-0346. **Fax:** 781/878-7944.
Contact: Human Resources. **World Wide Web address:**
http://www.hharnold.com. **Description:** A manufacturing company providing
quality machine parts & machine assemblers for over 90 years.

BOC EDWARDS
301 Ballardvale Street, Wilmington MA 01887. 978/658-5410x3154. **Toll-free
phone:** 800/848-9800. **Fax:** 978/988-9360. **Contact:** Zena Gerolimato, Human
Resources Manager. **E-mail address:** zina.gerolimato@Edwards.boc.com.
World Wide Web address: http://www.bocedwards.com. **Description:** Supplies
high vacuum manufacturing and process control equipment, industrial freeze
dryers, and thin-film coating systems used in a variety of applications including
pharmaceutical processing, microchip manufacturing, and vacuum packaging.
Founded in 1919. **NOTE:** Entry-level positions are offered. **Office hours:**
Monday - Friday, 8:30 a.m. - 5:00 p.m. **Corporate headquarters location:** This
location. **Other U.S. locations:** Fairfield CA; Tonawanda NY. **International
locations:** Worldwide. **Parent company:** BOC Group. **Listed on:** London Stock

Exchange. **President:** Mark Rosenzweig. **Annual sales/revenues:** More than $100 million. **Number of employees at this location:** 200. **Number of employees nationwide:** 700. **Number of employees worldwide:** 2,000.

BTU INTERNATIONAL
23 Esquire Road, North Billerica MA 01862. 978/667-4111. **Contact:** Human Resources. **E-mail address:** btuhr@btu.com. **World Wide Web address:** http://www.btu.com. **Description:** A manufacturer of thermal processing systems used in electronics packaging, metals and ceramics sintering, nuclear fuel sintering, and various nonelectronics applications. **Positions advertised include:** Electrical Wirer; Final Test Technician; Mechanical Assembler; Plumber. **Corporate headquarters location:** This location. **Operations at this facility include:** Administration; Manufacturing; Research and Development; Sales; Service. **Listed on:** NASDAQ. **Stock exchange symbol:** BTUI.

BARRY CONTROLS
40 Guest Street, Brighton MA 02135. 617/787-1555. **Fax:** 617/254-7381. **Contact:** Human Resources. **E-mail address:** resume@bcdi.com. **World Wide Web address:** http://www.barrycontrols.com. **Description:** Engaged in the design, manufacture, and sale of shock, noise, and vibration isolation and absorption products used in a wide variety of industrial applications. **Other U.S. locations:** Nationwide. **International locations:** Worldwide. **Parent company:** Hutchinson Worldwide. **Operations at this facility include:** Administration; Divisional Headquarters; Manufacturing; Research and Development; Sales.

BATTENFELD GLOUCESTER ENGINEERING COMPANY, INC.
Blackburn Industrial Park, P.O. Box 900, Gloucester MA 01931. 978/281-1800. **Contact:** Human Resources. **World Wide Web address:** http://www.battenfeld.com. **Description:** A manufacturer of plastics, processing machinery, and related components. **Other area locations:** Rockport MA. **Other U.S. locations:** Santa Ana CA; Woodstock GA; Algonquin IL; Medina OH; Frisco TX. **International locations:** Worldwide. **Parent company:** Battenfeld (Germany).

BIRD MACHINE COMPANY
100 Neponset Street, South Walpole MA 02071. 508/668-0400. **Fax:** 508/660-1385. **Contact:** Human Resources. **World Wide Web address:** http://www.bakerhughes.com. **Description:** Designs, develops, and manufactures centrifuges, filters, and other solid/liquid separation equipment systems for process industries. **Other U.S. locations:** Houston TX; Salt Lake City UT. **International locations:** Worldwide. **Parent company:** Baker Hughes Inc. **Annual sales/revenues:** More than $100 million. **Number of employees at this location:** 360. **Number of employees nationwide:** 500. **Number of employees worldwide:** 15,000.

BROOKFIELD ENGINEERING LABORATORIES, INC.
11 Commerce Boulevard, Middleborough MA 02346-1031. 508/946-6200. **Toll-free phone:** 800/628-8139. **Fax:** 508/946-6262. **Contact:** Human Resources. **E-mail address:** hr@brookfieldengineering.com. **World Wide Web address:** http://www.brookfieldengineering.com. **Description:** Designs, manufactures, sells, and services electromechanical instrumentation, viscometers, and accessories for a broad range of industries. Founded in 1934. **NOTE:** Second and third shifts are offered. **Special programs:** Co-ops; Summer Jobs. **Office hours:** Monday - Friday, 8:00 a.m. - 5:00 p.m. **Corporate headquarters location:** This location. **Subsidiaries include:** Brookfield Viscometers Ltd.

(England); Brookfield Engineering Laboratories Vertriebs, GmbH (Germany). **Listed on:** Privately held.

BUTLER AUTOMATIC INC.
41 Leona Drive, Middleboro MA 02346. 781/828-5450. **Toll-free phone:** 800/544-0070. **Fax:** 508/923-0885. **Contact:** Marilyn Kujala, Director of Personnel. **World Wide Web address:** http://www.butlerautomatic.com. **Description:** Manufactures automatic web-handling equipment for sale to the printing and corrugating industries. **Positions advertised include:** Field Services Representative. **Corporate headquarters location:** This location. **International locations:** Australia; France; Japan; Mexico.

DAVID CLARK COMPANY, INC.
360 Franklin Street, Box 15054, Worcester MA 01615-0054. 508/751-5800. **Fax:** 508/751-5827. **Recorded jobline:** 508/751-5861. **Contact:** Personnel. **E-mail address:** humanresc@davidclark.com. **World Wide Web address:** http://www.davidclark.com. **Description:** Manufacturers of air crew protective clothing, communication headsets, hearing protectors, and antishock trousers. Founded in 1935. **Positions advertised include:** Mechanical Designer. **NOTE:** Entry-level positions are offered. **Special programs:** Summer Jobs. **Office hours:** Monday - Friday, 8:00 a.m. - 4:30 p.m. **Corporate headquarters location:** This location. **Listed on:** Privately held. **President:** Robert Vincent. **Facilities Manager:** Vin Klimas. **Information Systems Manager:** James Grigos. **Purchasing Manager:** Gerry Leach. **Number of employees at this location:** 350.

CREO AMERICAS, INC.
8 Oak Park Drive, Bedford MA 01730. 781/275-5150. **Fax:** 781/275-3430. **Contact:** Human Resources. **E-mail address:** resume.america@creo.com. **World Wide Web address:** http://www.creo.com. **Description:** Designs, develops, manufactures, markets, and services electronic prepress systems for the printing and publishing industries. These systems automate the labor- and materials-intensive prepress process of converting graphic design specifications for color slides, text, and graphics into final color separation films. **Positions advertised include:** Marketing Manager; Product Marketing Engineer; Professional Success Team Lead; Manager Market Development. **Listed on:** NASDAQ. **Stock exchange symbol:** CREO.

CUMBERLAND ENGINEERING LLC
BROWN PLASTIC MACHINERY LLC
100 Roddy Avenue, South Attleboro MA 02703. 508/399-6400. **Fax:** 508/399-3057. **Contact:** Donna Welch, Director of Human Resources. **World Wide Web address:** http://www.cumberland-plastics.com. **Description:** Manufactures industrial and commercial machinery. **Corporate headquarters location:** This location. **Number of employees at this location:** 200. **Number of employees nationwide:** 1,250.

GODDARD VALVE
P.O. Box 765, Worcester MA 01613-0765. 508/852-2435. **Physical address:** 705 Plantation Street, Worcester MA 01605. 508/852-2435. **Contact:** Human Resources. **World Wide Web address:** http://www.goddardvalve.com. **Description:** Designs and manufactures cryogenic gate, globe, and check valves and control devices required for the handling of liquefied natural gas, liquid oxygen, and other liquefied gases. **Corporate headquarters location:** This location. **International locations:** Australia; England. **Parent company:** Goddard Industries, Inc.

HIGH VOLTAGE ENGINEERING CORP.
401 Edgewater Place, Suite 680, Wakefield MA 01880. 781/224-1001. **Fax:** 781/224-1011. **Contact:** Human Resources. **World Wide Web address:** http://www.hvec.com. **Description:** Owns and operates a diversified group of technology-based, middle market, industrial manufacturing businesses.

HONEYWELL SENSING AND CONTROL
100 Discovery Way, Acton MA 01720. 978/264-9550. **Contact:** Human Resources. **World Wide Web address:** http://content.honeywell.com/sensing/. **Description:** Honeywell is engaged in the research, development, manufacture, and sale of advanced technology products and services in the fields of chemicals, electronics, automation, and controls. The company's major businesses are home and building automation and control, performance polymers and chemicals, industrial automation and control, space and aviation systems, and defense and marine systems. **Corporate headquarters location:** Morristown NJ. **Operations at this facility include:** This location manufactures transducers and safety equipment for presses. **Listed on:** New York Stock Exchange. **Stock exchange symbol:** HON.

RODNEY HUNT COMPANY
46 Mill Street, Orange MA 01364. 978/544-2511. **Fax:** 978/544-7209. **Contact:** David Broghum, Manager of Human Resources. **World Wide Web address:** http://www.rodneyhunt.com. **Description:** Manufactures water control valves and related components. **Positions advertised include:** Design Hydraulic Engineer. **Parent company:** GA Industries.

ITW FOILMARK
5 Malcolm Hoyt Drive, Newburyport MA 01950. 978/462-7300. **Toll-free phone:** 800/468-7826. **Fax:** 978/462-0831. **Contact:** Human Resources. **E-mail address:** corporate@foilmark.com. **World Wide Web address:** http://www.foilmark.com. **Description:** Manufactures metallized, pigmented, and diffraction foils; and packaging films. **Office hours:** Monday - Friday, 8:00 a.m. - 5:00 p.m. **Corporate headquarters location:** This location.

IMTRAN FOILMARK
25 Hale Street, Newburyport MA 01950. 978/462-2722. **Contact:** Human Resources. **World Wide Web address:** http://www.foilmark.com. **Description:** Manufactures pad printing equipment and supplies, dies, tooling, and silicone rubber products. **Corporate headquarters location:** This location. **Parent company:** Foilmark, Inc. **Listed on:** NASDAQ. **Stock exchange symbol:** FLMK.

INSTRON CORPORATION
100 Royall Street, Canton MA 02021. 781/828-2500. **Toll-free phone:** 800/877-6674. **Fax:** 781/575-5776. **Contact:** Human Resources. **E-mail address:** careers@instron.com. **World Wide Web address:** http://www.instron.com. **Description:** Manufactures, markets, and services materials testing instruments, systems, software, and accessories used to evaluate the mechanical properties and performance of metals, plastics, composites, textiles, ceramics, rubber, adhesives, and other materials. Instron's applications technology is used by research scientists, design engineers, and quality control managers in industry, academia, and government. The systems include electromechanical and servohydraulic instruments, structural components, computer software, temperature chambers, and hardness testers. **Positions advertised include:** Field Service Engineer; Product Manager. **Corporate headquarters location:**

This location. **Other U.S. locations:** Nationwide. **International locations:** Worldwide. **Subsidiaries include:** Laboratory Microsystems (Troy NY). **Listed on:** American Stock Exchange. **Stock exchange symbol:** INSTRN. **Number of employees at this location:** 400.

IONICS INC.
P.O. Box 9131, Watertown MA 02472. 617/926-2500. **Physical address:** 65 Grove Street, Watertown MA 02472. **Contact:** Brenda Madden, Recruiter. **World Wide Web address:** http://www.ionics.com. **Description:** Designs, manufactures, and sells four groups of products: Water Processing Systems are used for water desalination, food processing, chemical manufacturing, and biological separations that include ion-exchange membranes and electrochemical cells. Membrane Cell Products include products used in food processing, the manufacture of chlorination chemicals, and products used by the food, pharmaceutical, and chemical industries for special process problems; Energy Related & Other Fabricated Products include products used in nuclear or fossil fuel power plants and heat recuperating systems; and Instruments & Medical Products include laboratory and process control instruments and medical products. **Positions advertised include:** Purchasing Agent. **NOTE:** Visit http://www.monster.com to search for open positions. **Corporate headquarters location:** This location. **Other U.S. locations:** Nationwide. **International locations:** Worldwide. **Operations at this facility include:** Administration; Manufacturing; Research and Development; Sales; Service. **Listed on:** New York Stock Exchange. **Stock exchange symbol:** ION. **Number of employees nationwide:** 800.

JACO, INC.
140 Constitution Boulevard, Franklin MA 02038. 508/553-1000. **Fax:** 508/553-1061. **Contact:** Human Resources. **E-mail address:** info@jaco.com. **World Wide Web address:** http://www.jacoinc.com. **Description:** Manufactures housings for computers and medical equipment. **Positions advertised include:** Assembler; Press Brake Operator; Grinder; Packer.

KENNAMETAL GREENFIELD IPG
34 Sanderson Street, Greenfield MA 01301. 413/772-3200. **Contact:** Esther M. Johnson, CPS/Human Resources Specialist. **World Wide Web address:** http://www.gfii.com. **Description:** Kennametal Greenfield IPG is also one of North America's leading producers of rotary cutting tools and suppliers of circuit board drills to the Far East. The company operates in four divisions: Industrial, Electronics, Oil Field Equipment, and Consumer. The company distributes its products to manufacturers, the federal government, electronic OEMs, electronic subcontractors, oil field pump manufacturers, do-it-yourself customers, and contractors. The company's product lines are sold under an array of national brand names. **Corporate headquarters location:** Augusta GA. **Other U.S. locations:** Nationwide. **Operations at this facility include:** This location manufactures cutting tools. **Listed on:** New York Stock Exchange. **Stock exchange symbol:** KMT. **Annual sales/revenues:** More than $100 million. **Number of employees at this location:** 160. **Number of employees nationwide:** 4,700.

KONICA BUSINESS TECHNOLOGIES
175 Great Road, Bedford MA 01730. 781/275-4643. **Contact:** Human Resources. **E-mail address:** philbins@kmbs.konicaminolta.com. **World Wide Web address:** http://www.konicabt.com. **Description:** Sells and services copier machines, duplicator equipment, and facsimile machines.

B.L. MAKEPEACE, INC.
125 Guest Street, Brighton MA 02135-2083. 617/782-3800. **Fax:** 617/782-9768. **Contact:** Human Resources. **E-mail address:** personel@makepeace.com. **World Wide Web address:** http://www.makepeace.com. **Description:** A firm specializing in supplying drafting room equipment and supplies. **Corporate headquarters location:** This location. **Other area locations:** Hopkinton MA.

MARKET FORGE INDUSTRIES, INC.
35 Garvey Street, Everett MA 02149. 617/387-4100. **Toll-free phone:** 800/227-2659. **Fax:** 617/387-4456. **Contact:** Human Resources. **E-mail address:** custserv@mfii.com. **World Wide Web address:** http://www.mfii.com. **Description:** Manufactures restaurant equipment including ranges, ovens, convection ovens, shelving, and tilting skillets.

MATEC INSTRUMENT COMPANIES
56 Hudson Street, Northborough MA 01532. 508/393-0155. **Fax:** 508/393-5476. **Contact:** Ed Antolino, Human Resources. **E-mail address:** eantolino@matec.com. **World Wide Web address:** http://www.matec.com. **Description:** Designs, manufactures, imports, and sells quartz crystals and oscillators; develops and manufactures computer-controlled, ultrasonic test equipment to perform real-time measurements and analysis; and produces and sells instruments to evaluate the stability of colloidal dispersions. **Corporate headquarters location:** This location. **Subsidiaries include:** Valpey-Fisher Corporation. **Listed on:** American Stock Exchange. **Stock exchange symbol:** MXC. **CEO:** Ted Valpey, Jr.

MESTEK INC.
260 North Elm Street, Westfield MA 01085. 413/568-9571. **Fax:** 413/562-7630. **Contact:** Karen Chartier, Personnel Manager. **E-mail address:** kchartier@mestek.com. **World Wide Web address:** http://www.mestek.com. **Description:** Manufactures industrial refrigeration and heating equipment. **Corporate headquarters location:** This location. **Listed on:** New York Stock Exchange. **Stock exchange symbol:** MCC. **Number of employees nationwide:** 2,000.

METSO AUTOMATION
P.O. Box 8044, Shrewsbury MA 01545. 508/852-0200. **Physical address:** 44 Bowditch Street, Shrewsbury MA 01545. **Contact:** Marcia Siart, Employment Manager. **World Wide Web address:** http://www.metsoautomation.com. **Description:** Manufactures valves and controls for the process control industry. **Positions advertised include:** Machinist; Industrial Controls Technician. **NOTE:** Entry-level positions and second and third shifts are offered. **Special programs:** Summer Jobs. **International locations:** Brazil; Finland; Singapore. **Parent company:** Metso Corporation. **Listed on:** New York Stock Exchange. **Stock exchange symbol:** MX. **Annual sales/revenues:** More than $100 million. **Number of employees at this location:** 450. **Number of employees nationwide:** 500. **Number of employees worldwide:** 750.

MICROCUT
18 Plymouth Drive, South Easton MA 02375. 508/230-9389. **Fax:** 508/230-0387. **Contact:** Human Resources. **E-mail address:** info@microcutusa.com. **World Wide Web address:** http://www.microcutusa.com. **Description:** A manufacturer of premium carbide end mills and special application rotary cutting tools.

MICROFLUIDICS INTERNATIONAL CORPORATION

30 Ossipee Road, Newton MA 02464. 617/969-5452. **Contact:** Human Resources. **World Wide Web address:** http://www.microfluidics.com. **Description:** Manufactures and distributes high-performance mixing equipment primarily for the chemical, pharmaceutical, biotechnology, food, and personal care products industries. **Corporate headquarters location:** This location.

MORGAN CONSTRUCTION COMPANY

15 Belmont Street, Worcester MA 01605. 508/755-6111. **Contact:** Human Resources. **World Wide Web address:** http://www.morganco.com. **Description:** Engineers and manufactures heavy machinery, ferrous and nonferrous rolling mills, and wire drawing machinery. **Positions advertised include:** Process Metallurgist. **Special programs:** Internships. **Other U.S. locations:** Chicago IL; Pittsburgh PA. **International locations:** Brazil; China; England; France; Japan; India. **Operations at this facility include:** Administration; Manufacturing; Sales.

NIDEC/POWER GENERAL

100 River Ridge Drive, Norwood MA 02062. 781/769-0619. **Fax:** 781/551-6825. **Contact:** Human Resources. **E-mail address:** jobs@nidecpg.com. **World Wide Web address:** http://www.nidec.com. **Description:** Develops, manufactures, and markets axial fans and motors, power supplies, and AC/DC converters. **Positions advertised include:** Administration Assistant; Engineer; Manufacturer; Sales. **Corporate headquarters location:** Torrington CT. **Parent company:** Nidec Corporation (Japan).**Operations at this facility include:** Manufacturing; Research and Development; Sales. **Number of employees at this location:** 300.

NORTON COMPANY

P.O. Box 15008, Worcester MA 01615-0008. 508/795-5000. **Physical address:** One New Bond Street, Worcester MA 01606. **Fax:** 508/795-2828. **World Wide Web address:** http://www.nortonabrasives.com. **Contact:** Human Resources. **Description:** The Norton Company is one of the world's largest manufacturers of abrasives. Founded in 1885. **Positions advertised include:** Accountant; Application Engineer; Application Developer; Customer Service Representative; Financial Analyst; Human Resources Specialist; Industrial Engineer; Manufacturing Engineer; Network Specialist; Quality Engineer; Process Engineer; Product Engineer; Purchasing Agent; Research & Development Engineer; Technical Sales Representative. **International locations:** Worldwide. **Parent company:** Saint-Gobain Corporation (Valley Forge PA) consists of Certainteed Corporation, Norton Company, and all of their subsidiaries. **Operations at this facility include:** This location is the headquarters for the Abrasives Branch. The Abrasives Branch is one of the only worldwide manufacturers to produce the three major types of abrasives: bonded abrasives including grinding wheels, coated abrasives including sandpaper, and superabrasives. The products of the Abrasives Branch are sold under several names including Amplex, Carborundum Abrasives, Clipper, Norton, Penhall, and Procut.

PERKINELMER

35 Congress Street, Salem MA 01970. 978/745-3200. **Contact:** Human Resources. **World Wide Web address:** http://www.perkinelmer.com. **Description:** Operates four separate business units. The Instruments Unit designs and manufactures products for detecting, measuring, and testing purposes, and markets them to the pharmaceuticals, food, chemical, plastics, and environmental industries. The Life Sciences Unit designs and manufactures bioanalytic and diagnostic instrument systems and markets them to medical

research facilities, hospitals, and clinics. The Fluid Sciences Unit manufactures sealing systems, advanced pneumatic components, and static and dynamic valves for use by OEMs and end users. The Optoelectronics Unit produces silicon-based sensor products, imaging technology, and a range of light sources. **Positions advertised include:** Global Risk Manager; Manager of Technical Accounting & Controls. **Other area locations:** Boston MA. **Other U.S. locations:** Beltsville MD; Norton OH. **International locations:** Belgium; Canada; England; Finland. **Listed on:** New York Stock Exchange. **Stock exchange symbol:** PKI.

F.C. PHILLIPS
471 Washington Street, Stoughton MA 02072. 781/344-9400. **Contact:** Human Resources. **World Wide Web address:** http://www.fcphillips.com. **Description:** Manufactures screw machines and cleat spikes for athletic shoes.

PHOENIX CONTROLS CORPORATION
55 Chapel Street, Newton MA 02458. 617/964-6670. **Fax:** 617/965-9450. **Contact:** Human Resources. **E-mail address:** hr@pheonixcontrols.com. **World Wide Web address:** http://www.phoenixcontrols.com. **Description:** A manufacturer of air-flow control devices for hospitals and laboratories.

REED-RICO
18 Industrial Drive, Holden MA 01520. 508/829-4491. **Contact:** Human Resources. **Description:** Produces thread-rolling machines, die attachments, thread rolls, and knurls. Reed-Rico has more than 2,000 registered trademarks, and more than 5,000 U.S. and foreign patents or patent applications. **Corporate headquarters location:** Portland OR. **Other U.S. locations:** Bristol RI; Gaffney SC. **Parent company:** Precision Castparts Corporation. **Listed on:** New York Stock Exchange. **Stock exchange symbol:** PCP. **Number of employees at this location:** 345.

SCHNEIDER AUTOMATION
One High Street, North Andover MA 01845. 978/794-0800. **Contact:** Human Resources. **World Wide Web address:** http://www.modicon.com. **Description:** Manufactures industrial instruments for measurement, display, and control of process variables and related products. **Positions advertised include:** Principal Product Leader.

STANDARD-THOMSON CORPORATION
152 Grove Street, Waltham MA 02453-8325. 781/894-7310. **Contact:** Louis Mollinedo, Human Resources. **E-mail address:** hr@Schrader-bridgeport.net. **World Wide Web address:** http://www.schrader-bridgeport.net. **Description:** Engaged in the production of original equipment and replacement engine temperature control devices. The company is also a producer of automotive electronic and fuel control devices. Other products include a specialized fuel heater for diesel truck and off-highway equipment. **Parent company:** Schrader-Bridgeport/Standard Thomson.

L.S. STARRETT COMPANY
121 Crescent Street, Athol MA 01331. 978/249-3551. **Fax:** 978/249-3457. **Contact:** Human Resources. **World Wide Web address:** http://www.starrett.com. **Description:** Manufactures industrial, professional, and consumer products. Among the items produced are precision tools, tape measures, levels, electronic gages, dial indicators, gage blocks, digital-readout measuring tools, granite surface plates, optical measuring projectors, and coordinate measuring vises. Much of the company's production is concentrated

in hand measuring tools and precision instruments. These products are sold throughout the United States and in over 100 foreign countries. **Corporate headquarters location:** This location. **Other U.S. locations:** NC; OH; PA; SC. **International locations:** Brazil; England; Puerto Rico; Scotland. **Listed on:** New York Stock Exchange. **Stock exchange symbol:** SCX.

J. STONE & SON INC.
23 Turcotte Memorial Drive, Rowley MA 01969. 978/948-7276. **Contact:** Human Resources. **Description:** Manufactures and distributes custom packaging including boxes, cups, and microwavable containers.

TECH-ETCH, INC
45 Aldrin Road, Plymouth MA 02360. 508/747-0300. **Fax:** 508/746-9639. **Contact:** Human Resources. **E-mail address:** hr@tech-etch.com. **World Wide Web address:** http://www.tech-etch.com. **Description:** A manufacturing company producing precision parts. **Positions advertised include:** Process Engineer; Product Engineer; Tool & Die Maker; Tool Designer; CAD Drafter; Technician. **Number of employees:** 600.

TEMPTRONIC CORPORATION
4 Commercial Street, Sharon MA 02067. 781/688-2300. **Fax:** 781/688-2301. **Contact:** Human Resources. **E-mail address:** info@temptronic.com. **World Wide Web address:** http://www.temptronic.com. **Description:** Produces controlled temperature test equipment. **NOTE:** Entry-level positions are offered. **Special programs:** Internships. **Corporate headquarters location:** This location. **Listed on:** Privately held. **Annual sales/revenues:** $11 - $20 million. **Number of employees at this location:** 100.

THYSSENKRUPP ELEVATOR
665 Concord Avenue, Cambridge MA 02138. 617/547-9000. **Contact:** Human Resources. **World Wide Web address:** http://www.thyssenkruppelevator.com. **Description:** Manufactures and installs elevators.

USFILTER
P.O. Box 36, Sturbridge MA 01566-0036. 508/347-7344. **Physical address:** 441 Main Street, Sturbridge MA 01518. **Contact:** Human Resources. **World Wide Web address:** http://www.usfilter.com. **Description:** Manufactures water pollution control pumps. **Positions advertised include:** Business Unit Sales Manager; Administrative Assistant; Plant Operator; Maintenance Specialist. **Parent company:** Vivendi.

VARIAN VACUUM TECHNOLOGIES
121 Hartwell Avenue, Lexington MA 02421. 781/861-7200. **Fax:** 781/860-5437. **Contact:** Human Resources. **World Wide Web address:** http://www.varianinc.com. **Description:** Produces vacuum products used in leak detection. **Positions advertised include:** Customer Care Supervisor; Technical Product Manager. **Corporate headquarters location:** Palo Alto CA. **Parent company:** Varian Associates has manufacturing facilities in seven nations and has sales and service offices worldwide. The company is organized around the following core businesses: Health Care Systems, Instruments, Electronic Devices, and Semiconductor Equipment. The company is a leading supplier of X-ray tubes for imaging systems of all types. Leading semiconductor chip manufacturers worldwide rely on Varian's manufacturing systems. The company's instruments also aid physicians and researchers in the fight against diseases such as AIDS. Varian is also a worldwide leader in the manufacture of devices that generate, amplify, and define signals for radio and television

broadcasting and satellite communications. These are also essential elements in air traffic control, navigation, radar, fusion energy, and other scientific research applications. **Listed on:** NASDAQ. **Stock exchange symbol:** VARI. **Number of employees nationwide:** 6,500.

WATTS REGULATOR COMPANY
815 Chestnut Street, North Andover MA 01845. 978/688-1811. **Fax:** 978/794-1848. **Contact:** Human Resources. **World Wide Web address:** http://www.wattsind.com. **Description:** Designs, manufactures, and sells an extensive line of valves for the plumbing and heating, water quality, municipal water, steam, industrial, and oil and gas markets. The company has 28 manufacturing plants worldwide. Major products include relief valves; water pressure regulators; backflow preventers; ball valves; hydronic heating valves; butterfly valves; steam specialty products; automatic control valves; drainage products; water supply stops; tubular and specialty water supply products; flexible water supply connectors, fittings, and tubing products; float valves; and water conditioning valves. **Listed on:** New York Stock Exchange. **Stock exchange symbol:** WTS.

WEB INDUSTRIES
1700 West Park Drive, Suite 110, Westborough MA 01581. 508/898-2988. **Toll-free phone:** 800/932-3213. **Fax:** 508/898-3329. **Contact:** Alan Harrington, Director of Human Resources. **World Wide Web address:** http://www.webconverting.com. **Description:** A custom contractor that converts various foils (including aluminum), plastics, and woven and nonwoven materials into different forms for use by other companies. **Corporate headquarters location:** This location. **Subsidiaries include:** Web Converting, 2272 Park Central Boulevard, Decatur GA 30035, 770/593-2004.

WESTERBEKE CORPORATION
150 John Hancock Road, Taunton MA 02780. 508/823-7677. **Fax:** 508/884-9688. **Contact:** Monica Corbeio, Human Resources Manager. **World Wide Web address:** http://www.westerbeke.com. **Description:** Designs, manufactures, and markets marine engine and air conditioning products. The company's products consist of diesel and gasoline engine-driven electrical generator sets; inboard propulsion engines; self-contained, reverse cycle air-conditioners; and associated spare parts and accessories. Westerbeke's generator sets are installed in powerboats, houseboats, large sailboats, and other types of pleasure and commercial boats to provide electricity for operating, safety, and convenience needs. The company's propulsion engines are installed as auxiliary power systems for sailboats. In addition, the company manufactures and markets a limited number of electrical generator sets for use in nonmarine applications. Westerbeke's products are marketed through a nationwide and international network of 54 distributors and approximately 400 dealers and through the company's direct sales personnel. Founded in 1930. **NOTE:** Entry-level positions are offered. **Special programs:** Co-ops. **Office hours:** Monday - Friday, 8:15 a.m. - 5:00 p.m. **Listed on:** NASDAQ. **Stock exchange symbol:** WTBK. **President:** Jack Westerbeke. **Facilities Manager:** Bob Bisanti. **Purchasing Manager:** Dennis Durkee. **Sales Manager:** Tom Sutherland. **Number of employees at this location:** 150.

XERIUM TECHNOLOGIES, INC.
1 Technology Drive, Westborough Technology Park, Westborough MA 01581. 508/616-9468. **Fax:** 508/616-9487. **Contact:** Human Resources. **World Wide Web address:** http://www.xerium.com. **Description:** A leading global manufacturer and supplier of consumable products used in the production of

paper. Operates 39 manufacturing facilities in 15 countries. **Corporate headquarters location:** This location. **Subsidiaries include:** Huyck; Mount Hope; Stowe Woodward; Wangner; Weavexx. **Listed on:** New York Stock Exchange. **Stock exchange symbol:** XRM. **Number of employees worldwide:** 4,000.

MINING, GAS, PETROLEUM, ENERGY RELATED

You can expect to find the following types of companies in this section:
Anthracite, Coal, and Ore Mining • Mining Machinery and Equipment • Oil and Gas Field Services • Petroleum and Natural Gas

ALVIN HOLLIS
One Hollis Street, South Weymouth MA 02190. 781/335-2100. **Toll-free phone:** 800/649-5090. **Contact:** Human Resources. **World Wide Web address:** http://www.alvinhollis.com. **Description:** A leading supplier of fuel and home heating oil to South Shore Massachusetts homes and businesses. **Corporate headquarters location:** This location.

CABOT CORPORATION
2 Seaport Lane, Suite 1300, Boston MA 02210. 617/345-0100. **Contact:** Human Resources. **World Wide Web address:** http://www.cabot-corp.com. **Description:** A supplier of liquefied natural gas; and Distrigas Corporation, which imports liquefied natural gas from Algeria. **Positions advertised include:** Corporate Accountant. **Corporate headquarters location:** This location. **Other area locations:** Billerica MA; Woburn MA. **Other U.S. locations:** Alpharetta GA; Tuscola IL; Franklin LA; Ville Platte LA; Midland MI; Pampa TX; The Woodlands TX; Waverly WV. **International locations:** Worldwide. **Listed on:** New York Stock Exchange. **Stock exchange symbol:** CBT.

DUKE ENERGY ALGONQUIN
1284 Soldiers Field Road, Brighton MA 02135. 617/254-4050. **Toll-free phone:** 800/USE-DUKE. **Contact:** Personnel. **World Wide Web address:** http://www.duke-energy.com. **Description:** A natural gas transmission company. The company pipes natural gas to utility companies. **Listed on:** New York Stock Exchange. **Stock exchange symbol:** DUK.

FRAMATOME AWP
400 Donald Lynch Boulevard, Marlborough MA 01752. 508/229-2100. **Contact:** Human Resources. **World Wide Web address:** http://www.framatome-awp.com. **Description:** A nuclear engineering company. **Parent company:** Areva.

GLOBAL PETROLEUM CORPORATION
P.O. Box 9161, Waltham MA 02454-9161. 781/894-8800. **Physical address:** 800 South Street, Suite 200, Waltham MA 02454. **Contact:** Human Resources. **Description:** Wholesale retailer of refined petroleum products and marketer of natural gas. **Corporate headquarters location:** This location.

A.R. SANDRI, INC.
P.O. Box 1578, Greenfield MA 01302-1578. 413/773-3658. **Physical address:** 400 Chapman Street, Greenfield MA 01301. **Contact:** Human Resources. **World Wide Web address:** http://www.sandrisunoco.com. **Description:** One of the largest regional distributors of Sunoco brand gasoline, heating oil, lubricants, and other petroleum products. **Corporate headquarters location:** This location.

PAPER AND WOOD PRODUCTS

**You can expect to find the following types of companies
in this section:**
Forest and Wood Products and Services • Lumber and Wood Wholesalers •
Millwork, Plywood, and Structural Members • Paper and Wood Mills

AMES SPECIALTY PACKAGING
12 Tyler Street, Somerville MA 02143. 617/776-3360. **Fax:** 617/776-6269.
Contact: Human Resources. **E-mail address:** jobs@amespage.com. **World
Wide Web address:** http://www.amespage.com. **Description:** Manufactures a
variety of paper products including file folders and X-ray jackets. **Positions
advertised include:** Master Development Scheduler; Master Code Writer; Digital
Print Sales Representative. **Parent company:** Ames Safety Envelope Company.

AMPAD CORPORATION
75 Appleton Street, Holyoke MA 01040. 413/536-3511. **Fax:** 972/578-3364.
NOTE: Fax # for Plano Office. **Contact:** Human Resources Manager. **World
Wide Web address:** http://www.ampad.com. **Description:** A paper converting
company that manufactures school and office supplies. **NOTE:** Resumes should
be sent to Plano Texas office, American Pad & Paper, Attention: Human
Resources. 3000 East Plano Parkway, Plano Texas, 75074. **Corporate
headquarters location:** Dallas TX. **Other U.S. locations:** Atlanta GA; Mattoon
IL; Marion IN; North Salt Lake City UT. **Parent company:** American Pad & Paper
Company. **Operations at this facility include:** Manufacturing. **Listed on:**
Privately held. **Number of employees at this location:** 350. **Number of
employees nationwide:** 900.

AVERY DENNISON CORPORATION
P.O. Box 7057, Chicopee MA 01022. 413/593-3963. **Physical address:** One
Better Way, Chicopee MA 02021. **Fax:** 413/593-3445. **Contact:** Human
Resources. **World Wide Web address:** http://www.averydennison.com.
Description: A manufacturer of stationery and office products. **Positions
advertised include:** Associate Project Manager; Director of Marketing; Financial
Analyst. **Corporate headquarters location:** Pasadena CA. **Operations at this
facility include:** Administration; Manufacturing. **Listed on:** New York Stock
Exchange. **Stock exchange symbol:** AVY. **Number of employees at this
location:** 300.

BOISE CASCADE CORPORATION
P.O Box 130, Nutting Lake Massachusetts 01865. 978/670-3800. **Physical
Address:** 32 Manning Road, Billerica MA 01821. **Contact:** Human Resources.
Description: A wholesale lumber company.

HOLLINGSWORTH & VOSE COMPANY
112 Washington Street, East Walpole MA 02032. 508/668-0295. **Fax:** 508/668-
3057. **Contact:** Human Resources. **E-mail address:** info@hovo.com. **World
Wide Web address:** http://www.hollingsworth-vose.com. **Description:**
Manufactures high-tech specialty filtration papers including nonwovens, battery
separators, and engine filtration products. Founded in 1843. **NOTE:** Entry-level
positions are offered. **Special programs:** Co-ops. **Corporate headquarters
location:** This location. **Other area locations:** West Groton MA. **Other U.S.
locations:** Concord CA; Hawkinsville GA; Hillsdale IL; Easton NY; Greenwich

NY; Charlotte NY; Brentwood TN; Floyd VA. **International locations:** Belgium; Brazil; England; Germany; India; Italy; Japan; Korea; Mexico. **Operations at this facility include:** Administration; Manufacturing; Research and Development; Sales; Service. **Listed on:** Privately held. **Annual sales/revenues:** More than $100 million. **Number of employees at this location:** 200. **Number of employees nationwide:** 750. **Number of employees worldwide:** 900.

MEADWESTVACO
40 Willow Street, South Lee MA 01260. 413/243-1231. **Contact:** Human Resources Manager. **World Wide Web address:** http://www.meadwestvaco.com. **Description:** Manufactures papers for decorative and industrial laminates, and papers made from various materials including mica, cotton, metal, and carbon. **Corporate headquarters location:** Stamford CT. **Other U.S. locations:** Nationwide. **Listed on:** New York Stock Exchange. **Stock exchange symbol:** MWV. **Number of employees worldwide:** 30,000.

XPEDX
613 Main Street, Wilmington MA 01887. 978/988-7447. **Fax:** 978/988-8595. **Contact:** Human Resources. **World Wide Web address:** http://www.xpedx.com. **Description:** Distributes office and printing papers. **Corporate headquarters location:** Denver CO. **Other U.S. locations:** City of Industry CA; Detroit MI.

PRINTING AND PUBLISHING

You can expect to find the following types of companies in this section:
Book, Newspaper, and Periodical Publishers • Commercial Photographers • Commercial Printing Services • Graphic Designers

---

ACME PRINTING COMPANY
30 Industrial Way, Wilmington MA 01887. 978/658-0800. **Contact:** Human Resources. **World Wide Web address:** http://www.acmeprinting.com. **Description:** A commercial printer.

ADAMS MEDIA, AN F+W PUBLICATIONS COMPANY
57 Littlefield Street, Avon MA 02322. 508/427-7100. **Toll-free phone:** 800/872-5627. **Fax:** 800/872-5628. **Contact:** Human Resources. **E-mail address:** hr@adamsmedia.com. **World Wide Web address:** http://www.adamsmedia.com. **Description:** A rapidly growing publisher of nonfiction books in a wide range of categories. Major book series include the Everything® series, Cup of Comfort®, JobBank, Knock 'em Dead, and Polka Dot Press. The company's line of business books includes the Adams Small Business series, the Adams Streetwise® series, and Platinum Press. Other nonfiction categories include self-help, weddings, humor, personal finance, parenting, and reference. Founded in 1980. **Positions advertised include:** Associate Editor; Editorial Assistant; Manufacturing Coordinator; Production Artist; Production Editor. **NOTE:** Refer to http://www.fwpublications.com for current employment opportunities. **Special programs:** Internships. **Internship information:** Adams Media's internship program runs throughout the year. **Office hours:** Monday - Friday, 8:00 a.m. - 5:00 p.m. **Corporate headquarters location:** Cincinnati OH. **Parent Company:** F&W Publications, Inc. **Operations at this facility include:** Accounting/Auditing; Administration; Customer Service; Editorial - Reference; Editorial - Trade; Marketing; Operations; Production; Publishing; Sales. **Listed on:** Privately held.

ADDISON WESLEY
75 Arlington Street, Suite 300, Boston MA 02116. 617/848-6000. **Contact:** Human Resources. **World Wide Web address:** http://www.awl.com. **Description:** Publishes and distributes educational materials for use in elementary and high schools, universities, and certain businesses. Addison Wesley publications cover all of the major disciplines. The company also publishes professional, reference, and nonfiction trade books. The company operates in three divisions: Higher Education; School; and General Books. **Positions advertised include:** Page Formatter; Project Manager; Sales Representative; Webmaster; Associate Media Producer; Designer; Development Editor; Editorial Assistant; Education Consultant; Executive Assistant; Managing Editor; Marketing Manager; Production Editor; Math Content Writer. **Corporate headquarters location:** Upper Saddle River NJ. **International locations:** England, Hong Kong. **Parent company:** Pearson Education

AMES ON-DEMAND
12 Tyler Street, Somerville MA 02143. 617/776-3360x1126. **Contact:** Human Resources. **World Wide Web address:** http://www.amesondemand.com. **Description:** A large commercial printer. **Parent company:** Ames Safety Envelope Company.

Tom Tom ?

BEACON PRESS
25 Beacon Street, Boston MA 02108. 617/742-2110. **Fax:** 617/723-3097. **Contact:** Human Resources. **World Wide Web address:** http://www.beacon.org. **Description:** An independent publisher of nonfiction and fiction books. Founded in 1854. **Special programs:** Internships. **Corporate headquarters location:** This location. **Parent company:** Unitarian Universalist Association. **Number of employees at this location:** 25.

CHANNING L. BETE COMPANY INC.
One Community Place, South Deerfield MA 01373-0200. 413/665-7611. **Toll-free phone:** 800/477-4776. **Fax:** 413/665-6397. **Contact:** Human Resources. **World Wide Web address:** http://www.channing-bete.com. **Description:** Publishers and printers of educational booklets, calendars, videos, coloring books, and posters. **Positions advertised include:** Copywriter; Advertising Direct Marketer; Product Manager; Market Research Specialist; Programming Analyst. **Corporate headquarters location:** This location. **Operations at this facility include:** Administration; Manufacturing; Research and Development; Sales. **Listed on:** Privately held. **Number of employees at this location:** 275.

BLACKWELL PUBLISHERS
350 Main Street, Malden MA 02148. 781/388-8200. **Fax:** 781/388-8210. **Contact:** Human Resources. **World Wide Web address:** http://www.blackwellpub.com. **Description:** Publishes books and journals on a variety of subjects including history, linguistics, and air pollution. **Positions advertised include:** Conference Services Marketing Manager; Telemarketing Coordinator; Journal Editor; Associate Publisher; Production Assistant; Conference Assistant; Editorial Coordinator. **International locations:** England.

BOSTON BUSINESS JOURNAL
200 High Street, Suite 4B, Boston MA 02110. 617/330-1000. **Fax:** 617/330-1015. **Contact:** Personnel. **E-mail address:** boston@bizjournals.com. **World Wide Web address:** http://www.amcity.com/boston. **Description:** Publishes a weekly business journal serving the Boston area. **Publisher:** James C. Menneto.

BOSTON COMMON PRESS
17 Station Street, Brookline MA 02445. 617/232-1000. **Contact:** David Mack, Circulation Director. **World Wide Web address:** http://www.cooksillustrated.com. **Description:** Publishes *Natural Health Magazine, Cooks Illustrated,* and *Handcraft* magazines.

THE BOSTON GLOBE
P.O. Box 2378, Boston MA 02107-2378. 617/929-2000. **Physical address:** 135 Morrissey Boulevard, Boston MA 02125. **Fax:** 617/929-3376. **Contact:** Human Resources. **World Wide Web address:** http://www.boston.com/. **Description:** One of New England's largest daily newspapers. Founded in 1872. **Special programs:** Internships; Co-ops. **Internship information:** The Boston Globe offers a Business Summer internship program to college sophomores and juniors. There are two internship positions available: one in advertising and one in accounting. The accounting intern is assigned to the Controller's Office and works on specific projects for the Credit, Accounting, and Payroll departments. The advertising intern is responsible for selling advertising space and servicing existing accounts. Summer interns work from June 1 through Labor Day and are paid approximately $550.00 per week. The deadline for applications (including resume and personal statement) is February 28. Questions about application procedures should be addressed to Human Resources. **Parent company:** New

York Times Company. **Listed on:** New York Stock Exchange. **Stock exchange symbol:** NYT. **Number of employees at this location:** 2,400.

BOSTON HERALD
P.O. Box 2096, Boston MA 02106. 617/426-3000. **Contact:** Human Resources. **World Wide Web address:** http://www.bostonherald.com. **Description:** One of New England's largest daily newspapers.

BOSTON MAGAZINE
300 Massachusetts Avenue, Boston MA 02115. 617/262-9700. **Contact:** Human Resources. **World Wide Web address:** http://www.bostonmagazine.com. **Description:** A monthly magazine focusing on local interest stories, politics, entertainment, theater, and dining. **Corporate headquarters location:** This location. **Parent company:** MetroCorp (Philadelphia PA).

BOWNE OF BOSTON
411 D Street, Boston MA 02210. 617/542-1926. **Fax:** 617/542-5790. **Contact:** Human Resources. **World Wide Web address:** http://www.bowne.com. **Description:** Engaged in financial and commercial printing services. Founded in 1775. **Positions advertised include:** Reprographic Associate; Hospitality Associate; Records Manager; Receptionist; Office Service Associate; Client Services Shift Supervisor; Estimator. **Corporate headquarters location:** New York NY. **Parent company:** Bowne & Company, Inc. is a financial printer. **Other area locations:** Cambridge MA. **Other U.S. locations:** Nationwide. **International locations:** Worldwide. **Listed on:** New York Stock Exchange. **Stock exchange symbol:** BNE.

CAPE COD TIMES
319 Main Street, Hyannis MA 02601. 508/775-1200. **Contact:** Human Resources. **World Wide Web address:** http://www.capecodtimes.com/cctimes. **Description:** A daily newspaper serving Cape Cod. **Parent company:** Ottaway Newspapers, Inc. (Campbell Hall NY). **Operations at this facility include:** Administration; Manufacturing; Sales; Service. **Number of employees at this location:** 300.

CHAMPAGNE/LAFAYETTE COMMUNICATIONS
7 Strathmore Road, Natick MA 01760. 508/651-0400. **Contact:** Human Resources. **World Wide Web address:** http://www.chamlaf.com. **Description:** Provides graphic design services. Champagne/Lafayette Communications is also involved in commercial printing and direct mail marketing. Founded in 1967. **Positions advertised include:** Sales; Prepress Supervisor.

CHARLESBRIDGE PUBLISHING
85 Main Street, Watertown MA 02472. 617/926-0329. **Toll-free phone:** 800/225-3214. **Fax:** 617/926-5720. **Contact:** Personnel. **E-mail address:** books@ charlesbridge.com. **World Wide Web address:** http://www.charlesbridge.com. **Description:** Publisher of educational materials for the classroom and both fiction and nonfiction books for children. Picture books cover a wide range of topics including math, nature, multiculturalism, animals, history, geography, and nursery rhymes. Charlesbridge Publishing also has two fiction imprints (Talewinds and Whispering Coyotes) as well as a diversity imprint (Shakti). **Special programs:** Internships. **Internship information:** Internship applications should be directed to Ms. Elena Wright in the School Department. **Corporate headquarters location:** This location. **President:** Brent Farmer. **Number of employees at this location:** 25.

CHRISTIAN SCIENCE MONITOR
Christian Science Center, One Norway Street, Boston MA 02115-3195. 617/450-2000. **Contact:** Human Resources. **World Wide Web address:** http://www.csmonitor.com. **Description:** A daily newspaper focusing primarily on national and international news. Founded in 1908. **Corporate headquarters location:** This location. **Operations at this facility include:** Publishing.

COMMUNITY NEWSPAPER COMPANY
72 Cherry Hill Drive, Beverly MA 01915. 978/739-1300. **Contact:** Human Resources. **Description:** Owns and operates several weekly newspapers in communities north of Boston. Publications include *Ipswich Chronicle.*

COMPUTERWORLD INC.
500 Old Connecticut Path, Framingham MA 01701. 508/879-0700. **Contact:** Human Resources. **World Wide Web address:** http://www.computerworld.com. **Description:** Publishes *Computerworld,* a weekly newspaper devoted to the computer industry, with a special emphasis on the Internet; and *ROI,* a magazine for CIOs.

COURIER EPIC, INC.
COURIER CORPORATION
15 Wellman Avenue, North Chelmsford MA 01863. 978/251-6000. **Contact:** Human Resources. **World Wide Web address:** http://www.courier.com. **Description:** As a division of Courier Corporation, Courier EPIC coordinates material for electronic publishers and software companies. Courier Corporation (also at this location) offers a full range of book production and distribution services. Publishing markets served include educational, religious, reference, medical, financial, trade, and software. Founded in 1824. **Positions advertised include:** Staff Accountant. **Corporate headquarters location:** This location. **Other area locations:** Stoughton MA; Westford MA. **Other U.S. locations:** Hayward CA; Buffalo Creek CO; Chicago IL; Kendallville IN; North Bergen NJ; North Caldwell NJ; Mineola NY; New York NY; Philadelphia PA. **Listed on:** NASDAQ. **Stock exchange symbol:** CRRC.

COURIER STOUGHTON, INC.
100 Alpine Circle, Stoughton MA 02072. 781/341-1800. **Contact:** Human Resources. **World Wide Web address:** http://www.courier.com. **Description:** Offers a full-range of book production and distribution services. Publishing markets served include educational, religious, reference, medical, financial, trade, and software. Founded in 1824. **Positions advertised include:** Bindery Cutter Operator. **Corporate headquarters location:** North Chelmsford MA. **Other area locations:** Hayward CA; Buffalo Creek CO; Chicago IL; Kendallville IN; North Bergen NJ; North Caldwell NJ; Mineola NY; New York NY; Philadelphia PA. **Listed on:** NASDAQ. **Stock exchange symbol:** CRRC. **Other U.S. locations:** Kendallville IN; Philadelphia PA. **Parent company:** Courier Corporation.

COURIER WESTFORD, INC.
22 Town Farm Road, Westford MA 01886. 978/692-6321. **Fax:** 978/692-7292. **Contact:** Human Resources. **World Wide Web address:** http://www.courier.com. **Description:** Offers a full-range of book production and distribution services. Publishing markets served include educational, religious, reference, medical, financial, trade, and software. Founded in 1824. **Positions advertised include:** Human Resources Manager; Casebinder Operator; Web Press Operator; Skidder; General Worker. **Corporate headquarters location:** North Chelmsford MA. **Other area locations:** Stoughton MA. **Other U.S.**

locations: Hayward CA; Buffalo Creek CO; Chicago IL; Kendallville IN; North Bergen NJ; North Caldwell NJ; Mineola NY; New York NY; Philadelphia PA. **Listed on:** NASDAQ. **Stock exchange symbol:** CRRC. **Parent company:** Courier Corporation.

DS GRAPHICS INC.
120 Stedman Street, Lowell MA 01851-2797. 978/970-1359. **Toll-free phone:** 800/536-8283. **Fax:** 978/970-1253. **Contact:** Human Resources. **World Wide Web address:** http://www.dsgraphics.com. **Description:** A commercial printer engaged in the printing of books, software documentation, and direct mail marketing materials. Founded in 1974. **Corporate headquarters location:** This location.

DAILY EVENING ITEM
38 Exchange Street, Lynn MA 01901. 781/593-7700. **Contact:** Allan Kort, Managing Editor. **World Wide Web address:** http://www.thedailyitem.com. **Description:** Publishes a daily newspaper with a weekday circulation of more than 20,000. **Parent company:** Ottaway Newspapers, Inc.

R.R. DONNELLEY FINANCIAL
20 Custom House Street, Suite 650, Boston MA 02110. 617/345-4300. **Contact:** Human Resources. **World Wide Web address:** http://www.rrdonnelley.com. **Description:** R.R. Donnelley & Sons is a world leader in managing, reproducing, and distributing print and digital information for publishing, merchandising, and information technology customers. The company is one of the largest commercial printers in the world, producing catalogs, inserts, magazines, books, directories, computer documentation, and financial materials. R.R. Donnelley has more than 180 sales offices and production facilities worldwide. Principal services offered by the company are conventional and digital prepress operations; computerized printing and binding; sophisticated pool shipping and distribution services for printed products; information repackaging into multiple formats including print, magnetic, and optical media; database management, list rental, list enhancement, and direct mail production services; turnkey computer documentation services including outsourcing, translation, printing, binding, diskette replication, kitting, licensing, republishing, and fulfillment; reprographics and facilities management; creative design and communication services; and digital and conventional map creation and related services. Founded in 1864. **Corporate headquarters location:** Chicago IL. **Other U.S. locations:** Nationwide. **International locations:** Worldwide. **Operations at this facility include:** This location prints financial materials. **Parent company:** R.R. Donnelley & Sons. **Listed on:** New York Stock Exchange. **Stock exchange symbol:** DNY. **Number of employees worldwide:** 35,000.

DYNAGRAF, INC.
5 Dan Road, Canton MA 02021. 781/575-1700. **Contact:** Human Resources. **World Wide Web address:** http://www.dynagraf.com. **Description:** A printing company. Dynagraf prints annual reports, educational materials, and financial documents.

THE ENTERPRISE
60 Main Street, P.O. Box 1450, Brockton MA 02303. 508/586-6200. **Contact:** Caroline Darosa, Personnel Director. **Description:** Publishes the *Enterprise,* a daily newspaper that is distributed throughout southeastern Massachusetts and has a daily circulation of over 60,000. **Parent company:** Newspaper Media LLC.

ESSEX COUNTY NEWSPAPERS, INC.
SALEM EVENING NEWS
32 Dunham Road, Beverly MA 01915. 978/922-1234. **Fax:** 978/927-1020. **Contact:** Kathy Melanson, Director of Human Resources. **World Wide Web address:** http://www.ecnnews.com. **Description:** Publishes the *Salem Evening News, Gloucester Daily Times,* and the *Daily News* of Newburyport. **NOTE:** Second and third shifts are offered. **Special programs:** Internships. **Corporate headquarters location:** Campbell Hall NY. **Parent company:** Ottaway Newspapers, Inc. (a subsidiary of Dow Jones & Company.) **Operations at this facility include:** Administration; Manufacturing; Regional Headquarters; Sales; Service. **Listed on:** New York Stock Exchange. **Stock exchange symbol:** DJ. **Annual sales/revenues:** $11 - $20 million. **Number of employees at this location:** 350.

FOUR STAR PRINTING COMPANY, INC.
P.O. Box 301, Lynn MA 01903-0301. 781/599-8772. **Physical address:** 82 Sanderson Avenue, Lynn MA 01902-1937. **Fax:** 781/581-3930. **Contact:** Doug Stewart, President. **Description:** A commercial printer. **Number of employees at this location:** 15.

GANNETT OFFSET BOSTON
565 University Avenue, Norwood MA 02062. 781/762-0277. **Contact:** Human Resources. **World Wide Web address:** http://www.gannett.com. **Description:** A full-service newspaper printer. **Corporate headquarters locations:** Springfield VA. **Parent company:** Gannett Company, Inc. is a nationwide news and information company that publishes 92 newspapers including *USA Today,* and is one of the largest outdoor advertising companies in North America. Gannett is also involved in marketing, television news and program production, and research satellite information systems. **Listed on:** New York Stock Exchange. **Stock exchange symbol:** GCI.

HCPRO
100 Hoods Lane, P.O. Box 1168, Marblehead MA 01945. 781/639-1872. **Fax:** 781/639-2982. **Contact:** Human Resources. **E-mail address:** hcprocustomerservice@hcpro.com. **World Wide Web address:** http://www.hcpro.com. **Description:** A publisher of health care newsletters and related materials.

HARVARD BUSINESS SCHOOL PUBLISHING CORPORATION
60 Harvard Way, Boston MA 02163. 617/783-7400. **Physical address:** 300 North Beacon Street, Watertown MA 02472. **Fax:** 617/783-7485. **Contact:** Human Resources. **World Wide Web address:** http://www.hbsp.harvard.edu. **Description:** Publishes *Harvard Business Review, Harvard Management Update,* and many books on business management. The company also produces videos and interactive CD-ROMs. **NOTE:** Entry-level positions are offered. **Number of employees at this location:** 190.

HARVARD UNIVERSITY PRESS
79 Garden Street, Cambridge MA 02138. 617/495-2600. **Contact:** Human Resources. **World Wide Web address:** http://www.hup.harvard.edu. **Description:** A publisher of scholarly books and journals. **Corporate headquarters location:** This location.

HOUGHTON MIFFLIN COMPANY
222 Berkeley Street, Boston MA 02116. 617/351-5180. **Fax:** 617/351-1106. **Contact:** Human Resources. **World Wide Web address:** http://www.hmco.com.

Description: A publisher of school textbooks; fiction, nonfiction, and reference works; educational software; and related multimedia products. **NOTE:** Entry-level positions are offered. **Positions advertised include:** Administrative Coordinator; Editor; Editorial Project Manager; Associate Editor Dictionaries; Image Producer; Designer; Editorial Project Manager; Lead Desktop Analyst; Project Manager; Helpdesk Supervisor; Sales & Service Coordinator. **Special programs:** Internships. **Corporate headquarters location:** This location. **Listed on:** New York Stock Exchange. **Stock exchange symbol:** HTN. **Annual sales/revenues:** More than $100 million. **Number of employees at this location:** 850. **Number of employees nationwide:** 2,300.

INC. MAGAZINE
38 Commercial Wharf, Boston MA 02110. 617/248-8000. **Contact:** Personnel Department. **E-mail address:** mail@inc.com. **World Wide Web address:** http://www.inc.com. **Description:** Publishes a financial and business news magazine that is distributed worldwide. **Special programs:** Internships. **Corporate headquarters location:** This location.

INTERNATIONAL DATA GROUP (IDG)
5 Speen Street, Framingham MA 01701. 508/872-8200. **Contact:** Human Resources Department. **World Wide Web address:** http://www.idg.com. **Description:** Publishes periodicals that primarily focus on computer-related topics. **Positions advertised include:** Advertising Sales Associate; Client Services Representative; Conference Coordinator; Premium Content Services Director; Editor in Chief; Features Writer; Graphic Designer; Staff Accountant; Market Development Manager; Managing Editor; Marketing Communications Coordinator; Program Manager; Research Analyst; Research Manager; Account Executive; Inquiry Analyst; Training & Development Coordinator; Vice President Interactive Products & Services.

LITTLE, BROWN AND COMPANY
3 Center Plaza, Boston MA 02108. 617/227-0730. **Contact:** Human Resources. **World Wide Web address:** http://www.littlebrown.com. **Description:** The publishing house has printed works by such well-known authors as Louisa May Alcott, Emily Dickinson, Oliver Wendell Holmes, Jr., J.D. Salinger, and Norman Mailer. Little, Brown and Company operates through two divisions: The Professional Division produces law and medical textbooks for students, and reference books and journals for professionals; The Trade Division consists of Adult Trade, and Children's Books including Joy Street Books, Bulfinch Press, and Arcade. In total, the company produces and publishes close to 400 new titles each year. The number of titles in print of all the divisions at any one time is approximately 3,000. Founded in 1837. **Other U.S. locations:** New York NY. **Parent company:** AOL Time Warner.

LOWELL SUN PUBLISHING COMPANY
P.O. Box 1477, Lowell MA 01853. 978/458-7100. **Contact:** Carmen Bellrose, Controller. **World Wide Web address:** http://www.newschoice.com. **Description:** Publishes the *Lowell Sun,* a daily newspaper with a weekday circulation of more than 56,000.

MIT PRESS
5 Cambridge Center, 4th Floor, Cambridge MA 02142-1493. 617/253-5646. **Contact:** Human Resources. **World Wide Web address:** http://www.mitpress.mit.edu. **Description:** Publishes scholarly books. Founded in 1962. **Corporate headquarters location:** This location.

NEW ENGLAND BUSINESS SERVICE INC. (NEBS)

500 Main Street, Groton MA 01471. 978/448-6111. **Fax:** 978/449-3841. **Contact:** Human Resources. **E-mail address:** hr@nebs.com. **World Wide Web address:** http://www.nebs.com. **Description:** A supplier of business forms and software for small businesses. The company's product line consists of over 1,000 standardized imprinted manual and computer business forms including billing forms, work orders, job proposals, and purchase orders; stationery including letterheads, envelopes, and business cards; checks and check writing systems; and marketing products including advertising labels, pricing tags and labels, signage, and greeting cards. The company offers a line of software that includes check writing, billing, and mailing applications, as well as a variety of simpler form-filling software; and One-Write Plus, a line of accounting software that integrates accounting and payroll functions with basic word processing, mail merge, a spreadsheet link, a backup utility, and a menu organizer. The computer forms are compatible with over 3,500 personal computer software packages developed by third parties and used by small businesses. **Positions advertised include:** Call Center Supervisor; Composition Artist; Corporate Legal Manager; Corporate Legal Manager; Corporate Paralegal; Customer Sales Consultant; Field Sales Support Representative; Field Sales Support Representative; Human Resources Director; Inbound Sales Representative; Data Mining Analyst. **Corporate headquarters location:** This location. **Other area locations:** Sudbury MA; Townsend MA; Woburn MA. **Other U.S. locations:** Flagstaff AZ; Maryville MO; Nashua NH; Peterborough NH. **International locations:** Canada; England; France. **Operations at this facility include:** Administration; Sales; Service. **Listed on:** New York Stock Exchange. **Stock exchange symbol:** NEB. **Number of employees at this location:** 800. **Number of employees nationwide:** 2,600.

NEWSEDGE CORPORATION

80 Blanchard Road, Burlington MA 01803. 781/229-3000. **Contact:** Human Resources. **World Wide Web address:** http://www.newsedge.com. **Description:** Provides customized, real-time news and information delivered to knowledge workers over their organizations' local area networks. The company's NewsEDGE service delivers more than 480 news and information sources, in real-time, to users' personal computers; automatically monitors and filters the news according to pre-established personal interest profiles; and alerts users to stories matching their profiles. The NewsEDGE service is used by executives, salespeople, marketers, lawyers, accountants, consultants, bankers, and financial professionals. News and information sources available on NewsEDGE include newswire from AFP/Extel News Limited; The Associated Press; Dow Jones; Knight-Ridder/Tribune Information Services; and the text of stories in the *Financial Post, Financial Times,* the *New York Times* News Service, *USA Today,* and the *Wall Street Journal.* Also available on NewsEDGE are the business sections of over 100 North American newspapers; periodicals such as *Forbes, Fortune, InfoWorld, MacWeek,* and *PC Week*; and newsletters such as those distributed by American Banker and Philips Business Information Services, Inc. **Positions advertised include:** Business Development Executive; Inside Sales Representative. **Corporate headquarters location:** This location. **Other U.S. locations:** Irvine CA; San Francisco CA; Washington DC; Miami FL; Chicago IL; Iselin NJ; New York NY; Addison TX; Burlington VT. **International locations:** Canada; England; France; Germany; Japan; The Netherlands; Switzerland. **Parent company:** The Thomson Corporation.

NORTHEAST PUBLISHING COMPANY
FALL RIVER HERALD NEWS
207 Pocasset Street, Fall River MA 02721. 508/676-8211. **Contact:** Dan Goodrich, Publisher. **World Wide Web address:** http://www.heraldnews.com. **Description:** Publishes a daily newspaper with a weekday circulation of more than 39,000.

ONE SOURCE INFORMATION SERVICES, INC.
300 Baker Avenue, Concord MA 01742. 978/318-4300. **Toll-free phone:** 800/333-8036. **Contact:** Human Resources. **E-mail address:** info@corptech.com. **World Wide Web address:** www.corptech.com. **Description:** Publishes company information in print and electronic formats. **Corporate headquarters location:** This location. **Listed on:** NASDAQ. **Stock exchange symbol:** ONES. **Number of employees at this location:** 60.

THE PATRIOT LEDGER
400 Crown Colony Drive, P.O. Box 699159, Quincy MA 02269-9159. 617/786-7246. **Fax:** 617/786-7259. **Contact:** Cynthia Papil, Human Resources Manager. **World Wide Web address:** http://www.southofboston.com. **Description:** Publishes a suburban daily newspaper, with a weekday circulation of more than 90,000. **NOTE:** Entry-level positions are offered. **Special programs:** Internships; Apprenticeships. **Corporate headquarters location:** This location. **Parent company:** Newspaper Media LLP. **Listed on:** Privately held. **Number of employees at this location:** 575.

PEARSON EDUCATION
160 Gould Street, Needham Heights MA 02494. 781/455-1200. **Contact:** Human Resources. **World Wide Web address:** http://www.pearsoned.com. **Description:** Publishes educational textbooks in the following divisions: elementary school reading and math, junior high school social studies, and college. **Positions advertised include:** Marketing Assistant. **Corporate headquarters location:** New York NY.

PHOENIX MEDIA/COMMUNICATIONS GROUP
126 Brookline Avenue, Boston MA 02215. 617/859-3339. **Fax:** 617/425-2615. **Contact:** Joe Goss, Human Resources. **E-mail address:** jobs@phx.com. **World Wide Web address:** http://www.bostonphoenix.com. **Description:** Publishes the *Boston Phoenix,* a weekly newspaper focusing on the art and entertainment industries in the greater Boston area. **Parent company:** Phoenix Media Group.

POHLY & PARTNERS
27 Melcher Street, 2nd Floor, Boston MA 02210. 617/451-1700. **Toll-free phone:** 877/687-6459. **Fax:** 617/338-7767. **Contact:** Human Resources. **World Wide Web address:** http://www.pohlypartners.com. **Description:** A full-service provider of end-to-end custom publishing services in the production of books, magazines, newsletters, and Websites. **Parent company:** Cadmus Communications Corporation is a graphic communications company offering specialized products and services in three broad areas: printing, marketing, and publishing. Cadmus is one of the largest graphic communications companies in North America. Product lines include annual reports, catalogs, direct marketing financial printing, point-of-sale marketing, promotional printing, publishing, research journals, specialty magazines, and specialty packaging. Subsidiaries of Cadmus Communications include Cadmus Color Center, Inc. (Sandston VA); Cadmus Consumer Publishing (Richmond VA); Cadmus Direct Marketing, Inc. (Charlotte NC); Cadmus Interactive (Tucker GA); Cadmus Journal Services (Linthicum MD; Easton MD; and Richmond VA); Cadmus Marketing Services

(Atlanta GA); Central Florida Press, L.C. (Orlando FL); Expert Brown (Sandston VA); Graftech Corporation (Charlotte NC); 3Score, Inc. (Tucker GA); Washburn Graphics, Inc. (Charlotte NC); and The William Byrd Press (Richmond VA).

PUBLISHERS CIRCULATION FULFILLMENT
P.O. Box 537, Waltham MA 02454. 781/466-1800. **Physical address:** 60 First Avenue, Waltham MA 02454. **Contact:** Human Resources. **Description:** Contracts home delivery of newspapers such as the *Wall Street Journal, Boston Globe,* and *New York Times.*

QUEBECOR WORLD
BOOK SERVICES DIVISION
1133 County Street, Taunton MA 02780. 508/823-4581. **Fax:** 508/828-4356. **Contact:** Human Resources. **World Wide Web address:** http://www.quebecorworld.com. **Description:** One of the largest commercial printers in the world. **Positions advertised include:** Production Worker. **NOTE:** Entry-level positions and second and third shifts are offered. **Special programs:** Co-ops. **Office hours:** Monday - Friday, 8:00 a.m. - 5:00 p.m. **Other U.S. locations:** Nationwide. **Listed on:** New York Stock Exchange. **Stock exchange symbol:** IQW. **Annual sales/revenues:** More than $100 million. **Number of employees at this location:** 450. **Number of employees nationwide:** 12,000. **Number of employees worldwide:** 16,000.

REED BUSINESS INFORMATION
275 Washington Street, Newton MA 02458-1630. 617/964-3030. **Contact:** Human Resources. **World Wide Web address:** http://www.reedbusiness.com. **Description:** A publisher whose offerings include over 50 magazines in both business and consumer markets. They also provide a variety of marketing and publishing services including direct mail, economic forecasting, and marketing research.

THE STANDARD-TIMES PUBLISHING COMPANY
25 Elm Street, New Bedford MA 02740. 508/997-7411. **Contact:** Human Resources. **World Wide Web address:** http://www.s-t.com. **Description:** Publishes a daily newspaper with a circulation of more than 48,000.

USA TODAY
100 Unicorn Park Drive, Woburn MA 01801. 781/932-0660. **Contact:** Kathi Bakas, Assistant to General Manager. **World Wide Web address:** http://www.usatoday.com. **Description:** Publishes *USA Today,* a nationally distributed newspaper. **Parent company:** Gannett Company, Inc. (Arlington VA). **Operations at this facility include:** Administration; Regional Headquarters; Sales; Service. **Number of employees at this location:** 45.

UNITED LITHOGRAPH
48 Third Avenue, Somerville MA 02143. 617/629-3200. **Contact:** Human Resources. **World Wide Web address:** http://www.unitedlithograph.com. **Description:** A commercial printer.

VERIZON INFORMATIONAL SERVICES
35 Village Road, Middleton MA 01949. 978/762-0350. **Contact:** Human Resources. **World Wide Web address:** http://www.bigyellow.com. **Description:** Verizon provides a wide variety of communications services ranging from local telephone services for the home and office to highly complex voice and data services for governments and commercial industries. **Operations at this facility include:** This location is engaged in Yellow Pages publishing.

WINTHROP PRINTING COMPANY
235 Old Colony Avenue, South Boston MA 02127. 617/268-9660. **Fax:** 617/268-6735. **Contact:** Human Resources. **World Wide Web address:** http://www.winprint.com. **Description:** A commercial printer. **Positions advertised include:** Sales Executive;.

WORCESTER TELEGRAM & GAZETTE
P.O. Box 15012, Worcester MA 01615-0012. 508/793-9260. **Physical address:** 20 Franklin Street, Worcester MA 01615. **Contact:** Victor A. DiNardo, Director of Human Resources. **World Wide Web address:** http://www.telegram.com. **Description:** Publishes the *Worcester Telegram & Gazette* with a daily circulation of over 107,000 and a Sunday circulation of over 133,000, and several weekly and semiweekly newspapers. The company also provides the *Telegram & Gazette* online, an Internet access service, and a wide range of online community information directories. **Parent company:** The New York Times Company.

WORLD TIMES INC.
225 Franklin Street 26th Floor, Boston MA 02110. 617/439-5400. **Fax:** 617/439-5415. **Contact:** Human Resources. **E-mail address:** info@worldtimes.com. **World Wide Web address:** http://www.worldtimes.com. **Description:** Publishes the monthly *WorldPaper,* an international newspaper. Founded in 1978. **Corporate headquarters location:** This location.

ZIFF-DAVIS PUBLISHING COMPANY
500 Unicorn Park Drive, Woburn MA 01801. 781/938-2600. **Fax:** 781/393-3038. **World Wide Web address:** http://www.zdnet.com. **Contact:** Human Resources. **Description:** A publisher of over 22 computer industry magazines in the United States and abroad. Titles published by Ziff-Davis include *PC Week* and *Computer Shopper.* **Positions advertised include:** Editor; Reporter.

REAL ESTATE

You can expect to find the following types of companies in this section:
Land Subdividers and Developers • Real Estate Agents, Managers, and Operators • Real Estate Investment Trusts

ACS DEVELOPMENT
80 Everett Avenue, Suite 319, Chelsea MA 02150. 617/889-6900. **Fax:** 617/889-6255. **Contact:** Patricia Simboli, Principal. **Description:** A real estate corporation with assets in the metropolitan Boston and Florida markets. Properties include retail, office, and industrial locations. **Corporate headquarters location:** This location. **Operations at this facility include:** Administration; Sales.

AYRE REAL ESTATE COMPANY, INC.
701 Main Street, Agawam MA 01001. 413/789-0812. **Fax:** 413/789-2427. **Contact:** Human Resources. **E-mail address:** ayrerealestate@ayrerealestate.com. **World Wide Web address:** http://www.ayrerealestate.com. **Description:** A commercial and residential real estate company serving the greater Springfield area.

CB RICHARD ELLIS INVESTORS
800 Boylston Street, Suite 1475, Boston MA 02199. 617/425-2800. **Fax:** 617/425-2801. **Contact:** Personnel. **World Wide Web address:** http://www.cbrichardellis.com. **Description:** Provides real estate services. **Positions advertised include:** Real Estate Analyst; Research Analyst; Network Engineer; Production Officer. **Corporate headquarters location:** Los Angeles CA. **Other U.S. locations:** Nationwide. **International locations:** Worldwide. **Listed on:** New York Stock Exchange. **Stock exchange symbol:** CBG.

CB RICHARD ELLIS/WHITTIER PARTNERS
Federal Reserve Building, 600 Atlantic Avenue, Boston MA 02210. 617/912-7000. **Fax:** 617/912-7001. **Contact:** Human Resources. **World Wide Web address:** http://www.cbrichardellis.com. **Description:** Provides real estate services. **Positions advertised include:** Real Estate Analyst; Research Analyst; Network Engineer; Production Officer, **Corporate headquarters location:** Los Angeles CA. **Other U.S. locations:** Nationwide. **International locations:** Worldwide. **Listed on:** New York Stock Exchange. **Stock exchange symbol:** CBG.

CENTURY 21 ANNEX REALTY
49 Beale Street, Quincy MA 02170. 617/472-4330. **Toll-free phone:** 800/345-4614. **Contact:** Human Resources. **World Wide Web address:** http://www.c21annex.com. **Description:** A real estate company. **Other area locations:** Hanover MA.

CENTURY 21 CAPE SAILS, INC.
133 Route 6A, Sandwich MA 02563. 508/888-2121. **Contact:** Human Resources. **World Wide Web address:** http://www.c21capesails.com. **Description:** A residential real estate company serving the Cape Cod area.

DEWOLFE NEW ENGLAND
326 Washington Street, Wellesley Hills MA 02481. 781/235-6885. **Contact:** Human Resources. **World Wide Web address:** http://www.dewolfenewengland.com. **Description:** An integrated residential real estate service company that provides sales and marketing services to residential real estate consumers. In addition, the company originates, processes, and closes residential mortgage loans; provides corporate and employee relocation services; and provides asset management services to a variety of clients. In residential real estate and marketing, the company acts as a broker or agent in transactions through independent sales associates. **Corporate headquarters location:** This location. **Other U.S. locations:** CT; NH. **Subsidiaries include:** DeWolfe Relocation Services, Inc. offers employers a variety of specialized services primarily concerned with facilitating the resettlement of transferred employees. **Listed on:** American Stock Exchange. **Stock exchange symbol:** DWL. **Number of employees nationwide:** 275.

EQUITY OFFICE PROPERTIES
100 Summer Street, 2nd Floor, Boston MA 02110. 617/425-7500. **Contact:** Human Resources. **World Wide Web address:** http://www.equityoffice.com. **Description:** Operates as a self-administered and self-managed real estate investment trust (REIT). The company specializes in property acquisitions, management, leasing, design, construction, and development. In addition to its own locations, the company manages properties for several third-party property owners. **Corporate headquarters location:** Chicago IL. **Other U.S. locations:** Atlanta GA. **Operations at this facility include:** Administration. **Listed on:** New York Stock Exchange. **Stock exchange symbol:** EOP.

FIRST WINTHROP CORPORATION
P.O. Box 9507, Boston MA 02114. 617/234-3000. **Contact:** Human Resources. **Description:** A real estate agency specializing in commercial properties. Founded in 1978. **Corporate headquarters location:** This location. **Listed on:** Privately held. **Number of employees at this location:** 30. **Number of employees nationwide:** 110.

FOREST CITY DEVELOPMENT
38 Sidney Street, Cambridge MA 02139. 617/225-0310. **Contact:** Human Resources. **World Wide Web address:** http://www.fceboston.com. **Description:** A real estate developer.

HEALTH AND RETIREMENT PROPERTIES TRUST
400 Centre Street, Newton MA 02458. 617/332-3990. **Fax:** 617/332-2261. **E-mail address:** ifno@hrpreit.com. **World Wide Web address:** http://www.hrpreit.com. **Contact:** Joyce Silver, Human Resources. **Description:** A real estate investment trust that invests primarily in retirement communities, assisted living centers, nursing homes, and other long-term care facilities. **Corporate headquarters location:** This location.

MEDITRUST CORPORATION
197 First Avenue, Needham Heights MA 02494. 781/433-6000. **Contact:** Human Resources. **Description:** A health care real estate investment trust. Meditrust invests primarily in health care facilities providing subacute and long-term care services. The company has investments in more than 400 health care facilities in 38 states. **Corporate headquarters location:** This location. **Other U.S. locations:** Palm Beach FL. **Parent company:** The Meditrust Companies (also at this location) also consists of Meditrust Operating Company. **Number of employees at this location:** 50.

NEW ENGLAND MANAGEMENT
375 Harvard Street, Brookline MA 02134. 617/566-5571. **Contact:** Human Resources. **Description:** Acquires, develops, operates, and sells residential and commercial real estate. **Corporate headquarters location:** This location.

NORTH RIVER REALTY
228 R. Columbia Road Suite #11, Hanover MA 02339. 781/829-9441. **Fax:** 781/829-9427. **Contact:** Paul Bourque, President. **E-mail address:** pbourque@northriverrealty.com. **World Wide Web address:** http://www.northriverrealty.com. **Description:** A full service real estate agency. **Positions advertised include.** Experienced Broker.

SPAULDING & SLYE COLLIERS
255 State Street, 4th Floor, Boston MA 02109. 617/523-8000. **Fax:** 617/531-4281. **Contact:** Catherine Spritca, Human Resources. **World Wide Web address:** http://www.spauldslye.com. **Description:** Corporate offices of a national, full-service real estate development firm. Services include development, construction, brokerage and property management, and advisory services. **Positions advertised include:** Project Manager; Property Manager; Associate; Administrative Assistant; Assistant Construction Manager; Graphic Designer; Tenant Coordinator; Superintendent; Construction Manager; Marketing Associate. **Other area locations:** Burlington MA. **Other U.S. locations:** Washington DC. **Operations at this facility include:** Administration; Sales. **Listed on:** Privately held. **Number of employees at this location:** 170. **Number of employees nationwide:** 235.

TORTO WHEATON RESEARCH
200 High Street, 3rd Floor, Boston MA 02110. 617/912-5200. **Fax:** 617/912-5240. **Contact:** Frank Moynihan, Human Resources Department. **E-mail address:** fmoyniham@tortowheatonresearch.com. **World Wide Web address:** http://www.twr.com. **Description:** Provides real estate services. **Corporate headquarters location:** Los Angeles CA. **Parent company:** CB Richard Ellis. **Stock exchange symbol:** CBG.

RETAIL

You can expect to find the following types of companies in this section:
Catalog Retailers • Department Stores, Specialty Stores • Retail Bakeries • Supermarkets

---

ROBERT ALLEN FABRICS
55 Cabot Boulevard, Mansfield MA 02048. 508/339-9151. **Fax:** 508/339-4057. **Contact:** Human Resources. **E-mail address:** careers@robertallendesign.com. **World Wide Web address:** http://www.robertallendesign.com. **Description:** Robert Allen Fabrics is a fabric retailer. **Office hours:** Monday - Friday, 8:30 a.m. - 5:00 p.m. **Corporate headquarters location:** This location. **Other U.S. locations:** Nationwide. **Operations at this facility include:** This location houses the corporate offices.

APPLESEED'S
30 Tozer Road, Beverly MA 01915. 978/922-2040. **Fax:** 978/922-7001. **Contact:** Human Resources. **E-mail address:** jobs@appleseeds.com. **World Wide Web address:** http://www.appleseeds.com. **Description:** A retailer of women's clothing through its stores and catalog.

BJ'S WHOLESALE CLUB
One Mercer Road, Natick MA 01760. 508/651-7400. **Contact:** Human Resources. **World Wide Web address:** http://www.bjs.com. **Description:** Membership club retailer of bulk merchandise from grocery items to electronics, automotive accessories and vacations. **Corporate headquarters location:** This location. **Listed on:** New York Stock Exchange. **Stock exchange symbol:** BJ.

BARNES & NOBLE BOOKSTORES
395 Washington Street, Boston MA 02108. 617/426-5184. **Contact:** Manager. **World Wide Web address:** http://www.bn.com. **Description:** A discount bookstore chain. **Corporate headquarters location:** New York NY. **Other U.S. locations:** Nationwide.

BARNES & NOBLE BOOKSTORES
150 Granite Street, Braintree MA 02184. 781/380-3655. **Fax:** 781/380-0665. **Contact:** Manager. **World Wide Web address:** http://www.bn.com. **Description:** A discount bookstore chain. **Corporate headquarters location:** New York NY. **Other U.S. locations:** Nationwide.

BIG Y FOODS INC.
2145 Roosevelt Avenue, Springfield MA 01102. 413/784-0600. **Fax:** 413/732-7350. **Contact:** Human Resources. **World Wide Web address:** http://www.bigy.com. **Description:** Operates a chain of over 40 supermarkets. **Positions advertised include:** Staff Accountant; Financial Representative Support; HVAC/R Technician; General Maintenance Mechanic; Food Service Equipment Technician; Computer Operator; Loss Prevention Representative. **NOTE:** Users may apply for positions online. **Special programs:** Internships. **Other area locations:** Statewide. **Other U.S. locations:** CT. **Corporate headquarters location:** This location. **Operations at this facility include:** Administration. **Listed on:** Privately held. **Number of employees nationwide:** 7,200.

BORDERS BOOKS & MUSIC
10-24 School Street, Boston MA 02108. 617/557-7188. **Fax:** 617/557-4476. **Contact:** Hiring Manager. **World Wide Web address:** http://www.borders.com. **Description:** One location of the discount bookstore chain offering over 200,000 book titles, as well as music and videos. Borders also provides year-round events including live musical performances, author readings, kids programs, book groups, and art exhibitions.

BORDERS BOOKS & MUSIC
255 Grossman Drive, Braintree MA 02184. 781/356-5111. **Contact:** Hiring Manager. **World Wide Web address:** http://www.borders.com. **Description:** One location of the discount bookstore chain offering over 200,000 book titles, as well as music and videos. Borders also provides year-round events including live musical performances, author readings, kids programs, book groups, and art exhibitions.

THE BRICK COMPUTER COMPANY
80 Turnpike Road, Ipswich MA 01938. 978/356-1228. **Contact:** Human Resources. **World Wide Web address:** http://www.brickcomputers.com. **Description:** Sells laptops through a mail-order catalog.

BRYLANE, INC.
35 United Drive, West Bridgewater MA 02379. 508/583-8110. **Fax:** 508/588-7994. **Contact:** Human Resources. **E-mail address:** chadwicksjobs@brylane.com. **World Wide Web address:** http://www.brylane.com. **Description:** A specialty catalog retailer. **Positions advertised include:** Control Buyer; Rebuyer; Collateral Projects Coordinator; Maintenance Mechanic Coordinator. **Corporate headquarters location:** New York NY.

CAMBRIDGE SOUNDWORKS, INC.
311 Needham Street, Newton MA 02464. 617/332-5936. **Fax:** 617/244-3743. **Contact:** Human Resources. **World Wide Web address:** http://www.hifi.com. **Description:** A factory-direct retailer that designs and manufactures stereo and home theater speakers under the Cambridge SoundWorks brand name. **Listed on:** NASDAQ. **Stock exchange symbol:** HIFI.

CASUAL MALE CORPORATION
555 Turnpike Street, Canton MA 02021. 781/828-9300. **Contact:** Human Resources. **World Wide Web address:** http://www.casualmale.com. **Description:** Engaged in the retail sale of footwear and apparel. Casual Male Corporation sells footwear through self-service licensed shoe departments in mass merchandising department stores, through full- and semiservice licensed shoe departments in department and specialty stores, on a wholesale basis, and through its Fayva and Parade of Shoes chains of shoe stores. The company is also involved in the retail sale of apparel through its chain of Casual Male Big & Tall men's stores and also through its chain of Work 'n Gear work clothing stores. **Special programs:** Internships. **Corporate headquarters location:** This location. **Operations at this facility include:** Administration; Service.

CHARRETTE CORPORATION
P.O. Box 4010, Woburn MA 01888-4010. 781/935-6000. **Physical address:** 31 Olympia Avenue, Woburn MA 01801. **Fax:** 781/933-6104. **Contact:** Lawrence Mansfield, Director of Human Resources. **E-mail address:** csullivan@charrette.com. **World Wide Web address:** http://www.charrette.com. **Description:** Offers a variety of products and services to design professionals.

Products include a wide range of art, design, and office products from mat boards and paints, to furniture and software. Services include digital imaging, offset printing, reprographics, and blueprinting. **NOTE:** Entry-level positions are offered. **Special programs:** Internships. **Corporate headquarters location:** This location. **Other U.S. locations:** Nationwide. **Operations at this facility include:** Administration; Sales; Service. **Listed on:** Privately held. **Annual sales/revenues:** $51 - $100 million. **Number of employees at this location:** 350. **Number of employees nationwide:** 750.

COLUMBIA MOTORS
1817 Washington Street, Hanover MA 02339. 781/826-8300. **Contact:** Human Resources. **E-mail address:** sales@columbiamotors.com. **World Wide Web address:** http://www.columbiamotors.com. **Description:** A Pontiac, GMC, Buick, car dealership.

CSN STORES
Two Copley Place, Floor 4, Boston MA 02116. 617/532-6100. **Fax:** 617/236-4761. **Contact:** Recruiting. **E-mail address:** jobs@csnstores.com. **World Wide Web address:** http://www.csnstores.com. **Description:** An online retailer. **Positions advertised include:** Customer Care Representative. **NOTE:** Mail resume to: CSN Stores, Attention Recruiting, Two Copley Place Floor 4, Boston MA, 02116.

CUMBERLAND FARMS, INC.
777 Dedham Street, Canton MA 02021. 781/828-4900. **Fax:** 781/828-9012. **Contact:** Human Resources. **World Wide Web address:** http://www.cumberlandfarms.com. **Description:** Cumberland Farms operates a chain of retail convenience stores and gas stations. **Positions advertised include:** Multi Unit Area Manager; Equipment Operator. **Corporate headquarters location:** This location. **Operations at this facility include:** Manufacturing; Sales. **Listed on:** Privately held. **Number of employees at this location:** 700. **Number of employees nationwide:** 8,000.

DEMOULAS SUPERMARKETS INC.
875 East Street, Tewksbury MA 01876. 978/851-8000. **Contact:** President of Operations. **Description:** Operates a grocery store chain with locations throughout northern and eastern Massachusetts. **Corporate headquarters location:** This location.

DUNKIN' DONUTS OF AMERICA INC.
P.O. Box 317, Randolph MA 02368. 781/961-4000. **Physical address:** 14 Pacella Park Drive, Randolph MA 02368. **Contact:** Human Resources. **World Wide Web address:** http://www.dunkindonuts.com. **Description:** Develops and franchises Dunkin' Donuts shops that sell coffee, donuts, and baked goods. **Corporate headquarters location:** This location. **Subsidiaries include:** Togo; Baskin Robbins. **Parent company:** Allied Domecq Retailing USA.

FILENE'S
426 Washington Street, Boston MA 02108. 617/357-2100. **Contact:** Human Resources. **World Wide Web address:** http://www.filenes.com. **Description:** A fashion department store with locations in the New England and New York areas. **NOTE:** Visit http://www.mayco.com for employment information. **Special programs:** Internships. **Corporate headquarters location:** St. Louis MO. **Parent company:** May Department Stores Company. **Other locations:** Hanover MA; Braintree MA; Kingston MA; Taunton MA; Framingham MA; Manchester NH; Middletown NY. Additional locations in CT, ME, & VT. **Operations at this**

facility include: Administration; Divisional Headquarters. **Listed on:** New York Stock Exchange. **Stock exchange symbol:** MAY.

FILENE'S BASEMENT CORPORATION
12 Gill Street, Woburn MA 01801. 617/348-7075. **Fax:** 617/348-7159. **Contact:** David Abelson, Personnel. **World Wide Web address:** http://www.filenesbasement.com. **Description:** Operates specialty stores offering assortments of fashionable, nationally recognized brands and private-label family apparel and accessories. **Corporate headquarters location:** This location. **Other U.S. locations:** CT; DC; IL; ME; MN; NH; NJ; NY; PA; RI; VA.

GEERLINGS & WADE
960 Turnpike Street, Canton MA 02021. 781/821-4152. **Toll-free phone:** 800/782-WINE. **Contact:** Human Resources Department. **World Wide Web address:** http://www.geerwade.com. **Description:** Provides personal wine-buying services to consumers through direct marketing. The company purchases imported and domestic wines and delivers them directly to the customer's home or office. **Corporate headquarters location:** This location.

GROSSMAN'S INC.
90 Hawes Way, Stoughton MA 02072. 781/297-3300. **Contact:** Human Resources. **Description:** Sells lumber, building materials, doors and windows, hardware, paint, plumbing, and electrical supplies. Grossman's Inc. operates five retail warehouse stores and has over 70 locations in nine states. **Subsidiaries include:** Builder's Mart and Contractors' Warehouse have large, drive-thru lumber yards and focus on the needs of contractors, remodelers, tradespeople, and other building professionals; Mr. 2nd's Bargain Outlet offers close-outs, seconds, and overstocks in a wide range of building materials; The Project-Pros provides materials and design and building services for a variety of home improvement projects including fencing, decks, windows and doors, siding and roofing, electric and alarms, painting, kitchens and baths, plumbing, landscaping, masonry, and additions.

J.L. HAMMETT COMPANY
P.O. Box 859057, Braintree MA 02185. 781/848-1000. **Toll-free phone:** 800/955-2200. **Physical address:** One Hammett Place, Braintree MA 02184. **Fax:** 781/848-3869. **Contact:** Human Resources. **World Wide Web address:** http://www.hammett.com. **Description:** Distributes educational supplies and equipment through catalog and retail stores. **Corporate headquarters location:** This location. **Operations at this facility include:** Administration; Regional Headquarters; Sales; Service.

THE HARVARD COOPERATIVE SOCIETY
1400 Massachusetts Avenue, Cambridge MA 02138. 617/499-2000. **Contact:** Human Resources. **World Wide Web address:** http://www.thecoop.com. **Description:** A member-owned, collegiate department store selling a broad range of merchandise from clothing, books, and music, to housewares, electronics, and prints. **Corporate headquarters location:** This location.

JANNELL MOTORS
2000 Washington Street, Hanover MA 02339. 781/982-4500. **Fax:** 781/982-4535. **Contact:** Human Resources. **E-mail address:** sales@jannell.com. **World Wide Web address:** http://www.jannell.com. **Description:** A Ford dealership on the South Shore.

JOAN FABRICS CORPORATION
100 Vesper Executive Park, Tyngsboro MA 01879-2710. 978/649-5626.
Contact: Human Resources. **World Wide Web address:**
http://www.joanfabrics.com. **Description:** Engaged in the manufacturing of
woven and knitted fabrics for furniture and automotive manufacturers. The
company also operates retail fabric stores nationwide. **Corporate headquarters
location:** This location. **Other U.S. locations:** Hickory NC; Troy MI.

KOHL'S
125 Church Street, Pembroke MA 02359. 781/826-3696. **Fax:** 781/982-4535.
Contact: Human Resources. **World Wide Web address:** http://www.kohls.com.
Description: A clothing department store. **Positions advertised include:** Cash
Office Associate; Customer Service Associate; Department Supervisor;
Housekeeper; Loss Prevention Associate; Register Operator; Sales Associate.

MACY'S
450 Washington Street, Boston MA 02111. 617/357-3000. **Recorded jobline:**
800/603-6229. **Contact:** Human Resources. **World Wide Web address:**
http://www.macys.com. **Description:** One location of the department store chain.
Positions advertised include: Beauty Advisor; Bridal Consultant; Cosmetic
Business Manager; Counter Manager; Fine Jewelry Service Associate; Furniture
Service Associate Selling Specialist; Women's Shoe Service Specialist;
Department Sales Manager; Group Sales Manager; Human Resources
Coordinator; Merchandise Manager. **Corporate headquarters location:** New
York City.

PRINCESS HOUSE, INC.
470 Myles Standish Boulevard, Taunton MA 02780. 508/823-0711. **Contact:**
Human Resources. **World Wide Web address:** http://www.princesshouse.com.
Description: A national direct sales company specializing in crystal and china.
Corporate headquarters location: This location. **Parent company:** Colgate-
Palmolive Company. **Operations at this facility include:** Administration;
Service.

RITZ CAMERA
South Shore Plaza, 250 Granite Street, Braintree MA 02184. 781/843-4619.
Contact: Hiring Manager. **World Wide Web address:**
http://www.ritzcamera.com. **Description:** One location of the camera shop and
photo developer chain.

SAKS FIFTH AVENUE
Prudential Center, Boston MA 02199. 617/262-8500. **Contact:** Human
Resources. **World Wide Web address:** http://www.saksincorporated.com.
Description: Saks Fifth Avenue is a 62-store chain emphasizing soft-goods
products, primarily apparel for men, women, and children. **Corporate
headquarters location:** New York NY. **Parent company:** Saks Incorporated is a
department store holding company that operates approximately 360 stores in 36
states. The company's stores include Saks Fifth Avenue, Parisian, Proffit's,
Younker's, Herberger's, Carson Pirie Scott, Boston Store, Bergner's, and Off 5th,
the company's outlet store. Saks Incorporated also operates two retail catalogs
and several retail Internet sites. **Listed on:** New York Stock Exchange. **Stock
exchange symbol:** SKS.

SEARS, ROEBUCK & CO.
Route 6 and 118, Swansea Mall Drive, Swansea MA 02777. 508/324-6500.
Contact: Human Resources. **World Wide Web address:** http://www.sears.com.

Description: One location of the department chain store. **Listed on:** NYSE. **Stock exchange symbol:** S.

SHAW'S SUPERMARKETS

P.O. Box 600, East Bridgewater MA 02333-0600. 508/378-7211. **Physical address:** 750 West Center Street, East Bridgewater MA. **Contact:** Human Resources. **World Wide Web address:** http://www.shaws.com. **Description:** Administrative offices of the New England supermarket chain. Shaw's Supermarkets has locations throughout New England. **Corporate headquarters location:** This location. **Other U.S. locations:** CT; ME; MA; NH; RI; VT. **Subsidiaries include:** Star Markets; Wild Harvest. **Parent company:** J Sainsbury plc.

STAPLES, INC.

500 Staples Drive, Framingham MA 01702. 508/253-5000. **Contact:** Human Resources. **World Wide Web address:** http://www.staples.com. **Description:** Staples is a leading retailer of discount office products. The company operates over 350 high-volume office superstores in 18 states and the District of Columbia. **Positions advertised include:** Recruiting Specialist; Loss Prevention Manager; Senior Business Analyst; Business Development Associate; Customer Relations Manager. **Corporate headquarters location:** This location. **Other U.S. locations:** Nationwide. **Operations at this facility include:** Administration. **Listed on:** NASDAQ. **Stock exchange symbol:** SPLS. **Number of employees at this location:** 850. **Number of employees nationwide:** 15,700.

THE STOP & SHOP COMPANIES, INC.

1385 Hancock Street, Quincy MA 02169. 781/380-8000. **Contact:** Human Resources. **World Wide Web address:** http://www.stopandshop.com. **Description:** A national supermarket retail chain. **Corporate headquarters location:** This location.

STRIDE-RITE CORPORATION

191 Spring Street, P.O. Box 9191, Lexington MA 02421. 617/824-6000. **Contact:** Mary Kuconis, Human Resources Director. **World Wide Web address:** http://www.striderite.com. **Description:** Manufactures and distributes children's footwear. The company also operates retail stores. **Corporate headquarters location:** This location. **Listed on:** New York Stock Exchange. **Stock exchange symbol:** SRR.

THE TJX COMPANIES, INC.

770 Cochituate Road, Framingham MA 01701. 508/390-1000. **Fax:** 508/390-2650. **Recorded jobline:** 888/JOB-S597. **Contact:** Staffing Specialist. **E-mail address:** jobs@tjx.com. **World Wide Web address:** http://www.tjx.com. **Description:** The TJX Companies, Inc. is one of the world's largest off-price retailers. It consists of T.J. Maxx, Marshall's, Home Goods, A.J. Wright, Winners Apparel Ltd. in Canada, and T.K. Maxx in Europe. **NOTE:** Entry-level positions, part-time jobs, and second and third shifts are offered. **Positions advertised include:** Administrative Assistant; Domestics Buyer. **Special programs:** Internships; Training; Co-ops; Summer Jobs. **Corporate headquarters location:** This location. **Other U.S. locations:** Nationwide. **International locations:** Canada; Europe. **Listed on:** New York Stock Exchange. **Stock exchange symbol:** TJX. **Annual sales/revenues:** More than $100 million. **Number of employees at this location:** 2,000. **Number of employees nationwide:** 60,000.

TALBOTS INC.

One Talbots Drive, Hingham MA 02043. 781/749-7600. **Contact:** Human Resources. **World Wide Web address:** http://www.talbots.com. **Description:** Talbots is a leading specialty retailer and cataloger of women's classic apparel, shoes, and accessories. Talbots operates more than 330 stores in North America and has 23 different catalogs with a total annual circulation of approximately 60 million. The company also operates a chain of Talbots for Kids stores. Founded in 1947. **Other U.S. locations:** Nationwide. **Listed on:** New York Stock Exchange. **Stock exchange symbol:** TLB.

VICTORY SUPERMARKETS

75 North Main Street, Leominster MA 01453. 978/840-2200. **Contact:** Human Resources. **World Wide Web address:** http://www.victorysupermarkets.com. **Description:** A grocery store chain with 20 outlets located in Massachusetts and New Hampshire. **Parent company:** Hannaford Supermarkets. **Other area locations:** Clinton MA; Fitchburg MA; Gardner MA; Marlborough MA; Uxbridge MA.

WEARGUARD CORPORATION

141 Longwater Drive, Norwell MA 02061. 781/871-4100. **Contact:** Kathy Gillis, Director of Training. **E-mail address:** employment@wearguard.com. **World Wide Web address:** http://www.wearguard.com. **Description:** WearGuard is a leading direct marketer of work clothing serving over 2 million businesses and individuals and, in association with Sears Shop at Home, markets Workwear and Big and Tall Men's Clothing catalogs under the Sears name. **Parent company:** ARAMARK (Philadelphia PA) is one of the world's leading providers of quality managed services. The company operates in all 50 states and 10 foreign countries, offering a broad range of services to businesses of all sizes including most *Fortune* 500 companies and thousands of universities, hospitals, and municipal, state, and federal government facilities. ARAMARK's major businesses include Food, Leisure & Support Services, including Campus Dining Services, School Nutrition Services, Leisure Services, Business Dining Services, International Services, Healthcare Support Services, Conference Center Management, and Refreshment Services; Facility Services, Correctional Services, and Industrial Services; Uniform Services, which includes Uniform Services and WearGuard; Health & Education Services, which includes Spectrum Healthcare Services and Children's World Learning Centers; and Book & Magazine Services, of which ARAMARK is one of the largest distributors in the country. **Positions advertised include:** Corporate Financial Officer; Business Sales Group Director; QSR Director; Program Manager; Staff Accountant; Human Resources Generalist; Account Coordinator Supervisor; Regional Sales Representative; Sales Representative; Market Center Developer; Business Sales Group Representative; Print Production Artist; Account Coordinator; Administrative Assistant; Sales Associate; Machine Operator; Trainer; Computerized Machine Operator; Incentive Packer; Quality Auditor. **NOTE:** Download latest job postings in Adobe Acrobat PDF format online. **Operations at this facility include:** This location is a retail store and catalog marketer.

WHITE HEN PANTRY, INC.

41 Montvale Avenue, Stoneham MA 02180. 781/438-1140. **Fax:** 781/438-9354. **Contact:** General Manager. **World Wide Web address:** http://www.whitehenpantry.com. **Description:** White Hen Pantry operates a chain of convenience food stores. **Corporate headquarters location:** Elmhurst IL. **Parent company:** Clark Retail Enterprises, Inc. **Operations at this facility include:** This location houses administrative offices.

WOODWORKERS WAREHOUSE
126 Oxford Street, Lynn MA 01901. 781/598-6393. **Contact:** Human Resources. **World Wide Web address:** http://www.woodworkerswarehouse.com. **Description:** A distributor of woodworkers tools and accessories. Products are sold through Woodworkers Warehouse retail stores, with 100 Northeast locations. Founded in 1981. **Corporate headquarters location:** This location.

STONE, CLAY, GLASS, AND CONCRETE PRODUCTS

**You can expect to find the following types of companies
in this section:**
Cement, Tile, Sand, and Gravel • Crushed and Broken Stone • Glass and Glass
Products • Mineral Products

AGGREGATE INDUSTRIES
1715 Broadway, Saugus MA 01906. 781/941-7200. **Fax:** 781/941-7228.
Contact: Human Resources. **World Wide Web address:**
http://www.aggregate.com. **Description:** A leading producer of crushed stone,
bituminous and ready-mixed concrete, and liquid asphalt. Aggregate Industries
also engages in a variety of general construction, asphalt and concrete recycling,
and soil remediation activities. **Corporate headquarters location:** Bethesda
MD. **Other area locations:** Stoughton MA.

AGGREGATE INDUSTRIES
1101 Turnpike Street, Stoughton MA 02072. 781/344-1100. **Contact:** Human
Resources. **World Wide Web address:** http://www.aggregate.com. **Description:**
A leading producer of crushed stone, bituminous and ready-mixed concrete, and
liquid asphalt. Aggregate Industries also engages in a variety of general
construction, asphalt and concrete recycling, and soil remediation activities.
Corporate headquarters location: Bethesda MD. **Other area locations:**
Saugus, MA.

AMERICAN FLAT GLASS DISTRIBUTORS, INC. (AFGD)
575 Currant Road, Fall River MA 02720. 508/675-9220. **Toll-free phone:**
800/666-2343. **Contact:** Branch Manager. **World Wide Web address:**
http://www.afgd.com. **Description:** Specializes in the manufacture of
architectural insulated units and custom tempering services. The firm
manufactures a complete line of insulated units for commercial and residential
applications including clear, tint, and reflective float glass; laminated, low-
emissivity, tempered, acrylic, mirror, obscure, insulated and polished wire glass;
and a complete line of glass handling, storage, and transportation equipment.
Positions advertised include: Inside Sales Representative. **Corporate
headquarters location:** Atlanta GA. **Other U.S. locations:** Nationwide.
Subsidiaries include: AFGD Canada. **Parent company:** AFG Industries, Inc.
Listed on: Privately held. **Number of employees at this location:** 150.
Number of employees nationwide: 1,000.

BOSTON SAND & GRAVEL COMPANY
169 Portland Street, P.O. Box 9187, Boston MA 02114. 617/227-9000. **Contact:**
Human Resources. **Description:** Produces ready-mixed concrete. **Corporate
headquarters location:** This location. **Operations at this facility include:**
Administration; Sales. **Listed on:** Privately held. **Number of employees at this
location:** 30. **Number of employees nationwide:** 250.

NORTHEAST CONCRETE PRODUCTS
P.O. Box 2189, Plainville MA 02762. 508/695-1737. **Fax:** 508/695-7596.
Physical address: 24 Cross Street, Plainville MA 02762. **Contact:** Human
Resources. **World Wide Web address;** http://www.necp.net. **Description:**
Manufactures concrete products for use in the building of parking lots and
bridges.

SAINT-GOBAIN CONTAINERS
One National Street, Milford MA 01757. 508/478-2500. **Contact:** Human Resources. **Description:** Manufactures glass bottles.

TRANSPORTATION AND TRAVEL

**You can expect to find the following types of companies
in this section:**
Air, Railroad, and Water Transportation Services • Courier Services • Local and
Interurban Passenger Transit • Ship Building and Repair • Transportation
Equipment • Travel Agencies • Trucking • Warehousing and Storage

AAA AUTO CLUB
900 Hingham Street, Rockland MA 02370. 781/871-5880. **Contact:** Human
Resources. **E-mail address:** humanresources@aaasne.com. **World Wide Web
address:** http://www.aaasne.com. **Description:** Provides insurance, travel, and
related services to motorists through a network of over 50 branch offices.
Positions advertised include: Dispatcher Road Services Call Center; Call
Counselor; Auto Travel Call Counselor; Insurance Customer Service
Representative; Travel Agent; Membership Processor; Security Guard; Auto
Travel Route Marker; Human Resource Assistant; Non Radio Dispatcher;
Executive Assistant.

ALL WORLD TRAVEL
COOPERS LIMOUSINE SERVICE
54 Canal Street, Suite 1, Boston MA 02114. 617/720-2000. **Contact:** Human
Resources. **Description:** All World Travel is a travel agency. Coopers Limousine
Service (also at this location) provides limousine transportation services.

AMERICAN EXPRESS TRAVEL RELATED SERVICES
One State Street, Ground Level, Boston MA 02109. 617/723-8400. **Contact:**
Human Resources. **World Wide Web address:**
http://www.americanexpress.com. **Description:** A full-service travel agency.
Founded in 1850. **Corporate headquarters location:** Cambridge MA. **Parent
company:** American Express is a diversified travel and financial services
company operating in 160 countries. The company offers consumers the
Personal, Gold, and Platinum credit cards, as well as revolving credit products
such as Optima Cards, which allow customers to extend payments. Other
products include the American Express Corporate Card, which helps businesses
manage their travel and entertainment expenditures; and the Corporate
Purchasing Card, which helps businesses manage their expenditures on
supplies, equipment, and services. American Express Financial Advisors
provides a variety of financial products and services to help individuals,
businesses, and institutions establish and achieve their financial goals. American
Express Financial Advisors employs more than 8,000 financial advisors in the
United States and offers products and services that include financial planning;
annuities; mutual funds; insurance; investment certificates; and institutional
investment advisory trust, tax preparation, and retail securities brokerage
services. American Express Bank seeks to meet the financial services needs of
wealthy entrepreneurs and local financial service institutions through a global
network of offices in 37 countries. **Positions advertised include:** Administrative
Assistant; Team Leader Consumer Travel. **NOTE:** Submit resumes and apply
online. **Listed on:** Privately held. **Number of employees nationwide:** 3,700.

AMERICAN OVERSEAS MARINE CORPORATION
116 East Howard Street, Quincy MA 02169. 617/786-8300. **Contact:** Human
Resources. **E-mail address:** hr@gdamsea.com. **World Wide Web address:**

http://www.gdamsea.com. **Description:** Provides supplies and support to ships for the U.S. Navy and maritime academies. **Positions advertised include:** Port Engineer; Program Manager. **Corporate headquarters location:** Falls Church VA. **Other U.S. locations:** CT; IL; MI; NJ; RI; SC. **Parent company:** General Dynamics is a major producer of nuclear submarines and land systems. The company has two main divisions: the Electric Boat Division designs and builds nuclear submarines including the Seawolf class attack submarine and the New Attack submarine; The Land Systems Division designs and builds armored vehicles such as the M1 Series of battle tanks for the U.S. Army, the U.S. Marine Corps, and a number of international customers. General Dynamics also has coal mining operations, provides ship management services for the U.S. government on prepositioning and ready reserve ships, and leases liquefied natural gas tankers. **Listed on:** New York Stock Exchange. **Stock exchange symbol:** GD.

CSL INTERNATIONAL
55 Tozer Road, Beverly MA 01915. 978/922-1300. **Fax:** 978/922-1772. **Contact:** Human Resources. **World Wide Web address:** http://www.csl.ca. **Description:** A bulk freight shipping company that specializes in self-unloading bulk carriers. **Parent company:** Canada Steamship Lines (Montreal, Quebec, Canada). **International locations:** Manitoba; Nova Scotia; Ontario; Singapore.

CAPE AIR/NANTUCKET AIRLINES
660 Barnstable Road, Hyannis MA 02601. 508/771-6944. **Toll-free phone:** 800/352-0714. **Contact:** Personnel. **World Wide Web address:** http://www.flycapeair.com. **Description:** An air transportation company with direct service to Cape Cod and the islands.

CAREY LIMOUSINE OF BOSTON
161 Broadway, Somerville MA 02145. 617/623-8700. **Contact:** Kevin Muldenatto, General Manager. **Description:** A limousine service and executive travel specialist. Carey Limousine offers services for business meetings, airport transfers, dinner/theater events, weddings, and sightseeing activities. **Positions advertised include:** Accountant/Auditor. **Corporate headquarters location:** This location. **Parent company:** Carey International. **Operations at this facility include:** Administration; Sales; Service. **Listed on:** Privately held. **Number of employees at this location:** 50.

GARBER TRAVEL
660 Beacon Street, Boston MA 02215. 617/353-2100. **Contact:** Paul Woods, Human Resources. **E-mail address:** pwoods@garbertravel.com. **World Wide Web address:** http://www.garber.com. **Description:** A travel agency. **Other U.S. locations:** Nationwide.

KELLAWAY TRANSPORTATION
One Kellaway Drive, P.O. Box 750, Randolph MA 02368. 781/961-8200. **Contact:** Human Resources. **E-mail address:** kellaway@kellaway.com. **World Wide Web address:** http://www.kellaway.com. **Description:** An intermodal distribution company. **Corporate headquarters location:** This location. **Parent company:** RoadLink USA.

LILY TRANSPORTATION CORPORATION
145 Rosemary Street, Needham MA 02494. 781/449-8811. **Toll-free phone:** 800/248-LILY. **Contact:** Human Resources. **E-mail address:** hr@lilytransportation.com. **World Wide Web address:** http://www.lily.com. **Description:** A truck rental and leasing company. **Positions advertised**

include: CDL Class A Truck Driver; CDL Class B Truck Driver; Truck Mechanic. **Corporate headquarters location:** This location. **Other U.S. locations:** CT; ME; NH; NJ; NY; RI; VT.

MASSACHUSETTS BAY TRANSPORTATION AUTHORITY (MBTA)
10 Park Plaza, Boston MA 02116. 617/222-5000. **Contact:** Human Resources. **World Wide Web address:** http://www.mbta.com. **Description:** Operates the subways, trolleys, buses, and commuter train lines.

MASSACHUSETTS PORT AUTHORITY (MASSPORT)
One Harborside Drive, Suite 200S, East Boston MA 02128-2909. 617/428-2800. **Contact:** Human Resources. **World Wide Web address:** http://www.massport.com. **Description:** Owns and operates Logan International Airport and the public terminals of the Port of Boston. The Massachusetts Port Authority operates an engineering department and environmental unit at this facility.

PROVIDENCE AND WORCESTER RAILROAD COMPANY
75 Hammond Street, Worcester MA 01610. 508/755-4000. **Contact:** Human Resources. **World Wide Web address:** http://www.pwrr.com. **Description:** Providence and Worcester Railroad Company is an interstate freight carrier conducting railroad operations in Massachusetts, Rhode Island, and Connecticut. The railroad operates on approximately 470 miles of track. Freight traffic is interchanged with Consolidated Rail Corporation (ConRail) at Worcester MA and New Haven CT; with Springfield Terminal Railway Company at Gardner MA; and with New England Central Railroad at New London CT. Through its connections, Providence and Worcester Railroad links approximately 78 communities through its lines. Founded in 1847. **Corporate headquarters location:** This location. **Other U.S. locations:** Plainfield CT; Cumberland RI. **Operations at this facility include:** This location is the main freight classification yard and the locomotive and car maintenance facility. **Listed on:** American Stock Exchange. **Stock exchange symbol:** PWX. **Number of employees nationwide:** 140.

ROLLS ROYCE NAVAL MARINE
110 Norfolk Street, Walpole MA 02081. 508/668-9610. **Fax:** 508/668-5638. **Contact:** Human Resources. **Description:** Manufactures marine propulsion systems.

TIGHE WAREHOUSING & DISTRIBUTION, INC.
45 Holton Street, Winchester MA 01890. 781/729-5440. **Fax:** 781/721-5862. **Contact:** Human Resources. **E-mail address:** personnel@tighe-co.com. **World Wide Web address:** http://www.tighe-co.com. **Description:** Provides warehousing, transportation, and related distribution services. **Positions advertised include:** Class A CDL Driver; Warehouse Forklift Operations.

UTILITIES: ELECTRIC, GAS, AND WATER

You can expect to find the following types of companies
in this section:
Gas, Electric, and Fuel Companies • Other Energy-Producing Companies •
Public Utility Holding Companies • Water Utilities

BAY STATE GAS COMPANY

300 Friberg Parkway, Westborough MA 01581-5039. 508/836-7000. **Contact:** Human Resources. **World Wide Web address:** http://www.baystategas.com. **Description:** A gas distribution utility. The company furnishes gas to 300,000 customers in more than 60 eastern Massachusetts communities. Through its subsidiary, Northern Utilities, Inc. it also serves 41 communities in New Hampshire and Maine. **Corporate headquarters location:** Merrillville IN. **Subsidiaries include:** Northern Utilities, Inc. **Parent company:** NiSource Inc.

THE BERKSHIRE GAS COMPANY

115 Cheshire Road, Pittsfield MA 01201. 413/445-0252. **Contact:** Human Resources. **World Wide Web address:** http://www.berkshiregas.com. **Description:** A public gas utility operating in western Massachusetts, eastern New York, and southern Vermont. The Berkshire Gas Company distributes natural gas to approximately 30,000 people in its service area. The Berkshire Propane Division sells and leases related gas-burning appliances, and markets liquefied petroleum. **NOTE:** Entry-level positions are offered. **Company slogan:** Energy you can count on. People you can trust. **Special programs:** Internships; Summer Jobs. **Corporate headquarters location:** This location. **Listed on:** NASDAQ. **Stock exchange symbol:** BGAS. **President/CEO:** Scott Robinson. **Information Systems Manager:** Joseph Bosworth. **Annual sales/revenues:** $21 - $50 million. **Number of employees at this location:** 130.

BLUESTONE ENERGY

871 Washington Street, Braintree MA 02184. 781/356-8865. **Fax:** 781/356-8864. **Contact:** Human Resources. **E-mail address:** blu@bluestoneenergy.com. **World Wide Web address:** http://www.bluestoneenergy.com. **Description:** Specializes in identifying and implementing products that improve energy efficiency.

KEYSPAN ENERGY DELIVERY

201 Rivermoor Street, West Roxbury MA 02132. 617/742-8400. **Fax:** 617/327-2865. **Contact:** Personnel. **World Wide Web address:** http://www.keyspanenergy.com. **Description:** The largest distributor of natural gas in the Northeast, serving residential, commercial, and industrial customers throughout eastern and central Massachusetts, New Hampshire, New York City, and Long Island. **Listed on:** New York Stock Exchange. **Stock exchange symbol:** KSE.

MASSACHUSETTS ELECTRIC COMPANY

55 Bearfoot Road, Northborough MA 01532. 508/421-7000. **Toll-free phone:** 800/322-3223. **Contact:** Personnel. **World Wide Web address:** http://www.masselectric.com. **Description:** An electric utility company. **Listed on:** New York Stock Exchange. **Stock exchange symbol:** NGG. **Parent company:** National Grid.

NSTAR

One NSTAR Way, SUMSE 150, Westwood MA 02090. 781/441-8000. **Toll-free phone:** 800/592-2000. **Fax:** 781/441-8886. **Recorded jobline:** 781/441-8091. **Contact:** Human Resources. **E-mail address:** resumes@nstaronline.com. **World Wide Web address:** http://www.nstaronline.com. **Description:** A public utility engaged in the generation, purchase, transmission, distribution, and sale of electric energy. The company supplies electricity to the city of Boston and 39 surrounding communities. The company also wholesales electricity to other utilities and municipal electric departments for resale. **Corporate headquarters location:** Boston MA. **Subsidiaries include:** NSTAR Communications, Inc.; Advanced Energy Systems, Inc.; NSTAR Steam Corporation; Hopkinton LNG Corp. **Listed on:** New York Stock Exchange. **Stock exchange symbol:** NST.

NATIONAL GRID

25 Research Drive, Westborough MA 01582. 508/389-2000. **Contact:** Human Resources. **World Wide Web address:** http://www.ngtgroup.com. **Description:** A public utility holding company. Founded in 1947. **Positions advertised include:** Analyst; Engineer; Information Technologist Engineer. **Corporate headquarters location:** This location. **Other U.S. locations:** NH; NY; RI. **Subsidiaries include:** Massachusetts Electric Company, Narragansett Electric Company, Nantucket Electric Company, Niagara Mohawk, and Granite State Electric Company are retail electric companies that provide electricity and related services to 1.3 million customers in 197 communities; New England Power Company is a wholesale electric generating company that operates 5 thermal generating systems, 14 hydroelectric generating stations, a pumped storage station, and 2,400 miles of transmission lines; New England Electric Resources, Inc. is an independent project development and consulting company; New England Electric Transmission Corporation, New England Hydro-Transmission Corporation, and New England Hydro-Transmission Electric Company, Inc. are electric transmission companies that develop, own, and operate facilities associated with high-voltage, direct current interconnection; Narragansett Energy Resources Company is a wholesale electric generating company; New England Energy Inc. is an oil and gas exploration and development company; and New England Power Services Company is a service company that provides administrative, legal, engineering, and other support to the subsidiaries. **Parent company:** National Grid USA. **Listed on:** New York Stock Exchange. **Stock exchange symbol:** NGG. **Number of employees at this location:** 1,200. **Number of employees nationwide:** 5,200.

NEW ENGLAND GAS COMPANY

155 North Main Street, Fall River MA 02720. 508/679-5271. **Toll-free phone:** 800/936-7000. **Contact:** Human Resources. **World Wide Web address:** http://www.negasco.com. **Description:** A public utility company selling natural gas at retail in Fall River, Somerset, Swansea, and Westport. **Corporate headquarters location:** This location.

PILGRIM NUCLEAR POWER PLANT

600 Rocky Hill Road, Plymouth MA 02360. 508/830-7000. **Contact:** Human Resources. **Description:** A 670-megawatt plant supplying energy to homes within New England.

MISCELLANEOUS WHOLESALING

**You can expect to find the following types of companies
in this section:**
Exporters and Importers • General Wholesale Distribution Companies

---

AIR COMPRESSOR ENGINEERING COMPANY INC.
P.O. Box 738, Westfield MA 01806. 413/568-2884. **Physical Address:** 17
Meadow Street, Westfield MA 01085-3221. **Contact:** Human Resources.
Description: Engaged in the wholesale of new and used metalworking
machinery.

BRAUN NORTH AMERICA
400 Unicorn Park Drive, Woburn MA 01801. 781/939-8300. **Toll-free phone:**
800/BRA-UN11. **Contact:** Human Resources. **World Wide Web address:**
www.braun.com. **Description:** Distributes a variety of consumer products
including coffee makers, juicers, and razors, all of which are manufactured by
Braun in Germany. **Parent company:** The Gillette Company.

IKON OFFICE SOLUTIONS
204 Second Avenue, Waltham MA 02451. 781/487-5100. **Contact:** Human
Resources. **World Wide Web address:** http://www.ikon.com. **Description:** A
wholesaler and distributor of copy machines, fax machines, and related office
supplies. **Positions advertised include:** Associate Sales Representative; On-
Site Support Specialist; Major Account Representative; Associate Sales
Representative; Account Executive; Operations Manager; Field Support
Specialist; Production Manager; Receptionist; Customer Service Representative.
Other U.S. locations: Nationwide. **International locations:** Worldwide. **Listed
on:** New York Stock Exchange. **Stock exchange symbol:** IKN.

W.B. MASON
P.O. Box 111, Brockton MA 02303-0111. 508/586-3434. **Physical address:** 59
Centre Street, Brockton MA 02301. **Contact:** Human Resources. **World Wide
Web address:** http://www.wbmason.com. **Description:** Distributes a wide range
of office supplies, primarily to businesses. **Positions advertised include:** Driver;
Picker Packer Warehouse Associate; Customer Service Representative; 3rd Shift
Supply Warehouse Worker; Desktop Publishing Marketing Department.
Corporate headquarters location: This location. **Other area locations:** Auburn
MA; Boston MA; Hyannis MA; Woburn MA. **Other U.S. locations:** North Haven
CT; Secaucus NJ; Cranston RI.

ACCOUNTING AND MANAGEMENT CONSULTING

AMERICAN ACCOUNTING ASSOCIATION
5717 Bessie Drive, Sarasota FL 34233-2399. 941/921-7747. **Fax:** 941/923-4093.
E-mail address: Office@aaahq.org. **World Wide Web address:**
http://aaahq.org. **Description:** A voluntary organization founded in 1916 to
promote excellence in accounting education, research and practice.

AMERICAN INSTITUTE OF CERTIFIED PUBLIC ACCOUNTANTS
1211 Avenue of the Americas, New York NY 10036. 212/596-6200. **Toll-free
phone:** 888/777-7077. **Fax:** 212/596-6213. **World Wide Web address:**
http://www.aicpa.org. **Description:** A non-profit organization providing resources,
information, and leadership to its members.

AMERICAN MANAGEMENT ASSOCIATION
1601 Broadway, New York NY 10019. 212/586-8100. **Fax:** 212/903-8168. **Toll-
free phone:** 800/262-9699. **E-mail address:** info@amanet.org. **World Wide
Web address:** http://www.amanet.org. **Description:** A non-profit association
providing its members with management development and educational services.

ASSOCIATION OF GOVERNMENT ACCOUNTANTS
2208 Mount Vernon Avenue, Alexandria VA 22301. 703/684-6931. **Toll-free
phone:** 800/AGA-7211. **Fax:** 703/548-9367. **World Wide Web address:**
http://www.agacgfm.org. **Description:** A public financial management
organization catering to the professional interests of financial managers at the
local, state and federal governments and public accounting firms.

ASSOCIATION OF MANAGEMENT CONSULTING FIRMS
380 Lexington Avenue, Suite 1700, New York NY 10168. 212/551-7887. **Fax:**
212/551-7934. **E-mail address:** info@amcf.org. **World Wide Web address:**
http://www.amcf.org. **Description:** Founded in 1929 to provide a forum for
confronting common challenges; increasing the collective knowledge of members
and their clients; and establishing a professional code conduct.

CONNECTICUT SOCIETY OF CERTIFIED PUBLIC ACCOUNTANTS
845 Brook Street, Building Two, Rocky Hill CT 06067-3405. 860/258-4800. **Fax:**
860/258-4859. **E-mail address:** info@cs-cpa.org. **World Wide Web address:**
http://www.cs-cpa.org. **Description:** A statewide professional membership
organization catering to CPAs.

INSTITUTE OF INTERNAL AUDITORS
247 Maitland Avenue, Altamonte Springs FL 32701-4201. 407-937-1100. **Fax:**
407-937-1101. **E-mail address:** iia@theiia.org. **World Wide Web address:**
http://www.theiia.org. **Description:** Founded in 1941 to serves members in
internal auditing, governance and internal control, IT audit, education, and
security worldwide.

INSTITUTE OF MANAGEMENT ACCOUNTANTS
10 Paragon Drive, Montvale NJ 07645-1718. 201/573-9000. **Fax:** 201/474-1600.
Toll-free phone: 800/638-4427. **E-mail address:** ima@imanet.org. **World Wide
Web address:** http://www.imanet.org. **Description:** Provides members personal
and professional development opportunities in management accounting, financial
management and information management through education and association

with business professionals and certification in management accounting and financial management.

INSTITUTE OF MANAGEMENT CONSULTANTS

2025 M Street, NW, Suite 800, Washington DC 20036-3309. 202/367-1134. **Toll-free phone:** 800/221-2557. **Fax:** 202/367-2134. **E-mail address:** office@imcusa.org. **World Wide Web address:** http://www.imcusa.org. **Description** Founded in 1968 as the national professional association representing management consultants and awarding the CMC (Certified Management Consultant) certification mark.

NATIONAL ASSOCIATION OF TAX PROFESSIONALS

720 Association Drive, PO Box 8002, Appleton WI 54912-8002. 800/558-3402. **Fax:** 800/747-0001. **E-Mail address:** natp@natptax.com. **World Wide Web address:** http://www.natptax.com. **Description:** Founded in 1979 as a nonprofit professional association dedicated to excellence in taxation with a mission to serve professionals who work in all areas of tax practice.

NATIONAL SOCIETY OF PUBLIC ACCOUNTANTS

1010 North Fairfax Street, Alexandria VA 22314. 703/549-6400. **Toll-free phone:** 800/966-6679. **Fax:** 703/549-2984. **Email address:** members@nsacct.org. **World Wide Web address:** http://www.nsacct.org. **Description:** For more than 50 years, NSA has supported its members with resources and representation to protect their right to practice, build credibility and grow the profession. NSA protects the public by requiring its members to adhere to a strict Code of Ethics.

ADVERTISING, MARKETING, AND PUBLIC RELATIONS

ADVERTISING RESEARCH FOUNDATION
641 Lexington Avenue, New York NY 10022. 212/751-5656. **World Wide Web address:** http://www.thearf.com. **Description:** Founded in 1936 by the Association of National Advertisers and the American Association of Advertising Agencies, the Advertising Research Foundation (ARF) is a nonprofit corporate-membership association, which is today the preeminent professional organization in the field of advertising, marketing and media research. Its combined membership represents more than 400 advertisers, advertising agencies, research firms, media companies, educational institutions and international organizations.

AMERICAN ASSOCIATION OF ADVERTISING AGENCIES
405 Lexington Avenue, 18th Floor, New York NY 10174-1801. 212/682-2500. **Fax:** 212/682-8391. **World Wide Web address:** http://www.aaaa.org. **Description:** Founded in 1917 as the national trade association representing the advertising agency business in the United States.

AMERICAN MARKETING ASSOCIATION
311 South Wacker Drive, Suite 5800, Chicago IL 60606. 312/542-9000. **Fax:** 312/542-9001. **Toll-free phone:** 800/AMA-1150. **E-mail address:** info@ama.org. **World Wide Web address:** http://www.marketingpower.com. **Description:** A professional associations for marketers providing relevant marketing information that experienced marketers turn to everyday.

DIRECT MARKETING ASSOCIATION
1120 Avenue of the Americas, New York NY 10036-6700. 212/768-7277. **Fax:** 212/302-6714. **E-mail address:** info@the-dma.org. **World Wide Web address:** http://www.the-dma.org. **Description:** Founded in 1917 as a non-profit organization representing professionals working in all areas of direct marketing.

INTERNATIONAL ADVERTISING ASSOCIATION
521 Fifth Avenue, Suite 1807, New York NY 10175. 212/557-1133. **Fax:** 212/983-0455. **E-mail address:** iaa@iaaglobal.org. **World Wide Web address:** http://www.iaaglobal.org. **Description:** A strategic partnership that addresses the common interests of all the marketing communications disciplines ranging from advertisers to media companies to agencies to direct marketing firms to individual practitioners.

MARKETING RESEARCH ASSOCIATION
1344 Silas Deane Highway, Suite 306, PO Box 230, Rocky Hill CT 06067-0230. 860/257-4008. **Fax:** 860/257-3990. **E-mail address:** email@mra-net.org. **World Wide Web address:** http://www.mra-net.org. **Description:** MRA promotes excellence in the opinion and marketing research industry by providing members with a variety of opportunities for advancing and expanding their marketing research and related business skills. To protect the marketing research environment, we will act as an advocate with appropriate government entities, other associations, and the public.

PUBLIC RELATIONS SOCIETY OF AMERICA
33 Maiden Lane, 11th Floor, New York NY 10038-5150. 212/460-1400. **Fax:** 212/995-0757. **E-mail address:** info@prsa.org. **World Wide Web address:** http://www.prsa.org. **Description:** A professional organization for public relations

practitioners. Comprised of nearly 20,000 members organized into 116 Chapters represent business and industry, counseling firms, government, associations, hospitals, schools, professional services firms and nonprofit organizations.

AEROSPACE

AMERICAN INSTITUTE OF AERONAUTICS AND ASTRONAUTICS
1801 Alexander Bell Drive, Suite 500, Reston VA 20191-4344. 703/264-7500.
Toll-free phone: 800/639-AIAA. **Fax:** 703/264-7551. **E-mail address:**
info@aiaa.org. **World Wide Web address:** http://www.aiaa.org. **Description:**
The principal society of the aerospace engineer and scientist.

NATIONAL AERONAUTIC ASSOCIATION OF USA
1815 N. Fort Myer Drive, Suite 500, Arlington VA 22209. 703/527-0226. **Fax:**
703/527-0229. **E-mail address:** naa@naa-usa.org. **World Wide Web address:**
http://www.naa-usa.org. **Description:** A non-parochial, charitable organization
serving all segments of American aviation whose membership encompass all
areas of flight including skydiving, models, commercial airlines, and military
fighters.

PROFESSIONAL AVIATION MAINTENANCE ASSOCIATION
717 Princess Street, Alexandria VA 22314. 703/683-3171. **Toll-free phone:**
866/865-PAMA. **Fax:** 703/683-0018. **E-mail address:** hq@pama.org. **World
Wide Web address:** http://www.pama.org. **Description:** A non-profit
organization concerned with promoting professionalism among aviation
maintenance personnel; fostering and improving methods, skills, learning, and
achievement in aviation maintenance. The association also conducts regular
industry meetings and seminars.

APPAREL, FASHION, AND TEXTILES

AMERICAN APPAREL AND FOOTWEAR ASSOCIATION
1601 North Kent Street, Suite 1200, Arlington VA 22209. 703/524-1864. **Fax:** 703/522-6741. **World Wide Web address:** http://apparelandfootwear.org. **Description:** The national trade association representing apparel, footwear and other sewn products companies, and their suppliers. Promotes and enhances its members' competitiveness, productivity and profitability in the global market.

THE FASHION GROUP
8 West 40th Street, 7th Floor, New York NY 10018. 212/302-5511. **Fax:** 212/302-5533. **E-mail address:** info@fgi.org. **World Wide Web address:** http://www.fgi.org. **Description:** A non-profit association representing all areas of the fashion, apparel, accessories, beauty and home industries.

INTERNATIONAL ASSOCIATION OF CLOTHING DESIGNERS AND EXECUTIVES
124 West 93rd Street, Suite 3E, New York NY 10025. 603/672-4065. **Fax:** 603/672-4064. **World Wide Web address:** http://www.iacde.com. **Description:** Founded in 1911, with the mission to serve as a global network for the sharing of information by its members on design direction and developments, fashion and fiber trends, and technical innovations affecting tailored apparel, designers, their suppliers, retailers, manufacturing executives and educational institutions for the purpose of enhancing their professional standing and interests.

NATIONAL COUNCIL OF TEXTILE ORGANIZATIONS
1776 I Street, NW, Suite 900, Washington DC 20006. 202/756-4878. **Fax:** 202/756-1520. **World Wide Web address:** http://www.ncto.org. **Description:** The national trade association for the domestic textile industry with members operating in more than 30 states and the industry employs approximately 450,000 people.

ARCHITECTURE, CONSTRUCTION, AND ENGINEERING

AACE INTERNATIONAL: THE ASSOCIATION FOR TOTAL COST MANAGEMENT
209 Prairie Avenue, Suite 100, Morgantown WV 26501. 304/296-8444. **Fax:** 304/291-5728. **E-mail address:** info@aacei.org. **World Wide Web address:** http://www.aacei.org. **Description:** Founded 1956 to provide its approximately 5,500 worldwide members with the resources to enhance their performance and ensure continued growth and success. Members include cost management professionals: cost managers and engineers, project managers, planners and schedulers, estimators and bidders, and value engineers.

AMERICAN ASSOCIATION OF ENGINEERING SOCIETIES
1828 L Street, NW, Suite 906, Washington DC 20036. 202/296-2237. **Fax:** 202/296-1151. **World Wide Web address:** http://www.aaes.org. **Description:** A multidisciplinary organization of engineering societies dedicated to advancing the knowledge, understanding, and practice of engineering.

AMERICAN CONSULTING ENGINEERS COMPANIES
1015 15th Street, 8th Floor, NW, Washington DC, 20005-2605. 202/347-7474. **Fax:** 202/898-0068. **E-mail address:** acec@acec.org. **World Wide Web address:** http://www.acec.org. **Description:** Engaged in a wide range of engineering works that propel the nation's economy, and enhance and safeguard America's quality of life. These works allow Americans to drink clean water, enjoy a healthy life, take advantage of new technologies, and travel safely and efficiently. The Council's mission is to contribute to America's prosperity and welfare by advancing the business interests of member firms.

AMERICAN INSTITUTE OF ARCHITECTS
1735 New York Avenue, NW, Washington DC 20006. 202/626-7300. **Fax:** 202/626-7547. **Toll-free phone:** 800/AIA-3837. **E-mail address:** infocentral@aia.org. **World Wide Web address:** http://www.aia.org. **Description:** A non-profit organization for the architecture profession dedicated to: Serving its members, advancing their value, improving the quality of the built environment. Vision Statement: Through a culture of innovation, The American Institute of Architects empowers its members and inspires creation of a better-built environment.

AMERICAN INSTITUTE OF CONSTRUCTORS
P.O. Box 26334, Alexandria VA 22314. 703/683-4999. **Fax:** 703/683-5480. **E-mail address:** admin@aicnet.org. **World Wide Web address:** http://www.aicnet.org. **Description:** Founded to help individual construction practitioners achieve the professional status they deserve and serves as the national qualifying body of professional constructor. The Institute AIC membership identifies the individual as a true professional. The Institute is the constructor's counterpart of professional organizations found in architecture, engineering, law and other fields.

AMERICAN SOCIETY FOR ENGINEERING EDUCATION
1818 N Street, NW, Suite 600, Washington DC, 20036-2479. 202/331-3500. **Fax:** 202/265-8504. **World Wide Web address:** http://www.asee.org. **Description:** A nonprofit member association, founded in 1893, dedicated to promoting and improving engineering and technology education.

AMERICAN SOCIETY OF CIVIL ENGINEERS
1801 Alexander Bell Drive, Reston VA 20191-4400. 703/295-6300. **Fax:** 703/295-6222. **Toll-free phone:** 800/548-2723. **World Wide Web address:** http://www.asce.org. **Description:** Founded to provide essential value to its members, their careers, partners and the public by developing leadership, advancing technology, advocating lifelong learning and promoting the profession.

AMERICAN SOCIETY OF HEATING, REFRIGERATION, AND AIR CONDITIONING ENGINEERS
1791 Tullie Circle, NE, Atlanta GA 30329. 404/636-8400. **Fax:** 404/321-5478. **Toll-free phone:** 800/527-4723. **E-mail address:** ashrae@ashrae.org. **World Wide Web address:** http://www.ashrae.org. **Description:** Founded with a mission to advance the arts and sciences of heating, ventilation, air conditioning, refrigeration and related human factors and to serve the evolving needs of the public and ASHRAE members.

AMERICAN SOCIETY OF MECHANICAL ENGINEERS
Three Park Avenue, New York, NY 10016-5990. 973-882-1167. **Toll-free phone:** 800/843-2763. **E-mail address:** infocentral@asme.org. **World Wide Web address:** http://www.asme.org. **Description:** Founded in 1880 as the American Society of Mechanical Engineers, today ASME International is a nonprofit educational and technical organization serving a worldwide membership of 125,000.

AMERICAN SOCIETY OF NAVAL ENGINEERS
1452 Duke Street, Alexandria VA 22314-3458. 703/836-6727. **Fax:** 703/836-7491. **E-mail address:** asnehq@navalengineers.org. **World Wide Web address:** http://www.navalengineers.org. **Description:** Mission is to advance the knowledge and practice of naval engineering in public and private applications and operations, to enhance the professionalism and well being of members, and to promote naval engineering as a career field.

AMERICAN SOCIETY OF PLUMBING ENGINEERS
8614 Catalpa Avenue, Suite 1007, Chicago IL 60656-1116. 773/693-2773. **Fax:** 773/695-9007. **E-mail address:** info@aspe.org. **World Wide Web address:** http://www.aspe.org. **Description:** The international organization for professionals skilled in the design, specification and inspection of plumbing systems. ASPE is dedicated to the advancement of the science of plumbing engineering, to the professional growth and advancement of its members and the health, welfare and safety of the public.

AMERICAN SOCIETY OF SAFETY ENGINEERS
1800 E Oakton Street, Des Plaines IL 60018. 847/699-2929. **Fax:** 847/768-3434. **E-mail address:** customerservice@asse.org. **World Wide Web address:** http://www.asse.org. **Description:** A non-profit organization promoting the concerns of safety engineers.

ASSOCIATED BUILDERS AND CONTRACTORS
4250 N. Fairfax Drive, 9th Floor, Arlington VA 22203-1607. 703/812-2000. **E-mail address:** gotquestions@abc.org. **World Wide Web address:** http://www.abc.org. **Description:** A national trade association representing more than 23,000 merit shop contractors, subcontractors, material suppliers and related firms in 80 chapters across the United States. Membership represents all specialties within the U.S. construction industry and is comprised primarily of firms that perform work in the industrial and commercial sectors of the industry.

ASSOCIATED GENERAL CONTRACTORS OF AMERICA, INC.
333 John Carlyle Street, Suite 200, Alexandria VA 22314. 703/548-3118. **Fax:** 703/548-3119. **E-mail address:** info@agc.org. **World Wide Web address:** http://www.agc.org. **Description:** A construction trade association, founded in 1918 on a request by President Woodrow Wilson.

THE ENGINEERING CENTER (TEC)
One Walnut Street, Boston MA 02108-3616. 617/227-5551. **Fax:** 617/227-6783. **E-mail address:** tec@engineers.org. **World Wide Web address:** http://www.engineers.org. **Description:** Founded with a mission to increase public awareness of the value of the engineering profession; to provide current information affecting the profession; to offer administrative facilities and services to engineering organizations in New England; and to provide a forum for discussion and resolution of professional issues.

ILLUMINATING ENGINEERING SOCIETY OF NORTH AMERICA
120 Wall Street, Floor 17, New York NY 10005. 212/248-5000. **Fax:** 212/248-5017(18). **E-mail address:** iesna@iesna.org. **World Wide Web address:** http://www.iesna.org. **Description:** To advance knowledge and to disseminate information for the improvement of the lighted environment to the benefit of society.

JUNIOR ENGINEERING TECHNICAL SOCIETY
1420 King Street, Suite 405, Alexandria VA 22314. 703/548-5387. **Fax:** 703/548-0769. **E-mail address:** info@jets.org. **World Wide Web address:** http://www.jets.org. **Description:** JETS is a national non-profit education organization that has served the pre-college engineering community for over 50 years. Through competitions and programs, JETS serves over 30,000 students and 2,000 teachers, and holds programs on 150 college campuses each year.

NATIONAL ACTION COUNCIL FOR MINORITIES IN ENGINEERING
440 Hamilton Avenue, Suite 302, White Plains NY 10601-1813. 914/539-4010. **Fax:** 914/539-4032. **E-mail address:** webmaster@nacme.org. **World Wide Web address:** http://www.nacme.org. **Description:** Founded in 1974 to provide leadership and support for the national effort to increase the representation of successful African American, American Indian and Latino women and men in engineering and technology, math- and science-based careers.

NATIONAL ASSOCIATION OF BLACK ENGINEERS
1454 Duke Street, Alexandria VA 22314. 703/549-2207. **Fax:** 703/683-5312. **E-mail address:** info@nsbe.org. **World Wide Web address:** http://www.nsbe.org. **Description:** A non-profit organization dedicated to increasing the number of culturally responsible Black engineers who excel academically, succeed professionally and positively impact the community.

NATIONAL ASSOCIATION OF HOME BUILDERS
1201 15th Street, NW, Washington DC 20005. 202/266-8200. **Toll-free phone:** 800/368-5242. **World Wide Web address:** http://www.nahb.org. **Description:** Founded in 1942, NAHB has been serving its members, the housing industry, and the public at large. A trade association that promotes the policies that make housing a national priority.

NATIONAL ASSOCIATION OF MINORITY ENGINEERING PROGRAM ADMINISTRATORS
1133 West Morse Boulevard, Suite 201, Winter Park FL 32789. 407/647-8839. **Fax:** 407/629-2502. **E-mail address:** namepa@namepa.org **World Wide Web**

address: http://www.namepa.org. **Description:** Provides services, information, and tools to produce a diverse group of engineers and scientists, and achieve equity and parity in the nation's workforce.

NATIONAL ELECTRICAL CONTRACTORS ASSOCIATION
3 Bethesda Metro Center, Suite 1100, Bethesda MD 20814. 301/657-3110. **Fax:** 301/215-4500. **World Wide Web address:** http://www.necanet.org. **Description:** Founded in 1901 as representative segment of the construction market comprised of over 70,000 electrical contracting firms.

NATIONAL SOCIETY OF PROFESSIONAL ENGINEERS
1420 King Street, Alexandria VA 22314-2794. 703/684-2800. **Fax:** 703/836-4875. **World Wide Web address:** http://www.nspe.org. **Description:** An engineering society that represents engineering professionals and licensed engineers (PEs) across all disciplines. Founded in 1934 to promote engineering licensure and ethics, enhance the engineer image, advocate and protect legal rights, publish industry news, and provide continuing education.

SOCIETY OF FIRE PROTECTION ENGINEERS
7315 Wisconsin Avenue, Suite 620E, Bethesda MD 20814. 301/718-2910. **Fax:** 301/718-2242. **E-mail address:** sfpehqtrs@sfpe.org. **World Wide Web address:** http://www.sfpe.org. **Description:** Founded in 1950 and incorporated as in independent organization in 1971, the professional society represents professionals in the field of fire protection engineering. The Society has approximately 3500 members in the United States and abroad, and 51 regional chapters, 10 of which are outside the US.

ARTS, ENTERTAINMENT, SPORTS, AND RECREATION

AMERICAN ASSOCIATION OF MUSEUMS
1575 Eye Street NW, Suite 400, Washington DC 20005. 202/289-1818. **Fax:** 202/289-6578. **World Wide Web address:** http://www.aam-us.org. **Description:** Founded in 1906, the association promotes excellence within the museum community. Services include advocacy, professional education, information exchange, accreditation, and guidance on current professional standards of performance.

AMERICAN FEDERATION OF MUSICIANS
1501 Broadway, Suite 600, New York NY 10036. 212/869-1330. **Fax:** 212/764-6134. **World Wide Web address:** http://www.afm.org. **Description:** Represents the interests of professional musicians. Services include negotiating agreements, protecting ownership of recorded music, securing benefits such as health care and pension, or lobbying our legislators. The AFM is committed to raising industry standards and placing the professional musician in the foreground of the cultural landscape.

AMERICAN MUSIC CENTER
30 West 26th Street, Suite 1001, New York NY 10010. 212/366-5260. **Fax:** 212/366-5265. **World Wide Web address:** http://www.amc.net. **Description:** Dedicated to fostering and composition, production, publication, and distribution of contemporary (American) music.

AMERICAN SOCIETY OF COMPOSERS, AUTHORS, AND PUBLISHERS (ASCAP)
One Lincoln Plaza, New York NY 10023. 212/621-6000. **Fax:** 212/724-9064. **E-mail address:** info@ascap.com. **World Wide Web address:** http://www.ascap.com. **Description:** A membership based association comprised of composers, songwriters, lyricists, and music publishers across all genres of music.

AMERICAN SYMPHONY ORCHESTRA LEAGUE
33 West 60th Street, 5th Floor, New York NY 10023-7905. 212/262-5161. **Fax:** 212/262-5198. **E-mail address:** league@symphony.org. **World Wide Web address:** http://www.symphony.org. **Description:** Founded in 1942 to exchange information and ideas with other orchestra leaders. The league also publishes the bimonthly magazine.

AMERICAN ZOO AND AQUARIUM ASSOCIATION
8403 Colesville Road, Suite 710, Silver Spring MD 20910-3314. 301/562-0777. **Fax:** 301/562-0888. **World Wide Web address:** http://www.aza.org. **Description:** Dedicated to establishing and maintaining excellent professional standards in all AZA Institutions through its accreditation program; establishing and promoting high standards of animal care and welfare; promoting and facilitating collaborative conservation and research programs; advocating effective governmental policies for our members; strengthening and promoting conservation education programs for our public and professional development for our members, and; raising awareness of the collective impact of its members and their programs.

ASSOCIATION OF INDEPENDENT VIDEO AND FILMMAKERS

304 Hudson Street, 6th floor, New York NY 10013. 212/807-1400. **Fax:** 212/463-8519. **E-mail address:** info@aivf.org. **World Wide Web address:** http://www.aivf.org. **Description:** A membership organization serving local and international film and videomakers including documentarians, experimental artists, and makers of narrative features.

NATIONAL ENDOWMENT FOR THE ARTS
1100 Pennsylvania Avenue, NW, Washington DC 20506. 202/682-5400. **E-mail address:** webmgr@arts.endow.com. **World Wide Web address:** http://www.nea.gov. **Description:** Founded in 1965 to foster, preserve, and promote excellence in the arts, to bring art to all Americans, and to provide leadership in arts education.

NATIONAL RECREATION AND PARK ASSOCIATION
22377 Belmont Ridge Road, Ashburn VA 20148-4150. 703/858-0784. **Fax:** 703/858-0794. **E-mail address:** info@nrpa.org. **World Wide Web address:** http://www.nrpa.org. **Description:** Works "to advance parks, recreation and environmental conservation efforts that enhance the quality of life for all people."

WOMEN'S CAUCUS FOR ART
P.O. Box 1498, Canal Street Station, New York NY 10013. 212/634-0007. **E-mail address:** info@nationalwca.com. **World Wide Web address:** http://www.nationalwca.com. **Description:** Founded in 1972 in connection with the College Art Association (CAA), as a national organization unique in its multi-disciplinary, multicultural membership of artists, art historians, students /educators, museum professionals and galleries in the visual arts.

AUTOMOTIVE

NATIONAL AUTOMOBILE DEALERS ASSOCIATION
8400 Westpark Drive, McLean VA 22102. 703/821-7000. **Toll-free phone:** 800/252-6232. **E-mail address:** nadainfo@nada.org. **World Wide Web address:** http://www.nada.org. **Description:** NADA represents America's franchised new-car and -truck dealers. Today there are more than 19,700 franchised new-car and -truck dealer members holding nearly 49,300 separate new-car and light-, medium-, and heavy-duty truck franchises, domestic and import. Founded in 1917.

NATIONAL INSTITUTE FOR AUTOMOTIVE SERVICE EXCELLENCE
101 Blue Seal Drive, SE, Suite 101, Leesburg VA 20175. 703/669-6600. **Toll-free phone:** 877/ASE-TECH. **World Wide Web address:** http://www.ase.com. **Description:** An independent, non-profit organization established in 1972 to improve the quality of vehicle repair and service through the testing and certification of repair and service professionals. More than 420,000 professionals hold current ASE credentials.

SOCIETY OF AUTOMOTIVE ENGINEERS
400 Commonwealth Drive, Warrendale PA 15096-0001. 724/776-4841. **E-mail address:** customerservice@sae.org. **World Wide Web address:** http://www.sae.org. **Description:** An organization with more than 84,000 members from 97 countries who share information and exchange ideas for advancing the engineering of mobility systems.

BANKING

AMERICA'S COMMUNITY BANKERS
900 Nineteenth Street, NW, Suite 400, Washington DC 20006. 202/857-3100. **Fax:** 202/296-8716. **World Wide Web address:** http://www.acbankers.org. **Description:** Represents the nation's community banks of all charter types and sizes providing a broad range of advocacy and service strategies to enhance their members' presence and contribution to the marketplace.

AMERICAN BANKERS ASSOCIATION
1120 Connecticut Avenue, NW, Washington DC 20036. 800/BANKERS. **World Wide Web address:** http://www.aba.com. **Description:** Founded in 1875 and represents banks on issues of national importance for financial institutions and their customers. Members include all categories of banking institutions, including community, regional and money center banks and holding companies, as well as savings associations, trust companies and savings banks.

BIOTECHNOLOGY, PHARMACEUTICALS, AND SCIENTIFIC R&D

AMERICAN ASSOCIATION FOR CLINICAL CHEMISTRY
2101 L Street, NW, Suite 202, Washington DC 20037-1558. 202/857-0717. **Fax:** 202/887-5093. **Toll-free phone:** 800/892-1400. **World Wide Web address:** http://www.aacc.org. **Description:** Founded in 1948 as an international scientific/medical society of clinical laboratory professionals, physicians, research scientists and other individuals involved with clinical chemistry and other clinical laboratory science-related disciplines. The society has 10,000 members.

AMERICAN ASSOCIATION OF COLLEGES OF PHARMACY
1426 Prince Street, Alexandria VA 22314. 703/739-2330. **Fax:** 703/836-8982. **E-mail address:** mail@aacp.org. **World Wide Web address:** http://www.aacp.org. **Description:** Founded in 1900 as the national organization representing the interests of pharmaceutical education and educators. Comprising all 89 U.S. pharmacy colleges and schools including more than 4,000 faculty, 36,000 students enrolled in professional programs, and 3,600 individuals pursuing graduate study, AACP is committed to excellence in pharmaceutical education.

AMERICAN ASSOCIATION OF PHARMACEUTICAL SCIENTISTS
2107 Wilson Boulevard, Suite 700, Arlington VA 22201-3042. 703/243-2800. **Fax:** 703/243-9650. **E-mail address:** aaps@aaps.org. **World Wide Web address:** http://www.aaps.org. **Description:** Founded in 1986 as professional, scientific society of more than 10,000 members employed in academia, industry, government and other research institutes worldwide. The association advances science through the open exchange of scientific knowledge; serves as an information resource; and contributes to human health through pharmaceutical research and development.

AMERICAN COLLEGE OF CLINICAL PHARMACY (ACCP)
3101 Broadway, Suite 650, Kansas City MO 64111. 816/531-2177. **Fax:** 816/531-4990. **E-mail address:** accp@accp.com **World Wide Web address:** http://www.accp.com. **Description:** A professional and scientific society providing leadership, education, advocacy, and resources enabling clinical pharmacists to achieve excellence in practice and research.

AMERICAN PHARMACISTS ASSOCIATION
2215 Constitution Avenue, NW, Washington DC 20037-2985. 202/628-4410. **Fax:** 202/783-2351. **E-mail address:** info@aphanet.org. **World Wide Web address:** http://www.aphanet.org. **Description:** Founded in 1852 as the national professional society of pharmacists. Members include practicing pharmacists, pharmaceutical scientists, pharmacy students, pharmacy technicians, and others interested in advancing the profession.

AMERICAN SOCIETY FOR BIOCHEMISTRY AND MOLECULAR BIOLOGY
9650 Rockville Pike, Bethesda MD 20814-3996. 301/634-7145. **Fax:** 301/634-7126. **E-mail address:** asbmb@asbmb.faseb.org. **World Wide Web address:** http://www.asbmb.org. **Description:** A nonprofit scientific and educational organization with over 11,900 members. Most members teach and conduct research at colleges and universities. Others conduct research in various government laboratories, nonprofit research institutions and industry. The Society's student members attend undergraduate or graduate institutions.

AMERICAN SOCIETY OF HEALTH-SYSTEM PHARMACISTS
7272 Wisconsin Avenue, Bethesda MD 20814. 301/657-3000. **Toll-free phone:** 866/279-0681. **World Wide Web address:** http://www.ashp.org. **Description:** A national professional association representing pharmacists who practice in hospitals, health maintenance organizations, long-term care facilities, home care, and other components of health care systems.

NATIONAL PHARMACEUTICAL COUNCIL
1894 Preston White Drive, Reston VA 20191-5433. 703/620-6390. **Fax:** 703/476-0904. **E-mail address:** main@npcnow.com. **World Wide Web address:** http://www.npcnow.org. **Description:** Conducts research and education programs geared towards demonstrating that the appropriate use of pharmaceuticals improves both patient treatment outcomes and the cost effective delivery of overall health care services.

NATIONAL SPACE BIOMEDICAL RESEARCH INSTITUTE
One Baylor Plaza, NA-425, Houston TX 77030. 713/798-7412. **Fax:** 713/798-7413. **E-mail address:** info@www.nsbri.org. **World Wide Web address:** http://www.nsbri.org. **Description:** Conducts research into health concerns facing astronauts on long missions.

BUSINESS SERVICES & NON-SCIENTIFIC RESEARCH

AMERICAN SOCIETY OF APPRAISERS
555 Herndon Parkway, Suite 125, Herndon VA 20170. 703/478-2228. **Fax:** 703/742-8471. **E-mail address:** asainfo@appraisers.org. **World Wide Web address:** http://www.appraisers.org. **Description:** Fosters professional excellence through education, accreditation, publication and other services. Its goal is to contribute to the growth of its membership and to the appraisal profession.

EQUIPMENT LEASING ASSOCIATION OF AMERICA
4301 North Fairfax Drive, Suite 550, Arlington VA 22203-1627. 703/527-8655. **Fax:** 703/527-2649. **World Wide Web address:** http://www.elaonline.com. **Description:** Promotes and serves the general interests of the equipment leasing and finance industry.

NATIONAL ASSOCIATION OF PERSONNEL SERVICES
The Village at Banner Elk, Suite 108, P.O. Box 2128, Banner Elk NC 28604. 828/898-4929. **Fax:** 828/898-8098. **World Wide Web address:** http://www.napsweb.org. **Description**: Serves, protects, informs, and represents all facets of the personnel services industry regarding federal legislation and regulatory issues by providing education, certification, and member services which enhance the ability to conduct business with integrity and competence.

CHARITIES AND SOCIAL SERVICES

AMERICAN COUNCIL FOR THE BLIND
1155 15th Street, NW, Suite 1004, Washington DC 20005. 202/467-5081. **Fax:** 202/467-5085. **Toll-free phone:** 800/424-8666. **World Wide Web address:** http://www.acb.org. **Description:** The nation's leading membership organization of blind and visually impaired people. It was founded in 1961.

CATHOLIC CHARITIES USA
1731 King Street, Alexandria VA 22314. 703/549-1390. **Fax:** 703/549-1656. **World Wide Web address:** http://www.catholiccharitiesusa.org. **Description:** A membership association of social service networks providing social services to people in need.

NATIONAL ASSOCIATION OF SOCIAL WORKERS
750 First Street, NE, Suite 700, Washington DC 20002-4241. 202/408-8600. **E-mail address:** membership@naswdc.org. **World Wide Web address:** http://www.naswdc.org. **Description:** A membership organization comprised of professional social workers working to enhance the professional growth and development of its members, to create and maintain professional standards, and to advance sound social policies.

NATIONAL COUNCIL ON FAMILY RELATIONS
3989 Central Avenue, NE, #550, Minneapolis MN 55421. 763/781-9331. **Fax:** 763/781-9348. **Toll-free phone:** 888/781-9331. **E-mail address:** info@ncfr.org. **World Wide Web address:** http://www.ncfr.org. **Description:** Provides a forum for family researchers, educators, and practitioners to share in the development and dissemination of knowledge about families and family relationships, establishes professional standards, and works to promote family well-being.

NATIONAL FEDERATION OF THE BLIND
1800 Johnson Street, Baltimore MD 21230-4998. 410/659-9314. **Fax:** 410/685-5653. **World Wide Web address:** http://www.nfb.org. **Description:** Founded in 1940, the National Federation of the Blind (NFB) is the nation's largest membership organization of blind persons. With fifty thousand members, the NFB has affiliates in all fifty states plus Washington D.C. and Puerto Rico, and over seven hundred local chapters. As a consumer and advocacy organization, the NFB is a leading force in the blindness field today.

NATIONAL MULTIPLE SCLEROSIS SOCIETY
733 Third Avenue, New York NY 10017. **Toll-free phone:** 800/344-4867. **World Wide Web address:** http://www.nmss.org. **Description:** Provides accurate, up-to-date information to individuals with MS, their families, and healthcare providers is central to our mission.

CHEMICALS, RUBBER, AND PLASTICS

AMERICAN CHEMICAL SOCIETY
1155 Sixteenth Street, NW, Washington DC 20036. 202/872-4600. **Fax:** 202/872-6067. **Toll-free phone:** 800/227-5558. **E-mail address:** help@acs.org. **World Wide Web address:** http://www.acs.org. **Description:** A self-governed individual membership organization consisting of more than 159,000 members at all degree levels and in all fields of chemistry. The organization provides a broad range of opportunities for peer interaction and career development, regardless of professional or scientific interests. The Society was founded in 1876.

AMERICAN INSTITUTE OF CHEMICAL ENGINEERS
3 Park Avenue, New York NY 10016-5991. 212/591-8100. **Toll-free phone:** 800/242-4363. **Fax:** 212/591-8888. **E-mail address:** xpress@aiche.org. **World Wide Web address:** http://www.aiche.org. **Description:** Founded in 1908 and provides leadership in advancing the chemical engineering profession; fosters and disseminates chemical engineering knowledge, supports the professional and personal growth of its members, and applies the expertise of its members to address societal needs throughout the world.

THE ELECTROCHEMICAL SOCIETY
65 South Main Street, Building D, Pennington NJ 08534-2839. 609/737-1902. **Fax:** 609/737-2743. **World Wide Web address:** http://www.electrochem.org. **Description:** Founded in 1902, The Electrochemical Society has become the leading society for solid-state and electrochemical science and technology. ECS has 8,000 scientists and engineers in over 75 countries worldwide who hold individual membership, as well as roughly 100 corporate members.

SOCIETY OF PLASTICS ENGINEERS
14 Fairfield Drive, PO Box 403, Brookfield CT 06804-0403. 203/775-0471. **Fax:** 203/775-8490. **E-mail address:** info@4spe.org. **World Wide Web address:** http://www.4spe.org. **Description:** A 25,000-member organization promoting scientific and engineering knowledge relating to plastics. Founded in 1942.

THE SOCIETY OF THE PLASTICS INDUSTRY, INC.
1667 K Street, NW, Suite 1000, Washington DC 20006. 202/974-5200. **Fax:** 202/296-7005. **World Wide Web address:** http://www.socplas.org. **Description:** Founded in 1937, The Society of the Plastics Industry, Inc., is the trade association representing one of the largest manufacturing industries in the United States. SPI's members represent the entire plastics industry supply chain, including processors, machinery and equipment manufacturers and raw materials suppliers. The U.S. plastics industry employs 1.4 million workers and provides more than $310 billion in annual shipments.

COMMUNICATIONS:TELECOMMUNICATIONS AND BROADCASTING

ACADEMY OF TELEVISION ARTS & SCIENCES
5220 Lankershim Boulevard, North Hollywood CA 91601-3109. 818/754-2800. **Fax:** 818/761-2827. **World Wide Web address:** http://www.emmys.com. **Description:** Promotes creativity, diversity, innovation and excellence though recognition, education and leadership in the advancement of the telecommunications arts and sciences.

AMERICAN DISC JOCKEY ASSOCIATION
20118 North 67th Avenue, Suite 300-605, Glendale AZ 85308. 888/723-5776. **E-mail address:** office@adja.org. **World Wide Web address:** http://www.adja.org. **Description:** Promotes ethical behavior, industry standards and continuing education for its members.

AMERICAN WOMEN IN RADIO AND TELEVISION, INC.
8405 Greensboro Drive, Suite 800, McLean VA 22102. 703/506-3290. **Fax:** 703/506-3266. **E-mail address:** info@awrt.org. **World Wide Web address:** http://www.awrt.org. **Description:** A non-profit, professional organization of women and men who work in the electronic media and allied fields.

COMPTEL/ASCENT
1900 M Street, NW, Suite 800, Washington DC 20036. 202/296-6650. **Fax:** 202/296-7585. **World Wide Web address:** http://www.comptelascent.org. **Description:** An association representing competitive telecommunications companies in virtually every sector of the marketplace: competitive local exchange carriers, long-distance carriers of every size, wireless service providers, Internet service providers, equipment manufacturers, and software suppliers.

MEDIA COMMUNICATIONS ASSOCIATION-INTERNATIONAL
7600 Terrace Avenue, Suite 203, Middleton WI 53562. 608/827-5034. **Fax:** 608/831-5122. **E-mail address:** info@mca-i.org. **World Wide Web address:** http://www.itva.org. **Description:** A not-for-profit, member-driven organization that provides opportunities for networking, forums for education and the resources for information to media communications professionals.

NATIONAL ASSOCIATION OF BROADCASTERS
1771 N Street, NW, Washington DC 20036. 202/429-5300. **Fax:** 202/429-4199. **E-mail address:** nab@nab.org. **World Wide Web address:** http://www.nab.org. **Description:** A trade association that represents the interests of free, over-the-air radio and television broadcasters.

NATIONAL CABLE & TELECOMMUNICATIONS ASSOCIATION
1724 Massachusetts Avenue, NW, Washington DC 20036. 202/775-3550. **E-mail address:** webmaster@ncta.com. **World Wide Web address:** http://www.ncta.com. **Description:** The National Cable and Telecommunications Association is the principal trade association of the cable and telecommunications industry. Founded in 1952, NCTA's primary mission is to provide its members with a strong national presence by providing a single, unified voice on issues affecting the cable and telecommunications industry.

PROMAX & BDA
9000 West Sunset Boulevard, Suite 900, Los Angeles CA 90069. 310/788-7600.
Fax: 310/788-7616. **World Wide Web address:** http://www.promax.org.
Description: A non-profit association dedicated to advancing the role and effectiveness of promotion, marketing, and broadcast design professionals in the electronic media.

U.S. TELECOM ASSOCIATION
1401 H Street, NW, Suite 600, Washington DC 20005-2164. 202/326-7300. **Fax:** 202/326-7333. **E-mail address:** membership@usta.org. **World Wide Web address:** http://www.usta.org. **Description:** A trade association representing service providers and suppliers for the telecom industry. Member companies offer a wide range of services, including local exchange, long distance, wireless, Internet and cable television service.

COMPUTER HARDWARE, SOFTWARE, AND SERVICES

ASSOCIATION FOR COMPUTING MACHINERY
1515 Broadway, New York NY, 10036. 212/626-0500. 212/626-0500. **Toll-free phone:** 800/342-6626. **World Wide Web address:** http://www.acm.org. **Description:** A 75-000-member organization founded in 1947 to advance the skills of information technology professionals and students worldwide.

ASSOCIATION FOR MULTIMEDIA COMMUNICATIONS
PO Box 10645, Chicago IL 60610. 773/276-9320. **E-mail address:** info@amcomm.org. **World Wide Web address:** http://www.amcomm.org. **Description:** A networking and professional organization for people who create New Media, including the Web, CD-ROMs and DVDs, interactive kiosks, streaming media, and other digital forms. The association promotes understanding of technology, e-learning, and e-business.

ASSOCIATION FOR WOMEN IN COMPUTING
41 Sutter Street, Suite 1006, San Francisco CA 94104. 415/905-4663. **Fax:** 415/358-4667. **E-mail address:** info@awc-hq.org. **World Wide Web address:** http://www.awc-hq.org. **Description:** A not-for-profit, professional organization for individuals with an interest in information technology. The association is dedicated to the advancement of women in the computing fields, in business, industry, science, education, government, and the military.

BLACK DATA PROCESSING ASSOCIATES
6301 Ivy Lane, Suite 700, Greenbelt MD 20770. 301/220-2180. **Fax:** 301/220-2185. **Toll-free phone:** 800/727-BDPA. **World Wide Web address:** http://www.bdpa.org. **Description:** A member-focused organization that positions its members at the forefront of the IT industry. BDPA is committed to delivering IT excellence to our members, strategic partners, and community.

INFORMATION TECHNOLOGY ASSOCIATION OF AMERICA
1401 Wilson Boulevard, Suite 1100, Arlington VA 22209. 703/522-5055. **Fax:** 703/525-2279. **Wide Web address:** http://www.itaa.org. **Description:** A trade association representing the U.S. IT industry and providing information about its issues, association programs, publications, meetings, and seminars.

INTERNATIONAL WEBMASTER'S ASSOCIATION- HTML WRITERS GUILD
119 E. Union Street, Suite F, Pasadena CA 91030. **World Wide Web address:** http://www.hwg.org. **Description:** Provides online web design training to individuals interested in web design and development.

NETWORK PROFESSIONAL ASSOCIATION
17 South High Street, Suite 200, Columbus OH 43215. 614/221-1900. **Fax:** 614/221-1989. **E-mail address:** npa@npa.org. **World Wide Web address:** http://www.npa.org. **Description:** A non-profit association for professionals in Network Computing.

SOCIETY FOR INFORMATION MANAGEMENT
401 North Michigan Avenue, Chicago IL 60611. 312/527-6734. **E-mail address:** sim@simnet.org **World Wide Web address:** http://www.simnet.org. **Description:** With 3,000 members, SIM is a network for IT leaders including CIOs, senior IT executives, prominent academicians, consultants, and others. SIM is a community of thought leaders who share experiences and knowledge, and who explore future IT direction. Founded in 1968.

SOCIETY FOR TECHNICAL COMMUNICATION
901 North Stuart Street, Suite 904, Arlington VA 22203-1822. 703/522-4114. **Fax:** 703/522-2075. **World Wide Web address:** http://www.stc.org. **Description:** A 25,000-member organization dedicated to advancing the arts and sciences of technical communication

SOFTWARE & INFORMATION INDUSTRY ASSOCIATION
1090 Vermont Avenue, NW, Sixth Floor, Washington DC 20005-4095. 202/289-7442. **Fax:** 202/289-7097. **World Wide Web address:** http://www.siia.net. **Description:** The SIIA is the principal trade association for the software and digital content industry. SIIA provides services in government relations, business development, corporate education and intellectual property protection to leading companies.

USENIX ASSOCIATION
2560 Ninth Street, Suite 215, Berkeley CA, 94710. 510/528-8649. **Fax:** 510/548-5738. **E-mail address:** office@usenix.org. **World Wide Web address:** http://www.usenix.org. **Description:** Founded in 1975 the association fosters technical excellence and innovation, supports and disseminates practical research, provides a neutral forum for discussion of technical issues, and encourages computing outreach to the community. USENIX brings together engineers, system administrators, scientists, and technicians working on the cutting edge of the computing world.

EDUCATIONAL SERVICES

AMERICAN ASSOCIATION OF SCHOOL ADMINISTRATORS
801 North Quincy Street, Suite 700, Arlington VA 22203-1730. 703/528-0700.
Fax: 703/841-1543. **E-mail address:** info@aasa.org. **World Wide Web address:** http://www.aasa.org. **Description:** The professional organization for more than 14,000 educational leaders in the U.S. and other countries. The association supports and develops effective school system leaders who are dedicated to the highest quality public education for all children.

AMERICAN ASSOCIATION FOR HIGHER EDUCATION
One Dupont Circle, Suite 360, Washington DC 20036-1143. 202/293-6440. **Fax:** 202/293-0073. **E-mail address:** info@aahe.org. **World Wide Web address:** http://www.aahe.org. **Description:** An independent, membership-based, nonprofit organization dedicated to building human capital for higher education.

AMERICAN FEDERATION OF TEACHERS
555 New Jersey Avenue, NW, Washington DC 20001. 202/879-4400. **E-mail address:** online@aft.org. **World Wide Web address:** http://www.aft.org. **Description:** Improves the lives of its members and their families, gives voice to their professional, economic and social aspirations, brings together members to assist and support one another and to promote democracy, human rights and freedom.

COLLEGE AND UNIVERSITY PROFESSIONAL ASSOCIATION FOR HUMAN RESOURCES
Tyson Place, 2607 Kingston Pike, Suite 250, Knoxville TN 37919. 865/637-7673. **Fax:** 865/637-7674. **World Wide Web address:** http://www.cupa.org. **Description:** Promotes the effective management and development of human resources in higher education and offers many professional development opportunities.

NATIONAL ASSOCIATION FOR COLLEGE ADMISSION COUNSELING
1631 Prince Street, Alexandria VA 22314-2818. 703/836-2222. **Fax:** 703/836-8015. **World Wide Web address:** http://www.nacac.com. **Description:** Founded in 1937, NACAC is an organization of 8,000 professionals dedicated to serving students as they make choices about pursuing postsecondary education. NACAC supports and advances the work of college admission counseling professionals.

NATIONAL ASSOCIATION OF COLLEGE AND UNIVERSITY BUSINESS OFFICERS
2501 M Street, NW, Suite 400, Washington DC 20037. 202/861-2500. **Fax:** 202/861-2583. **World Wide Web address:** http://www.nacubo.org. **Description:** A nonprofit professional organization representing chief administrative and financial officers at more than 2,100 colleges and universities across the country.

NATIONAL SCIENCE TEACHERS ASSOCIATION
1840 Wilson Boulevard, Arlington VA 22201-3000. 703/243-7100. **World Wide Web address:** http://www.nsta.org. **Description:** Promotes excellence and innovation in science teaching and learning.

ELECTRONIC/INDUSTRIAL ELECTRICAL EQUIPMENT AND COMPONENTS

AMERICAN CERAMIC SOCIETY
P.O. Box 6136, Westerville OH 43086-6136. 614/890-4700. **Fax:** 614/899-6109. **E-mail address:** info@ceramics.org. **World Wide Web address:** http://www.acers.org. **Description:** Provides technical, scientific and educational information to its members and others in the ceramics and related materials field, structures its services, staff and capabilities to meet the needs of the ceramics community, related fields, and the general public.

ELECTRONIC INDUSTRIES ALLIANCE
2500 Wilson Boulevard, Arlington VA 22201. 703/907-7500. **World Wide Web address:** http://www.eia.org. **Description:** A national trade organization including 2,500 U.S. manufacturers. The Alliance is a partnership of electronic and high-tech associations and companies whose mission is promoting the market development and competitiveness of the U.S. high-tech industry through domestic and international policy efforts.

ELECTRONICS TECHNICIANS ASSOCIATION, INTERNATIONAL
5 Depot Street, Greencastle IN 46135. 765/653-8262. **Fax:** 765/653-4287. **Toll-free phone:** 800/288-3824. **E-mail address:** eta@tds.net. **World Wide Web address:** http://www.eta-sda.org. **Description:** A not-for-profit, worldwide professional association founded by electronics technicians and servicing dealers in 1978. Provides professional credentials based on an individual's skills and knowledge in a particular area of study.

FABLESS SEMICONDUCTOR ASSOCIATION
Three Lincoln Center, 5430 LBJ Freeway, Suite 280, Dallas TX 75240. 972/866-7579. **Fax:** 972/239-2292. **World Wide Web address:** http://www.fsa.org. **Description:** An industry organization aimed at achieving an optimal balance between wafer supply and demand.

INSTITUTE OF ELECTRICAL AND ELECTRONICS ENGINEER (IEEE)
3 Park Avenue, 17th Floor, New York NY 10016-5997. 212/419-7900. **Fax:** 212/752-4929. **E-mail address:** ieeeusa@ieee.org. **World Wide Web address:** http://www.ieee.org. **Description:** Advances the theory and application of electrotechnology and allied sciences, serves as a catalyst for technological innovation and supports the needs of its members through a wide variety of programs and services.

INTERNATIONAL SOCIETY OF CERTIFIED ELECTRONICS TECHNICIANS
3608 Pershing Avenue, Fort Worth TX 76107-4527. 817/921-9101. **Fax:** 817/921-3741 **Toll-free phone:** 800/946-0201 **E-mail address:** info@iscet.org **World Wide Web address:** http://www.iscet.org. **Description:** Prepares and tests technicians in the electronics and appliance service industry. Designed to measure the degree of theoretical knowledge and technical proficiency of practicing technicians.

NATIONAL ELECTRONICS SERVICE DEALERS ASSOCIATION
3608 Pershing Avenue, Fort Worth TX 76107-4527. 817/921-9061. **Fax:** 817/921-3741. **World Wide Web address:** http://www.nesda.com. **Description:** A trade organization for professionals in the business of repairing consumer electronic equipment, appliances, or computers.

ENVIRONMENTAL & WASTE MANAGEMENT SERVICES

AIR & WASTE MANAGEMENT ASSOCIATION
One Gateway Center, 3rd Floor, 420 Fort Duquesne Boulevard, Pittsburgh PA 15222-1435. 412/232-3444. **Fax:** 412/232-3450. **E-mail address:** info@awma.org. **World Wide Web address:** http://www.awma.org. **Description:** A nonprofit, nonpartisan professional organization providing training, information, and networking opportunities to thousands of environmental professionals in 65 countries.

AMERICAN ACADEMY OF ENVIRONMENTAL ENGINEERS
130 Holiday Court, Suite 100, Annapolis MD 21401. 410/266-3311. **Fax:** 410/266-7653. **World Wide Web address:** http://www.aaee.net. **Description:** AAEE was founded in 1955 for the principal purpose of serving the public by improving the practice, elevating the standards, and advancing public recognition of environmental engineering through a program of specialty certification of qualified engineers.

INSTITUTE OF CLEAN AIR COMPANIES
1660 L Street, NW, Suite 1100, Washington DC 20036. 202/457-0911. **Fax:** 202/331-1388. **World Wide Web address:** http://www.icac.com. **Description:** The nonprofit national association of companies that supply air pollution monitoring and control systems, equipment, and services for stationary sources.

NATIONAL SOLID WASTES MANAGEMENT ASSOCIATION
4301 Connecticut Avenue, NW, Suite 300, Washington DC 20008-2304. 202/244-4700. **Fax:** 202/364-3792. **Toll-free phone:** 800/424-2869. **World Wide Web address:** http://www.nswma.org. **Description:** A non-profit, trade association that represents the interests of the North American waste services industry.

WATER ENVIRONMENT FEDERATION
601 Wythe Street, Alexandria VA 22314-1994. 703/684-2452. **Fax:** 703/684-2492. **Toll-free phone:** 800/666-0206. **World Wide Web address:** http://www.wef.org. **Description:** A not-for-profit technical and educational organization, founded in 1928, with members from varied disciplines. The federation's mission is to preserve and enhance the global water environment. The WEF network includes water quality professionals from 79 Member Associations in over 30 countries.

FABRICATED METAL PRODUCTS AND PRIMARY METALS

ASM INTERNATIONAL: THE MATERIALS INFORMATION SOCIETY
9639 Kinsman Road, Materials Park OH 44073-0002. 440/338-5151. **Fax:** 440/338-4634. **Toll-free phone:** 800/336-5152. **E-mail address:** cust-srv@asminternational.org. **World Wide Web address:** http://www.asm-intl.org. **Description:** An organization for materials engineers and scientists, dedicated to advancing industry, technology and applications of metals and materials.

AMERICAN FOUNDRYMEN'S SOCIETY
1695 Penny Lane, Schaumburg IL 60173-4555. 847/824-0181. **Fax:** 847/824-7848. **Toll-free phone:** 800/537-4237. **World Wide Web address:** http://www.afsinc.org. **Description:** An international organization dedicated to provide and promote knowledge and services that strengthen the metalcasting industry. AFS was founded in 1896 and has approximately 10,000 members in 47 countries.

AMERICAN WELDING SOCIETY
550 NW LeJeune Road, Miami FL 33126. 305/443-9353. **Toll-free phone:** 800/443-9353. **E-mail address:** info@aws.org. **World Wide Web address:** http://www.aws.org. **Description:** Founded in 1919 as a multifaceted, nonprofit organization with a goal to advance the science, technology and application of welding and related joining disciplines.

FINANCIAL SERVICES

THE BOND MARKET ASSOCIATION
360 Madison Avenue, New York NY 10017-7111. 646/637-9200. **Fax:** 646/637-9126. **World Wide Web address:** http://www.bondmarkets.com. **Description:** The trade association representing the largest securities markets in the world. The Association speaks for the bond industry, advocating its positions and representing its interests in New York; Washington, D.C.; London; Frankfurt; Brussels and Tokyo; and with issuer and investor groups worldwide. The Association represents a diverse mix of securities firms and banks, whether they are large, multi-product firms or companies with special market niches.

FINANCIAL EXECUTIVES INSTITUTE
200 Campus Drive, PO Box 674, Florham Park NJ 07932-0674. 973/765-1000. **Fax:** 973/765-1018. **E-mail address:** conf@fei.org. **World Wide Web address:** http://www.fei.org. **Description:** An association for financial executives working to alert members to emerging issues, develop the professional and management skills of members, provide forums for peer networking, advocate the views of financial executives, and promote ethical conduct.

NATIONAL ASSOCIATION FOR BUSINESS ECONOMICS
1233 20th Street, NW, #505, Washington DC 20036. 202/463-6223. **Fax:** 202/463-6239. **E-mail address:** nabe@nabe.com. **World Wide Web address:** http://www.nabe.com. **Description:** An association of professionals who have an interest in business economics and who want to use the latest economic data and trends to enhance their ability to make sound business decisions. Founded in 1959.

NATIONAL ASSOCIATION OF CREDIT MANAGEMENT
8840 Columbia 100 Parkway, Columbia MD 21045. 410/740-5560. **Fax:** 410/740-5574. **E-mail address:** nacm_info@nacm.org. **World Wide Web address:** http://www.nacm.org. **Description:** Founded in 1896 to promote good laws for sound credit, protect businesses against fraudulent debtors, improve the interchange of credit information, develop better credit practices and methods, and establish a code of ethics.

NATIONAL ASSOCIATION OF REAL ESTATE INVESTMENT TRUSTS
1875 Eye Street, NW, Washington DC 20006. 202/739-9400. **Fax:** 202/739-9401. **E-mail address:** info@nareit.org. **World Wide Web address:** http://www.nareit.com. **Description:** NAREIT is the national trade association for REITs and publicly traded real estate companies. Members are real estate investment trusts (REITs) and other businesses that own, operate and finance income-producing real estate, as well as those firms and individuals who advise, study and service these businesses.

SECURITIES INDUSTRY ASSOCIATION
120 Broadway, 35th Floor, New York NY 10271-0080. 212/608-1500. **Fax:** 212/968-0703. **E-mail address:** info@sia.com. **World Wide Web address:** http://www.sia.com. **Description:** The Securities Industry Association (SIA) was established in 1972 through the merger of the Association of Stock Exchange Firms (1913) and the Investment Banker's Association (1912). The Securities Industry Association brings together the shared interests of more than 600 securities firms to accomplish common goals. SIA member-firms (including

investment banks, broker-dealers, and mutual fund companies) are active in all U.S. and foreign markets and in all phases of corporate and public finance.

WOMEN'S INSTITUTE OF FINANCIAL EDUCATION
PO Box 910014, San Diego CA 92191. 760/736-1660. **E-mail address:** info@wife.org. **World Wide Web address:** http://www.wife.org. **Description:** A non-profit organization dedicated to providing financial education to women in their quest for financial independence.

FOOD AND BEVERAGES/AGRICULTURE

AMERICAN ASSOCIATION OF CEREAL CHEMISTS (AACC)
3340 Pilot Knob Road, St. Paul MN 55121-2097. 651/454-7250. **Fax:** 651/454-0766. **World Wide Web address:** http://www.aaccnet.org. **Description:** A non-profit international organization of nearly 4,000 members who are specialists in the use of cereal grains in foods. The association gathers and disseminates scientific and technical information to professionals in the grain-based foods industry worldwide for over 85 years.

AMERICAN BEVERAGE ASSOCIATION
1101 16th Street, NW, Washington DC 20036. 202/463-6732. **Fax:** 202/659-5349. **World Wide Web address:** http://www.ameribev.org. **Description:** An association for America's non-alcoholic beverage industry, serving the public and its members for more than 75 years.

AMERICAN FROZEN FOOD INSTITUTE
2000 Corporate Ridge, Suite 1000, McLean VA 22102. 703/821-0770. **Fax:** 703/821-1350. **E-mail address:** info@affi.com. **World Wide Web address:** http://www.affi.com. **Description:** A national trade association representing all aspects of the frozen food industry supply chain, from manufacturers to distributors to suppliers to packagers; the Institute is industry's voice on issues crucial to future growth and progress.

AMERICAN SOCIETY OF AGRICULTURAL ENGINEERS
2950 Niles Road, St. Joseph MI 49085. 269/429-0300. **Fax:** 269/429-3852. **World Wide Web address:** http://www.asae.org. **Description:** An educational and scientific organization dedicated to the advancement of engineering applicable to agricultural, food, and biological systems.

AMERICAN SOCIETY OF BREWING CHEMISTS
3340 Pilot Knob Road, St. Paul MN 55121-2097. 651/454-7250. **Fax:** 651/454-0766. **World Wide Web address:** http://www.asbcnet.org. **Description:** Founded in 1934 to improve and bring uniformity to the brewing industry on a technical level.

CIES – THE FOOD BUSINESS FORUM
8455 Colesville Road, Suite 705, Silver Spring MD 20910. 301/563-3383. **Fax:** 301/563-3386. **E-mail address:** us.office@ciesnet.com. **World Wide Web address:** http://www.ciesnet.com. **Description:** An independent global food business network. Membership in CIES is on a company basis and includes more than two thirds of the world's largest food retailers and their suppliers.

CROPLIFE AMERICA
1156 15th Street, NW, Suite 400, Washington DC 20005. 202/296-1585. **Fax:** 202/463-0474. **World Wide Web address:** http://www.croplifeamerica.org. **Description:** Fosters the interests of the general public and member companies by promoting innovation and the environmentally sound manufacture, distribution, and use of crop protection and production technologies for safe, high-quality, affordable and abundant food, fiber and other crops.

INTERNATIONAL DAIRY FOODS ASSOCIATION
1250 H Street, NW, Suite 900, Washington DC 20005. 202/737-4332. **Fax:** 202/331-7820. **E-mail address:** membership@idfa.org. **World Wide Web**

address: http://www.idfa.org. **Description:** IDFA represents more than 500 dairy food manufacturers, marketers, distributors and industry suppliers in the U.S. and 20 other countries, and encourages the formation of favorable domestic and international dairy policies.

NATIONAL BEER WHOLESALERS' ASSOCIATION

1101 King Street, Suite 600, Alexandria VA 22314-2944. 703/683-4300. **Fax:** 703/683-8965. **E-mail address:** info@nbwa.org. **World Wide Web address:** http://www.nbwa.org. **Description:** Founded in 1938 as a trade association for the nations' beer wholesalers. NBWA provides leadership which enhances the independent malt beverage wholesale industry; advocates before government and the public on behalf of its members; encourages the responsible consumption of beer; and provides programs and services that will enhance members' efficiency and effectiveness.

NATIONAL FOOD PROCESSORS ASSOCIATION

1350 I Street, NW, Suite 300, Washington DC 20005. 202/639.5900. **E-mail address:** nfpa@nfpa-food.org. **World Wide Web address:** http://www.nfpa-food.org. **Description:** NFPA is the voice of the $500 billion food processing industry on scientific and public policy issues involving food safety, nutrition, technical and regulatory matters and consumer affairs.

HEALTH CARE SERVICES, EQUIPMENT, AND PRODUCTS

ACCREDITING COMMISSION ON EDUCATION FOR HEALTH SERVICES ADMINISTRATION

2000 14th Street North, Arlington VA 22201. 703/894-0960. **Fax:** 703/894-0941. **World Wide Web address:** http://www.acehsa.org. **Description:** An association of educational, professional, clinical, and commercial organizations devoted to accountability and quality improvement in the education of health care management and administration professionals.

AMERICAN ACADEMY OF ALLERGY, ASTHMA, AND IMMUNOLOGY

555 East Wells Street, Suite 1100, Milwaukee WI 53202-3823. 414/272-6071. **E-mail address:** info@aaaai.org. **World Wide Web address:** http://www.aaaai.org. **Description:** A professional medical specialty organization representing allergists, asthma specialists, clinical immunologists, allied health professionals, and other physicians with a special interest in allergy. Established in 1943.

AMERICAN ACADEMY OF FAMILY PHYSICIANS

11400 Tomahawk Creek Parkway, Leawood KS 66211-2672. 913/906-6000. **Toll-free phone:** 800/274-2237. **E-mail address:** fp@aafp.org. **World Wide Web address:** http://www.aafp.org. **Description:** Founded in 1947, the Academy represents family physicians, family practice residents and medical students nationwide. AAFP's mission is to preserve and promote the science and art of family medicine and to ensure high quality, cost-effective health care for patients of all ages.

AMERICAN ACADEMY OF PEDIATRIC DENTISTRY

211 East Chicago Avenue, Suite 700, Chicago IL 60611-2663. 312/337-2169. **Fax:** 312/337-6329. **World Wide Web address:** http://www.aapd.org. **Description:** A membership organization representing the specialty of pediatric dentistry.

AMERICAN ACADEMY OF PERIODONTOLOGY

737 North Michigan Avenue, Suite 800, Chicago IL 60611-2690. 312/787-5518. **Fax:** 312/787-3670. **World Wide Web address:** http://www.perio.org. **Description:** A 7,900-member association of dental professionals specializing in the prevention, diagnosis and treatment of diseases affecting the gums and supporting structures of the teeth and in the placement and maintenance of dental implants. The Academy's purpose is to advocate, educate, and set standards for advancing the periodontal and general health of the public and promoting excellence in the practice of periodontics.

AMERICAN ACADEMY OF PHYSICIANS ASSISTANTS

950 North Washington Street, Alexandria VA 22314-1552. 703/836-2272. **Fax:** 703/684-1924. **E-mail address:** aapa@aapa.org. **World Wide Web address:** http://www.aapa.org. **Description:** Promotes quality, cost-effective, accessible health care, and the professional and personal development of physician assistants.

AMERICAN ASSOCIATION FOR CLINICAL CHEMISTRY

2101 L Street, NW, Suite 202, Washington DC 20037-1558. 202/857-0717. **Fax:** 202/887-5093. **Toll-free phone:** 800/892-1400. **World Wide Web address:**

http://www.aacc.org. **Description:** Founded in 1948 as an international scientific/medical society of clinical laboratory professionals, physicians, research scientists and other individuals involved with clinical chemistry and other clinical laboratory science-related disciplines. The society has 10,000 members.

AMERICAN ASSOCIATION FOR ORAL AND MAXILLOFACIAL SURGEONS
9700 West Bryn Mawr Avenue, Rosemont IL 60018-5701. 847/678-6200. **E-mail address:** inquiries@aaoms.org. **World Wide Web address:** http://www.aaoms.org. **Description:** The American Association of Oral and Maxillofacial Surgeons (AAOMS), is a not-for-profit professional association serving the professional and public needs of the specialty of oral and maxillofacial surgery.

AMERICAN ASSOCIATION FOR RESPIRATORY CARE
9425 North MacArthur Boulevard, Suite 100, Irving TX 75063-4706. 972/243-2272. **Fax:** 972/484-2720. **E-mail address:** info@aarc.org. **World Wide Web address:** http://www.aarc.org. **Description:** Advances the science, technology, ethics, and art of respiratory care through research and education for its members and teaches the general public about pulmonary health and disease prevention.

AMERICAN ASSOCIATION OF COLLEGES OF OSTEOPATHIC MEDICINE
5550 Friendship Boulevard, Suite 310, Chevy Chase MD 20815-7231. 301/968-4100. **Fax:** 301/968-4101. **World Wide Web address:** http://www.aacom.org. **Description:** Promotes excellence in osteopathic medical education throughout the educational continuum, in research and in service; to enhance the strength and quality of the member colleges; and to improve the health of the American public.

AMERICAN ASSOCIATION OF COLLEGES OF PODIATRIC MEDICINE
15850 Crabbs Branch Way, Suite 320, Rockville MD 20855. **Fax:** 301/948-1928. **Toll-free phone:** 800/922-9266. **E-mail address:** aacpmas@aacpm.org. **World Wide Web address:** http://www.aacpm.org. **Description:** An organization advancing podiatric medicine and its education system.

AMERICAN ASSOCIATION OF HEALTHCARE CONSULTANTS
5938 North Drake Avenue, Chicago IL 60659. **Fax:** 773/463-3552. **Toll-free phone:** 888/350-2242. **E-mail address:** info@aahc.net. **World Wide Web address:** http://www.aahc.net. **Description:** Founded in 1949 as the professional membership society for leading healthcare consultants and consulting firms.

AMERICAN ASSOCIATION OF HOMES AND SERVICES FOR THE AGING
2519 Connecticut Avenue, NW, Washington DC 20008. 202/783.2242. **Fax:** 202/783-2255. **World Wide Web address:** http://www.aahsa.org. **Description:** The American Association of Homes and Services for the Aging (AAHSA) is committed to advancing the vision of healthy, affordable, ethical aging services for America. The association represents 5,600 not-for-profit nursing homes, continuing care retirement communities, assisted living and senior housing facilities, and home and community-based service providers.

AMERICAN ASSOCIATION OF MEDICAL ASSISTANTS
20 North Wacker Drive, Suite 1575, Chicago IL 60606. 312/899-1500. **World Wide Web address:** http://www.aama-ntl.org. **Description:** The mission of the American Association of Medical Assistants is to enable medical assisting professionals to enhance and demonstrate the knowledge, skills and

professionalism required by employers and patients; protect medical assistants' right to practice; and promote effective, efficient health care delivery through optimal use of multiskilled Certified Medical Assistants (CMAs).

AMERICAN ASSOCIATION OF NURSE ANESTHETISTS
222 South Prospect Avenue, Park Ridge IL 60068. 847/692-7050. **World Wide Web address:** http://www.aana.com. **Description:** Founded in 1931 as the professional association representing more than 30,000 Certified Registered Nurse Anesthetists (CRNAs) nationwide. The AANA promulgates education, and practice standards and guidelines, and affords consultation to both private and governmental entities regarding nurse anesthetists and their practice.

AMERICAN CHIROPRACTIC ASSOCIATION
1701 Clarendon Boulevard, Arlington VA 22209. **Fax:** 703/243-2593. **Toll-free phone:** 800/986-4636. **E-mail address:** memberinfo@amerchiro.org. **World Wide Web address:** http://www.americhiro.org. **Description:** A professional association representing doctors of chiropractic that provides lobbying, public relations, professional and educational opportunities for doctors of chiropractic, funds research regarding chiropractic and health issues, and offers leadership for the advancement of the profession.

AMERICAN COLLEGE OF HEALTH CARE ADMINISTRATORS
300 North Lee Street, Suite 301, Alexandria VA 22314. 703/739-7900. **Fax:** 703/739-7901. **Toll-free phone:** 888/882-2422. **E-mail address:** membership@achca.org. **World Wide Web address:** http://www.achca.org. **Description:** A non-profit membership organization that provides educational programming, certification in a variety of positions, and career development for its members. Founded in 1962.

AMERICAN COLLEGE OF HEALTHCARE EXECUTIVES
One North Franklin Street, Suite 1700, Chicago IL 60606-4425. 312/424-2800. **Fax:** 312/424-0023. **World Wide Web address:** http://www.ache.org. **Description:** An international professional society of nearly 30,000 healthcare executives who lead our nation's hospitals, healthcare systems, and other healthcare organizations.

AMERICAN COLLEGE OF MEDICAL PRACTICE EXECUTIVES
104 Inverness Terrace East, Englewood CO 80112-5306. 303/799-1111. **Fax:** 303/643-4439. **Toll-free phone:** 877/275-6462. **E-mail address:** acmpe@mgma.com. **World Wide Web address:** http://www.mgma.com/acmpe. **Description:** Established in 1956, the ACMPE offers board certification, self-assessment and leadership development for medical practice executives.

AMERICAN COLLEGE OF OBSTETRICIANS AND GYNECOLOGISTS
409 12th Street, SW, PO Box 96920, Washington DC 20090-6920. **World Wide Web address:** http://www.acog.org. **Description:** Founded in 1951, the 46,000-member organization is the nation's leading group of professionals providing health care for women.

AMERICAN COLLEGE OF PHYSICIAN EXECUTIVES
4890 West Kennedy Boulevard, Suite 200, Tampa FL 33609. 813/287-2000. **Fax:** 813/287-8993. **Toll-free phone:** 800/562-8088. **E-mail address:** acpe@acpe.org. **World Wide Web address:** http://www.acpe.org. **Description:** A specialty society representing physicians in health care leadership. Provides educational and career development programs.

AMERICAN DENTAL ASSOCIATION
211 East Chicago Avenue, Chicago IL 60611-2678. 312/440-2500. **World Wide Web address:** http://www.ada.org. **Description:** A dental association serving both public and private physicians. Founded in 1859.

AMERICAN DENTAL EDUCATION ASSOCIATION
1400 K Street, NW Suite 1100, Washington DC 20005. 202/289-7201. **Fax:** 202/289-7204. **World Wide Web address:** http://www.adea.org. **Description:** A national organization for dental education. Members include all U.S. and Canadian dental schools, advanced dental education programs, hospital dental education programs, allied dental education programs, corporations, faculty, and students.

AMERICAN DENTAL HYGIENISTS ASSOCIATION
444 North Michigan Avenue, Suite 3400, Chicago IL 60611. 312/440-8900. **E-mail address:** mail@adha.net. **World Wide Web address:** http://www.adha.org. **Description:** Founded in 1923, the association develops communication and mutual cooperation among dental hygienists and represents the professional interests of the more than 120,000 registered dental hygienists (RDHs) in the United States.

AMERICAN HEALTH INFORMATION MANAGEMENT ASSOCIATION
233 North Michigan Avenue, Suite 2150, Chicago IL 60601-5800. 312/233-1100. **Fax:** 312/233-1090. **E-mail address:** info@ahima.org. **World Wide Web address:** http://www.ahima.org. **Description:** Represents more than 46,000 specially educated health information management professionals who work throughout the healthcare industry. Health information management professionals serve the healthcare industry and the public by managing, analyzing, and utilizing data vital for patient care -- and making it accessible to healthcare providers when it is needed most.

AMERICAN HOSPITAL ASSOCIATION
One North Franklin, Chicago IL 60606-3421. 312/422-3000. **Fax:** 312/422-4796. **World Wide Web address:** http://www.aha.org. **Description:** A national organization that represents and serves all types of hospitals, health care networks, and their patients and communities. Approximately 5,000 institutional, 600 associate, and 27,000 personal members belong to the AHA.

AMERICAN MEDICAL ASSOCIATION
515 North State Street, Chicago IL 60610. **Toll-free phone:** 800/621-8335. **World Wide Web address:** http://www.ama-assn.org. **Description:** American Medical Association speaks out on issues important to patients and the nation's health. AMA policy on such issues is decided through its democratic policy-making process, in the AMA House of Delegates, which meets twice a year.

AMERICAN MEDICAL INFORMATICS ASSOCIATION
4915 St. Elmo Avenue, Suite 401, Bethesda MD 20814. 301/657-1291. **Fax:** 301/657-1296. **World Wide Web address:** http://www.amia.org. **Description:** The American Medical Informatics Association is a nonprofit membership organization of individuals, institutions, and corporations dedicated to developing and using information technologies to improve health care. Founded in 1990.

AMERICAN MEDICAL TECHNOLOGISTS
710 Higgins Road, Park Ridge IL 60068. 847/823-5169. **Fax:** 847/823-0458. **Toll-free phone:** 800/275-1268. **World Wide Web address:** http://www.amt1.com. **Description:** A nonprofit certification agency and

professional membership association representing nearly 27,000 individuals in allied health care. Provides allied health professionals with professional certification services and membership programs to enhance their professional and personal growth.

AMERICAN MEDICAL WOMEN'S ASSOCIATION
801 North Fairfax Street, Suite 400, Alexandria VA 22314. 703/838-0500. **Fax:** 703/549-3864. **E-mail address:** info@amwa-doc.org. **World Wide Web address:** http://www.amwa-doc.org. **Description:** An organization of 10,000 women physicians and medical students dedicated to serving as the unique voice for women's health and the advancement of women in medicine.

AMERICAN NURSES ASSOCIATION
8515 Georgia Avenue, Suite 400 West, Silver Spring MD 20910. 301/628-5000. **Fax:** 301//628-5001. **Toll-free phone:** 800/274-4ANA. **World Wide Web address:** http://www.nursingworld.org. **Description:** A professional organization representing the nation's 2.6 million Registered Nurses through its 54 constituent state associations and 13 organizational affiliate members. Fosters high standards of nursing practice, promotes the economic and general welfare of nurses in the workplace, projects a positive and realistic view of nursing, and by lobbies Congress and regulatory agencies on health care issues affecting nurses and the public.

AMERICAN OCCUPATIONAL THERAPY ASSOCIATION
4720 Montgomery Lane, PO Box 31220, Bethesda MD 20824-1220. 301/652-2682. **Fax:** 301/652-7711. **Toll-free phone:** 800/377- 8555. **World Wide Web address:** http://www.aota.org. **Description:** A professional association of approximately 40,000 occupational therapists, occupational therapy assistants, and students of occupational therapy.

AMERICAN OPTOMETRIC ASSOCIATION
243 North Lindbergh Boulevard, St. Louis MO 63141. 314/991-4100. **Fax:** 314/991-4101. **World Wide Web address:** http://www.aoanet.org. **Description:** The American Optometric Association is the acknowledged leader and recognized authority for primary eye and vision care in the world.

AMERICAN ORGANIZATION OF NURSE EXECUTIVES
325 Seventh Street, NW, Washington DC 20004. 202/626-2240. **Fax:** 202/638-5499. **E-mail address:** aone@aha.org. **World Wide Web address:** http://www.aone.org. **Description:** Founded in 1967, the American Organization of Nurse Executives (AONE), a subsidiary of the American Hospital Association, is a national organization of nearly 4,000 nurses who design, facilitate, and manage care. Its mission is to represent nurse leaders who improve healthcare.

AMERICAN ORTHOPAEDIC ASSOCIATION
6300 North River Road, Suite 505, Rosemont IL 60018-4263. 847/318-7330. **Fax:** 847/318-7339. **E-mail address:** info@aoassn.org **World Wide Web address:** http://www.aoassn.org. **Description:** Founded in 1887, The American Orthopaedic Association is the oldest orthopaedic association in the world.

AMERICAN PHYSICAL THERAPY ASSOCIATION
1111 North Fairfax Street, Alexandria VA 22314-1488. 703/684-2782. **Fax:** 703/684-7343. **Toll-free phone:** 800/999-2782. **World Wide Web address:** http://www.apta.org. **Description:** The American Physical Therapy Association (APTA) is a national professional organization representing more than 63,000

members. Its goal is to foster advancements in physical therapy practice, research, and education.

AMERICAN PODIATRIC MEDICAL ASSOCIATION
9312 Old Georgetown Road, Bethesda MD 20814. 301/571-9200. **Fax:** 301/530-2752. **Toll-free phone:** 800/FOOTCARE. **World Wide Web address:** http://www.apma.org. **Description:** The American Podiatric Medical Association is the premier professional organization representing the nation's Doctors of Podiatric Medicine (podiatrists). The APMA represents approximately 80 percent of the podiatrists in the country. APMA includes 53 component societies in states and other jurisdictions, as well as 22 affiliated and related societies.

AMERICAN PSYCHIATRIC ASSOCIATION
1000 Wilson Boulevard, Suite 1825, Arlington VA.22209-3901. 703/907-7300. **E-mail address:** apa@psych.org **World Wide Web address:** http://www.psych.org. **Description:** With 35,000 members, the American Psychiatric Association is a medical specialty society recognized worldwide.

AMERICAN PUBLIC HEALTH ASSOCIATION
800 I Street, NW, Washington DC 20001. 202/777-2742. **Fax:** 202/777-2534. **E-mail address:** comments@apha.org. **World Wide Web address:** http://www.apha.org. **Description:** The American Public Health Association (APHA) is the oldest and largest organization of public health professionals in the world, representing more than 50,000 members from over 50 occupations of public health.

AMERICAN SOCIETY OF ANESTHESIOLOGISTS
520 N. Northwest Highway, Park Ridge IL 60068-2573. 847/825-5586. **Fax:** 847/825-1692. **E-mail address:** mail@asahq.org. **World Wide Web address:** http://www.asahq.org. **Description:** An educational, research and scientific association of physicians organized to raise and maintain the standards of the medical practice of anesthesiology and improve the care of the patient. Founded in 1905.

AMERICAN SPEECH-LANGUAGE-HEARING ASSOCIATION
10801 Rockville Pike, Rockville MD 20852-3226. **Toll-free phone:** 800/638-8255. **E-mail address:** actioncenter@asha.org. **World Wide Web address:** http://www.asha.org. **Description:** The professional, scientific, and credentialing association for more than 110,000 audiologists, speech-language pathologists, and speech, language, and hearing scientists with a mission to ensure that all people with speech, language, and hearing disorders have access to quality services to help them communicate more effectively.

AMERICAN VETERINARY MEDICAL ASSOCIATION
1931 North Meacham Road, Suite 100, Schaumburg IL 60173. 847/925-8070. **Fax:** 847/925-1329. **E-mail address:** avmainfo@avma.org. **World Wide Web address:** http://www.avma.org. **Description:** A not-for-profit association founded in 1863 representing more than 69,000 veterinarians working in private and corporate practice, government, industry, academia, and uniformed services.

ASSOCIATION OF AMERICAN MEDICAL COLLEGES
2450 N Street, NW, Washington DC 20037-1126. 202/828-0400. **Fax:** 202/828-1125. **World Wide Web address:** http://www.aamc.org. **Description:** A non-profit association founded in 1876 to work for reform in medical education. The association represents the nation's 126 accredited medical schools, nearly 400

major teaching hospitals, more than 105,000 faculty in 96 academic and scientific societies, and the nation's 66,000 medical students and 97,000 residents.

ASSOCIATION OF UNIVERSITY PROGRAMS IN HEALTH ADMINISTRATION
2000 North 14th Street, Suite 780, Arlington VA 22201. 703/894-0940. **Fax:** 703/894-0941. **E-mail address:** aupha@aupha.org. **World Wide Web address:** http://www.aupha.org. **Description:** A not-for-profit association of university-based educational programs, faculty, practitioners, and provider organizations. Its members are dedicated to continuously improving the field of health management and practice. It is the only non-profit entity of its kind that works to improve the delivery of health services throughout the world - and thus the health of citizens - by educating professional managers.

HEALTH INFORMATION AND MANAGEMENT SYSTEMS SOCIETY
230 East Ohio Street, Suite 500, Chicago IL 60611-3269. 312/664-4467. **Fax:** 312/664-6143. **World Wide Web address:** http://www.himss.org. **Description:** Founded in 1961 and provides leadership for the optimal use of healthcare information technology and management systems for the betterment of human health.

HEALTHCARE FINANCIAL MANAGEMENT ASSOCIATION
2 Westbrook Corporate Center, Suite 700, Westchester IL 60154-5700. 708/531-9600. **Fax:** 708/531-0032. **Toll-free phone:** 800/252-4362. **World Wide Web address:** http://www.hfma.org. **Description:** A membership organization for healthcare financial management professionals with 32,000 members.

NATIONAL ASSOCIATION FOR CHIROPRACTIC MEDICINE
15427 Baybrook Drive, Houston TX 77062. 281/280-8262. **Fax:** 281/280-8262. **World Wide Web address:** http://www.chiromed.org. **Description:** A consumer advocacy association of chiropractors striving to make legitimate the utilization of professional manipulative procedures in mainstream health care delivery.

NATIONAL MEDICAL ASSOCIATION
1012 Tenth Street, NW, Washington DC 20001. 202/347-1895. **Fax:** 202/898-2510. **World Wide Web address:** http://www.nmanet.org. **Description:** Promotes the collective interests of physicians and patients of African descent with a mission to serve as the collective voice of physicians of African descent and a leading force for parity in medicine, elimination of health disparities and promotion of optimal health.

HOTELS AND RESTAURANTS

AMERICAN HOTEL AND LODGING ASSOCIATION
1201 New York Avenue, NW, #600, Washington DC 20005-3931. 202/289-3100.
Fax: 202/289-3199. **World Wide Web address:** http://www.ahla.com.
Description: Provides its members with assistance in operations, education, and communications, and lobbies on Capitol Hill to provide a business climate in which the industry can continue to prosper. Individual state associations provide representation at the state level and offer many additional cost-saving benefits.

THE EDUCATIONAL FOUNDATION OF THE NATIONAL RESTAURANT ASSOCIATION
175 West Jackson Boulevard, Suite 1500, Chicago IL 60604-2702. 312/715-1010. **Toll-free phone:** 800/765-2122. **E-mail address:** info@nraef.org. **World Wide Web address:** http://www.nraef.org. **Description:** A not-for-profit organization dedicated to fulfilling the educational mission of the National Restaurant Association. Focusing on three key strategies of risk management, recruitment, and retention, the NRAEF is the premier provider of educational resources, materials, and programs, which address attracting, developing and retaining the industry's workforce.

NATIONAL RESTAURANT ASSOCIATION
1200 17th Street, NW, Washington DC 20036. 202/331-5900. 202/331-5900.
Fax: 202/331-2429. **Toll-free phone:** 800/424-5156. **World Wide Web address:** http://www.restaurant.org. **Description:** Founded in 1919 as a business association for the restaurant industry with a mission to represent, educate and promote a rapidly growing industry that is comprised of 878,000 restaurant and foodservice outlets employing 12 million people.

INSURANCE

AMERICA'S HEALTH INSURANCE PLANS
601 Pennsylvania Avenue, NW, SOuth Building, Suite 500, Washington DC 20004. 202/778-3200. **Fax:** 202/331-7487. **World Wide Web address:** http://www.ahip.org. **Description:** A national association representing nearly 1,300 member companies providing health insurance coverage to more than 200 million Americans.

INSURANCE INFORMATION INSTITUTE
110 William Street, New York NY 10038. 212/346-5500. **World Wide Web address:** http://www.iii.org. **Description:** Provides definitive insurance information. Recognized by the media, governments, regulatory organizations, universities and the public as a primary source of information, analysis and referral concerning insurance.

NATIONAL ASSOCIATION OF PROFESSIONAL INSURANCE AGENTS
400 North Washington Street, Alexandria VA 22314. 703/836-9340. **Fax:** 703/836-1279. **E-mail address:** piaweb@pianet.org. **World Wide Web address:** http://www.pianet.com. **Description:** Represents independent agents in all 50 states, Puerto Rico and the District of Columbia. Founded in 1931.

PROPERTY CASUALTY INSURERS ASSOCIATION OF AMERICA
2600 South River Road, Des Plaines IL 60018-3286. 847/297-7800. **Fax:** 847/297-5064. **World Wide Web address:** http://www.pciaa.net. **Description:** A property/casualty trade association representing more than 1,000 member companies, PCI advocates its members' public policy positions at the federal and state levels and to the public.

LEGAL SERVICES

AMERICAN BAR ASSOCIATION
321 North Clark Street, Chicago IL 60610. 312/988-5000. **E-mail address:** askaba@abanet.org. **World Wide Web address:** http://www.abanet.org. **Description:** A voluntary professional association with more than 400,000 members, the ABA provides law school accreditation, continuing legal education, information about the law, programs to assist lawyers and judges in their work, and initiatives to improve the legal system for the public.

FEDERAL BAR ASSOCIATION
2215 M Street, NW, Washington DC 20037. 202/785-1614. **Fax:** 202/785-1568. **E-mail address:** fba@fedbar.org. **World Wide Web address:** http://www.fedbar.org. **Description:** The professional organization for private and government lawyers and judges involved in federal practice.

NATIONAL ASSOCIATION OF LEGAL ASSISTANTS
1516 South Boston, #200, Tulsa OK 74119. 918/587-6828. **World Wide Web address:** http://www.nala.org. **Description:** A professional association for legal assistants and paralegals, providing continuing education and professional development programs. Founded in 1975.

NATIONAL FEDERATION OF PARALEGAL ASSOCIATIONS
2517 Eastlake Avenue East, Suite 200, Seattle WA 98102. 206/652-4120. **Fax:** 206/652-4122. **E-mail address:** info@paralegals.org. **World Wide Web address:** http://www.paralegals.org. **Description:** A non-profit professional organization representing more than 15,000 paralegals in the United States and Canada. NFPA is the national voice and the standard for excellence for the paralegal profession through its work on the issues of regulation, ethics and education.

MANUFACTURING: MISCELLANEOUS CONSUMER

ASSOCIATION FOR MANUFACTURING EXCELLENCE
380 Palantine Road West, Wheeling IL 60090-5863. 847/520-3282. **Fax:** 847/520-0163. **World Wide Web address:** http://www.ame.org. **Description:** A not-for-profit organization founded in 1985 consisting of 6000 executives, senior and middle managers who wish to improve the competitiveness of their organizations.

ASSOCIATION FOR MANUFACTURING TECHNOLOGY
7901 Westpark Drive, McLean VA 22102-4206. 703/893-2900. **Fax:** 703/893-1151. **Toll-free phone:** 703/893-2900. **World Wide Web address:** http://www.amtonline.org. **Description:** Supports and promotes American manufacturers of machine tools and manufacturing technology. Provides members with industry expertise and assistance on critical industry concerns.

ASSOCIATION OF HOME APPLIANCE MANUFACTURERS
1111 19th Street, NW, Suite 402, Washington DC 20036. 202/872-5955. **Fax:** 202/872-9354. **World Wide Web address:** http://www.aham.org. **Description:** Represents the manufacturers of household appliances and products/services associated with household appliances.

SOCIETY OF MANUFACTURING ENGINEERS
One SME Drive, Dearborn MI 48121. 313/271-1500. **Fax:** 313/425-3401. **Toll-free phone:** 800/733-4763. **World Wide Web address:** http://www.sme.org. **Description:** Promotes an increased awareness of manufacturing engineering and helps keep manufacturing professionals up to date on leading trends and technologies. Founded in 1932.

MANUFACTURING: MISCELLANEOUS INDUSTRIAL

ASSOCIATION FOR MANUFACTURING EXCELLENCE
380 Palantine Road West, Wheeling IL 60090-5863. 847/520-3282. **Fax:** 847/520-0163. **World Wide Web address:** http://www.ame.org. **Description:** A not-for-profit organization founded in 1985 consisting of 6000 executives, senior and middle managers who wish to improve the competitiveness of their organizations.

INSTITUTE OF INDUSTRIAL ENGINEERS
3577 Parkway Lane, Suite 200, Norcross GA 30092. 770/449-0460. **Fax:** 770/441-3295. **Toll-free phone:** 800/494-0460. **World Wide Web address:** http://www.iienet.org. **Description:** A non-profit professional society dedicated to the support of the industrial engineering profession and individuals involved with improving quality and productivity. Founded in 1948.

NATIONAL ASSOCIATION OF MANUFACTURERS
1331 Pennsylvania Avenue, NW, Washington DC 20004-1790. 202/637-3000. **Fax:** 202/637-3182. **E-mail address:** manufacturing@nam.org. **World Wide Web address:** http://www.nam.org. **Description:** With 14,000 members, NAM's mission is to enhance the competitiveness of manufacturers and to improve American living standards by shaping a legislative and regulatory environment conducive to U.S. economic growth, and to increase understanding among policymakers, the media and the public about the importance of manufacturing to America's economic strength.

NATIONAL TOOLING AND MACHINING ASSOCIATION
9300 Livingston Road, Fort Washington MD 20744-4998. 800/248-6862. **Fax:** 301/248-7104. **World Wide Web address:** http://www.ntma.org. **Description:** A trade organization representing the precision custom manufacturing industry throughout the United States.

SOCIETY OF MANUFACTURING ENGINEERS
One SME Drive, Dearborn MI 48121. 313/271-1500. **Fax:** 313/425-3401. **Toll-free phone:** 800/733-4763. **World Wide Web address:** http://www.sme.org. **Description:** Promotes an increased awareness of manufacturing engineering and helps keep manufacturing professionals up to date on leading trends and technologies. Founded in 1932.

MINING, GAS, PETROLEUM, ENERGY RELATED

AMERICAN ASSOCIATION OF PETROLEUM GEOLOGISTS
P.O. Box 979, Tulsa OK 74101-0979. 918/584-2555. **Physical address:** 1444 South Boulder, Tulsa OK 74119. **Fax:** 918/560-2665. **Toll-free phone:** 800/364-2274. **E-mail address:** postmaster@aapg.org. **World Wide Web address:** http://www.aapg.org. **Description:** Founded in 1917, the AAPG's purpose is to foster scientific research, advance the science of geology, promote technology, and inspire high professional conduct. The AAPG has over 30,000 members.

AMERICAN GEOLOGICAL INSTITUTE
4220 King Street, Alexandria VA 22302-1502. 703/379-2480. **Fax:** 703/379-7563. **World Wide Web address:** http://www.agiweb.org. **Description:** A nonprofit federation of 42 geoscientific and professional associations that represents more than 100,000 geologists, geophysicists, and other earth scientists. Provides information services to geoscientists, serves as a voice of shared interests in the profession, plays a major role in strengthening geoscience education, and strives to increase public awareness of the vital role the geosciences play in society's use of resources and interaction with the environment.

AMERICAN NUCLEAR SOCIETY
555 North Kensington Avenue, La Grange Park IL 60526. 708/352-6611. **Fax:** 708/352-0499. **World Wide Web address:** http://www.ans.org. **Description:** A not-for-profit, international, scientific and educational organization with a membership of 10,500 engineers, scientists, administrators, and educators representing 1,600 corporations, educational institutions, and government agencies.

AMERICAN PETROLEUM INSTITUTE
1220 L Street, NW, Washington DC 20005-4070. 202/682-8000. **World Wide Web address:** http://www.api.org. **Description:** Functions to insure a strong, viable U.S. oil and natural gas industry capable of meeting the energy needs of our Nation in an efficient and environmentally responsible manner.

GEOLOGICAL SOCIETY OF AMERICA
3300 Penrose Place, P.O. Box 9140, Boulder CO 80301. 303/447-2020. **Fax:** 303/357-1070. **Toll-free phone:** 888/443-4472. **E-mail address:** gsaservice@geosociety.org. **World Wide Web address:** http://www.geosociety.org. **Description:** The mission of GSA is to advance the geosciences, to enhance the professional growth of its members, and to promote the geosciences in the service of humankind.

SOCIETY FOR MINING, METALLURGY, AND EXPLORATION
8307 Shaffer Parkway, Littleton CO 80127-4102. 303/973-9550. **Fax:** 303/973-3845. **Toll-free phone:** 800/763-3132. **E-mail address:** sme@smenet.org. **World Wide Web address:** http://www.smenet.org. **Description:** An international society of professionals in the mining and minerals industry.

SOCIETY OF PETROLEUM ENGINEERS
P.O. Box 833836, Richardson TX 75083-3836. 972/952-9393. **Physical address:** 222 palisades Creek Drive, Richardson TX 75080. **Fax:** 972/952-9435. **E-mail address:** spedal@spe.org. **World Wide Web address:** http://www.spe.org. **Description:** SPE is a professional association whose

60,000-plus members worldwide are engaged in energy resources development and production. SPE is a key resource for technical information related to oil and gas exploration and production and provides services through its publications, meetings, and online.

PAPER AND WOOD PRODUCTS

AMERICAN FOREST AND PAPER ASSOCIATION
1111 Nineteenth Street, NW, Suite 800, Washington DC 20036. **Toll-free phone:** 800/878-8878. **E-mail address:** info@afandpa.org. **World Wide Web address:** http://www.afandpa.org. **Description:** The national trade association of the forest, pulp, paper, paperboard and wood products industry.

FOREST PRODUCTS SOCIETY
2801 Marshall Court, Madison WI 53705-2295. 608/231-1361. **Fax:** 608/231-2152. **E-mail address:** info@forestprod.org. **World Wide Web address:** http://www.forestprod.org. **Description:** An international not-for-profit technical association founded in 1947 to provide an information network for all segments of the forest products industry.

NPTA ALLIANCE
500 Bi-County Boulevard, Suite 200E, Farmingdale NY 11735. 631/777-2223. **Fax:** 631/777-2224. **Toll-free phone:** 800/355-NPTA. **World Wide Web address:** http://www.gonpta.com. **Description:** An association for the $60 billion paper, packaging, and supplies distribution industry.

PAPERBOARD PACKAGING COUNCIL
201 North Union Street, Suite 220, Alexandria VA 22314. 703/836-3300. **Fax:** 703/836-3290. **E-mail address:** http://www.ppcnet.org. **World Wide Web address:** http://www.ppcnet.org. **Description:** A trade association representing the manufacturers of paperboard packaging in the United States.

TECHNICAL ASSOCIATION OF THE PULP AND PAPER INDUSTRY
15 Technology Parkway South, Norcross GA 30092. 770/446-1400. **Fax:** 770/446-6947. **Toll-free phone:** 800/332-8686. **World Wide Web address:** http://www.tappi.org. **Description:** The leading technical association for the worldwide pulp, paper, and converting industry.

PRINTING AND PUBLISHING

AMERICAN BOOKSELLERS ASSOCIATION
828 South Broadway, Tarrytown NY 10591. 914/591-2665. **Fax:** 914/591-2720. **Toll-free phone:** 800/637-0037. **E-mail address:** info@bookweb.org. **World Wide Web address:** http://www.bookweb.org. **Description:** A not-for-profit organization founded in 1900 devoted to meeting the needs of its core members of independently owned bookstores with retail storefront locations through advocacy, education, research, and information dissemination.

AMERICAN INSTITUTE OF GRAPHIC ARTS
164 Fifth Avenue, New York NY 10010. 212/807-1990. **Fax:** 212/807-1799. **E-mail address:** comments@aiga.org. **World Wide Web address:** http://www.aiga.org. **Description:** Furthers excellence in communication design as a broadly defined discipline, strategic tool for business and cultural force. AIGA is the place design professionals turn to first to exchange ideas and information, participate in critical analysis and research and advance education and ethical practice. Founded in 1914.

AMERICAN SOCIETY OF NEWSPAPER EDITORS
11690B Sunrise Valley Drive, Reston VA 20191-1409. 703/453-1122. **Fax:** 703/453-1133. **E-mail address:** asne@asne.org. **World Wide Web address:** http://www.asne.org. **Description:** A membership organization for daily newspaper editors, people who serve the editorial needs of daily newspapers and certain distinguished individuals who have worked on behalf of editors through the years.

ASSOCIATION OF AMERICAN PUBLISHERS, INC.
71 Fifth Avenue, 2nd Floor, New York NY 10003. 212/255-0200. **Fax:** 212/255-7007. **World Wide Web address:** http://www.publishers.org. **Description:** Representing publishers of all sizes and types located throughout the U.S., the AAP is the principal trade association of the book publishing industry.

ASSOCIATION OF GRAPHIC COMMUNICATIONS
330 Seventh Avenue, 9th Floor, New York NY 10001-5010. 212/279-2100. **Fax:** 212/279-5381. **E-mail address:** info@agcomm.org. **World Wide Web address:** http://www.agcomm.org. **Description:** The AGC serves as a network for industry information and idea exchange, provides graphic arts education and training, promotes and markets the industry, and advocates legislative and environmental issues.

BINDING INDUSTRIES OF AMERICA
100 Daingerfield Road, Alexandria VA 22314. 703/519-8137. **Fax:** 703/548-3227. **World Wide Web address:** http://www.bindingindustries.org. **Description:** A trade association representing Graphic Finishers, Loose-Leaf Manufacturers, and suppliers to these industries throughout the United States, Canada, and Europe.

THE DOW JONES NEWSPAPER FUND
P.O. Box 300, Princeton NJ 08543-0300. 609/452-2820. **Fax:** 609/520-5804. **E-mail address:** newsfund@wsj.dowjones.com. **World Wide Web address:** http://djnewspaperfund.dowjones.com. **Description:** Founded in 1958 by editors of The Wall Street Journal to improve the quality of journalism education and the pool of applicants for jobs in the newspaper business. It provides internships and scholarships to college students, career literature, fellowships for high school

journalism teachers and publications' advisers and training for college journalism instructors. The Fund is a nonprofit foundation supported by the Dow Jones Foundation, Dow Jones & Company, Inc. and other newspaper companies.

GRAPHIC ARTISTS GUILD

90 John Street, Suite 403, New York NY 10038-3202. 212/791-3400. **World Wide Web address:** http://www.gag.org. **Description:** A national union of illustrators, designers, web creators, production artists, surface designers and other creatives who have come together to pursue common goals, share their experience, raise industry standards, and improve the ability of visual creators to achieve satisfying and rewarding careers.

INTERNATIONAL GRAPHIC ARTS EDUCATION ASSOCIATION

1899 Preston White Drive, Reston VA 20191-4367. 703/758-0595. **World Wide Web address:** http://www.igaea.org. **Description:** An association of educators in partnership with industry, dedicated to sharing theories, principles, techniques and processes relating to graphic communications and imaging technology.

MAGAZINE PUBLISHERS OF AMERICA

810 Seventh Avenue, 24th Floor, New York NY 10019. 212/872-3746. **E-mail address:** infocenter@magazine.org. **World Wide Web address:** http://www.magazine.org. **Description:** An industry association for consumer magazines representing more than 240 domestic publishing companies with approximately 1,400 titles, more than 80 international companies and more than 100 associate members.

NATIONAL ASSOCIATION FOR PRINTING LEADERSHIP

75 West Century Road, Paramus NJ 07652-1408. 201/634-9600. **Fax:** 201/986-2976. **E-mail address:** information@napl.org. **World Wide Web address:** http://www.napl.org. **Description:** A not-for-profit trade association founded in 1933 for commercial printers and related members of the Graphic Arts Industry.

NATIONAL NEWSPAPER ASSOCIATION

P.O. Box 7540,, Columbia MO 65205-7540. 573/882-5800. **Fax:** 573/884-5490. **Toll-free phone:** 800/829-4662. **World Wide Web address:** http://www.nna.org. **Description:** A non-profit association promoting the common interests of newspapers.

NATIONAL PRESS CLUB

529 14th Street, NW, Washington DC 20045. 202/662-7500. **Fax:** 202/662-7512. **World Wide Web address:** http://npc.press.org. **Description:** Provides people who gather and disseminate news a center for the advancement of their professional standards and skills, the promotion of free expression, mutual support and social fellowship. Founded in 1908.

NEWSPAPER ASSOCIATION OF AMERICA

1921 Gallows Road, Suite 600, Vienna VA 22182-3900. 703/902-1600. **Fax:** 703/917-0636. **World Wide Web address:** http://www.naa.org. **Description:** A nonprofit organization representing the $55 billion newspaper industry.

THE NEWSPAPER GUILD

501 Third Street, NW, Suite 250, Washington DC 20001. 202/434-7177. **Fax:** 202/434-1472. **E-mail address:** guild@cwa-union.org. **World Wide Web address:** http://www.newsguild.org. **Description:** Founded as a print journalists' union, the Guild today is primarily a media union whose members are diverse in their occupations, but who share the view that the best working conditions are achieved by people who have a say in their workplace.

TECHNICAL ASSOCIATION OF THE GRAPHIC ARTS
200 Deer Run Road, Sewickley PA 15213. 412/259-1813. **Fax:** 412/741-2311. **E-mail address:** jallen@piagatf.org. **World Wide Web address:** http://www.taga.org. **Description:** A professional technical association founded in 1948 for the graphic arts industries.

WRITERS GUILD OF AMERICA WEST
7000 West Third Street, Los Angeles CA 90048. 323/951-4000. **Fax:** 323/782-4800. **Toll-free phone:** 800/548-4532. **E-mail address: World Wide Web address:** http://www.wga.org. **Description:** Represents writers in the motion picture, broadcast, cable and new technologies industries.

REAL ESTATE

INSTITUTE OF REAL ESTATE MANAGEMENT
430 North Michigan Avenue, Chicago IL 60611-4090. 312/329-6000. **Fax:** 800/338-4736. **Toll-free phone:** 800/837-0706. **E-mail address:** custserv@irem.org. **World Wide Web address:** http://www.irem.org. **Description:** IREM, an affiliate of the National Association of Realtors, is an association of professional property and asset managers who have met strict criteria in the areas of education, experience, and a commitment to a code of ethics.

INTERNATIONAL REAL ESTATE INSTITUTE
1224 North Nokomis, NE, Alexandria MN 56308. 320/763-4648. **Fax:** 320/763-9290. **E-mail address:** irei@iami.org. **World Wide Web address:** http://www.iami.org/irei. **Description:** A real estate association with members in more than 100 countries, providing media to communicate on an international basis.

NATIONAL ASSOCIATION OF REALTORS
30700 Russell Ranch Road, Westlake Village CA 91362. 805/557-2300. **Fax:** 805/557-2680. **World Wide Web address:** http://www.realtor.com. **Description:** An industry advocate of the right to own, use, and transfer real property; the acknowledged leader in developing standards for efficient, effective, and ethical real estate business practices; and valued by highly skilled real estate professionals and viewed by them as crucial to their success.

RETAIL

INTERNATIONAL COUNCIL OF SHOPPING CENTERS
1221 Avenue of the Americas, 41st floor, New York NY 10020-1099. 646/728-3800. **Fax:** 732/694-1755. **E-mail address:** icsc@icsc.org. **World Wide Web address:** http://www.icsc.org. **Description:** A trade association of the shopping center industry founded in 1957.

NATIONAL ASSOCIATION OF CHAIN DRUG STORES
413 North Lee Street, PO Box 1417-D49, Alexandria VA 22313-1480. 703/549-3001. **Fax:** 703/836-4869. **World Wide Web address:** http://www.nacds.org. **Description:** Represents the views and policy positions of member chain drug companies accomplished through the programs and services provided by the association.

NATIONAL RETAIL FEDERATION
325 7th Street, NW, Suite 1100, Washington DC 20004. 202/783-7971. **Fax:** 202/737-2849. **Toll-free phone:** 800/NRF-HOW2. **World Wide Web address:** http://www.nrf.com. **Description:** A retail trade association, with membership that comprises all retail formats and channels of distribution including department, specialty, discount, catalog, Internet and independent stores as well as the industry's key trading partners of retail goods and services. NRF represents an industry with more than 1.4 million U.S. retail establishments, more than 20 million employees - about one in five American workers - and 2003 sales of $3.8 trillion.

STONE, CLAY, GLASS, AND CONCRETE PRODUCTS

THE AMERICAN CERAMIC SOCIETY
PO Box 6136, Westerville OH 43086-6136. 614/890-4700. **Fax:** 614/899-6109.
E-mail address: info@ceramics.org. **World Wide Web address:**
http://www.acers.org. **Description:** An organization dedicated to the
advancement of ceramics.

NATIONAL GLASS ASSOCIATION
8200 Greensboro Drive, Suite 302, McLean VA 22102-3881. 866/342-5642. **Fax:**
703/442-0630. **World Wide Web address:** http://www.glass.org. **Description:** A
trade association founded in 1948 representing the flat (architectural and
automotive) glass industry. The association represents nearly 5,000 member
companies and locations, and produces the industry events and publications.

TRANSPORTATION AND TRAVEL

AIR TRANSPORT ASSOCIATION OF AMERICA
1301 Pennsylvania Avenue, NW, Suite 1100, Washington DC 20004-1707. 202/626-4000. **Fax:** 301/206-9789. **Toll-free phone:** 800/497-3326. **E-mail address:** ata@airlines.org. **World Wide Web address:** http://www.air-transport.org. **Description:** A trade organization for the principal U.S. airlines.

AMERICAN SOCIETY OF TRAVEL AGENTS
1101 King Street, Suite 200, Alexandria VA 22314. 703/739-2782. **Fax:** 703/684-8319. **World Wide Web address:** http://www.astanet.com. **Description:** An association of travel professionals whose members include travel agents and the companies whose products they sell such as tours, cruises, hotels, car rentals, etc.

AMERICAN TRUCKING ASSOCIATIONS
2200 Mill Road, Alexandria VA 22314. 703/838-1700. **Toll-free phone:** 888/333-1759. **World Wide Web address:** http://www.trucking.org. **Description:** Serves and represents the interests of the trucking industry with one united voice; positively influences Federal and State governmental actions; advances the trucking industry's image, efficiency, competitiveness, and profitability; provides educational programs and industry research; promotes highway and driver safety; and strives for a healthy business environment.

ASSOCIATION OF AMERICAN RAILROADS
50 F Street, NW, Washington DC 20001-1564. 202/639-2100. **World Wide Web address:** http://www.aar.org. **Description:** A trade associations representing the major freight railroads of the United States, Canada and Mexico.

INSTITUTE OF TRANSPORTATION ENGINEERS
1099 14th Street, NW, Suite 300 West, Washington DC 20005-3438. 202/289-0222. **Fax:** 202/289-7722. **E-mail address:** ite_staff@ite.org. **World Wide Web address:** http://www.ite.org. **Description:** An international individual member educational and scientific association whose members are traffic engineers, transportation planners and other professionals who are responsible for meeting society's needs for safe and efficient surface transportation through planning, designing, implementing, operating and maintaining surface transportation systems worldwide.

MARINE TECHNOLOGY SOCIETY
5565 Sterrett Place, Suite 108, Columbia MD 21044. 410/884-5330. **Fax:** 410/884-9060. **E-mail address:** mtsmbrship@erols.com. **World Wide Web address:** http://www.mtsociety.org. **Description:** A member-based society supporting all the components of the ocean community: marine sciences, engineering, academia, industry and government. The society is dedicated to the development, sharing and education of information and ideas.

NATIONAL TANK TRUCK CARRIERS
2200 Mill Road, Alexandria VA 22314. 703/838-1960. **Fax:** 703/684-5753. **E-mail address:** inquiries@tanktruck.org. **World Wide Web address:** http://www.tanktruck.net. **Description:** A trade association founded in 1945 and composed of approximately 180 trucking companies, which specialize in the nationwide distribution of bulk liquids, industrial gases and dry products in cargo tank motor vehicles.

UTILITIES: ELECTRIC, GAS, AND WATER

AMERICAN PUBLIC GAS ASSOCIATION
201 Massachusetts Avenue, NE, Suite C-4 Washington DC 20002. 202/464-2742. **Fax:** 202/464-0246. **E-mail address:** website@apga.org. **World Wide Web address:** http://www.apga.org. **Description:** A nonprofit trade organization representing publicly owned natural gas local distribution companies (LDCs). APGA represents the interests of public gas before Congress, federal agencies and other energy-related stakeholders by developing regulatory and legislative policies that further the goals of our members. In addition, APGA organizes meetings, seminars, and workshops with a specific goal to improve the reliability, operational efficiency, and regulatory environment in which public gas systems operate.

AMERICAN PUBLIC POWER ASSOCIATION (APPA)
2301 M Street, NW, Washington DC 20037-1484. 202/467-2900. **Fax:** 202/467-2910. **World Wide Web address:** http://www.appanet.org. **Description:** The service organization for the nation's more than 2,000 community-owned electric utilities that serve more than 40 million Americans. Its purpose is to advance the public policy interests of its members and their consumers, and provide member services to ensure adequate, reliable electricity at a reasonable price with the proper protection of the environment.

AMERICAN WATER WORKS ASSOCIATION
6666 West Quincy Avenue, Denver CO 80235. 303/794-7711. **Fax:** 303/347-0804. **Toll-free phone:** 800/926-7337. **World Wide Web address:** http://www.awwa.org. **Description:** A resource for knowledge, information, and advocacy to improve the quality and supply of drinking water in North America. The association advances public health, safety and welfare by uniting the efforts of the full spectrum of the drinking water community.

NATIONAL RURAL ELECTRIC COOPERATIVE ASSOCIATION
4301 Wilson Boulevard, Arlington VA 22203. 703/907-5500. **E-mail address:** nreca@nreca.coop. **World Wide Web address:** http://www.nreca.org. **Description:** A national organization representing the national interests of cooperative electric utilities and the consumers they serve. Founded in 1942.

MISCELLANEOUS WHOLESALING

NATIONAL ASSOCIATION OF WHOLESALER-DISTRIBUTORS (NAW)
1725 K Street, NW, Washington DC 20006-1419. 202/872-0885. **Fax:** 202/785-0586. **World Wide Web address:** http://www.naw.org. **Description:** A trade association that represents the wholesale distribution industry active in government relations and political action; research and education; and group purchasing.

INDEX OF PRIMARY EMPLOYERS

Your Job Hunt
Your Feedback

Comments, questions, or suggestions? We want to hear from you!
Please complete this questionnaire and mail it to:

The JobBank Staff
Adams Media
57 Littlefield Street
Avon, MA 02322

Did this book provide helpful advice and valuable information that you used in your job search? What did you like about it?

_____

_____

_____

How could we improve this book to help you in your job search? Is there a specific company we left out or an industry you'd like to see more of in a future edition? No suggestion is too small or too large.

_____

_____

_____

Would you recommend this book to a friend beginning a job hunt?

_____

_____

Name: _____

Occupation: _____

Which JobBank did you use? _____

Mailing address: _____

E-mail address: _____

Daytime phone: _____

SH.